William Inge

William Inge

Essays and Reminiscences on the Plays and the Man

Edited by JACKSON R. BRYER *and* MARY C. HARTIG

McFarland & Company, Inc., Publishers
Jefferson, North Carolina

Frontispiece: William Inge at George Peabody College in Nashville, 1935 (Vanderbilt University Special Collections and University Archives).

LIBRARY OF CONGRESS CATALOGUING-IN-PUBLICATION DATA

William Inge : essays and reminiscences on the plays and the man / edited by Jackson R. Bryer and Mary C. Hartig.
   p.   cm.
Includes bibliographical references and index.

ISBN 978-0-7864-7647-3 (softcover : acid free paper) ♾
ISBN 978-1-4766-1632-2 (ebook)

1. Inge, William—Criticism and interpretation.   I. Bryer, Jackson R., editor of compilation.   II. Hartig, Mary C., editor of compilation.
PS3517.N265Z955 2014
812'.54—dc23   2014015914

BRITISH LIBRARY CATALOGUING DATA ARE AVAILABLE

© 2014 Jackson R. Bryer and Mary C. Hartig. All rights reserved

No part of this book may be reproduced or transmitted in any form or by any means, electronic or mechanical, including photocopying or recording, or by any information storage and retrieval system, without permission in writing from the publisher.

On the cover: Playwright William Inge, circa early 1950s (Photofest)

Printed in the United States of America

McFarland & Company, Inc., Publishers
  Box 611, Jefferson, North Carolina 28640
  www.mcfarlandpub.com

Table of Contents

Introduction	1
Editors' Note	8
Chronology	10

• Critical Essays •

American Theater in the 1950s and Inge's Plays ALBERT WERTHEIM	13
The Inside-Outsider ROBERT PATRICK	25
Come Back, Little Sheba and Mass Culture JANE COURANT	30
The Two Texts of *Picnic* DAVID RICHMAN	55
Picnic, Summer Brave, and the Peace of Staying KERK FISHER	73
Robert Brustein's "Men-Taming Women of William Inge": A Re-Examination RALPH F. VOSS	96
Structures of Violence: Gender Roles in Inge's Plays LINDA WAGNER-MARTIN	120
Inge and the Empty Stage SUSAN KOPRINCE	127
Life with Father in Four Inge Plays ROBERT A. MARTIN	137

"Going Next Door": Placing Inge
BARRY GROSS   152

Another Kansan in the Land of Oz: Inge as Screenwriter
THOMAS P. ADLER   162

Build-Up to *Natural Affection*
R. BAIRD SHUMAN   173

Unnatural Affection: Sons and Mothers
THERESE JONES   185

• Reminiscences •

Memories of Happier Times
HELENE INGE CONNELL   201

Loving Memories of a Kindly Uncle
LUTHER C. INGE   207

Billy
JEANNE SEYMOUR MITCHAM   214

My Teacher
WILLIAM STUCKEY   218

Shadows on Success
AUDREY WOOD   221

Hampton Sundays
HORTON FOOTE   223

Inward Bound
JEROME LAWRENCE *and* ROBERT E. LEE   226

Counted Among His Friends
ROBERT ANDERSON   229

Directing *Picnic*
JOSHUA LOGAN   231

Designing *Picnic*
JO MIELZINER   235

On the Verge
N. RICHARD NASH   237

What Remains Behind
RICHARD H. GOLDSTONE   240

A Softness That Never Toughened
    WILLIAM GIBSON   245

Driving Inge
    JOHN CONNOLLY   248

That Was Bill
    ROBERT WHITEHEAD   255

Gestures of Love, Gestures of Despair
    JO ANN MAHAN KIRCHMAIER   259

Waiting for Inge
    JACK B. WRIGHT   263

The Stairs to Darkness
    PHILIP CLARKSON   266

He Knew the Poetry of Life
    JACK GARFEIN   273

Notes on Contributors   281

Index   287

Introduction

It is often forgotten, some sixty years later, that during the 1950s William Inge was not only the most commercially successful American playwright of the decade but also one of the most highly esteemed among critics. Between February 15, 1950, when Inge made his Broadway debut with *Come Back, Little Sheba*, and January 17, 1959, when his fourth successive hit play, *The Dark at the Top of the Stairs*, closed, no other dramatist matched his success. While *Come Back, Little Sheba* had a highly respectable but relatively modest run of 191 performances, *Picnic*, *Bus Stop*, and *Dark at the Top of the Stairs* each ran for more than 450 performances. When one adds to these statistics the fact that, in each case, a successful film version of the play, often with such major movie stars of the day as Burt Lancaster, Marilyn Monroe, and William Holden, appeared within a year or two following its stage debut, one can begin to understand Inge's prominence. Typical of the high regard in which he was held by critics are Walter Kerr's remark, in his review of *Dark at the Top of the Stairs*, that Inge is "one of the three or four ablest dramatists now working in the American theater" (1) and Gilbert Millstein's observation in a 1958 *Esquire* article that "[t]here is little question that Inge is today one of America's three leading writers for the stage, his compeers being Arthur Miller and Tennessee Williams" (60).

Inge's success can be attributed to a number of factors. The seemingly simple humanity of his characters and the honesty and empathy with which he depicted them in easily identifiable, mostly domestic, situations certainly struck a responsive chord with a 1950s post–World War II audience that was living through the Eisenhower years and emerging chastened from the horrors and traumas of the 1930s and 1940s. On one level, Inge's plays seemed to be just the sort of homespun, easily understood depictions of American life that appealed to a generation weary of political conflict and social upheaval. Sophisticated and urban New York audiences also undoubtedly found something vaguely exotic and refreshing in the small-town Midwest settings and predicaments depicted in Inge's plays. Whatever the reasons, the plays were extremely popular on stage and on screen during the decade of the 1950s; that the mood of the time had something to do with Inge's success is testified to further by the fact that, as the 1950s ended and the 1960s, a very different decade, began, Inge's fortunes declined precipitously. His last play of the 1950s, *A Loss of Roses*, which opened on November 28, 1959 (a mere ten months after *Dark at the Top of the Stairs* ended its highly successful run), lasted less than a month (for many years thereafter, Inge referred to it as his favorite among his plays).

As the 1960s began, Inge felt the changes that were occurring and believed that he had to adjust to them. As he explained to Digby Diehl in 1967, "I think any creative person who is going to survive more than a decade or so has to find himself anew periodically because he has to change with the times. I know that the kind of play that was being done in the 'fifties has no audience now. And I know that I don't have the same kind of approach to writing as I did in the 'fifties.... I seem to be dealing with more metaphysical material" (Inge, "William Inge" 51). Whatever his motives, Inge's attempts to "change with the times" and deal with "more metaphysical material" failed. Although his screenplay for *Splendor in the Grass* (1961), which won him an Academy Award, was set in the rural Midwestern milieu that had brought him so much recognition, his two Broadway plays of the 1960s, *Natural Affection* (1963) and *Where's Daddy?* (1966), each abandoned that setting in favor of urban locations, Chicago and New York, respectively; the former attempted to be relevant by emphasizing the violence of the day and the latter did the same by including a black couple and an openly gay character. Both closed shortly after they opened; and the one-act plays he wrote during this period, many of which—presumably in a similar effort to reflect the less repressive atmosphere of the time—dealt directly with such subjects as homosexuality and depression, topics central personally to Inge that he had not felt able to confront in the 1950s, were not produced. While these later plays are arguably simply not as good as his four hits—probably because Inge veered away from the settings, characters, and situations about which he felt most deeply in favor of what he thought the times demanded—it is also true that the audiences of the 1960s wanted a theater very different from what Inge offered, no matter the shift in his subject matter. Where realism was the stock in trade in the 1950s, the 1960s saw the rise of the Theater of the Absurd and of a far more experimental theater than that presented in any Inge play.

Although he had suffered for many years from depression, alcoholism, and the anguish of being a deeply closeted homosexual, these difficulties intensified in the 1960s and early 1970s, culminating on June 10, 1973, when he committed suicide. At the time of his death, while his four successful plays were being done quite frequently by amateur groups, the professional theater had pretty much forgotten about him. In 1982, Margaret Goheen, a speech and theater teacher at the community college in Inge's hometown of Independence, Kansas—he had attended the college briefly in 1931–32 during a depression-enforced return home—wanting to publicize the college's acquisition of Inge's papers (some left in his will and others donated by his sister Helene), organized a one-day Inge Festival on May 3rd in celebration of the playwright's 69th birthday. In 1983, the Festival was expanded to three days and featured the selection of Inge's close friend, fellow playwright Jerome Lawrence, as the recipient of the first William Inge Award for Lifetime Achievement. Three decades later, the annual William Inge Festival, now a four-day event, is thriving; and the recipients of the Inge Award have included virtually every major American playwright of the past six decades, all of whom were present to receive the honor. The Festival has attracted increased media attention in recent years; and there is little doubt that it contributed to a gradual resurgence of interest in Inge and his plays. There have been major New York revivals of *Come Back, Little Sheba* (1984, 2008), *Picnic* (1994, 2013), *Bus Stop* (1996), *Dark at the Top of the Stairs* (1979), and *Natural Affection* (2013), as well as frequent productions in regional theaters; and in 1989 the first comprehensive Inge biography, *A Life of William Inge: The Strains of Triumph* by Ralph F. Voss, was published.

As we try to explain this increased attention to Inge, we can, to a large extent, attribute it to the very aspects of his artistry that made him so successful in the 1950s. His own assertion that "the kind of play that was being done in the 'fifties has no audience now" has in fact been largely disproven. If we look at the praise reviewers lavished on his plays when they first appeared and at Inge's own comments on his aims as a dramatist, we can begin to identify the qualities of his work that have endured. Ironically, two of the most trenchant analyses of Inge's achievement came in reviews of his later, unsuccessful plays. Brooks Atkinson, in a review of *A Loss of Roses,* commented, "The drama in which he is interested lies beneath the surface"; and John Gassner, assessing *Natural Affection*, called Inge "a poet who has been more than commonly attuned to the still, small voice of humanity; ... he moves best when he seems to stand still with the deprived and feebly, sometimes comically, aspiring souls of people he knows with uncommon perception and sympathy" (186). Throughout the contemporary commentaries run the words "sympathy," "compassion," "understanding," "modesty," "truth," "integrity," and "dignity." As Atkinson noted in his review of *Dark at the Top of the Stairs*, Inge "is not judging.

He does not indicate whether he thinks his segment of life is good or bad. He does not suggest that the characters are the salt of the earth or that they are mediocrities." In a similar vein, he contended, in his review of *Picnic*, that "Mr. Inge seems to have no personal point of view, but only a knowledge of people and an instinct for the truth of the world they live in." Louis Sheaffer, in his review of *Picnic*, identified yet another source of Inge's talent: "[B]y the time the play is over you know everything important there is to know about [his characters]." Calling Inge's plays "delicate work," Robert Hatch, reviewing *Bus Stop*, pointed to "the night-club girl who is vulgar but not cheap; the cowboy who is absurd but not ridiculous; the professor who is pitiable but not maudlin; [and] the restaurant owner who is tough but not callous" (246). In his obituary tribute to his good friend, Tennessee Williams wrote, "Bill ... loved his characters, he wrote of them with a perfect ear for their homely speech, he saw them through their difficulties with the tenderness of a parent for suffering children" (8).

The most incisive contemporary commentary on Inge's work came, not surprisingly, from Harold Clurman, who was not only one of the major dramatic critics of his generation but also one of its leading directors—he directed the Broadway productions of *Bus Stop* and *Where's Daddy*. In his review of a 1974 off-Broadway production of Inge's late play *Overnight*, Clurman's analysis of the playwright's achievement rings as eloquently true today as it did then:

> Inge was the dramatist of the ordinary. He plumbed no great depths, but this limitation does not negate the honesty or genuineness of his endeavor. Inge really knew and felt his people; he was kin to them. His plays provide insight into their childlike bewilderment, for their profound if largely unconscious loneliness. His touch was popular, but never "commercial." His plays reflect a perturbed spirit modestly but nonetheless authentically groping for alleviation from the burdens of our society, particularly as they affect simple or un-sophisticated citizens outside our big cities or on their fringes. As such, Inge's plays are perceptive and touching. The narrowness of their scope, their American "provincialism" is in his case an asset rather than a liability. There was very little synthetic in what he had to say; his plays were born of his own distress [92].

Inge's own comments also offer important indications of why his plays have survived. Echoing Atkinson's two reviews noted above, Inge, in a 1953 interview, asserted, "I hate a play that tells me what to think. I have to leave my characters for the audience to make their own judgments of" (Bracker 3). Just as tellingly, in a 1954 essay, he described what impelled him to write a play:

> I am moved to write a play only when I find, sometimes with a little shock to myself, that I have seen inside a person's heart. Then, with a little feeling of

identification, I can begin. And then I love more than anything to bring people together, to relate them in whatever way possible and find something meaningful in the relationship, something that brings out the depth of their feelings. I want my plays only to provide the audience with an experience they can enjoy (and people can enjoy themselves crying as much as laughing) and which shocks them with the unexpected in human nature, with the deep inner life that exists primarily behind the life that is publicly presented [Inge, "From 'Front Porch'"].

* * *

This collection is designed to illuminate the virtues of William Inge's plays as well as give some insight into the man behind the work. As is often the case, the writing and the writer are inextricably bound; and as Clurman's comment above indicates, this connection is especially relevant to an understanding and appreciation of Inge's achievement. That it has been 100 years since Inge's birth makes an examination of the man and his work particularly appropriate.

The critical essays in this volume take a fresh look at some of his best-loved work as well as the later, more unfamiliar plays. Whereas some critics and academics continue to dismiss Inge's plays as out-of-date and old-fashioned, Jane Courant, Kerk Fisher, and others suggest Inge's work was often ahead of its time—in that he understood and foreshadowed the influence of popular media and advertising (Courant on *Come Back, Little Sheba*) as well as anticipated—without judgment—the sexual revolution and the women's movement (Fisher on *Summer Brave* and Courant on Marie Buckholder in *Come Back, Little Sheba*). Decidedly *not* placing Inge ahead of his time with regard to gender politics, however, is Linda Wagner-Martin who looks at "themes of household control and sexual alignment" as well as at the link between sex and violence in Inge's plays. Therese Jones examines the relationship between Inge's having undergone years of psychoanalysis and both his work and his view of himself. And while Inge's homosexuality is not central to her essay, Jones certainly addresses its relevance to her discussion of psychoanalytic theory in Inge.

Kerk Fisher and David Richman both engage in useful comparative studies of versions of *Picnic* and the antecedent and descendant versions of the play as they attempt to determine Inge's true intent in this much reworked (by Inge) material. Susan Koprince examines Inge's use of the "empty stage"— that is, his intentional pauses prior to characters' entrances and following their exits. Robert A. Martin scrutinizes the fathers in four of Inge's plays. R. Baird Shuman gives an overview of events in Inge's life leading up to the writing of *Natural Affection*, followed by an analysis of that play, the violent ending of which Shuman discussed with Inge himself. A 2013 off–Broadway revival of

Natural Affection, which received more positive reviews than did the 1963 production, makes Shuman's essay particularly relevant.

Essays by Albert Wertheim and Barry Gross set Inge's work in the contexts of the drama of the 1950s and the twentieth century, respectively. Thomas P. Adler's essay analyzes Inge's screenplays. And Inge's biographer Ralph F. Voss re-examines the devastating (to Inge and his career) Robert Brustein article that appeared in *Harper's* in 1958 and essentially dismissed Inge's work; Voss contends that Brustein's article is not only a "misinterpretation of Inge's plays" but is misogynistic as well. A short piece by fellow playwright Robert Patrick asserts that the keen observation that Inge was able to bring to his scrutiny of the heterosexual world arose from his being an "outsider"—in the sense that he was a gay man most often writing about heterosexual relationships—who like most gay men of his generation had to pass as an "insider."

While the critical essays attest to Inge's exceptional talent, the reminiscences in the second section of the book shed light on how this brilliant and troubled man suffered and why he eventually took his own life. We hear from close relatives—his sister Helene, his niece Jo Ann Mahan Kirchmaier, and his nephew Luther C. Inge; from people who worked closely with him—his secretary John Connolly, his agent Audrey Wood, legendary set designer Jo Mielziner, director Joshua Logan, and producer Robert Whitehead; two former students—William Stuckey, who knew him when Inge was a young teacher, and Jack B. Wright, who encountered him later in his career; Philip Clarkson, whose graduate thesis on Inge brought him into contact with the playwright in the early 1960s; fellow playwrights Robert Anderson, Horton Foote, William Gibson, Jerome Lawrence and Robert E. Lee, and N. Richard Nash; and friends Jack Garfein and Richard H. Goldstone. All contribute to the multi-faceted portrait of Inge that emerges from this collage of memories. Together they give us a sense of a talented, often fragile human being, a closeted homosexual whose personal life might have been quite different had he been born a few decades later. Through these people who knew him we get glimpses of his vulnerability, his frequent self-doubt, his eccentricities, and his neuroses—but also his gifts, his humor, his generosity, his gentility, and his affection for those closest to him. We hear from people who knew him as a teenager and young man, from others who knew him at the peak of his success; and Kirchmaier, Connolly, and Garfein speak directly and poignantly about his final days and suicide.

This book certainly does not constitute the final word on William Inge—nor should it. The fact that his plays are now receiving increased attention will bring more critical and scholarly scrutiny to them and to the complex human being who wrote them. We hope that this collection will provide an incentive for a new generation of scholars to take a second look at one of the twentieth century's most important playwrights.

J. R. B.
M. C. H.
Kensington, MD
October 24, 2013

WORKS CITED

Atkinson, Brooks. "At the Theatre." Rev. of *Picnic*, by William Inge. *New York Times* 20 Feb. 1953: L14. Print.

―――. "Midseason Blues." Rev. of *A Loss of Roses*, by William Inge. *New York Times* 6 Dec. 1959, sec. 2: 5. Print.

―――. "Mr. Inge in Top Form." Rev. of *The Dark at the Top of the Stairs*, by William Inge. *New York Times* 15 Dec. 1957, sec. 2: 3. Print.

Bracker, Milton. "Boy Actor to Broadway Author." *New York Times* 22 Mar. 1953, sec. 2: 1, 3. Print.

Clurman, Harold. "Theatre." Rev. of *Overnight*, by William Inge. *The Nation* 3 Aug. 1974: 91–93. Print.

Gassner, John. "Broadway in Review." Rev. of *Natural Affection*, by William Inge. *Educational Theatre Journal* 15.2 (May 1963): 181–87. Print.

Hatch, Robert. "Theatre." Rev. of *Bus Stop*, by William Inge. *The Nation* 19 Mar. 1955: 245–46. Print.

Inge, William. "From 'Front Porch' to Broadway." *Theatre Arts* Apr. 1954: 33. Print.

―――. "William Inge—A Playwright in Transition: A Conversation with Digby Diehl." Interview with Digby Diehl. *Transatlantic Review* 26 (Fall 1967): 51–56. Print.

Kerr, Walter. "The Dark at the Top of the Stairs." Rev. of *The Dark at the Top of the Stairs*, by William Inge. *New York Herald Tribune* 15 Dec. 1957, sec. 4: 1, 3. Print.

Millstein, Gilbert. "The Dark at the Top of William Inge." *Esquire* Aug. 1958: 60–63. Print.

Sheaffer, Louis. "'Picnic' Fine, Honest Play by Inge of Smalltown Life." Rev. of *Picnic*, by William Inge. *Brooklyn Daily Eagle* 20 Feb. 1953: 8. Print.

Williams, Tennessee. "To William Inge: An Homage." *New York Times* 1 July 1973, sec. 2: 1, 8. Print.

Editors' Note

Each of the critical essays in this collection began as a paper delivered in the scholars' conference segment of the annual William Inge Theatre Festival in Independence, Kansas; most of them were substantially revised for their first publication here. The personal reminiscences by Robert Anderson, Philip Clarkson, Horton Foote, Luther C. Inge, Jerome Lawrence and Robert E. Lee, Jeanne Seymour Mitcham, William Stuckey, and Jack B. Wright were commissioned for this collection. The reminiscence by Helene Inge Connell is partially drawn from a manuscript in the Inge Collection at the Independence Community College Library and is published here with the permission of James A. Mahan, Executor of the William Inge Literary Trust; other portions are drawn from an interview conducted by Mike Wood on September 19, 1981, and are published with the permission of Mike Wood and the Independence Community College Library where an audiotape of the full interview is deposited. The reminiscence by John Connolly is partially drawn from the text of a panel discussion, "Remembering Bill Inge," that was presented at the 1990 William Inge Festival; other portions are drawn from an interview conducted by Mike Wood on September 13, 1981, and are published here with the permission of Mike Wood and the Independence Community College Library where an audiotape of the full interview is deposited. The reminiscences by Jack Garfein, Joshua Logan, and Robert Whitehead are excerpted from interviews conducted by Mike Wood in 1981 and are published with the permission of Mike Wood and the Independence Community College Library where audiotapes of the full interviews are deposited. The reminiscences by Jo Ann Mahan Kirchmaier, Jo Mielziner, and Audrey Wood are excerpted from interviews conducted by Tim Emert in 1975 (Mielziner and Wood) and 1981 (Kirchmaier) and are published with the permission of Tim Emert and the Independence Community College Library where audiotapes of the full interviews are deposited. A brief section of the Audrey Wood reminiscence is drawn from pages 226 and 227 of *Represented by Audrey Wood*, by Audrey Wood, with Max Wilk (Garden City, NY: Doubleday, 1981).

For significant assistance in the preparation of this book, we wish to thank Paula L. K. Brown, Susannah Compton, Elizabeth Stuckey French, Andrew Gans, the late William Gibson, the late Richard H. Goldstone, Ann Gurton-Wachter, Tim Haynes, Jean Inge, Kathryn Mahan Kirchmaier, James A. Mahan, Robert Patrick, Marvin J. Taylor, Kerri Wood Thomson, and Calvin Webb. We are particularly grateful to Lily Morgan, the librarian of Independence Community College, who performed a variety of tasks expeditiously and cheerfully.

Chronology

May 3, 1913	William Motter Inge born in Independence, Kansas, fifth child of Maude Sarah Gibson and Luther Clayton Inge
November 12, 1920	Brother, Luther Clayton Inge, Jr., dies
1926	Enters Independence High School
1930, Fall	Enrolls at University of Kansas as a freshman; pledges Sigma Nu
1931	Returns for one year to Independence Community Junior College
1933–34	Drops out of University of Kansas and tours as juvenile in tent shows
1935, Spring	Graduates from University of Kansas; enters master's program in English at George Peabody College in Nashville
1936, Summer	Works on highway crew in Kansas
1936, Fall	Works as news announcer and scriptwriter at KFH radio in Wichita, Kansas
1937	Teaches at Columbus High School, Columbus, Kansas
1938, Summer	Returns to Peabody to finish MA degree; thesis entitled "David Belasco and the Age of Photographic Realism in the American Theatre"
1938, Fall	Starts teaching English composition and drama at Stephens College in Columbia, Missouri

1943–46	Serves as art, music, and drama critic for *St. Louis Star-Times*
1944	Meets Tennessee Williams; goes to Chicago and sees *Glass Menagerie*
1945	Writes first play, *Farther Off from Heaven*
1946	Teaches English at Washington University in St. Louis until 1949
1947	*Farther Off from Heaven* produced at Margo Jones's Theatre '47 in Dallas, June 3–10
February 15–July 29, 1950	*Come Back, Little Sheba* runs for 191 performances at the Booth Theatre, New York; wins George Jean Nathan Award
1952	*Come Back, Little Sheba* (film version) released
February 19, 1953–April 10, 1954	*Picnic* runs for 477 performances at the Music Box Theatre, New York; wins Pulitzer Prize, Drama Critics' Circle Award, and Donaldson Award
1955	*Picnic* (film version) released
March 2, 1955–April 21, 1956	*Bus Stop* runs for 478 performances at the Music Box Theatre, New York
1956	*Bus Stop* (film version) released
December 5, 1957–January 17, 1959	*The Dark at the Top of the Stairs* runs for 468 performances at the Music Box Theatre, New York
November 28–December 19, 1959	*A Loss of Roses* runs for 25 performances at the Eugene O'Neill Theatre, New York
1960	*The Dark at the Top of the Stairs* (film version) released
1961	*Splendor in the Grass* (film), with screenplay by Inge, released
1962	*All Fall Down* (film), with screenplay by Inge, released; Inge wins Academy Award for Best Original Screenplay for *Splendor in the Grass*
1963	*The Stripper* (film version of Inge's play *A Loss of Roses*) released

January 31– March 2, 1963	*Natural Affection* runs for 36 performances at the Booth Theatre, New York
November 6, 1964	*Out on the Outskirts of Town* (Bob Hope Chrysler Theatre) broadcast on television; teleplay by Inge
1965	*Bus Riley's Back in Town* (film), with screenplay by Inge (under pseudonym Walter Gage), released
1968, Fall	Teaches Playwriting at University of California, Irvine
March 2– March 19, 1966	*Where's Daddy* runs for 22 performances at Billy Rose Theatre, New York
1970	*Good Luck, Miss Wyckoff* (novel) published
1971	*My Son Is a Splendid Driver* (novel) published
1972	*The Last Pad* staged in Phoenix, Arizona
June 10, 1973	Dies of carbon monoxide poisoning at age 60 at Los Angeles home
October 26– November 9, 1975	*Summer Brave* runs for 18 performances at ANTA Playhouse, New York
1979	*Good Luck, Miss Wyckoff* (film version) released
April 21– May 29, 1994	*Picnic* (revival) runs for 45 performances at Criterion Center Stage Right, New York
February 22– March 17, 1996	*Bus Stop* (revival) runs for 29 performances at the Circle in the Square Theatre, New York
January 24– March 16, 2008	*Come Back, Little Sheba* (revival) runs for 58 performances at the Biltmore Theatre, New York
January 13– February 24, 2013	*Picnic* (revival) runs for 49 performances at the American Airlines Theatre, New York
September 17– October 26, 2013	*Natural Affection* (revival) runs for 42 performances at the Actors Company Theatre, New York

CRITICAL ESSAYS

American Theater in the 1950s and Inge's Plays
Albert Wertheim

In his review of William Inge's *Come Back, Little Sheba*, Brooks Atkinson, of the *New York Times* wrote, "Having been a drama critic, Mr. Inge naturally knows more about more things than most people, including the sort of material worth writing about in the theatre" ("At the Theatre"). Although Atkinson never goes into detail about what he means, he does touch on a truth about the sensitivity of William Inge as a playwright, for Inge wrote plays that were very much attuned to the concerns of the 1950s and to the questions that Americans were then asking about their lives and the way they lived them. William Inge did not write revolutionary political drama nor did he write about bizarre and tragic situations of the kind described in the plays of Tennessee Williams. He wrote instead about the lives and decisions, the failures and fears, the sexual impulses and sexual compromises of Americans during the decade or so after World War II. He wrote about Americans living in mid–America because he knew them best. Yet he did not write of them because he was a so-called "regional" playwright, but because he wanted his characters, who live close to the geographic center of the United States, to be indicative of the central issues shaping American life in the 1950s. Those years were special ones in American life and American drama, and William Inge's plays go far in illuminating them. The importance and specialness of Inge's plays, however, only becomes clear when one sees their place within the general context of post-war American drama.

Like the paradoxically urbane and innocent Washingtonians of Lillian Hellman's 1941 play, *Watch on the Rhine*, Americans before World War II seemed largely complacent with their relative isolation from world affairs and from the horrors of the persecution and the oppression occurring on the other side of the Atlantic. World War II was to change all that, for American soldiers were to see first hand what Hitler and the Japanese had wrought while those at home deeply felt world events as they lost loved ones and as streams of refugees came to American shores bringing their tragic histories with them. But after the war, American innocence and isolationism did not give way to new, politic sophistication but rather to new post-war fears of Hitler-like evil lurking within the bowels of American society, of political subversion in the land perpetrated by the proponents of Communist totalitarianism. Although on opposite ends of a political spectrum, Fascists and Communists alike seemed for post-war America to share the ideas of dictatorship, persecution, and commitment to the overthrow of the American democratic way of life.

This post-war paranoia was given shape and support by the now famous proceedings of the House Un-American Activities Committee and later by the infamous hearings led by the junior senator from Wisconsin, Joseph McCarthy. In the theater, the dangers of Communism were made manifest in Sidney Kingsley's 1951 dramatic version of Arthur Koestler's *Darkness at Noon* and in Maxwell Anderson's 1951 parable *Barefoot in Athens*. In the latter, the democracy of ancient Athens becomes pitted against the ruthless Communism of Sparta, and the philosopher Socrates dies a martyr for Athenian democracy and the American way of life.

Equally concerned with the suspicion of evil in the land but less with the evil itself than with the threat of those who would take justice into their own hands to root out a malignancy they only suspected to be there were several important plays and two notable revivals of the 1950s. Archibald MacLeish's *The Trojan Horse* (1952), Robert Ardrey's *Sing Me No Lullaby* (1955), and the 1952 revivals of Lillian Hellman's *The Children's Hour* (1934) and James Thurber and Elliott Nugent's *The Male Animal* (1940) all deal fairly directly with what they characterize as anti–Communist witch-hunting. Though more obliquely, that is also the implicit subject of Robert Anderson's *Tea and Sympathy* (1953) and Jerome Lawrence and Robert E. Lee's *Inherit the Wind* (1955). And surely the most well-known and successful post-war play about witch-hunting in general and what is viewed as 1950s witch-hunting in particular is Arthur Miller's *The Crucible* (1953), which neatly pinpoints the recurrent need in civilization to exorcise the evil perceived to be harbored in society and which suggests that that need had surfaced with particular force in the America of the 1950s. Within his dramatic text, Miller interweaves his own commentary, in which he clearly connects the Salem witch trial events onstage with the events being staged in Washington in the early 1950s. Miller writes:

> Like Reverend Hale and the others on this stage, we conceive the Devil as a necessary part of a respectable view of cosmology. Ours is a divided empire in

which certain ideas and emotions and actions are of God, and their opposites are of Lucifer.... Since 1692 a great but superficial change has wiped out God's beard and the Devil's horns, but the world is still gripped between two diametrically opposed absolutes....

.... In the countries of the Communist ideology, all resistance of any import is linked to the totally malign capitalist succubi, and in America any man who is not reactionary in his views is open to the charge of alliance with the Red hell. Political opposition, thereby, is given an inhumane overlay which then justifies the abrogation of all normally applied customs of civilized intercourse. A political policy is equated with moral right, and opposition to it with diabolical malevolence. Once such an equation is effectively made, society becomes a congerie of plots and counterplots, and the main role of government changes from that of arbiter to that of the scourge of God [33, 34].

What all the playwrights writing about the Communist threat suggest, but what no one describes and explains so well as Miller is the sense that America felt it harbored a destructive sickness within its organs, a sickness that seemed to have something to do with the cancerous disease of Communism.

Surely the plays of William Inge are a far cry from the Salem witch trials, the House Un-American Activities Committee, or fears of Communist disease. But they are *not* so far away if one sees that the political plays like *The Crucible* are, together with Inge's plays—and particularly *Come Back, Little Sheba* and *Dark at the Top of the Stairs*—part and parcel of a larger questioning in American drama and in American society about post-war sickness—not merely political, but physical, psychological, and marital. "Why does America's sickness exist and how can health or rehabilitation occur?" are questions playwrights posed and attempted to answer. One could argue that many playwrights of the 1950s, including William Inge, willfully averted their gaze from political events, and consciously wrote instead about personal problems. It is also possible, and likely more correct, to say that the political plays are merely one aspect of a larger issue. Surveying the considerable corpus of American drama in the 1950s, it is possible to see that an underlying concern of many plays and playwrights of the period was the existence of social and personal evils and imperfections, and the ability of men either to overcome or fail to overcome calamity and evil. Whereas some playwrights used historical settings or cosmic allegories to present these matters, others projected them through the metaphors of physical illness or of psychological, sexual, and marital maladjustment. The frequent implicit suggestion, moreover, is that the road to personal or societal health is one that can be forged by individual will.

The Crucible presents the questions of social illness within the context of the Puritan theocracy and the witch-hunting madness it inspired. The theological issues that are part of Miller's play are echoed more boldly and cosmically through the biblical and quasi-biblical matters presented in 1954 by Clifford Odets in *The Flowering Peach*, a not altogether successful comic parable based on the Noah story, and in 1958 by Archibald MacLeish in *J.B.*, an impressive modern dramatic reworking of the Job story and of the questions of good and evil it raises. Both Odets's Noah and MacLeish's J.B. insist that men can and will endure, that civilization's sickness and man's calamities, that civilization's health and man's restoration ultimately lie not in God's but in mankind's and man's own hands. Noah concludes Odets's play exclaiming, "Yes, I hear You, God—now it's in man's hands to make or destroy the world" (85). And in the final moments of MacLeish's play, J.B. and his wife Sarah register the specialness of humanity and the need for mankind and not God to kindle the light that will extinguish the darkness and evil the world is heir to:

> J.B.: He [God] does not love. He Is.
> SARAH: But we do. That's the wonder.
> ....
> J.B.: It's too dark to see....
> ....
> SARAH: Then blow on the coal of the heart, my darling....
> Blow on the coal of the heart.
> The candles in churches are out.
> The lights have gone out in the sky.
> Blow on the coal of the heart
> And we'll see by and by ... [152, 153].

Although the context is different, the darkness MacLeish alludes to here is not so very different from Inge's dark at the top of the stairs.

The idea of calamity and restoration is brought down to a more mundane and specific plane in a number of excellent 1950s plays about sickness and health. In those plays, the American political situation and abstract theological or philosophical debate are replaced by the fight against physical debilitations as a way of projecting the idea of overcoming the world's ills and adversities. Those plays include Odets's *The Country Girl* (1955), about the comeback of an alcoholic actor; Michael V. Gazzo's *A Hatful of Rain* (1955), about a drug addict who must face himself and his addiction; Dore Schary's *Sunrise at Campobello* (1958), which depicts FDR's fight against the debilitation of infantile paralysis; and William Gibson's *The Miracle Worker* (1957), which depicts the way Helen Keller is taught the first steps in finding her own humanity and reaching beyond the diseases that have afflicted her and left her little better than an animal. In Tennessee Williams's *Cat on a Hot Tin Roof* (1955), too, Big Daddy is led to face the pain of his dying and that is perhaps the prelude to his son Brick's ultimately facing the pain of his alcoholism and concomitant escape from reality. Surely the alcoholism of Doc and his move to admit the realities of his life and his marriage link Inge's *Come Back, Little Sheba* with these 1950s plays of debility and restoration.

Linked to the presentation of political, social, and physiological illness and health is often the analogous presentation of marital sickness and health. It is important that Miller's *The Crucible* is as much about the Proctor marriage and the reasons behind John Proctor's illicit sexual relations as it is about witches. And when Elizabeth Proctor can openly admit, "It needs a cold wife to prompt lechery" (137), it becomes obvious that matters of sexuality and love are very much under discussion. Likewise, *The Country Girl* and *A Hatful of Rain* are, finally, plays about marriage as much as or more than they are about alcohol or drug abuse. Again in *Cat on a Hot Tin Roof* blending with Big Daddy's cancer and Brick's attempt to run from life through liquor is the central concern of Maggie's unfulfilled sexuality and sexual neurosis.

It is precisely in this area of sexual maladjustment and sexual health that William Inge has so much to tell us. But before looking more closely at Inge's plays, it is important to say something about the relative frankness of his plays. Looking back over the years, one can now see that Inge's plays were heralds of what we now know as the sexual revolution in America. Perhaps a playwright like Tennessee Williams with his presentation of sexual dynamics in plays like *Streetcar Named Desire* (1949), *Summer and Smoke* (1950), *The Rose Tattoo* (1951), *Camino Real* (1953), and *Cat on a Hot Tin Roof* cleared the path for his contemporaries. Nowadays the famous lines spoken by Deborah Kerr in *Tea and Sympathy* as she prepares to introduce the prep school boy accused of homosexuality to the intimacies of heterosexuality—"Years from now ... when you talk about this ... and you will ... be kind" (182)—seem stilted, but in 1953 they shocked Broadway audiences. Of course sex has always been the food for drama both tragic and comic, but frank discussion of sexual attraction, sex drive, and coital fulfillment or frustration were new and daring in the 1950s. Perhaps Inge's greatest achievement as a dramatist was to bring sexual matters to the stage in such a way that they were neither grotesque nor obscene but could be discussed in a theater so as to illumine the private lives of the spectators. In a sense, Inge was largely responsible for bringing a mature, honest discussion of sexual matters out of the closet and into the playhouse.

The drama of the 1950s explored the purgation of subversion in American political and social life; it discussed in the abstract the causes of inexplicable evil and holocaust; and it dramatized the attempts to overcome addiction, handicap, and disease. With plays by Tennessee Williams and Robert Anderson, with Lillian Hellman's *The Autumn Garden* (1951) and later *Toys in the Attic* (1960), and with, most of all, William Inge's major plays, the drama of the

1950s explored the maladies that can affect sexual relationships, and, in some instances, the means for overcoming those maladies. When Tennessee Williams's Big Mama recognizes that Brick and Maggie's marriage is in trouble, she points to their bed and exclaims with peasant wisdom, "When a marriage goes on the rocks, the rocks are there, right there" (37). Matters are not quite that simple in a Tennessee Williams play nor are they in the plays of Inge, yet Big Mama's words have an appropriateness for the sexual issues that Williams, Anderson, Hellman, and Inge were to explore in the 1950s.

The post-war changes in American sexual mores are not merely presented in Inge's plays, they are frequently at the heart of what has made characters and their marriages fail. In *Come Back, Little Sheba*, Lola and Doc present a case of arrested sexual development. Their premarital sex, Lola's abortion, and their consequent exile from their small Midwestern hometown have not merely colored but shaped their wasted lives. They have been and remain victims of small town, narrow-minded sexual codes and gender roles, tragically but sometimes even comically so. When Lola questions the fact that female models pose in the nude but males do not, Doc—with classic double standard and predictable attitude—explains, "Well, that's the way it should be, honey. A man, after all, is a man, and he ... well, he has to protect himself" (*4 Plays* 26). Likewise, Doc objects to Lola's lack of refinement when she exclaims that she's "pooped" (29).

Doc's perception of female gender roles is limited and narrow. For him, a woman is pure or impure, virgin or whore. And his inability to find an area of acceptability between those extremes leads him ultimately to become physically ill, go out on a bender, and even attempt murder when he recognizes that Marie, whom he had seen (as her name suggests) as a virgin figure, has had casual sex with Turk and that, moreover, she never had any intention of having more than casual sex with him. Suddenly, Marie, who is roughly the age that Doc and Lola's baby, lost through miscarriage, would have been, goes in Doc's mind from virgin to whore. And when Lola then tells him that Marie plans to marry her boyfriend Bruce, Doc can hold back no longer. Conflating his reaction to Marie with his long pent up feelings about his own marriage to Lola, he shouts, "He probably *has* to marry her, the poor bastard. Just 'cause she's pretty and he got amorous one day.... Just like I had to marry *you*.... You and Marie are both a couple of sluts" (56). And with that he grabs a hatchet and threatens violence.

The near-tragic dilemma in which Doc and Lola find themselves stems from the fact that they have accepted entirely the sexual rules and gender typing by which their parents lived, rules that have forced them into exile. But both the virgin/whore dichotomy and the sexual double standards Lola and

Doc have accepted no longer shape modern lives and Inge's main characters seem, therefore, tragically locked in a situation marked by obsolete codes of conduct and punishments. Their fate seems curiously obsolete particularly when set against the casual coital relations of Marie and Turk. Sexual morals have changed but Doc and Lola have not changed with them. Marie, Turk, and Bruce are there as a measure of the next generation and of new permissive sexual attitudes and standards. For Doc and Lola, the old sexual standards that governed their youth have wrecked their lives, but they are too timid to change. Instead, Lola hangs on to an imagined past, symbolized by Sheba, a puppy that, like Lola herself, has not grown to maturity; and Doc attempts to obliterate both past and present with alcohol. Only at the end of the play do they begin to recognize their failure to mature and begin to see as well their need to do so now, however late. As Lola relates her dream, filled with obvious sexual symbols, she gives up her past, acknowledging that Sheba is dead and never coming back; and she helps Doc to find the words he needs, "You kept saying, 'We can't stay here, honey; we gotta go on. We gotta go on'" (69).

That idea of change as it relates to sexual behavior and sexual attitudes is also at the heart of *The Dark at the Top of the Stairs*, in which Inge carefully reveals that both Cora and Lottie are the products of their parents' narrow-minded, restrictive sexual upbringing. The result is that Cora after her marriage has become an inadequate sexual partner and that Lottie has never enjoyed sex or achieved orgasm. The frank discussion of their sex lives between the two sisters is one of the best such discussions the American theater has produced. And in that discussion, the women come to reveal for themselves how the restrictive views of their parents have led to their own sexual inadequacies and failures. As in *Come Back, Little Sheba*, the conservative and censorious attitudes toward sexual relationships and sexual fulfillment held by the previous generation have disastrous results for the present generation. Such attitudes have, moreover, served as roadblocks to both sexual satisfaction and frank discussion of sexuality:

> CORA: Sometimes you talk shamefully, Lottie, and when I think of the way Mama and Papa brought us up....
> LOTTIE: Oh, Mama and Papa, Mama and Papa! Maybe they didn't know as much as we gave them credit for [277].

After the two sisters begin to work through their sexual inhibitions, Lottie leaves the house with her tight girdle removed, rubbing, as the stage directions tell us, "*the flesh on her stomach in appreciation of its new freedom*" (281). Clearly the act is a symbolic one. Likewise, at the end of the play, Cora can enter into a new relationship with her husband, one climaxed in the bedroom at the top of the stairs. And in *Dark*, both Cora and Rubin must grow and develop, must climb the stairs in their lives if they are to find satisfaction in marriage. In a way, the new standards that Doc and Lola must accept, the frank discussion Cora and Lottie are able to have, and the casting off of Lottie's restrictive girdle are important not merely for the characters of Inge's drama but for Inge himself as a playwright. Like his characters, he is, as a writer of the 1950s, casting off the restrictions placed on writers in the past to find a way to dramatize and discuss the new sexual morality and openness of post-war America.

What Inge shows best in *The Dark at the Top of the Stairs* is the way the forging of new, healthy sexual relationships goes hand in hand with accepting the changes in society. In the marriage of Rubin and Cora Flood, the problem is only partially *her* upbringing, for the problem lies with his as well. The play is set in the early 1920s in Oklahoma, which became a state in 1907, about the time Rubin and Cora married. Rubin has remained fixed in old ways, in the ways of the ranchers and the rough, colorful homesteaders who settled the Oklahoma territory. A dashing, handsome cowboy lover in his youth, Rubin has failed to change with the times. He is as resistant to the statehood and settlement of Oklahoma as he is to the familial domestication that his wife and her values represent for him. Oklahoma has entered the modern automotive age, but Rubin continues to sell harnesses. Similarly, male-female relationships have changed, as the younger generation in the play suggest, but Rubin clings to an anachronistic self-image and sexual attitude. In an assertion of his reactionary idea of masculinity, Rubin strikes his wife in Act 1. He returns in Act 3, however, ready to change and prepared to alter the conservative gender roles that have shaped his life and marriage. And the self-discoveries and self-revelations of Lottie and Cora in the intervening act of the play echo the internal decisions of Rubin not shown on stage. With Rubin's acceptance of Oklahoma and of modern life in that state as well as his acceptance of changing definitions of manhood and womanhood, and with Cora's concomitant enlightenment about her husband, a new marriage seems enacted, one based on mutuality in both domestic and coital relations.

Although Hal and Madge, and Cherie and Bo tend to dominate *Picnic* and *Bus Stop*, respectively, both plays are panoramas of sexual attitudes and ways of loving. In *Picnic*, Helen Potts, whose marriage was annulled by her restrictive parents, has led an unfulfilled, sexually frustrated life. Flo Owens has been frightened by her failed marriage and thus attempts to expunge sex and sexuality from both her life and that of her children. Rosemary Sydney is the unmarried schoolteacher fighting a desperate battle to achieve some sort of sexual fulfillment before reaching her sunset years. And Millie and Madge Owens are the two young girls who must accept or reject the sexual attitudes conveyed to them by their three female role models. These attitudes become galvanized with the appearance of Hal Carter, who comes to mean sexuality for all the women of the play. Although the influence of Williams on Inge is often noted, it seems clear that the influence worked both ways. In 1959, six years after *Picnic*, Tennessee Williams in *Sweet Bird of Youth* transformed Hal Carter into Chance Wayne. But whereas Williams creates a sexual athlete of almost mythic proportions in a decadent Gulf of Mexico town, Inge far more successfully presents a young man only partially aware of the extent of his sexuality and turns him loose in a believable, small Kansas town.

What becomes important in *Picnic* is the way Hal acts as a catalyst forcing the women of the play to become what they are and have to be. He is as much responsible, finally, for Rosemary's marriage to Howard Bevans and for Millie Owens's inebriation as he is for Madge's sexual surrender. The final version of *Picnic* has Madge leaving her home to follow Hal and her sexual commitment. Inge, however, presented a rather different and perhaps more plausible ending, in a version of the play entitled *Summer Brave*. In *Summer Brave*, Hal leaves town and Madge does not follow him, remaining behind presumably to become an easy conquest for the rather sleazy young men of the town. In both versions, however, what is important is that Hal and his potent aura of sexuality blow through the play's Kansas town much like the tornadoes indigenous to that area, leaving in his wake a town and women forever changed. Surely Hal is also Inge's unforgettable personification of the winds of new sexuality, sexual freedom, and sexual candor that blew through America in the 1950s.

Whereas *Picnic* presented a group of women energized by Hal, the cynosure of the play, *Bus Stop* depicts a wider range of love and sexual attitudes. Perhaps taking his cue from Shakespeare, who is quoted frequently in *Bus Stop* by Dr. Lyman and Elma, Inge has created a play that has similarities to *A Midsummer Night's Dream* in its display of various kinds and levels of love. Framing the play—like the marriage of Theseus and Hippolyta in Shakespeare—is the casual sexual encounter of Grace, the owner of the roadside eatery in which the play takes place, and Carl the bus driver en route from Kansas City to points west. For most of the play these two characters are in an upstairs bedroom engaged in sex while in the restaurant below Bo and Cherie and Elma and Dr. Lyman are engaged in a sexual learning process. Added to those dramatic possibilities are the enactment of Romeo and Juliet's balcony scene, the Shakespearean tragedies and love sonnets quoted, and the descriptions of Grace's marriage and Cherie's family.

In *Bus Stop*, Inge attempts to range beyond the possibilities of multiple plot to present a true, integrated panorama of sexual attitudes and discovery. Because Kim Stanley dominated the original stage version and Marilyn Monroe the movie, the Cherie and Bo plot overshadowed the rest of the play both on Broadway and in Hollywood. And because Cherie and Bo are far more colorful characters than the others in the play, they tend to corner audience attention even without the help of Stanley or Monroe. Although *Bus Stop* does not, as Inge seemed to wish, finally manage to transcend multiple plots, it does nonetheless present well Inge's discussion of the learning that must take place before sexual maturity can be achieved. Judgment and personal maturity are what Elma must learn. Mutuality and respect must be learned by Bo and Cherie. And an acceptance of occasional coitus, sex without commitment, seems to be learned by Carl and Grace. Inge appears to be well ahead of his time in defining new and liberal sexual values, and thus it is impressive that in 1955 he was able to write so sensitive a play and to present it to an accepting audience. The panorama of *Bus Stop* was probably accepted by theater and film audiences because the play's *dramatis personae* are not finally bizarre types involved in sexual grotesqueries. Set near Topeka, Kansas, the geographic middle of the U.S., *Bus Stop* presents not so much characters as human types. As Brooks Atkinson was to say of them in his review, "Being completely human, they are the salt of the earth" ("Theatre").

Drama in the 1950s was preoccupied with illness and maladjustment, and with the means for proper health, a health projected in terms of the body, the body politic, or the body joined in wedlock or sexual congress. In relation to that general preoccupation, it explored the concerns of the times such as anti–Communism and the Cold War, the military conflict in Korea, and the debilitations that were in part the legacy of World War II: physical handicaps, mental illness, alcoholism and drug addiction. The 1950s brought to the stage the extreme situations and often bizarre characters of Tennessee Williams and the political thrust of Arthur Miller's 1950s plays *The Crucible* and *A View from the Bridge* (1955) as well as his adaptation of Ibsen's *An Enemy of the People* (1951). Audiences in the 1950s saw Korean War plays like Mac Hyman's *No Time for Sergeants* (1954) and Henry Denker and Ralph Berkey's *Time Limit!* (1956) as well as those about the McCarthy era's war against Communism. A national preoccupation with what seemed to be a contemporary version of the ageless Armageddon between good and evil was projected not only in the cosmic drama of *J.B.* and *The Flowering Peach* but in a multitude of courtroom dramas that included Herman Wouk's *The Caine Mutiny Court-Martial* (1954), *Darkness at Noon*, *The Crucible*, and Saul Levitt's *The Andersonville Trial* (1959), to name but a few. Amid the 1950s concerns for spiritual, moral, physical, and mental health, William Inge made an important contribution to American theater by presenting openly and maturely, without an interest in sensationalism, the new plea for sexual health. He recorded for his audiences and posterity the new sexual morality that was just beginning to be felt as well as the newly realized need for openness and mutuality as the path to sexual adjustment and happiness. Showing these things through the lives of ordinary people in mid–America, Inge was able to speak clearly, meaningfully, and lastingly to the American theater public.

WORKS CITED

Anderson, Maxwell. *Barefoot in Athens*. New York: Sloane, 1951. Print.
Anderson, Robert. *Tea and Sympathy*. New York: Random House, 1953. Print.
Ardrey, Robert. *Sing Me No Lullaby: A Play in Three Acts*. New York: Dramatists Play Service, 1955. Print.
Atkinson, Brooks. "At the Theatre." Rev. of *Come Back, Little Sheba*, by William Inge. *New York Times* 16 Feb. 1950: 28. Print.
———. "Theatre: 'Bus Stop.'" Rev. of *Bus Stop*, by William Inge. *New York Times* 3 Mar. 1955: 23. Print.
Denker, Henry, and Ralph Berkey. *Time Limit!* New York: French, 1956. Print.
Gazzo, Michael V. *A Hatful of Rain*. New York: Random House, 1955. Print.
Gibson, William. *Dinny and the Witches [and] the Miracle Worker: Two Plays*. New York: Atheneum, 1960. Print.
Hellman, Lillian. *The Autumn Garden: A Play in Three Acts*. Boston: Little, Brown, 1951. Print.
———. *The Children's Hour*. New York: Knopf, 1934. Print.
———. *Toys in the Attic*. New York: Random House, 1960. Print.
———. *Watch on the Rhine*. New York: Random House, 1939. Print.
Hyman, Mac. *No Time for Sergeants*. New York: Random House, 1954. Print.
Inge, William. *4 Plays [Come Back, Little Sheba; Picnic; Bus Stop; The Dark at the Top of the Stairs]*. New York: Random House, 1958. Print.
———. *Summer Brave*. New York: Dramatists Play Service, 1962. Print.
Kingsley, Sidney. *Darkness at Noon*. New York: Random House, 1951. Print.
Lawrence, Jerome, and Robert E. Lee. *Inherit the Wind*. New York: Random House, 1955. Print.
Levitt, Saul. *The Andersonville Trial*. New York: Random House, 1960. Print.
MacLeish, Archibald. *J.B.* Boston: Houghton, 1957. Print.
———. *The Trojan Horse*. Boston: Houghton, 1952. Print.
Miller, Arthur. *The Crucible*. New York: Viking, 1953. Print.
———. *An Enemy of the People*. New York: Viking, 1951. Print.
———. *A View from the Bridge*. New York: Viking, 1955. Print.
Odets, Clifford. *The Country Girl*. New York: Viking, 1951. Print.
———. *The Flowering Peach*. New York: Dramatists Play Service, 1954. Print.
Schary, Dore. *Sunrise at Campobello*. New York: Random House, 1958. Print.
Thurber, James, and Elliott Nugent. *The Male Animal*. New York: Random House, 1940. Print.
Williams, Tennessee. *Camino Real*. Norfolk, CT: New Directions, 1953. Print.
———. *Cat on a Hot Tin Roof*. 1955. New York: New American Library, 1985. Print.

―――. *The Rose Tattoo.* New York: New Directions, 1951. Print.
―――. *A Streetcar Named Desire.* New York: New Directions, 1947. Print.
―――. *Summer and Smoke.* New York: New Directions, 1948. Print.
Wouk, Herman. *The Caine Mutiny Court-Martial.* Garden City, NY: Doubleday, 1954. Print.

The Inside-Outsider
Robert Patrick

The 1950s in America evinced a remarkable and unique situation with regards to the cultural influence of the stage. In this period, literacy in America reached its peak; technology provided abundant wealth, leisure time, and communications devices; the population was steadily increasing; and the experiences of the Great Depression and World War II had aroused questioning minds and encouraged greater sophistication. At this time, the stage still maintained its ancient prestige—it had not yet been displaced from the cultural center by the electronic media. The playwrights of the 1950s enjoyed sudden and widespread fame and power. Their work was widely reviewed and criticized. Paperback editions appeared in every drugstore. Intensely publicized film versions were automatically made of stage successes. Never have playwrights enjoyed such prestige and power simultaneously.

While many dramatists continued to produce inconsequential works, and many others maintained the tradition of social consciousness and criticism, others brought a new seriousness to the exploration of sex. The affluence, mobility, literacy, and much younger average age of the population in this period brought about new questioning of sexual relationships. Broadway playwrights were at the forefront, providing new images and ideas on the subject. One could say that the very nature of heterosexual meeting, mating, and parting were put to the test by the 1950s playwrights as never before—and to greater effect. The major explorers of these themes were, surprisingly, male homosexuals.

The outsider has often had an edge on the insider in the arts. Whether it is because the determination needed for an outsider to succeed gives greater drive and lasting power, or because the accent of another culture or subculture gives fresh flavor to familiar themes, or because detachment and objectivity support clarity—the economically, socially, racially, religiously, and sexually oppressed tend to supply a disproportionate number of a culture's major artists.

The homosexual's exclusion has a special quality. When we said, in the past, that ours was a white, male, Anglo-Saxon, protestant, capitalist culture, we meant that the red, brown, yellow, black, and tan races, women, Jews and Catholics, and the poor were not admitted to the corridors of power, did not know the inner workings of the power structure. But the homosexual was not outside. He was hidden within. While other out-groups struggled to escape their ghettoes, the homosexual was not, until recent years, permitted to have one. While it might be terrifying to be a black or Jew, humiliating to be a woman, limiting to be poor, it was not illegal to be any of them.

The homosexual had to hide, and he hid within heterosexuality. What an opportunity to gather material for a play! To be not only able, but ordered, to learn everything the oppressor taught his children! To have access to every moment of schooling, every nuance of relationships, every weapon of maintenance of the major force which sought your life!

The homosexual had to know every rite and sacrament, all ceremony and etiquette, of an essentially alien race—and to know them better, more consciously, and with more understanding and intellectual attention, than those around him. In many more cases than might generally be believed, even the essential and intimate patterns of heterosexuality were open to him. Who, then, was better equipped to depict the heterosexual's world?

This is not, obviously, a situation that arose in the 1950s, nor was the 1950s playwright's position as principal portraitist of heterosexuality an historically unique one. While historical prudery and politics mask the private lives of past playwrights, what we know about Euripides, Shakespeare, Marlowe, Dumas, Wilde, and Wilder in no way contradicts our thesis. What was new and unique to the 1950s was the substantial increase in authority given to the living stage by the enlarged media's contemporaneous respect for it. Tennessee Williams, William Inge, Arthur Laurents, John Van Druten—these four, and others who have not chosen to be named in their company—offered minutely detailed observations of straight behavior that brought to immense audiences laughter of recognition, cries of shock, roars of agreement, and endless discussions both in learned journals and college dorms of the need for reaffirmation and change. They materially contributed to the sexual attitudes of the so-called "Beats" and helped form the images of influential actors whose sexual presence was emulated by millions.

William Inge created, in the characters of Bo and Cherie in *Bus Stop* and Hal and Madge in *Picnic*, two of the archetypal couples of his time. In *Come Back, Little Sheba* and *Dark at the Top of the Stairs* he presented older married couples successfully and unsuccessfully attempting to seal the marriage vow. *Picnic*, especially, his undoubted masterpiece, puts heterosexual romance, heterosexual hypocrisy, heterosexual cowardice and courage, under a biologist's microscope and catches virtually every second of a complexly interwoven set of man/woman, young/old, rich/poor, sanctioned/taboo interactions. No other play is more consistent in its social, psychological, and moral qualities. It is a great achievement and stung the young into imitation.

Dark at the Top of the Stairs stands near to *Picnic* in its lapidarian creation of a behavioral mosaic utterly defining a time, a place, a human situation. *Bus Stop*, dominated by the boisterous courtship of Bo and Cherie, depicts its secondary characters less vividly, and shows Inge somewhat less at ease with oversized poetical romance than with the dryer schematization of *Picnic* and *Dark at the Top of the Stairs*, but lives on its core couple's highly colored and endearing shenanigans.

Come Back, Little Sheba most successfully combines the analytical insight of *Picnic* and *Dark* with the richer organic erotic interplay of *Bus Stop* (though in darker colors here) and draws sweet and sincere sentiment out of the memorably three-dimensional Lola. Doc is Inge's most detailed male character and his single finest creation. Perhaps only because its sexual content is recessed into secondary characters, *Sheba* lacks something of the tingling erotic charge of Inge's other work.

The outsider inside, the homosexual, watched and saw and remembered, analyzed, distilled and idealized, criticized, satirized, commemorated, blessed, and cursed the beauty, passion, pain, poetry, harmonies, and contradictions of the all-encompassing heterosexual hegemony.

But what of this observer himself? Where is he in this world so often dependent on him for the image of its identity? We do not find him in Inge's plays produced in the 1950s, and that is our subject here. We do not find him, or her, in fact, in any of the works by homosexuals which we examine today. One author, Robert Anderson, who disclaims personal involvement in homosexuality, did dare depict in *Tea and Sympathy* one character who might be homosexual, and another who is accused of it, with, one suspects, the author's intention being that we should believe the accusation. Perhaps Anderson felt safe in doing so. Tennessee Williams, with the bravado that came, perhaps, from a greater gift than Inge's, dared discuss three offstage dead characters who had been gay, and was allowed to show two probable but highly euphemistic Lesbians in a curtain-raiser. Carson McCullers mentions a transvestite. That is it. The homosexual could not appear in his own work. Forbidden. Out of the question. Taboo. Simon Stimson (Inge's last acting job), the drunken choirmaster, staggers through the streets of *Our Town* with much "tsk-tsking" from the proper principals, but his problems never emerge and he dies bitter and hateful. The witches of *Bell, Book, and Candle* sneer at mortals. But bitterness and hatred are not characteristic of these homosexual works—rather, what strikes us in all the works in question is their overwhelming compassion. Tough and true as they are, they are not unkind. This achievement—to maintain that degree of compassion under the stress of such self-abnegation—is perhaps the most striking feat of these authors.

But the self cannot be abnegated by the artist or there will be no character or style to the work. All of these playwrights included elements of their specific personal experience, through many veils and ruses. As their particular outgroup could not be presented directly, most of our subjects transferred their isolation and rejection to other unfortunates. Men attracted to young girls appear in *Bus Stop* and Williams's *The Night of the Iguana*; blacks surge forward in *The Member of the Wedding*. The Jew in *The Dark at the Top of the Stairs*, the artist in *The Fugitive Kind*; the schoolteachers in *Picnic* are typical of a generalized sympathy for the rejected.

The transference of homosexual attitudes to heterosexual characters was much-remarked on among the cognoscenti. Hal in *Picnic* was caustically described as a gay hustler; Blanche in *Streetcar* was much poo-poohed as an aging homosexual in drag; the lady who runs the diner in *Bus Stop* and has one-night stands was clucked at. Tom in *Glass Menagerie*, with his mysterious nights out, was checked off. Bo's non-participant buddy in *Bus Stop* was taken to be an abdicating gay lover; some saw the Jewish cadet in *Dark* as a symbol of the unassimilable gay.

But the device most often used to inject the gay observer's presence was the wistful, intellectual, alienated child or young teenager. The little sister in *Picnic* walled off from her world with books and pictures; the little boy in *Dark at the Top of the Stairs* hunched over his movie-star scrapbook; the gender-switching children in *The Member of the Wedding*—these were the little signature figures of the silent lonely gay, denied the avenues of self-realization and the whole means of maturing, forever outside-inside, watching the world go 'round, of necessity honing their minds, watching their steps, bewailing and applauding the climaxes of the more permissible dramas they lived among.

For what was the alternative? Inge has left us one play, *A Loss of Roses*, with a down-at-the-bottom down-on-her-luck stripper reaching out for a pretty young boy and fleeing for his sake; and in a filmscript, *Bus Riley's Back in Town*, we see a lonely undertaker reach for the hero's knee. Of adult gay life, that is all the hint we have—that and Bo's chum receding into the background.

Let us leave this inquiry with one last image—the little boy in *The Dark at the Top of the Stairs*, climbing that stairway with his mother, only to be forced to separate from her at the landing—already separated from his sister and his father and the wonderful sympathetic cadet—holding the hopefully varied images of Hollywood stars, hoping to find some image for his own, and not yet knowing that he would instead shape them for others, and that the next generation of sisters and cadets, mommies and daddies, would take images from him.

Good night, lonely little dreaming Midwest boy; sleep well, and may you hear this benediction in your dreams.

Come Back, Little Sheba and Mass Culture
Jane Courant

In the introduction to *Understanding Media, The Extensions of Man*, Marshall McLuhan writes:

> The power of the arts to anticipate future social and technological developments—has long been recognized. In this century, Ezra Pound called the artist "the antennae of the race." Art as radar acts as "an early warning system" as it were.... This concept of the arts as prophetic, contrasts with popular ideas of them as mere self-expression [xi].

Throughout his career and in the years that followed, most critics of William Inge's plays have been inclined to view them in psychological rather than political or social terms, as "mere self-expression" rather than as sensitive "radar" registering new social or cultural phenomena not yet apparent to the rest of society. This is especially true of his first play to receive national attention, *Come Back, Little Sheba*, which prompted a good deal of commentary on its supposed "Freudian" imagery, but limited discussion of its broader social implications.[1] Historical distance, however, elucidates an "early warning system" in the play about deep social inequities that would be challenged in the decades to follow. As Jeff Johnson, author of the only recent, in-depth critical study of Inge, notes, the playwright's exposure of sexual stereotyping was "certainly culturally subversive: in fact, it may have signaled the beginning of a general tearing of the social fabric of the '50s" (25).

Beginning with his first play to reach Broadway in 1950, Inge directly confronted not only sexual stereotyping but the cultural media that so emphatically reinforced these values in American society. Social scientists would not define the broader social and psychic problems troubling the playwright's characters for at least a decade after he created them. McLuhan's own books, appearing in the middle of the 1960s, heralded a new approach to the study of popular media. A flood of critical and historical commentary on motion pictures and broadcasting ushered in new academic disciplines in Popular Culture and Media Studies, while university departments in gender- and ethnic-based studies emerged in response to political and social upheavals of the era.

Although the contradiction between illusion and reality has long been drama's domain, Inge was the first major American playwright to explore the paradox in relation to a society oriented toward manufacturing images and illusion for an increasingly leisured populace. The mass media play an important role in all his drama, motivating action, shaping character, and establishing norms by which people measure their lives, and none of his contemporaries gave this emerging national consciousness so prominent a role in their work. The power of movies, radio, and mass advertising to shape popular ideals about feminine and masculine roles is especially marked in Inge's first major success for the stage.

In *Come Back, Little Sheba*, as in all his plays of the 1950s, Inge conveyed with precision the disparity between the myth and the reality of American life during an optimistic, consumer-oriented decade when television first developed its hold on the public, and a lagging film industry vigorously fought to compete. Yet, Inge's cultural critique was as subtle as the insidious powers that drove his frustrated, often bewildered characters. Inge's central dramatic theme of thwarted spiritual and emotional development, particularly among ordinary American women, represented an unusual departure in subject matter which puzzled critics who dismissed his work for focusing on what they considered trivial domestic or psychological concerns. Ironically, these plays would begin to take on greater political resonance in years to come as the social order began to change—since, as a popular feminist credo would later proclaim, "the personal *is* political."

Inge's deliberate use of American mass culture as the mythological center of his characters' lives came, in part, from intense observation of the popular arts in the years immediately preceding and coinciding with his first attempts at playwriting. From 1943 to 1946, the aspiring dramatist served as entertainment critic for the *St. Louis Star-Times,* where the great majority of his assignments were film reviews. He frequently criticized Hollywood's conventional treatment of women on the screen, and this excerpt from his review of a 1944 film, *American Romance,* specifically anticipates the prophetic departures in his own drama:

> ... when the picture narrows to an intimate study of American family life, it becomes as ordinary and trite as a magazine novel.... When is the American wife going to be represented as something besides the passive, understanding woman,

incapable of registering anything on her face but an insipid sweetness? How about character or intelligence for a change?

Rather than exploring the male-dominated realms of business, labor, and politics, as did many of his immediate predecessors in American drama, Inge concentrated on the domestic domain, a female arena that would take on broader social implications in later years when questions concerning sexual freedom and equality would become intensely political. Although his homosexuality remained hidden in his works of the 1950s, Inge closely observed the prevailing heterosexual hegemony with an acute eye toward its potential eruptions. This submerged sexual orientation forged a strong perspective on stereotypes operating in the dominant culture and a sense that relations between women and men would become one of the most significant issues of years to come. As one whose own sexual inclinations were emphatically condemned by his culture, Inge was especially attuned to the inequities of the "double standard" on the stage. Female characters in his drama clash with puritanical codes and oppressive convention, but, in comic rather than tragic manner, their sexuality does not defeat them. With regard to both the female and male roles Inge created, Johnson observes that his "most dynamic characters actually refuse their cookie-cutter roles ... and emerge as ... free-floating agents of subversion" (48).

Inge's faithful rendering of clichés of culture, language, and behavior during a period characterized by extreme social conformity—together with his enormous popularity with the public—made him especially vulnerable to criticism. Although most newspaper reviewers celebrated his plays of the 1950s, "those with pretensions beyond journalism," as Alan Downer describes them (28),[2] accused him of "pandering" to popular tastes. His candid treatment of sex was viewed as an effort to win the favor of a public intrigued with Freud's theories and Kinsey's recent studies of human sexuality. Moreover, concerns about mass communication's expanding role in society were coupled with fears about the encroaching power of women. Still relegated to their traditional roles as homemakers, women were nonetheless gaining in influence as a major consumer group in the United States and especially as consumers of culture and entertainment. Their mythological power—far different from their actual status—was suggested in the sex goddesses that Hollywood created as it strove to regain its former ascendancy in public entertainment

Anxieties about the feminization of culture can be detected in commentary that not only dismissed Inge as a serious playwright but viewed his popularity as a symptom of a declining dramatic tradition—indeed of a declining civilization. Robert Brustein derisively proclaimed Inge the "first spokesman for a matriarchal America" (57) at the close of the 1950s, specifically attacking him for writing "she-dramas" (53) in his influential essay, "The Men-Taming Women of William Inge." R. H. Gardner wrote in 1965, that, in *Picnic*, its "heavy emphasis upon sex and female frustration creates a suffocating atmosphere of sickness that ... subverts most of its good qualities" (99). Discussing *Come Back, Little Sheba* in 1967, Martin Gottfried complained, "What replaced the prewar socialistic content of drama was the postwar psychological content," and he attacked the play for its "elementary pop psychology" (*Theater* 257). Gottfried finally concluded that Inge's "concern with love and sex blossomed into a theory worthy of any ladies' discussion group" (259).[3] Ironically, Inge shared his harshest critics' fears about mass culture's power to thwart artistic and spiritual aspiration, but his sensitivity to its unique demoralization of women was not yet widely shared nor articulated in popular or intellectual discourse.

Though unremarkable by today's standards, Inge's sexual emphasis was indeed unusual for its time, especially because, beginning with Marie Buckholder in *Come Back, Little Sheba*, he allowed his female characters new freedom without subjecting them to traditional dramatic consequences. The advertising and motion picture industries were increasingly exploiting sex to further their aims, and many reviewers and critics seem to have confused the playwright's concerns with this trend. Yet, the image-molding power of the media—and especially its emphasis on youth, physical appearance, and material status—is a prominent theme in all of Inge's writing and is perhaps most striking in his Broadway debut.

Although Inge focuses on one family household in *Come Back, Little Sheba*, as he would in later works, domestic problems are a microcosm of a troubled world in which men and women live together in an uneasy, precarious balance. Having lost the baby that forced them to marry and unable to bear more children during a period of unprecedented population boom, the Delaneys are misfits in a postwar nation that cherished home life and idealized the nuclear family. Their troubled lives reflect the social retrenching of the era that brought women home from munitions factories and confined them once again to housekeeping, as men strove to fulfill unrealistic ideals of breadwinning power. The characters in *Sheba* accept their roles without question, but none are a very good fit: Doc Delaney is haunted by guilt and professional failure; the young college student must choose between a sexually attractive man and one whom she can depend upon financially; and Lola is completely without direction, as she herself explains early in the play: "When I lost my baby and found out I couldn't have any more, I didn't know what to do with myself. I wanted to get a job, but Doc wouldn't hear of it" (*4 Plays* 13). Consequently, Lola's days are spent in aimless chatter and childish fantasy, while

Doc projects his own guilt upon the young boarder in their home and grows more distant from his wife.

The claustrophobic world of the Delaneys is tightly restricted in *Come Back, Little Sheba*, but the dark undercurrent of their domestic arrangement reflects a wider national landscape. The editors of *The Nation* declared 1950, the year the play opened, to be America's "darkest time" since the war (qtd. in Oakley 7), reflecting upon the rampant anti–Communism sweeping the country and recent atomic bomb explosions. Nonetheless, the opening of the decade was also a time of great promise, and after many years of depression and war, America enjoyed greater prosperity than ever before, with a vast array of consumer goods to enjoy. Historian J. Ronald Oakley writes that the immediate postwar era was both auspicious and frightening: "To many Americans, at the beginning of 1950, the world appeared to have been turned upside down" (5), and Lola and Doc Delaney are among the most troubled, confused characters that Inge ever created. The playwright describes Lola as having "*a look of … emptiness, as though she were unable to understand anything that ever happened to her*" (*4 Plays* 21–22), and Doc, although more educated than his wife, is also "*mystified*" by the illusions which drive him to despair (29).

In his Foreword to *4 Plays*, Inge described his first major play as "a fabric of life in which the two central characters … were species of the environment" (vii). This postwar American environment placed enormous value on social status and material success, values unabashedly proclaimed by the expanding mass media. Doc's alcoholism in *Come Back, Little Sheba* is related to his loss of both; ironically, he still retains the nickname related to his abandoned profession, having given up medical school for the less prestigious pursuit of chiropractic. Forced to quit college in order to marry Lola, he then began drinking heavily, squandering the twenty-five-thousand-dollar inheritance that his mother left him when she died.

The expensive china that the Delaneys received from Doc's mother as a wedding gift becomes the concrete stage image of their disappointments and shattered ideals when Lola uses it to serve dinner to Marie and her future husband. The young woman's plans for the future represent all the conventional measures of success that Lola and Doc have failed to achieve, in that her fiancé "comes from one of the best families in Cincinnati, … makes three hundred dollars a month," and as she brightly adds, they plan to have "lots and lots of children" (13). Having cleaned house in anticipation of his visit, Lola happily busies herself with preparations, oblivious to her husband's distress about Marie's sexual relationship with another boyfriend. She tells the young bride-to-be, "The china's Havelin. I'm so proud of it. It's the most valuable possession we own" (47).

Inge first calls attention to this important scenic detail when Lola tells her admiring neighbor, "I got to get out all the silver and china. I like to set the table early, so I can spend the rest of the day looking at it" (45). The expensive tableware heightens expectation about the awaited dinner from the moment it appears on stage. When mealtime approaches, Lola is concerned that Doc has not returned, and, offering cocktails to the young couple, discovers that her recovering alcoholic husband has taken their one bottle of whiskey. Rather than joining the couple at the table with her own husband, as she had happily planned, the curtain falls on the distraught woman watching the young people eat from the other room. When Doc returns the next morning to find the dinner's remains, he begins his violent, drunken rampage by pulling off the cloth and smashing the table's contents. His action punctuates the play's most bitter and violent line: "My mother didn't buy these dishes for whores to eat off of" (56). Inge fuses contemporary illusions about conventional success and feminine purity that unify the play with a familiar domestic symbol of social and economic status.

In most manuscripts of *Come Back, Little Sheba*, Doc is alone on stage when the curtain rises, as he is in the final published version, but his very first action is to switch on the radio, from which a "news announcer" reads "headlines of universal sweep and magnitude"; each relates to wartime dislocation: "news from Palestine, news of the Russians in Berlin, startling stories of the atomic bomb."[4] Although Doc ignores the broadcast, it is the only sound the audience hears, and attention is immediately focused on the troubled outside world. Giving the radio such prominence in the opening moments, Inge immediately injects the mass media into his stage image. In several early drafts, Lola also makes her first entrance as the radio plays. Before she speaks a line, an anonymous broadcaster introduces the drama's central theme in an advertisement for "Dream of Youth" tissue cream. The frumpy, middle-aged woman descends the same center staircase from which Doc emerged, and which the young Marie has just ascended to take her morning bath, as the announcer's voice again fills the stage:

> (... When she gets to the bottom of the stairs her attention is caught by the radio. The newscast has ended and the announcer is interjecting his most sincere feelings into the commercial. LOLA listens)
> ANNOUNCER: Are you tired? Does life seem to have lost its zest? its meaning? Do you no longer find any fun in doing all those foolish, but exciting, terribly exciting little things that used to make life one happy, carefree dream? Is your skin dry? Have your eyes lost their glistening sparkle? Are your pores getting bigger every day? Do the facial muscles sag? Hundreds of women have found DREAM OF YOUTH TISSUE CREAM the answer to these very problems. Recapture your Dream of Youth. Find your youth again. Dream of

Youth tissue cream is to be found at ... (*With petulant annoyance,* LOLA *walks over and snaps the radio off. Then she shuffles into the kitchen.*) [*Come* 2 1–4].

Inge's sensitivity to the media's power to shape behavior and values is explicit in these early versions in which he introduces his bored housewife and her husband subject to the fears exploited by what they hear on their radio. He eventually cut both broadcasts from the play, but retained the soap opera which Lola listens to later in the first scene, the radio broadcast of "Ave Maria" which moves Doc so profoundly, and the dance band music which triggers the couple's nostalgic memories about their courtship. The role of the media is subtler in the final version of *Sheba*, as it would be in Inge's succeeding work, but he continued to expose the anxieties it exploited, and particularly the desperation with which women turn to consumer goods to preserve their youthful beauty. A jar of "Ponsella Three-Way Tissue Cream" eventually finds its way into the feminine world of *Picnic,* when Rosemary Sydney, who is frantic to marry, makes her entrance massaging the cream into her face (*4 Plays 86*). Long before others looked to mass culture as the subject of creative exploration, Inge incorporated its insidious messages into his art. His vision consistently encompassed traditional feminine and masculine polarities of beauty and power reinforced by Madison Avenue and Hollywood to this day.

In 1967, Inge discussed his feelings about mass advertising in connection with "a short 'pop play'" that he "composed almost entirely of TV commercials." The piece, entitled "Bad Breath," makes explicit Inge's artistic self-consciousness about American popular culture, and his attitudes toward that culture are strong:

> I'm fascinated by the ads on television. They repel me so; I feel that I have to do something about them. The reality that they imply, or that they *create,* out of American life is so appalling that I just had to show it.... It reminds me a bit of Andy Warhol's Coca-Cola bottles and Lichtenstein's work: it's so horrible it's funny. When you look at TV commercials in this way on-stage they take on a pretty awesome meaning. Remember those dreadful commercials where a girl's whole success in life depends upon some new deodorant or breath purifier? The desperate importance that the commercial gives to this nonsense is fascinating [Inge, "A Conversation" 51–52].

Early manuscripts of *Come Back, Little Sheba* from the late 1940s confirm Inge's sensitivity to the media's power over ordinary Americans as it developed during the age of print advertising and radio. Like that of many other Americans, Lola's cultural experience is limited to what the mass media provides. Historical hindsight reveals glaring contradictions between provocative female imagery and prevailing ideals of feminine purity in movies of the 1940s and 1950s, and Inge consistently chooses his Hollywood icons with care. In the opening scene of *Come Back, Little Sheba,* Doc tells Lola that he cannot take her to a Rita Hayworth movie because he has an Alcoholics Anonymous meeting. In movies such as *Gilda* (1946) and *The Lady from Shanghai* (1947), Hayworth epitomized the "destructive femininity" that film historians trace in many films of the decade (Haskell 209), and Doc appropriately rejects Lola's invitation, suggesting that the attractive Marie accompany her. Michael Wood writes that *Gilda* is "as sour and lucid a picture of romantic love as Hollywood has ever given us" and further notes that the powerful Hollywood conception of the beautiful woman as "lethal weapon" was objectified when "the bomb dropped on Bikini was called Gilda and had a picture of Rita Hayworth painted on it (51).[5] Hayworth conveyed the conflicting images of sexual promise and virginal purity that Hollywood had projected about women ever since Inge's movie-going boyhood in the 1920s, and the star aptly reflects Doc Delaney's own fears and illusions about women.

Unaware of the depth of her husband's repulsion over Marie's affair with a handsome athlete, Lola cheerfully discusses the young people in Hollywood terms. Despite her own inclination toward fantasy, she puts her finger on her husband's illusions:

> DOC: A big brawny bozo like Turk, he probably forces her to kiss him.
> LOLA: Daddy, that's not so at all. I came in the back way once when they were in the living room, and she was kissing him like he was Rudolph Valentino.
> DOC: (*An angry denial*) Marie is a nice girl.
> LOLA: I know she's nice. I just said she and Turk were doing some tall spooning. It wouldn't surprise me any if....
> DOC: Honey, I don't want to hear any more about it.
> LOLA: You try to make out like every young girl is Jennifer Jones in the *Song of Bernadette.*
> DOC: I do not. I just like to believe that young people like her are clean and decent ... [*4 Plays* 10–11].

Later, when Lola observes the young people "spooning" in their living room, she fails to distinguish her voyeuristic pleasure from the entertainment that movies provide. Inge's two-room, divided set is the scenic vehicle for her dependence upon others for stimulation, a dependence that grows out of her own thwarted marriage:

> LOLA: Come and look, Daddy.
> DOC: (*Shocked and angry*) No!
> LOLA: Just one little look. They're just kids, Daddy. It's sweet. (*Drags him by arm*)
> DOC: Stop it, Baby. I won't do it. It's not decent to snoop around spying on people like that. It's cheap and mischievous and mean.
> ....

> LOLA: You watch young people make love in the movies, don't you, Doc? There's nothing wrong with that. And I *know* Marie and I like her, and Turk's nice, too. They're both so young and pretty. Why shouldn't I watch them?
> DOC: I give up [37–38].

In "giving up," Doc registers some awareness that, for his wife, the lines between illusion and reality are blurred. A romantic movie is going on in her own home, and she accepts the role of observer with no notion of interfering. In contrast, Doc is anxious to impose his own confused morality, as if stopping the liaison could somehow absolve his own youthful indiscretions. Not daring to intervene, however, he inappropriately places responsibility for Marie's behavior on Lola, warning her at the close of the first scene, "If anything happens to the girl I'll never forgive you" (27). His deluded accusations that his wife is actually encouraging the affair intensifies as the action progresses and eventually provokes his violent attack that climaxes the play.

Doc's unconscious attraction for Marie is mirrored in Lola's fascination with Marie's handsome boyfriend Turk, whom she compliments by comparing him to another Hollywood figure. Admiring his exposed physique, as Marie sketches him, Lola tells the young track star that he "should be out in Hollywood making those Tarzan movies" (15). This remark pleases Turk, and Lola "*couldn't be more flattered*" when he returns the compliment in crude, popular metonymy, telling her that she is "a swell skirt" (16). Soon after, she wins the friendship of the muscular milkman by giving him the same career advice (20), and both the Valentino and Tarzan imagery anticipate Hal Carter's stories about his aborted Hollywood career in Inge's next play, *Picnic*:

> Yah! They took a lotta pictures of me with my shirt off. Real rugged. Then they dressed me up like the Foreign Legion. Then they put me in a pair of tights—and they gave me a big hat with a plume, and had me makin' with the sword play.... It was real crazy! [*4 Plays* 91].

Later, Hal tells his former college buddy about a hitchhiking incident with two women who "musta thought I was Superman" (93). In *Summer Brave* and early versions of *Picnic*, Inge changes the reference to Tarzan. The neighborhood boys torment the awkward Millie Owens with the epithet, "Mrs. Tarzan" in *Picnic* (*4 Plays* 77) and "Madam Tar-zan" in the published revision, *Summer Brave* (5). As in *Come Back, Little Sheba*, the dramatist carefully selected popular culture references that would convey great mythic resonance. The masculine icons that figure prominently in Inge's drama are examined by Rupert Wilkinson in his study, *American Tough: The Tough-Guy Tradition and American Character*: "Although many societies have had their strong-man heroes, only America has developed in such loving, muscular detail the superhero tradition of Tarzan and Superman" (11).

Inge exposes such "superhero" images by presenting them in an ironic or comic manner. Alan is highly skeptical of Hal's Hollywood stories in *Picnic*, and the body-building milkman, like the athlete/lover Turk in *Come Back, Little Sheba*, is humorously conceived. Initially in a hurry to get his job done, he barely tolerates Lola's meandering conversation about Doc's alcoholism as she leisurely checks off items on the dairy delivery list. When she comments on his "husky" physique and pays him the Tarzan compliment, however, he immediately becomes friendly, brags to her about sending his "physique study" photograph to *"Strength and Health"* magazine, and even drops to the floor to do push-ups (*4 Plays* 21). The scene prefigures Turk's pose as a javelin thrower in Lola's living room, his bare chest more directly suggestive of Tarzan.

Late in the second act, when the milkman returns with the items that Lola specifically ordered to help Doc overcome his craving for alcohol, it is after the climactic explosion and immediately before his sober return from the hospital. Inge brings back this comic figure to intensify the violent emotions that Lola has experienced in the interim. Her interest in him is significantly diminished and their scene creates a striking moment of comic pathos as he narcissistically boasts about his fame in the popular media:

> MILKMAN: ... Remember, I told you my picture was going to appear in *Strength and Health*. (*Showing her magazine*) Well, see that pile of muscles? That's me.
> LOLA: My goodness. You got your picture in a magazine.
> MILKMAN: Yes, ma'am. See what it says about my chest development? For the greatest self-improvement in a three months' period.
> LOLA: Goodness sakes. You'll be famous, won't you?
> MILKMAN: If I keep busy on these bar-bells. I'm working now for "muscular separation."
> LOLA: That's nice [66].

The printed media will also play a role in Inge's later plays. In *Picnic*, the *Reader's Digest*, one of the most popular magazines of the 1950s, is a ready point of reference, and Madge Owens, as town beauty queen, gets her picture published in the local Sunday supplement. Bo's first boast in *Bus Stop* concerns his rodeo photographs in *Life*, and the aspiring cabaret singer Cherie passes the time by reading movie magazines. The living room set of *Dark at the Top of the Stairs* incorporates movie fan magazines and signed photographs cherished by young Sonny Flood to escape the grim reality of his family home.

In *Sheba*, Inge links the primitive jungle imagery of the Tarzan figures who visit Lola's home with her temporary refuge in a favorite soap opera, "Taboo," whose title reflects the sexual repression that eventually triggers Doc's outburst. Having failed to retain the company of her Tarzan-like visitors, she turns on her radio show which directly proclaims its purpose of sweeping away reality:

> ... *A pulsating tom-tom is heard as a theme introduction. Then the* ANNOUNCER)
> ANNOUNCER (*In dramatic voice*) TA-BOOoooo! (*Now in a very soft, highly personalized voice.* LOLA *sits on couch, eats candy*) It's Ta-boo, radio listeners, your fifteen minutes of temp*t*ation. (*An alluring voice*) Won't you join me? (LOLA *swings feet up*) Won't you leave behind your routine, the dull cares that make up your day-to-day existence, the little worries, the uncertainties, the confusions of the work-a-day world and follow me where pagan spirits hold sway, where lithe natives dance on a moon-enchanted isle, where palm trees sway with the restless ocean tide, restless *tom-tom. Now, in an oily voice*) But remember, it's TA-BOOOOOO-OOOOOOO! (*Now the tom-tom again, going into a sensual, primitive rhythm melody.* LOLA *has been transfixed from the beginning of the program....*) [22].

Gilbert Seldes's pioneering study of the American mass media, *The Great Audience* (1951), is one of the few such sociological works in Inge's personal library. Like Inge, Seldes was especially sensitive to the media's insidious influence on women, and his description of the radio soap opera is especially pertinent to *Come Back, Little Sheba*:

> The daytime serial, which began between two wars ... took advantage of the loss of confidence during the depression as it takes advantage of the loss of direction in the years of the cold war. Moreover, it exists in the atmosphere of jeopardy induced by much of radio's advertising: cosmetics, laxatives, and other commodities to a degree, constantly threaten women with the loss of their husbands unless they act promptly ... it holds the threat of a lonely future over women ... it has the psychological strength of all glamorization of the past [240–43].

Seldes contends that the characters in radio serials "become friends with their listeners ... and 'visit' several hours a day" (240), and Inge appropriately notes that the "Taboo" announcer speaks in "*a very soft, highly personalized voice.*" It is only when Lola's flesh-and-blood guests have abandoned her that she turns to her electronic visitor.

In the next scene, the radio again plays an important role, this time to punctuate Lola's success in drawing her husband into nostalgic fantasy about the years when they enjoyed an active sexual life together. Having burst his "spell," listening to a broadcast of "*Ave Maria*," she asks for "some peppy music," and Doc obliges by turning the dial. He finds some "*sentimental dance band*" music (29), which stimulates mutual reminiscences about their courtship, but when Lola becomes "*very coy and flirtatious now, an old dog playing old tricks*" (30), Doc grows uncomfortable and tries to stop her by shutting off the radio. "That's all forgotten now" (31), he asserts, but Lola persists and even momentarily recaptures him in a reverie. When she next tries to confront him with the truth about their forced marriage, he deflects her with repressive finality. Appropriately, the radio's world of illusion is momentarily silenced as Lola attempts to face reality with her husband:

> LOLA: .... Are you sorry you married me, Doc?
> DOC: Of course not.
> LOLA: I mean, are you sorry you *had* to marry me?
> DOC: (*Goes to the porch*) We were never going to talk about that, Baby [32–33].

Lola persists and confronts him with more painful questions about their lost child, but as she gets no response and to change the gloomy mood, she again flicks on the radio. The world of illusion once more blocks out the painful reality of their present life, hurling them into nostalgic reverie. As the radio plays, Lola and Doc enjoy their happiest moment together in the play, but their temporary joy is shattered by Marie's arrival:

> LOLA: ... What are we sitting round here so serious for? (*Turns to radio*) Let's have some music. (LOLA *gets a lively fox trot on the radio, dances with* DOC. *They begin dancing vigorously as though to dispense with the sadness of the preceding dialogue, but slowly it winds them and leaves* LOLA *panting*) We oughta go dancing ... all the time, Docky.... It'd be good for us. Maybe if I danced more often, I'd lose ... some of ... this fat. I remember ... I used to be able to dance like this ... all night ... and not even notice ... it. (LOLA *breaks into a Charleston routine as of yore*) Remember the Charleston, Daddy? (DOC *is clapping his hands in rhythm. Then* MARIE *bursts in through the front door, the personification of the youth that* LOLA *is trying to recapture.*)
> MARIE: What are you trying to do, a jig, Mrs. Delaney? (MARIE *doesn't intend her remark to be cruel, but it wounds* LOLA. LOLA *stops abruptly in her dancing, losing all the fun she has been able to create for herself. She feels she might cry; so to hide her feelings she hurries quietly out to kitchen....*) [34–35].

Inge juxtaposes the cultural modes of different generations in this poignant dance centerpiece of *Come Back, Little Sheba*. Through self-referential theatricality and allusions to popular culture in each of his following plays, he creates similar moments of revelation for his older characters. Rosemary's happy reminiscence about being a "dancin' fool" (*4 Plays* 118) is sharply aborted in the central scene of *Picnic* when Hal frees himself from her grasp to dance with a woman of his own age, to the accompanying teenage band music. Professor Lyman halts his "meaningless little act" (*4 Plays* 196), playing Romeo to a much younger Juliet, midway through *Bus Stop* in a floorshow that also features the young torch singer's rendition of "That Old Black Magic" (197). Lottie Lacey is unsettled by the young couple dancing suggestively to the "Shiek of Araby" music halfway through *The Dark at the Top of the Stairs*

(*4 Plays* 266), and the pathetic Vince Brinkman performs a *"crude burlesque of rock and roll"* to twist music in *Natural Affection* (85), as his mortified young wife looks on.

Through these jarring or inappropriate performances of popular entertainment, Inge theatrically objectifies the arrested adolescence characteristic of American culture and conveys a powerful stage image of the nation's glorification of youth. His tender portrayal of Lola in *Come Back, Little Sheba* represents the first in a series of middle-aged characters who illustrate Seldes's warning that American movies, radio, and advertising "conspire to prolong adolescence until we are in danger of becoming a nation of teenagers" (23). Her longing for the past and her fascination with the young people in her home are reinforced by media images that prevent her from fully maturing or playing a productive role in adult life. Like other Inge characters, her predicament illustrates Seldes's contention that

> the exploitation of the insecurity of women joins with another powerful theme in American society, of which one aspect is properly called the glorification of youth, the other phase being the prevention of maturity ... [241].
> ... a determined effort to perpetuate the adolescent mind. In this the share of the popular arts is one of the dominant factors....
> The exploitation of the anxieties of middle-aged women by the daytime serial is matched by the exploitation of youth in the movies. What happens in the movies is chiefly love, and it happens to the young looking if not to the young. This corresponds to one form of reality, since the subconscious message of a vast amount of advertising reduces all sex attraction to one age level (for women); it is not the consuming fire of grown men and women, but the flash-point of adolescents. This is the promise-and-threat that sells cosmetics and girdles [243].

As in each of his succeeding plays, Inge interweaves contrasting realms of American culture into the fabric of Lola's disenchantment and Doc's distorted illusions about women, using popular and more established forms to highlight their differences. The virginal ideal that Doc unrealistically attaches to their young boarder (aptly named Marie) is linked to Schubert's "Ave Maria," which issues from the same radio that plays Lola's sexually romantic soap opera, the couple's favorite evening show, "Fibber McGee and Molly," and popular music. In early drafts of the play, Inge opens the second scene of Act I, with the Schubert piece (Inge, *Come* 1, 2–1; Inge, *Come* July 1949), and it remains an important moment in the final version of the play. Inge carefully selects a work of "high culture," whose overexposure he complained about as a St. Louis reporter, but Doc is appropriately unfamiliar with it. The selection reinforces the disappointed man's idealized notion of women and images of motherhood promulgated by the media in the postwar era. His temporary retreat to the world of illusion is abruptly halted by the reality of his wife's "vulgar" presence:

.... *At the radio* DOC *starts twisting the dial. He rejects one noisy program after another, then very unexpectedly he comes across a rendition of Schubert's famous "Ave Maria," sung in a high soprano voice. Probably he has encountered the piece before somewhere, but it is now making its first impression on him. Gradually he is transported into a world of ethereal beauty which he never knew existed. He listens intently. The music has expressed some ideal of beauty he never fully realized and he is even a little mystified. Then* LOLA *comes in the back door, letting it slam, breaking the spell, and announcing in a loud, energetic voice*) Isn't it funny? I'm not a bit tired tonight. You'd think after working so hard all day I'd be pooped.

DOC: (*In the living room; he cringes*) Baby, don't use that word.

LOLA: .... I'm sorry Doc. I hear Marie and Turk say it all the time, and I thought it was kinda cute.

DOC: It ... it sounds vulgar.

LOLA: (*Kisses* DOC) I won't say it again, Daddy. Where's Fibber McGee?

DOC: Not quite time yet [29].

Into his cultural fabric, Inge intertwines a double standard in the visual art world that feminists would identify some two decades later. Turning off her soap opera when Marie and Turk arrive for a sketching session, Lola questions the art student about her model, who is posing in his track suit, and she is confused by the fact that

the women pose naked but the men don't. (*This strikes her as a startling inconsistency*) If it's all right for a woman, it oughta be for a man [23].

Lola is so perplexed that she brings the subject up again with Doc, hoping for a more complete explanation:

LOLA: Why is that?

DOC: (*Stumped*) Well...

LOLA: If it's all right for a woman it oughta be for a man. But the man always keeps covered. That's what she said.

DOC: Well, that's the way it should be, honey. A man, after all, is a man, and he ... well, he has to protect himself.

LOLA: And a woman doesn't?

DOC: It's different, honey.

LOLA: Is it? ... [26].

In her ignorance and childlike innocence, Lola questions a double standard in a cultural world beyond her reach, whereas those with pretensions of understanding accept its social conventions without question. Complimenting Marie on her drawing, Lola further expresses a wistful yearning for her own creative fulfillment: "It ... it's real artistic. (*Pause*) I wish *I* was artistic" (24). In the world that the playwright so faithfully records, there is little possibility that she will ever have the opportunity to find out.

Mothers, housewives, and objects of sexual desire are the only female roles that the characters in *Come Back, Little Sheba* can fathom, and Inge's sensitivity to mass culture's reinforcement of these conventional roles represented "an early warning system" in an expanding realm of American life. Doc worships a spiritual ideal of womanhood objectified in "Ave Maria" that issues from the same radio that broadcasts "Taboo"; and he views sexuality as dangerous, a dichotomy sanctioned by the contemporary media and epitomized in the contemporary icon, Rita Hayworth. Lola depends upon its images, confusing real people with film stars, whereas the pragmatic Marie, who is busy enjoying life's pleasures, never once mentions movies or radio throughout the play.

Lola's immaturity is directly conveyed through the Delaneys' pet names for each other, "Baby" and "Daddy," or the deferential "Doc." Her boredom and arrested development as a housewife, and especially as a childless wife at a time when Americans were reproducing in record numbers, present a striking example of what Betty Friedan would identify thirteen years later as "The Problem That Has No Name" in her landmark polemic, *The Feminine Mystique*:

> The problem lay buried, unspoken, for many years in the minds of American women. It was a strange stirring, a sense of dissatisfaction, a yearning that women suffered in the middle of the twentieth century in the United States. Each suburban wife struggled with it alone ... [15].
>
> ....
> ... In the fifteen years after World War II ... [m]illions of women lived their lives in the image of those pretty pictures of the American suburban housewife, kissing their husbands goodbye in front of the picture window, depositing their stationwagonsful of children at school, and smiling as they ran the new electric waxer over the spotless kitchen floor ... [18].

Lola's isolation is highlighted by her visiting neighbor, Mrs. Coffman, a mother of seven, who nonetheless manages to keep an immaculate home. This secondary character's excessive, almost frantic concern about housekeeping is underlined when her admiration of Lola's transforming her home for Marie's visiting suitor is comically converted to envy. Winifred Dusenbury, one of the few female critics of *Come Back, Little Sheba*, points out that Lola and Doc are "both failures according to magazine advertising standards" (14), and Inge's set description together with Mrs. Coffman's contrasting habits, underscore the gap between Lola's attitudes toward homemaking and the media's ideal. Her childless, messy domicile clearly defies standards set by mass advertising which projected images of bright, sparkling appliances, presided over by orderly homemakers:

> *What sun could come through the window ... is dimmed by the smoky glass curtains. In the kitchen there is a table, center. On it are piled dirty dishes from supper the night before. Woodwork in the kitchen is dark and grimy. No industry whatsoever*

has been spent in making it one of those white, cheerful rooms that we commonly think kitchens should be [5].

In one of his earliest articles on playwriting, for *Theatre Arts*, Inge defended Lola's housekeeping habits and her friendly encounters with her morning visitors that several reviewers described as "slatternly" or "slovenly":

> ... she is certainly as well off having fun with the postman and milkman as she would be at bridge parties and teas. If she keeps a messy house, that is strictly her business and Doc doesn't seem to mind seriously [Inge, "Schizophrenic" 23].

He also called attention to harsh critical judgments leveled against both Lola and Marie. The older woman's vicarious pleasure in the college student's dual romantic life provoked scorn and even outrage in several reviews. As in *Bus Stop* and the Broadway production of *Picnic*, a sexually active young woman is rewarded with a "happy ending," and the reconciliation between the older couple, although much more qualified, also conveys a note of optimism which troubled reviewers accustomed to a different dramatic tradition.[6] An analysis of the divided critical opinion about *Come Back, Little Sheba* reveals a direct connection between the vocabulary of misogyny and dismissal, a relation that can be traced through reviews and criticism of Inge's later works and their revivals.[7]

In the most negative reviews of *Come Back, Little Sheba*, Marie is variously described as an "artful little hussy" (Norton), a "sex-driven girl" (Bolton), or a "wench who takes on all comers" (Barnes); *Time* offered the following plot summary: "discovering that their college-age boarder is turning, like Lola, into a slut, [Doc] goes on another drunken rampage" ("The Theater"). R. Baird Shuman, author of an early book on Inge, writes that Marie has "the morals of a cat" ([1965] 38).[8] To these analyses, Inge responded and noted the class prejudice at work as well:

> The only personal rancor I was induced to feel ... was for those who carelessly referred to Lola as a 'slut'.... [D]espite her love of dreaming and disregard for household responsibilities (childish rather than slovenly), she is *not* a slut; .... Nor is Marie a "slut." Surely we are thinking in very Victorian terms if we refer to a girl in this way just because she has been seduced before marriage. I cannot help thinking we still are unable to separate low morals from low incomes and perhaps low mentalities when we resort so abusively to such terms ["Schizophrenic" 23].

Perplexed by repressive illusions about female purity, it is Doc who attacks Lola and Marie as "whores" and "a couple of sluts" in his drunken frenzy (*4 Plays* 56), yet many contemporary reviewers, and even later critics, seem to regard these epithets as appropriate. Such moral judgments inevitably contribute to their finding flaws in the play, especially in the qualified, "happy ending" in which Lola and Doc make their tenuous peace. Responding to adverse reviews that described Doc as having been "trapped into disastrous marriage" (Bolton), Inge again expressed his egalitarian views:

> Doc, because he is pompous and self-righteous should not fool people into regarding him as a fallen aristocrat who has married beneath his station. If Lola is uneducated, lax, and not very intelligent, she possesses enough human warmth and compassion to make her his equal in basic human worth ["Schizophrenic" 23].

This attitude toward the sexually and economically oppressed runs through all Inge's work. Exposing conditions that made both sexes uneasy, he portrayed women trapped in a rigid social order and a moral code that was unforgiving with regard to sexual pleasure. In early one-acts, such as "The Boy in the Basement" and "The Tiny Closet," Inge portrayed homosexuals subjected to bigotry and oppression, and by the 1960s, he would dare to create sympathetic, gay characters in his Broadway plays *Natural Affection* and *Where's Daddy?* But in his drama of the 1950s, beginning with *Come Back, Little Sheba*, he confined his compassion to the dominated half of the heterosexual world.

Because women were still held to more rigid prohibitions than their male partners in the mid-twentieth century, Inge's matter-of-fact approach to Marie's romances, Cherie's past promiscuity in *Bus Stop*, and Madge's impulsive sex with Hal in *Picnic* were still unusual on the American stage. Sidney Howard was one of his rare predecessors in American realism to deal so objectively with sexual indiscretion by a working-class woman in the comic play, *They Knew What They Wanted* (1924). Like Howard's San Francisco waitress, Amy, Marie also knows precisely what she wants—security in marriage as well as a sexual "fling" before settling down; she is a pragmatic young woman who knows the limits of her world.

Early drafts of the play provide the explicit background on Marie's romantic life that troubled male critics so; in fact, these scenes are among the most reworked portions of the play. Since Marie embodies the attractive girl that Lola once was but moves in a modern world that she cannot comprehend, Inge carefully strove to create the right balance in their attitudes. He eventually chose to keep the young woman's romances somewhat ambiguous to emphasize Lola's disillusion but ultimate acceptance of her choice of mates. In the final version of *Come Back, Little Sheba*, Lola and Marie have two brief conversations about her fiancé and her current boyfriend. After offering her the living room in which to entertain Turk in the first act, Lola suddenly asks about Bruce:

> MARIE: .... Well, he comes from one of the best families in Cincinnati. And they have a great big house. And they have a maid, too. And he's got a wonderful personality. He makes three hundred dollars a month.

LOLA: That so?
MARIE: And he stays in the best hotels. His company insists on it....
LOLA: Do you like him as well as Turk? (*Buttoning up back of Marie's blouse*)
MARIE: (*Evasive*) Bruce is so dependable and ... he's a gentleman, too [*4 Plays* 13].

In several drafts, Marie repeats the banality, "Bruce is my ideal" (see *Come* 1 1-12; *Come* July 1949; *Sheba* 1 1-9), elaborating only on his financial attributes that will offer her a secure place in conventional society. In the final version, just prior to Bruce's arrival, the discussion of her dual romantic life continues, and Marie's pragmatic view is even linked to her fiancé's business values:

LOLA: What if Bruce finds out that you've been going with someone else?
MARIE: Bruce and I had a very businesslike understanding before I left for school that we weren't going to sit around lonely just because we were separated.
LOLA: Aren't you being kind of mean to Turk?
MARIE: I don't think so.
LOLA: How's he going to feel when Bruce comes?
MARIE: He may be sore for a little while, but he'll get over it.
LOLA: Won't he feel bad?
MARIE: He's had his eye on a pretty little Spanish girl in his history class for a long time. I like Turk, but he's not the marrying kind.
LOLA: No! Really? (LOLA *with a look of sad wonder on her face, sits on arm of couch. It's been a serious disillusionment*) [49-50].

Having observed Turk and Marie's affair progress in her home as she would watch a movie, Lola has momentary difficulty accepting the idea that it will not end in the neat resolution characteristic of the medium's convention. Although Lola quickly shifts her attention to the new suitor, she tells Marie in several early versions, that she liked Turk because "the two of you looked so nice together, he so big and strong [or "healthy looking" in another draft (*Come* 2 4-4)] and you so pretty and cute" (*Come* 1 1-12; *Sheba* 1 1-9), underlining the idealized, superficial Hollywood image of her fantasy. In one early version of their exchange, Inge develops dialogue that later becomes the crux of Madge Owens' dilemma regarding to her two contrasting suitors in *Picnic*:

MARIE: I guess Turk is the sort of boy every girl falls in love with *some* time ... while she's young. If he came in the room now with a justice of the peace and wanted me to marry him, I probably would. But he's not going to. And besides I don't think we'd stay in love very long.... And I'd be worried married to a man like Turk. The only thing he's interested in is sports; he doesn't study. I don't see how he'll ever hold a job, and he'll probably be chasing pretty girls as long as he lives.

> LOLA: That's too bad.
> MARIE: (*Fondly*) But I'll always remember him; and they'll be nice memories to keep. I won't regret a one of them [*Come* Dec. 1949 4-4].

In this draft, Bruce is described as "a small, thin young man, who early has assumed the right businessman's dress and attitude" (*Come* Dec. 1949 4-6), emphasizing the differences between the two men who will take center stage in *Picnic*. In another version of *Sheba*, Inge creates a scene in which Marie tries to convince Turk to propose to her, explicitly conveying her preference for the physically attractive athlete over the successful businessman and establishing that her choice of mates is an unambiguous compromise (*Come* Oct. 1949 Insert 1-3-22). In yet another version, Marie tells Lola that Turk has "known all along" about Bruce, and this draft especially illuminates Inge's commitment to his original ending for *Picnic* in which Madge does *not* follow the man who provides her sexual initiation. Moreover, it conveys a practical attitude toward female dependence upon a male breadwinner and striking defiance of the era's double standard:

> Turk's just the kind of a boy you have fun with while you're young, the kind of boy every girl has to get out of her system, I suppose, if she's ever going to grow up. But it never occurred to me to marry Turk; I want a thoughtful, dependable husband who'll look after me, so I can have a home and children [*Come* 2 4-5].

In this version, Marie is also more adamant about her "businesslike understanding" with her fiancé, telling the confused Lola: "what happens *before* we're married is none of Bruce's affair" (*Come* 2 4-5). Inge perhaps recognized that such attitudes were too advanced for acceptance on the post–World War II stage, and he eventually permits Marie's choices to speak for themselves. As the critics' reactions demonstrate, the result was often confusion and moral indignation; rather than recognizing her catalytic role in the primary dramatic action between the middle-aged couple, they insisted on judging the character and adopted Doc's distorted attitudes.

In 1966, Inge looked back on his first experience as a playwright in New York and modestly addressed the uniqueness of his Broadway debut:

> When I moved here in 1949, I had written an unassuming play, *Come Back, Little Sheba*, so close to me ('though never autobiographical) its writing had been like the painful removal of some malignancy; it was even painful and a little embarrassing for me to watch the play on the stage. Across the street from my theater the Lunts were playing in a picturesque romance with almost a dozen magnificent settings.... I felt very humbled returning to my own play with its one drab interior, so convincingly real, I could almost smell the bacon drippings. Was this poor thing really my own? Was this melancholy atmosphere all that I could create for an audience to behold? [Inge, "On New York" 27].

When *Sheba* opened in 1950, Inge disarmed critics by his "unassuming" and "drab" little play. In contrast to dramatic predecessors who chose untamed beasts as their central symbols—foxes, tigers, seagulls, larks, and wild ducks—his domesticated house pet was an unusual, even daring variation. In his first play to receive national attention, the frustrations of the Delaneys comprised "a problem that had no name," and some believed their dilemma too trivial for dramatic presentation. However, as Jeff Johnson writes a half-century later, "the virtue of [*Sheba*] lies in the way Inge details the lives of people cast into stereotypical roles they cannot maintain" (50). Lola's stymied development, especially, renders her the first of Inge's striking "anti-heroines" overwhelmed by a sophisticated cultural environment that locks her into a rigid social structure she cannot escape.

As in his other works of the 1950s, Inge surrounds his thwarted, middle-aged characters with youngsters who are experiencing the joys of life that they have lost. Marie, Turk, and Bruce belong to a new generation that their elders have difficulty comprehending. This juxtaposition also underscores the broader national context of *Come Back, Little Sheba*, as the new subculture of the teenager began to emerge in postwar years. Into the Delaneys' unhappy home comes a girl with *"the cheerfulness only youth can feel in the morning"* (*4 Plays* 5), as Inge describes Marie. In a review of a 1984 revival of *Sheba*, Benedict Nightingale writes about the playwright's unique dramatic treatment of that relationship between youth and age:

> Inge was always much concerned with the sexual force-field invisibly projected by the young, and its power to unsettle and disturb those of maturer years.... [W]hat gives the play its main interest nowadays is the sensitivity and insight Inge brings to precisely this subject, the embarrassing attraction the young hold for those they'd regard as their mother figures, father figures.... It is, if you think about it, something that hasn't often been treated by the drama.

The "embarrassing attraction" of the young is a central theme in *Picnic*, whose middle-aged characters are both stimulated by and fearful of the youthful sexuality in their midst. The dramatic impact of the central romance in *Bus Stop* also depends upon the darker counterpoint of its frame of older spectators. In *The Dark at the Top of the Stairs*, this counterpoint is reversed, as the suicide of a lonely teenager stuns his elders into recognizing the need to find fulfillment in their own lives. In *A Loss of Roses*, Lila Green actually engages in sexual activity with a young man whom she once cared for in childhood. Each of these painful congruities create powerful dramatic images of American society's "glorification of youth," a theme which first emerges in *Come Back, Little Sheba*. As Nightingale notes, Inge's consistent focus on this subject was unusual and reflects his unique portrayal of the decade when an identifiable youth culture first became apparent in American society.

Inge's exploration of the theme of generational conflict, begun in *Sheba*, takes central focus in *Picnic*, and several reviewers in the popular press seemed to sense the new play's prophetic power when it opened in 1953. John Chapman of the *New York Daily News* wrote, "the playwright sends his audience home with a feeling that somehow, some time, something more is going to happen." Brooks Atkinson, in the *New York Times*, pointed to the broad social and cultural transformation that Inge's action suggested:

> .... *Picnic* is a deadly serious play. Before it is over, the vagrant with the loud mouth and the unsavory past has altered the whole landscape.... Given a wayward brute who has a certain sincerity of his own, ... a flimsy world of lazy illusions blows apart.... Forces get loose that no one will ever again put under control.

As in *Sheba*, Inge creates a dynamic interplay of innocent optimism and dark repression in *Picnic* that reflects the anxious expectancy of the United States in the early 1950s. Such anxiety was manifest in the emerging perception of youth as a threat to traditional values, a symptom of the broader political conservatism and paranoia of the period. Once again, Inge particularly explored anxieties that beset American women. Creating a young female character who questions her sole value as a beauty queen—and asks, "[W]hat good is it to be pretty?" (*4 Plays* 84)—he pioneered new dramatic territory in exploring the era's unique oppression of women. That his teenager's first step in defying convention is taken on the dance floor with a socially unacceptable partner resonates in the nation's cultural history of succeeding years. The central musical climax, when Hal Carter wreaks havoc on the delicate equilibrium of the small community, is remarkably prophetic of the coming of rock and roll, a revolution in popular music led by the broadcast media that would not begin to emerge for at least another year.

The characters in Inge's next two plays are also highly susceptible to the media's impact. In *Bus Stop*, the nightclub singer, Cherie, explains that she "picked up" her singing style by "listenin' to the radio, seein' movies, tryin' to put over my songs as good as them people did" (*4 Plays* 166), and Inge notes that "*her make-up has been applied under the influence of having seen too many movies*" (157). Movies and celebrities are a point of reference for the more educated young waitress whose literary interests, like Millie's in *Picnic*, do not preclude a fascination with popular stars. Hollywood iconography establishes the foreground of *The Dark at the Top of the Stairs*, Inge's portrait of the 1920s, the era in which motion pictures and mass advertising first emerged as significant cultural influences. The frozen smiles on the movie stars in little Sonny

Flood's photo collection serve as concrete images of the illusions that haunt each of the play's characters.

Cherie's sexual experience and Bo's naiveté in *Bus Stop* further undermined powerful gender stereotypes of the decade. Set against the bitter musings of the aging professor, an alcoholic like Doc, their union suggested that real love had little to do with conventional values. Cherie's sense of herself as an artist is an important aspect of her character and heightens the pathos— and comedy—of her climactic performance of "That Old Black Magic" which so enraptures the lovesick cowboy. Although she recognizes her limitations, her aspirations recall Lola's abstracted artistic longing, "I wish *I* was artistic" (*4 Plays* 24). Most interesting is Inge's pointed defiance of the traditional double standard in *Bus Stop,* the culmination of the freedom that he granted Marie in *Come Back, Little Sheba*. A young woman with "a past" looks forward to a happy marriage, and the older diner owner engages in a casual affair with no serious consequences. Although the play proved popular, this sexual freedom again provoked criticism. Richard Hayes wrote of the play's "moral anarchy," and Eric Bentley complained about its "vulgar" emphasis on "sex, sex, sex." In an inversion of the convention that denied happiness to Camille and countless women on European and American stages, the divulged information that leads to the romantic resolution concerns the virginity of the male pursuer. Inge, thus, deliberately replaces the traditional "well-made" play's revelation of a secret pertaining to a fallen woman with a past to that of a man *without* a past.

Like Inge's writing for the theater, *Splendor in the Grass* departs from traditional dramatic convention on the movie screen. The action does not ultimately lead to tragedy for the thwarted young couple, nor does the film conclude with their romantic pairing. In his study of adolescence in film, David Considine notes that Inge's screenplay "significantly advanced the depiction of adolescent sexuality and brought a new maturity ... to American films" (219, 226). Carrying the first "R" rating the MPAA ever assigned, in 1961, *Splendor in the Grass* portrayed materialism's unique demoralization of women more starkly than Inge's earlier plays. Two years later, in 1963, Inge would create a successful business woman in his play *Natural Affection,* whose live-in lover refuses to marry her because she earns a higher salary.

Beginning with his first major work for the stage, William Inge exposed conditions lacking political or historical definition at the time that he wrote. His domestic emphasis on the plight of bewildered female protagonists represented an unusual departure in modern American drama, more often concerned with the economic struggles of male providers. With acute insight into impending social change, he brought the struggles of ordinary women and men to the stage with striking clarity. In each of his plays, the unattainable ideals purveyed by the mass media haunt their behavior, their speech, and their dreams. For Inge and for many of his characters, issues of sexuality and gender *were* political and moral issues; the personal was indeed political. William Inge's status as a sexual outsider forged a dramatic perspective on an obsessively materialistic, heterosexual world, and his artistic "antennae" registered significant warnings about the fundamental social upheavals that succeeding decades would bring.

NOTES

1. See especially Gardner's discussion in *The Splintered Stage: The Decline of the American Theater* (97–98); Lewis, *American Plays and Playwrights of the Contemporary Theatre* (146–51); and Weales, *American Drama Since World War II* (44–45).

2. Downer writes, "Inge's plays have not been so generally acclaimed by critics who have some pretensions beyond journalism. He has been described as flattering the prejudices of his audiences, of complying with demands of ... the box office. The final decision must, of course, be left to the future" (28).

3. See also discussions of Inge's work by Lewis and Weales, previously cited in note 1.

4. This broadcast is retained through the prompt script version, dated December 31, 1949, in the Billy Rose Theatre Collection at the New York Public Library Performing Arts Research Center and the latest version at Independence Community College (*Come* Dec. 1949 1-1-2). Of the six variant manuscripts in the William Inge Collection at Independence Community College and at the University of Kansas Library, three are undated and three are dated July 1949, October 1949, and December, 1949.

5. See especially Wood's chapter, "The Blame on Mame" (51–74), for a discussion of the "imaginary female hegemony" in the movies of the 1940s and 1950s. When the gawky younger sister enjoys her first dance with the handsome stranger in *Picnic*, she also cries out in delight, "I feel like Rita Hayworth!" (*4 Plays* 118).

6. Among them was George Jean Nathan, who liked the play, but described the closing scene as "a piece of candy dropped into its tragic pattern superficially to sweeten things a little for the box office."

7. In the harshest review of the 1975 Broadway production of *Summer Brave*, Inge's rewritten version of *Picnic*, Gottfried writes of Madge's "small time bitchiness" as a "rural hotpants."

8. In Shuman's 1989 revised edition, the reference (24) is unchanged.

WORKS CITED

Atkinson, Brooks. "At the Theatre." Rev. of *Picnic*, by William Inge. *New York Times* 20 Feb. 1953: 14. Print.

Barnes, Howard. "The Theaters: 'Come Back, Little Sheba.'" Rev. of *Come Back, Little Sheba*, by William Inge. *New York Herald Tribune* 16 Feb. 1950: 18. Print.

Bentley, Eric. "Theatre." Rev. of *Bus Stop*, by William Inge. *New Republic* 2 May 1955: 22. Print.

Bolton, Whitney. "Blackmer and Booth Make 'Little Sheba' Noteworthy." Rev. of *Come Back, Little Sheba*, by William Inge. *New York Morning Telegraph*, 17 Feb. 1950: 2. Print.
Brustein, Robert. "The Men-Taming Women of William Inge." *Harper's* Nov. 1958: 52–57. Print.
Chapman, John. "Inge's 'Picnic,' Absorbing Comedy, Given an Admirable Performance." Rev. of *Picnic*, by William Inge. *New York Daily News* 20 Feb. 1953: 53. Print.
Considine, David. M. *The Cinema of Adolescence*. Jefferson, NC: McFarland, 1985. Print.
Downer, Alan. *Recent American Drama*. Minneapolis: University of Minnesota Press, 1961. Print.
Dusenbury, Winifred. *The Theme of Loneliness in Modern American Drama*. Gainesville: University Press of Florida, 1960. Print.
Friedan, Betty. *The Feminine Mystique*. 1963. New York: Dell, 1983. Print.
Gardner, R. H. *The Splintered Stage: The Decline of the American Theater*. New York: Macmillan, 1965. Print.
Gottfried, Martin. "'Summer Brave' a Corny Revival." Rev. of *Summer* Brave, by William Inge. *New York Post* 27 Oct. 1975: 15. Print.
_____. *A Theater Divided: The Postwar American Stage*. Boston: Little, Brown, 1967. Print.
Haskell, Molly. *From Reverence to Rape: The Treatment of Women in the Movies*. Baltimore: Penguin, 1974. Print.
Hayes, Richard. "The Stage: Bus Stop." Rev. of *Bus* Stop, by William Inge. *Commonweal* 8 Apr. 1955: 14. Print.
Howard, Sidney. *They Knew What They Wanted*. Garden City, NY: Doubleday, 1925. Print.
Inge, William. "'American Romance' Is Typical Epic.'" Rev. of *American Romance* [film]. *St. Louis Star-Times* 17 Nov. 1944: 17. Print.
_____. "The Boy in the Basement." In *Summer Brave and Eleven Short Plays*. New York: Random House, 1962. 161–85. Print.
_____. *Come Back, Little Sheba* [*Sheba* 1]. TS. N.d. William Inge Collection. Independence Community College, Independence, KS. Print.
_____. *Come Back, Little Sheba* [*Come* July 1949]. TS. July 1949. William Inge Collection, Kansas Collection. Kenneth Spencer Research Library, University of Kansas Libraries, Lawrence. Print.
_____. *Come Back, Little Sheba* [*Come* Oct. 1949]. TS. Oct. 1949. William Inge Collection, Kansas Collection. Kenneth Spencer Research Library, University of Kansas Libraries, Lawrence. Print.
_____. *Come Back, Little Sheba* [*Come* Dec. 1949]. TS. Dec. 1949. William Inge Collection. Independence Community College, Independence, KS. Print.
_____. *Come Back, Little Sheba* [prompt script]. TS. Dec. 31, 1949. Billy Rose Theatre Collection, New York Public Library Performing Arts Research Center, New York, NY. Print.
_____. *Come Back, Little Sheba: A Play in Six Scenes* [*Come* 1]. TS. N.d. William Inge Collection. Independence Community College, Independence, KS. Print.
_____. *Come Back, Little Sheba: A Play in Six Scenes* [*Come* 2]. TS. N.d. William Inge Collection, Kansas Collection. Kenneth Spencer Research Library, University of Kansas Libraries, Lawrence. Print.

———. *4 Plays by William Inge* [*Come Back, Little Sheba*; *Picnic*; *Bus Stop*; *The Dark at the Top of the Stairs*]. New York: Random House, 1958. Print.
———. *A Loss of Roses*. New York: Random House, 1960. Print.
———. *Natural Affection*. New York: Random House, 1963. Print.
———. "On New York—and a New Play." *New York Herald Tribune* 27 Feb. 1966: 27. Print.
———. "The Schizophrenic Wonder." *Theatre Arts* May 1950: 22–23. Print.
———. *Splendor in the Grass* [screenplay]. *Men and Women*. Ed. Richard A. Maynard. New York: Scholastic, 1974. 12–74. Print.
———. *Summer Brave and Eleven Short Plays*. New York: Random House, 1962. Print.
———. "The Tiny Closet." In *Summer Brave and Eleven Short Plays*. New York: Random House, 1962. 187–200. Print.
———. *Where's Daddy?* New York: Random House, 1966. Print.
———. "William Inge—A Playwright in Transition: A Conversation with Digby Diehl." Interview with Digby Diehl. *Transatlantic Review* 26 (Fall 1967): 51–56. Print.
Johnson, Jeff. *William Inge and the Subversion of Gender*. Jefferson, NC: McFarland, 2005. Print.
Lewis, Allan. *American Plays and Playwrights of the Contemporary Theatre*. New York: Crown, 1965. Print
McLuhan, Marshall. *Understanding Media: The Extensions of Man*. 1964. New York: New American Library, 1965. Print.
Nathan, George Jean. "How to Fail in One Easy Lesson." Rev. of *Come Back, Little Sheba*, by William Inge. *New York Journal-American* 27 Feb. 1950: 12. Print.
Nightingale, Benedict. "Will Critics of a Later Day Give Inge His Due?" Rev. of *Come Back, Little Sheba*, by William Inge. *New York Times* 29 July 1984, sec. 4:3. Print.
Norton, Elliot. "New Drama Opens at the Colonial: 'Come Back, Little Sheba' Aimed at Heart." Rev. of *Come Back, Little Sheba*, by William Inge. *Boston Post* 31 Jan. 1950: 17. Print.
Oakley, J. Ronald. *God's Country, America in the Fifties*. New York: Dembner, 1986. Print.
Seldes, Gilbert. *The Great Audience*. New York: Viking, 1951. Print.
Shuman, R. Baird. *William Inge*. New York: Twayne, 1965. Print.
———. *William Inge*. Rev. ed. New York: Twayne, 1989. Print.
"The Theater: New Play in Manhattan." Rev. of *Come Back, Little Sheba*, by William Inge. *Time* 27 Feb. 1950: 81. Print.
Weales, Gerald. *American Drama Since World War II*. New York: Harcourt, Brace and World, 1962. Print.
Wilkinson, Rupert. *American Tough: The Tough-Guy Tradition and American Character*. New York: Harper and Row, 1984. Print.
Wood, Michael. *America in the Movies*. New York: Basic, 1975. Print.

The Two Texts of *Picnic*
David Richman

William Inge's *Picnic* was published by Random House in 1953, the year of the premiere production. In 1955, an acting edition was brought out by Dramatists Play Service. This volume, with its costume and property plots and expanded stage directions, has become the standard text on which productions of the play are based. In 1958, Random House brought out an omnibus volume of Inge's four best-known plays with a new foreword by the author. This volume, incorporating the 1953 Random House text of *Picnic*, has become for the reading public the most widely accessible edition of Inge's plays. Thus, as with most well-known American plays, *Picnic* has an acting edition and a reading edition.

That numerous differences exist between actors' scripts and readers' texts will come as no surprise to most theater artists and some general readers. Plays inevitably change in the crucible of rehearsal and performance, and their acting editions, based on their premiere productions, reflect those changes. The reading edition of a play is usually the exclusive work of its author, and it often incorporates passages that were cut or altered in production. A comparison between the acting edition and the reading edition of nearly any play of our time will yield a somber object lesson in the essential instability and fluidity of dramatic texts.

But anyone setting out to study *Picnic*, or to stage it, will be astonished to discover how substantial are the differences between that play's authoritative texts. Though the characters and large actions remain the same in both editions, the play changes radically in tone, texture, and emphases from edition to edition. The diverging texts of *Picnic* may constitute the most enduring legacy of the turbulent relations between Inge and Joshua Logan, who directed the initial production. The Random House text is closer to Inge's vision of the play, while the Dramatists Play Service text is a record of the dialogue and staging for the Logan production. Indeed, Inge's pre-production typescript, housed in the William Inge Collection at Independence Community College in Independence, Kansas, is virtually identical to the Dramatists Play Service text. The existence of this typescript, very close to what was played in the premiere production and quite different from the text that Random House published, suggests that even as the play was in rehearsal, Inge was planning to publish a version that varied from that on the stage in 1953. I offer this suggestion very tentatively; I think the typescript is a pre-production, but not a pre-publication document.

In the wake of the play's popular and critical success, Inge became guarded in his public utterances about Logan (Voss 126). Even so, it was no secret that the playwright was unhappy with what the director had wrought. Logan writes in his memoirs that he strove mightily with Inge to let the drama end with Madge following Hal to Tulsa. In the original ending, characterized by Logan as an "endlessly slow dim-out," a besmirched Madge remained behind (277). The battle over the ending was perhaps the most important point of contention between playwright and director.

But even as *Picnic* was enjoying its successful Broadway run, reviewers such as George Jean Nathan and Harold Clurman, who was subsequently to direct *Bus Stop*, were arguing that Logan had had a far more pervasive and damaging effect on Inge's play than the mere reversal of the ending. Nathan wrote that Inge was "bombarded with hundreds of suggestions from outside sources and was prevailed upon to incorporate many of them into his script" (15). Clurman, who had read *Front Porch*, the original script that Inge had submitted to Logan in 1951, was scathing in his assessment of what Logan had done to the play:

> In the attempt to make the author's particular kind of sensibility thoroughly acceptable, the play has been vulgarized.... Here at any rate is a solid success. But I am not sure whether the author should get down on his knees to thank the director for having made it one or punch him in the nose for having altered the play's values [213].

Ample evidence that the play's values were indeed altered in production can be found in the hundreds of differences between the two published texts of *Picnic*.

When it came time for Inge to prepare the play for its Random House publication, he wanted to print his original ending. Inge biographer Ralph F. Voss notes that the playwright considered the published versions of his plays quite important because they represented the "best possible piece" he could write: "The published play, after all, was wholly his, as he wanted it recorded for posterity; it did not necessarily reflect alterations that came via the production process" (118). Since Logan's ending was the alteration to which Inge most violently objected, he would naturally have wanted it struck from the published text. Logan writes, "I warned him that would hurt his chances for the Pulitzer and the critics' prizes, which were still pending, so he reluctantly stuck to our playing script" (285; cf. Voss 137–38).

That Inge did not, in fact, "stick to" Logan's playing script in the Random House text, in spite of his agreeing to keep Logan's ending, is suggested by that text's differences from his own pre-production typescript and the subsequently published Dramatists Play Service edition apparently based on that typescript. Eileen Heckart, who played Rosemary in the premiere production of *Picnic*, explained in a letter to me dated January 16, 1990, why two versions of the play were published:

> Josh was so quick—he was constantly saying to Bill: "Give us another line here." And Bill couldn't do that. He needed to go by himself and work it out. Often when he returned, a change had already been made. Then Josh would cajole him into the change. Bill was obviously unhappy, which is why he published the first version to *his* liking, and not what we played. Then it was Josh's turn to be hurt, and Audrey Wood talked Bill into publishing what we *were* playing.

That even the Random House text did not satisfy its author is suggested by his 1962 publication of *Summer Brave*; the title page identifies it as the "*rewritten and final version of the romantic comedy PICNIC.*" The appearance of *Summer Brave* added further complications to a textual history already Byzantine in its complexity.

The differences between *Summer Brave* and either or both texts of *Picnic* make for an interesting story, as do the differences between *Picnic* in either version and the earlier, unpublished treatments of events on Flo Owens's porch, *Front Porch* and *The Man in Boots* (manuscript versions of both are available in the William Inge Collection at Independence Community College in Independence, Kansas). However, my concern in this essay is with differences between the published texts of *Picnic*. Examining these texts is of more than historical interest. Directors and editors of Shakespeare, another playwright whose authoritative texts diverge, are well advised to consult the Quarto and Folio versions of his plays in preparing their editions or productions (Granville-Barker 69–74; cf. Urkowitz 304). Directors of *Picnic* would derive a similar advantage from examining both published texts of that play as they prepare their productions. My aim is to discuss a few of the hundreds of differences between these texts. Since my interest in this question grew out of my own production of *Picnic*, I will call attention to implications for staging and acting in the variant scenes. For convenience of reference, I will designate the Dramatists Play Service text as DPS and the Random House text as RH.

The reasons for undertaking this discussion can legitimately be questioned. If DPS is a record of Logan's playing script, and if that script is a vulgarization of Inge's vision, why should DPS be consulted at all—especially when the author's vision is at least partially preserved in RH? An open-minded comparison of DPS to RH will reveal that not all of Logan's changes were for the worse. *Picnic* in both its published texts is superior to *Front Porch*, the sprawling script that Inge gave Logan in 1951. Whatever else Logan was or was not, he was a shrewd and canny director, and he did help *Picnic* to achieve its success. As Tennessee Williams observed about Elia Kazan's changes to *Cat on a Hot Tin Roof*:

> The reception of the playing script has more than justified, in my opinion, the adjustments made to that influence. A failure reaches fewer people, and touches fewer, than a play that succeeds [125].

Knowledge of what the first successful director of *Picnic* did right, as well as what he did wrong, can constitute a useful resource for any student of the play.

Since the most violently disputed aspect of Logan's influence on Inge's play involves Madge's final disposition towards Hal, it is not surprising that the most interesting variants in the published texts of *Picnic* concern Hal's and Madge's relations to each other and Hal's relation to the audience. One such variant can be found in a startling comic sequence that occurs early in both texts. Hal is offstage, burning Mrs. Potts's leaves and her trash, while the ladies admire or reprove him from Flo's porch. When a sudden explosion is heard, Mrs. Potts rushes off to investigate.

Random House text:

> MRS. POTTS: (*Running off stage*) Pshaw! I'm not afraid.
> ALAN (*Looking off at* HAL) Who did that guy say he was? (*No one hears* ALAN)
> MRS. POTTS: (*Coming back and facing* FLO) I was a bad girl.
> FLO: What *is* it, Helen?
> MRS. POTTS: I threw the *new* bottle of cleaning fluid into the trash.
> FLO: You're the limit! ...
> ....
> MRS. POTTS: Come help me, Millie. The young man ran into the clothesline [90].

The sequence is expanded in DPS. Between Mrs. Potts's exit and her reentrance, offstage dialogue is added that clarifies Hal's relation to the explosion. Though he remains blameless, the added dialogue has the effect of obliquely implicating him in the minds of both characters and audience.

Dramatists Play Service text:

> (*Mrs. Potts breaks away and runs off* D.L.)
> MRS. POTTS: (*Off* L.) What happened out here, young man?

> HAL: (*Off* L.) Gee, I don't know, Mam, I just lit this stuff and the whole thing went up.
> ALAN: (*As he looks off* L.) Say, that guy looks like—No, it couldn't be.
> ROSEMARY: Isn't that a shame? She'll have to do her whole wash over again.
> MRS. POTTS: (*Off* L.) Well, was that bottle in it?
> HAL: (*Off* L.) Yeah, I guess so [20].

This sequence provides better comedy and richer illustration of the characters' motives and relationships than does its counterpart in RH. The lines invite the actress playing Mrs. Potts, Hal's staunchest defender, to show that she cannot keep a note of exasperation out of her voice as she bawls to him to learn what has happened. Rosemary should get a responsive chuckle from the audience with the added line of sympathy for the calamity of another, mixed with characteristic gloating over someone else's troubles, in DPS.

After Mrs. Potts makes her confession and elicits from Flo and the audience her due of exasperated affection, there is a further addition in DPS which enriches the audience's perception of Hal's well-intentioned clumsiness.

Dramatists Play Service text:

> MRS. POTTS: Millie, come help me. The young man ran into the clothesline trying to get away. (*She and Millie exit* D.L.)
> ....
> MRS. POTTS: (*Off* L.) You go ahead, young man. We'll take care of this.
> HAL: (*Off* L.) Gee, I'm awful sorry, Mam. I didn't mean to—
> MRS. POTTS: (*Off* L.) That's all right. Millie will help me [21].

Hal's reason for running into the clothesline, not given in RH, is made explicit in DPS. Moreover, Mrs. Potts's fervent insistence that Millie will help her, forestalling Hal from rooting about in her scattered clothes, is another fine laugh line. All in all, this sequence in DPS is clearer, funnier, and richer than its counterpart in RH.

Excepting Mrs. Potts and, of course, Madge, the other characters have little love for Hal. One cause of this general dislike is the vagabond's propensity to brag and swagger. His scenes of showing off are treated slightly differently in DPS than in RH. His public greeting of Millie, his putative date for the picnic, is a representative example.

Random House text:

> I wouldn't admit this to many people, but she does a jackknife almost as good as me! (*Realizes that this sounds bragging so goes on to explain*) You see, I was diving champion on the West Coast, so I know what I'm talking about! (*He laughs to reassure himself and sits beside* MILLIE *on doorstep*) [110].

The possibilities suggested by this speech are clarified in DPS by a bit of business that communicates a more complex impression of Hal.

Dramatists Play Service text:

> Oh, you see, I was diving champion on the West Coast, so I know what I'm talking about! (*This remark is a failure, too, and Hal admits as much by holding his nose and taking a flying leap on to the steps.*) [41].

The aggressive posing is hardly mitigated, but this Hal shows himself possessed of some self-knowledge and capable of self-irony. Though audiences are inclined to bristle at Hal, they may be persuaded by the stage business in DPS to laugh generously with a character who is able to laugh at himself.

Flo is one character who never laughs at Hal. Both texts depict her unequivocal dislike of him. Yet both texts display interesting differences in the first two brief encounters between these natural antagonists.

Random House text:

> FLO: Young man, this is *my* house. Is there something you want?
> HAL: Just loafin', ma'am.
> FLO: This is a busy day for us. We have no time to loaf. (*There is a quick glance between* HAL *and* FLO, *as though each sized up the other as a potential threat*)
> HAL: You the mother?
> FLO: Yes. You better run along now.
> HAL: Like you say, lady. It's your house. (*With a shrug of the shoulders, he saunters off stage*) [78–79].

Again, the sequence is expanded in DPS, though the descriptions of character and motive in RH are dropped. As is often the case in DPS, these are replaced by precise descriptions of activity.

Dramatists Play Service text:

> FLO: Young man, this is my house and these are my daughters.
> HAL: (*Turns and crosses to C. as Flo speaks.*) They are?
> FLO: (*She nods.*) Is there something you want?
> HAL: Just loafin', Mam.
> FLO: This is a busy day for us. You better run along.
> HAL: It's your house, lady. (*Crosses L. to shed, turns to Flo.*) You're their mother? (*Flo nods. Hal shakes his head in admiration and walks off to Mrs. Potts' yard.*) [10].

The version of Flo's opening line in DPS reveals her perception that Hal is a threat to her daughters, and the schoolteacherish "We have no time to loaf" in RH is dropped. Hal's final line and action enable him to display his masculine appreciation of mother and daughters. They can make for a moment electric with sexual antagonism, and they prove superior in production to the pedestrian exit line in RH.

DPS also intensifies the sexual tension between Hal and Flo in its version of their second encounter. In both versions, Hal interrupts an intimate conversation between Flo and Madge to ask whether he can burn leaves on such a hot day.

Random House text:

HAL: The nice lady, she said it's a hot enough day already and maybe you'd object
FLO: (*Matter-of-factly*) I guess we can stand it.
HAL: Thank you, ma'am. (HAL *runs off*) [84].

Dramatists Play Service text:

(*She looks up, sees that Hal is bare chested. She steps to L. of Madge shielding Hal from view.*)
HAL: The nice lady said it's a hot enough day already and maybe you'd object. How about it, Mam—mind a little fire? (*Madge manages a look past Flo at Hal.*)
FLO: (*She is cold towards him.*) No, I don't mind.
HAL: (*Hangs his jacket on shed door, closes door.*) I didn't think you would. (*He is suddenly conscious of his bare chest. He covers his chest modestly with his hands and walks off* D. L.) [15].

The threat inherent in Hal's sexuality and implied by his final lines is mitigated by his sudden embarrassment. The additions of dialogue and action in DPS make an arresting moment out of what in RH is a fairly routine encounter.

In all the examples I have given thus far, the Dramatists Play Service edition improves upon the Random House edition. As Eileen Heckart's letter to me confirms, the improvements were the work of Joshua Logan and his cast, and they probably grew out of discoveries made in rehearsal and performance. Indeed, Logan describes one vital discovery that he made about the play while it was in preview, en route to its New York opening. Logan's account bears directly on the play's diverging texts. He begins by describing his chagrin at the mixed reaction the play was receiving during its try-outs.

> I asked [producer David] Merrick for the reason for this dichotomy of opinion. "I'm not sure, but it has something to do with the Meeker character [Hal was played by Ralph Meeker]. Every time he comes on, I bristle. I can't stand the way he swaggers, brags, poses all over the place." I listened to him, but was still puzzled. That night, two men came up the aisle, talking excitedly. I heard only two vehemently spoken words. "*Some hero!*" ... Hero? *They* think *we* think he's a hero? *We*, the creators, think this *slob's* heroic!! They don't realize that *we see* those unattractive things about him as clearly as they do.... I called Bill Inge and told him what I had discovered. "Josh, if you can think of anything to do, do it. Write it down and I'll okay it. In the meantime, just put it in if you feel it will help." He obviously thought it was a disaster. Lawrence [Langner of the Theatre Guild, producers of the premiere production] and I decided that the most reliable character to put across our attitude towards Hal was Alan. All the ladies

adored Paul Newman. Here are the lines we put in, although they were changed later for publication:

FLO: But a fraternity! Don't these boys have more breeding?
ALAN: Maybe, but fraternities like to pledge big athletes. But I know what you're thinking, Mrs. Owens.
FLO: How do the other boys feel about him?
ALAN: They didn't like him, Mrs. Owens. When he came around, every man on that campus seemed to bristle! When I first met him, I couldn't stand the way he bragged and swaggered and posed all over the place. And then I found out that Hal's really a nice guy, believe it or not.

We checked it with Bill Inge by the phone. He changed a word or two and we put it in. From that night on, the play was a hit. The audience knew exactly where we stood on the subject of Hal, and where they stood [283–84].

Alan's crucial speech does not appear in either text in precisely the version Logan quotes. He notes that the speech was changed for publication, but to which publication is he referring?

Random House text:

ALAN: (*Reluctantly*) They didn't like him, Mrs. Owens. They were pretty rough on him. Every time he came into a room, the other fellows seemed to *bristle*. I didn't like him either, at first. Then we shared a room and I got to know him better. Hal's really a nice guy. About the best friend I ever had [99].

The language is toned down from the version Logan quotes. We lose "swagger" and "pose," though the speech asserts the paradox that Alan likes Hal in spite of his initial bristling. In DPS, the lines are expanded and strengthened.

Dramatists Play Service text:

ALAN: They didn't like him, Mrs. Owens. They were pretty rough on him. (*Takes foot down.*) When he came around, every man on that campus seemed to bristle. When I first met him, I couldn't stand the way he bragged and swaggered and posed all over the place, and then I found out he's done most of the things he says he's done. He's a fabulous character!
FLO: Do you like him now, Alan?
ALAN: Yes. Hal's really a nice guy, believe it or not. We shared the same room till he flunked out. He told me some of the things he was up against as a kid. It was pretty typical [30].

Of the three versions, RH, DPS, and that quoted by Logan, DPS is the best. The DPS lines give a sense that there is more truth than the audience might otherwise have thought in Hal's bragging, without in any way mitigating the sense that the production's creators are bristling along with the spectators. Indeed, the bristling is expressed in stronger terms. Moreover, the DPS lines give a credible motive for Alan's affection for Hal, and they help set up the near-tragic betrayal and loss that Alan endures toward the play's end. Thus, the acting edition yields the most theatrically effective version of these lines.

Many of the DPS sequences, clarified and enriched by telling lines or inventive pieces of stage business, prove more theatrically effective than their counterparts in RH. But further comparison of the two texts leads one to the disheartening conclusion that theatrical effectiveness, especially in a number of Hal's most important scenes, is sometimes achieved at the cost of dramatic integrity. The play in performance is nowhere more emotionally complex than in its treatment of Hal. In their different ways, both texts seek to balance the conflicting feelings so that spectators can comprehend and sympathize both with Madge's growing love for Hal and with her mother's growing antipathy. Both texts adhere to the basic elements of the plot: Hal and Madge do not go on the picnic; they spend an illicit night together; in the morning, Hal leaves by freight and Madge follows him by bus. But Hal and Madge take very different paths to the same end in the two texts, and the two texts taken together often force producers, directors, and actors to choose between what both Inge and his reviewers called the show and the play (Inge, "Picnic: From," 33; Nathan 15).

Harold Clurman, who, as noted earlier, had read *Front Porch*, decried the production's alterations of the play's values. Writing about Logan's and Meeker's treatment of Hal, he noted that the "boy in the script who was a rather pathetic, confused, morbidly explosive and bitter character is now a big goof of a he-man whom the audience can laugh at or lust after" (213). Support for Clurman's indictment can unfortunately be gleaned from a comparison of some of Hal's corresponding scenes in both texts.

Both DPS and RH open with a small vignette featuring Hal and Mrs. Potts. In both sequences, he is emptying her trash and preparing to take a few other odd jobs in payment for the breakfast she has given him. He is embarrassed about begging for a meal, and she comforts him. At this point, the scenes diverge.

Random House text:

MRS. POTTS: Now, stop being embarrassed because you asked for breakfast.
HAL: I never did it before.
MRS. POTTS: What's the difference? We all have misfortune part of the time.
HAL: Seems to me, ma'am, like I have it *lots* of the time [76].

This quiet moment encourages us to form an initially sympathetic impression of Hal before he encounters Rosemary, Flo, or Madge. The audience may still bristle at his subsequent bragging and posing, but the RH opening may help ensure that the bristling will be tempered by something of Alan's understanding and affection.

64 Critical Essays

Mrs. Potts and Hal do not talk about shared misfortune in DPS. Instead, there is a passage of dialogue that does not appear in RH.

Dramatists Play Service text:

> MRS. POTTS: You're going to be awfully hot working in that jacket.
> HAL: My shirt's awful dirty, Mam.
> MRS. POTTS: I'll wash it while you're burning the trash.
> HAL: I sure would like to feel clean. (*He looks around, worried.*) Would anybody object?
> MRS. POTTS: Of course not! You're a man! What's the difference? [7].

In the stage directions in both texts, Hal is described as wearing a "T-shirt, dungarees, and cowboy boots" (7). There is no mention of a jacket. Yet the DPS dialogue clearly calls for a jacket. That the DPS stage directions contradict its dialogue suggests a conflict of opinion about Hal's costuming. Such conflict is further suggested by the fact that the initial stage direction in Inge's pre-production typescript is crossed out, while the typescript's dialogue includes the lines about Hal's jacket and dirty shirt subsequently published in DPS. The jacketed Hal in DPS will make a very different first impression on the audience than the T-shirted Hal in RH.

More important, the lines in DPS call for an action. Hal's jacket and his dirty shirt presumably come off, and a sort of continuing striptease is underway. In both texts, much is made of Hal's bare-chested appearance later in the act. The DPS opening scene ends with the arresting spectacle of a handsome man beginning to take his clothes off. It may make for a better show than the wistful remarks about misfortune in RH. Corroborating Clurman's criticism, the pathetic, confused boy in RH contrasts with the character in DPS, after whom the audience is being encouraged to lust.

At Madge and Hal's first meeting, DPS and RH again present variant actions. In both texts, Millie is teasing Hal because he has had to ask Mrs. Potts for breakfast, and Madge tells her little sister to mind her own business.

Random House text:

> HAL: (*Turning to* MADGE, *his face lighting*) Hi.
> MADGE: Hi. (MADGE *and* HAL *stand looking at each other, awkward and self-conscious....*) [78]

Dramatists Play Service text:

> HAL: (*Turning to Madge—quick smile.*) Hi.
> MADGE: (*Returning smile.*) Hi.
> HAL: (*Turning U. L., to himself.*) Hi hi! [9–10].

There is sexual comedy in the "hi hi" in DPS but it is achieved at the cost of the moment of arresting stillness in RH. Hal in DPS is becoming at this moment the "big goof of a he-man" to whom Clurman objects. Hal and Madge in RH, on the other hand, can look at each other for a beat of stillness, while the tension mounts.

These variants suggest that RH gives a more compelling account than DPS of the sexual tension between Hal and Madge. When one compares the DPS version of the conclusion of the second act to the corresponding sequence in RH, this suggestion becomes a virtual certainty. The two sequences differ in almost every particular. Here, directors and performers cannot pick and choose, adopting a line from RH and a bit of business from DPS. One must choose to perform one scene or the other, recognizing that the diverging scenes represent fundamentally different choices about the nature of the play's central relationship.

In both texts, Hal's rejection of Rosemary has prompted her terrible tirade against him. He is alone on stage, suffering deep humiliation, when Madge enters toward the end of the act.

Dramatists Play Service text:

> MADGE: Don't feel bad. Women like Miss Sydney make me disgusted with the whole female sex. (*Recalling something, smiling.*) Last year she and some of the other teachers made such a fuss about a statue in the library. It was a gladiator and all he had on was a shield on his arm. Those teachers kept hollering about that statue, they said it was an insult to them every time they walked into the library. Finally, they made the principal—I don't know how to say it, but one of the janitors got busy with a chisel and then they weren't insulted any more. The next day there was a sign hanging on the statue—"Miss Sydney was here." I know you're not in the mood for funny stories, but you just have to laugh at Miss Sydney.
> HAL: What's the use, Baby? She saw through me like an X-ray machine. I'm a *bum*! There's just no place in the world for a guy like me.
> MADGE: I know how you feel. Millie's so smart and talented. I get to feeling so jealous of her and worthless when I try to be like her. Then I tell myself that I'm not Millie—I'm *me*! And I feel lots better [54–55].

This version contains at least two major shortcomings. One of these involves Madge's mention of Millie. Relations between the sisters constitute a significant theme in both texts, and Madge's final lines in both texts startlingly reveal her paradoxical love for her smart sister. But her assertion to Hal "I tell myself I'm not Millie—I'm *me*" oversimplifies and sentimentalizes that relationship. It is as if a Hallmark card is being clumsily grafted on to a complex drama.

A greater blemish is Madge's telling of the story about Miss Sydney and the statue. The hesitations written into her lines suggest that the character herself recognizes the story's awkwardness and inappropriateness. The story does not suit the character, and whatever laughter it might elicit in performance may be choked off by the audience's sense of her discomfort. As she herself perceives, it does not represent the best strategy for comforting Hal. There is an uncharacteristic awkwardness in the writing, suggesting that the dramatist has momentarily lost his grip on the material.

Yet the story of Rosemary, the statue, and the chisel should not be lost. It reveals much about Rosemary's violent, sexual nature. More important, it is Rosemary's story and not Madge's. It is dramatically appropriate for Rosemary to tell it, just as it is dramatically inappropriate for Madge to tell it. In the RH version of Rosemary's dance with Hal earlier in this act, Rosemary does tell the story. It is excised from the corresponding scene in DPS, and the blemish created by this excision is compounded by the transferring of the story to Madge in DPS. Thus the authorized acting edition of *Picnic* contains two flawed sequences that considerably weaken the play.

In both versions of the Rosemary-Hal dance, she tells him about the cowboy who took her up into the mountains. But the DPS version is truncated, lacking its center.

Dramatists Play Service text:

> Wanted me to marry him right there on the mountaintop. Said God'd be our preacher, the moon our best man. Ever here such talk? Didja? Didja? (*Hal pulls away from her.*) Where you goin'? You gotta dance with me! (*Rosemary holds on desperately.*)
> HAL: Mam, I guess I just don't feel like dancing [51].

The difference between this sequence and the corresponding sequence in the Random House text is the difference between assertion and revelation.

Random House text:

> .... Wanted me to marry him right there on the mountain top. Said God'd be our preacher, the moon our best man. Ever hear such talk?
> HAL: (*Trying to get away*) Ma'am, I'd like another li'l drink now.
> ROSEMARY: (*Jerking him closer to her*) Dance with me, young man. Dance with me. I can keep up with you. You know what? You remind me of one of those ancient statues. There was one in the school library until last year. He was a Roman gladiator. All he had on was a shield. (*She gives a bawdy laugh*) A shield over his arm. That was all he had on. All we girls felt insulted, havin' to walk past that statue every time we went to the library. We got up a petition and made the principal do something about it. (*She laughs hilariously during her narration*) You know what he did? He got the school janitor to fix things right. He got a chisel and made that statue decent. (*Another bawdy laugh*) Lord, those ancient people were depraved.
> HAL: (*He seldom has been made so uncomfortable*) Ma'am, I guess I just don't feel like dancin' [121–22].

As Rosemary tells it, the story is at once funny and threatening. She is symbolically castrating Hal, and the text suggests that he is aware of the connection between himself and the mutilated statue. He is repelled by her desire for him and terrified by her display of sexual antipathy. When the play is performed, these lines encourage the spectators to guffaw along with Rosemary, until they recognize with appropriate shock her story's painful implications. Her narrative and its accompanying action result in what Eugene O'Neill described in another context as the "big kind of comedy that doesn't stay funny very long" (qtd. in Cohn and Dukore 405). In comparison, the DPS version of this scene is a diminished thing.

Not surprisingly, the RH version of the scene between Hal and Madge at the end of the second act is also a superior piece of dramatic writing. That version is blemished neither by Madge's awkward telling of the chisel story nor by her bathetic description of the difference between herself and her sister. Instead, she comforts Hal far more appropriately and at the same time creates greater sexual tension by praising his dancing. Her compliments on his dancing are weakened in DPS, being subordinated to her telling of the chisel story.

In both versions, she wrings from Hal a confession that he spent a year in reform school. At this point, the two texts once again greatly diverge.

Dramatists Play Service text:

> (*Madge suddenly kisses him. After the kiss he looks at her a moment.*) Gee, baby, you come out here on the porch lookin' like a pretty little doll, but you're a real woman, aren't you?
> MADGE: I want to be.
> HAL: You are.
> MADGE: Am I? (*Now Hal kisses her. After a moment Madge breaks away and walks over near Mrs. Potts' steps. Hal follows to her R., turns her to him.*) We gotta go on the picnic.
> HAL: Do we? There's other places ... with not so many people. (*He pulls her to him and kisses her passionately. He releases her, then goes upstage and looks off R. and L. to see that no one is around. He turns to Madge and holds out his hand to her. After a moment she gives him her hand and they walk off slowly together through alley R.*) [56].

There is as much of romance as of seduction in this version.

The RH version also contains its element of romance. Madge kisses Hal as a result of his confession, though her reason for kissing him is expressed with greater strength and clarity. But what in DPS proceeds by mutual consent, in RH turns into near rape.

Random House text:

> HAL: .... (*There is a silence. Then* MADGE, *suddenly and impulsively, takes his face in her hands and kisses him. Then she returns her hands to her lap and feels embarrassed.* HAL *looks at her in amazement*) Baby! What'd you do?
> MADGE: I ... I'm proud you told me.
> HAL: (*With humble appreciation*) Baby!
> MADGE: I ... I get so tired of being told I'm pretty.
> HAL: (*Folding her in his arms caressingly*) Baby, baby, baby.
> MADGE: (*Resisting him, jumping to her feet*) Don't. We have to go. We have all the baskets in our car and they'll be waiting. (HAL *gets up and walks slowly to her, their eyes fastened and* MADGE *feeling a little thrill of excitement as he draws nearer*) Really—we have to be going. (HAL *takes her in his arms and kisses her passionately. Then* MADGE *utters his name in a voice of resignation*) Hal!
> HAL: Just be quiet, baby.
> MADGE: Really ... we have to go. They'll be waiting.
> HAL: (*Picking her up in his arms and starting off. His voice is deep and firm*) We're not goin' on no goddamn picnic [127].

In this version, Madge is part lover, part victim. She is sexually vulnerable, just as Hal has been sexually vulnerable to Rosemary earlier in the act. Madge's inchoate love for Hal is as clearly revealed in the RH version as in DPS, and RH gives a stronger sense of Hal's menace and a more disturbing harbinger of the sort of life Madge can be expected to lead with him. Finally, RH leads to a far more compelling second-act curtain.

In an interview for *Theatre Arts* in July 1953 about the time the Random House *Picnic* was published, Inge commented on the relation between Hal and Madge. His remarks need to be taken with the proverbial grain of salt, because he downplays his friction with Logan, and indeed gives the director a great deal of credit for the play's success. Yet his remarks apply with far more aptness to the RH Hal and Madge than to the DPS couple:

> "A girl who has been told all her life simply how pretty she is must sometimes wonder about herself as a human being."
> Hal, who is masculinely attractive on the outside and weak and frightened on the inside, Inge thinks, brings out the awareness that she is a woman. He is the first person to ever reveal himself frankly to her, to need her. In the first version of the play Inge had him go off at the end, leaving Madge to go back to her job at the five-and-dime. That had seemed more natural. He was even going to publish the play with two endings. But now that the two characters have grown to the point where Hal so vitally disturbs her whole life, the old ending falls flat. Now he feels that Madge has to follow him [Inge, "William Inge" 67].

The RH Madge, unlike the DPS Madge, makes it clear that she kisses Hal because she is proud of his revealing his fear and shame to her. She significantly tells him that she gets tired of being told she is pretty.

Equally revealing is Inge's acknowledgement in this interview of the connection between this sequence and the new ending to which he has acceded. Madge cannot stay behind after Hal has so vitally disturbed her life. In *Front Porch*, there is no such scene of disturbance. Hal simply tells Madge that he has a "hot news flash" that they are "not going on no goddamn picnic." When Inge published *Summer Brave*, a play that ends with Madge staying behind, he excised the scene in which Hal and Madge reveal their mutual needs. The second act of that play reverts to the brief, stark encounter in *Front Porch*. As Inge himself may have fitfully realized, Madge's decision to follow Hal to Tulsa is an inevitable consequence of their extended second-act scene in either of its two versions.

The two texts diverge even more widely in their treatments of Hal and Madge during the play's third and final act. A romantic and to my taste sentimentalized affection dominates their scenes in the Dramatists Play Service text, while the Random House text continues to explore sexual love tainted by sexual threat and vulnerability. The DPS version of Hal and Madge's return after their stolen evening of not going to the picnic would fit seamlessly into a romantic movie.

Dramatists Play Service text:

> (*Then Hal enters through alley L., comes on quietly to L. of stump. He looks around, then turns and beckons.*)
> HAL: Okay. (*Madge enters from alley L., touches him—he responds. She passes him to D. R. of stump.*) I'll take the car back to where we were and get a little sleep. I can't go back to Seymour's house now.
> MADGE: No.
> HAL: I didn't even think of Seymour 'til just this second.
> MADGE: I don't think either of us thought much about anything [60–61].

The corresponding sequence in RH depicts the tension between sexual yearning and realistic resignation that characterizes much of Inge's best writing.

Random House text:

> (.... *Then* MADGE *runs on from the back, right. Her face is in her hands. She is sobbing.* HAL *follows fast behind. He reaches her just as she gets to the door, and grabs her by the wrist. She resists him furiously.*)
> HAL: Baby ... You're not sorry, are you? (*There is a silence.* MADGE *sobs*)
> MADGE: Let me go.
> HAL: Please, baby. If I thought I'd done anything to make you unhappy, I ... I'd almost wanta die.
> MADGE: I ... I'm so ashamed [132].

Mutual shame and self-loathing, as well as mutual attraction, dominate this sequence.

In both texts, the couple's mutual attraction holds and Madge follows Hal to Tulsa. The spectators are left to conclude that she will repeat her mother's sad destiny. Yet one of the most striking differences in the two texts' respective treatments of this troubled relationship occurs in Hal's final moments onstage, just before he hops the freight.

Dramatists Play Service text:

> HAL: (*Beseeching.*) Look, Baby, I'm a poor bastard, and I gotta claim what's mine! And you're mine, Baby! You're the only real thing I ever had—ever! Baby, kiss me good-bye! (*He crosses D. to U. R. of stump. Madge turns and throws herself into his arms and they kiss violently. The train whistle is heard loudly, very close now. Hal breaks the kiss and holding her hands, looking down into her face.*) I feel like a freak to say this, but—I love you! [71].

Random House text:

> HAL: I'm a poor bastard, baby. I've gotta claim the things in this life that're mine. Kiss me good-bye. (*He grabs her and kisses her*) Come with me, baby. They gimme a room in the basement of the hotel. It's kinda crummy but we could share it till we found something better.
> FLO: (*Outraged*) Madge! Are you out of your senses?
> MADGE: I couldn't. (*The train whistles in the distance*)
> FLO: Young man, you'd better get on that train as fast as you can.
> HAL: (*To* MADGE) When you hear that train pull outa town and know I'm on it, your little heart's gonna be busted, 'cause you love me, God damn it! You love me, you love me, you love me [143].

There can be no starker illustration of the divergence between these corresponding relationships than the fact that in the Dramatists Play Service version Hal says, "I love you" while in the Random House version Hal says, "You love me."

Throughout this account, I have been displaying my preference for the Random House text's treatment of this relationship. The Madge-Hal scenes in the Dramatists Play Service text are internally consistent and, in the main, theatrically effective. But the Random House text's treatment of this couple is possessed of greater moral complexity and dramatic power. That text, but not the Dramatists Play Service text, presents a tragicomic depiction of mutual sexual threat and vulnerability that lies, I believe, at the core of the play Inge conceived.

In an April 1953 interview for *The New Yorker*, Inge articulated this theme:

> "As a child, I was struck by the fact that the women there were always protesting, while men pursued. I got the idea that women hated man. I later came to the conclusion that this was an act—that there was a certain artificiality in their attitude. Some women love so passionately that they're embarrassed about it, because it makes them dependent on men" ["Picnic's Provider" 24].

This idea is central to the Madge of the Random House text, and in that text—though not in the Dramatists Play Service text—the idea is given voice by Flo early in the first act. One has the impression that the mother is coming fully to terms with the ruin of her life as she is forced to articulate that ruin for her daughter. Her words parallel Inge's remarks for *The New Yorker.*

Random House text:

> FLO: (*After a long pause of summing up*) Some women are humiliated to love a man.
> MADGE: Why?
> FLO: (*Thinking as she speaks*) Because—a woman is weak to begin with, I suppose, and sometimes—her love for him makes her feel—almost helpless. And maybe she fights him—'cause her love makes her seem so dependent [83–84].

The fact that this speech is dropped from the Dramatists Play Service edition may be taken as a measure of how far that text falls away from what is strongest in Inge's achievement.

Yet, as I have shown, that text offers many superior sequences that would clarify and enrich the play in production. Neither text, taken alone, is wholly satisfactory. And despite Inge's claim that the subsequently published *Summer Brave* fulfilled his original intentions regarding *Picnic*, it should be borne in mind that *Summer Brave* is a play different in many of its essentials from *Picnic* in either version. Students and directors of *Picnic* must try to come to terms with both that play's texts. Responding to a similar textual situation, Harley Granville-Barker advised directors of *King Lear* to base their productions on the Folio, but to incorporate selected passages from the Quarto (69). Directors of *Picnic* might similarly base their productions on the Random House text and incorporate selected passages from the Dramatists Play Service text. Whatever their conclusions, directors of this play will do well judiciously to juggle both extant texts.

WORKS CITED

Clurman, Harold. "Theater." Rev. of *Picnic*, by William Inge. *Nation* 7 March 1953: 212–13. Print.
Cohn, Ruby, and Bernard F. Dukore, eds. *Twentieth Century Drama: England, Ireland and the United States.* New York: Random House, 1966. Print.
Granville-Barker, Harley. *Prefaces to Shakespeare.* Vol. 2. Princeton: Princeton University Press, 1946. Print.
Heckart, Eileen. MS. Letter to the author, 16 Jan. 1990.
Inge, William. *4 Plays by William Inge [Come Back, Little Sheba; Picnic; Bus Stop; The Dark at the Top of the Stairs].* New York: Random House, 1958. Print.

_____. *Front Porch.* TS. N.d. William Inge Collection. Independence Community College, Independence, KS.
_____. *The Man in Boots.* TS. N.d. William Inge Collection. Independence Community College, Independence, KS.
_____. *Picnic* [pre-production typescript]. TS. N.d. William Inge Collection. Independence Community College, Independence, KS.
_____. *Picnic.* New York: Dramatists Play Service, 1955. Print.
_____. "*Picnic*: From 'Front Porch' to Broadway." *Theatre Arts.* April, 1953: 32–33. Print.
_____. "*Picnic*'s Provider." Interview. *New Yorker* 4 Apr. 1953: 24–25. Print.
_____. *Summer Brave and Eleven Short Plays.* New York: Random House, 1962. Print.
_____. "William Inge Talks About *Picnic.*" Interview by Naomi Barko. *Theatre Arts* July 1963: 66–67. Print.
Logan, Joshua. *Josh: My Up and Down, In and Out Life.* New York: Delacorte, 1976. Print.
Nathan, George Jean. "Director's Picnic." Rev. of *Picnic*, by William Inge. *Theatre Arts*, May 1953: 14–15. Print.
Urkowitz, Steven. "Five Women Eleven Ways: Changing Images of Shakespearean Characters in the Earliest Texts." In *Images of Shakespeare: Proceedings of the Third Congress of the International Shakespeare Association.* Ed. Werner Habicht, D. J. Palmer, and Roger Pringle. Newark: University of Delaware Press, 1988. 292–304.
Voss, Ralph F. *A Life of William Inge: The Strains of Triumph.* Lawrence: University Press of Kansas, 1989. Print.
Williams, Tennessee. *Cat on a Hot Tin Roof.* New York: New American Library, 1955. Print.

Picnic, Summer Brave, and the Peace of Staying
Kerk Fisher

In the final moments of *Picnic*, Madge comes onto the front porch from the house with suitcase in hand and announces that she is going to Tulsa. She is leaving to join Hal, the drifter who entered the town, made love to her, and was chased out of town by the police. Madge's mother warns her of the disappointment that lies ahead if she leaves: "Maybe you think you love him now," she says, "but in a few years you'll hate the day he set foot on our porch!" (Inge, *Picnic* 73). After a tearful scene, Madge *"pulls away from Flo who holds her hands until both their arms are outstretched and Madge has to pull hard to break away"* (74). This gesture mirrors a scene earlier in the play in which Hal holds out his hand to Madge as he leads her away from the house. She finds herself pulled in both directions, torn between staying and leaving. In the end, *"Madge looks at her mother for a moment then crosses* U[pstage] *picks up her things and walks determinedly off..."* (74).

Inge always felt uncomfortable with, and even betrayed by, this ending, in which Madge leaves home and the town in order to pursue her dream. The ending was developed through the process of rehearsals for the Broadway opening of *Picnic* in 1953. However, in all versions of the play predating *Picnic*, beginning with the first, titled *Front Porch*, Madge does not leave with Hal. So, in 1962, nine years after the opening of *Picnic*, Inge changed "what some considered a fortuitous ending" so that Madge would, once again, remain home. *Summer Brave* resulted, a play which Inge felt to be "more humorously true than *Picnic*," and which fulfilled his "original intentions" (*Summer Brave* [1962] 4).

Joshua Logan, director of the Broadway production, reports in his memoirs that Inge rewrote the last act of *Picnic* "hundreds of times," and called the return to the original ending "one of the saddest moves in a pitiful life. It's as though he killed his favorite child just before killing himself" (356). As this essay will show, *Summer Brave* does not kill Madge but, quite to the contrary, gives her new and meaningful life, and provides instead a powerful vision of the peace of staying.

The differences between *Picnic* and *Summer Brave* are many and have not gone unnoticed by scholars, although the extant analyses stop short of noting the paramount importance of the ending which obsessed Inge throughout his life. Philip Bayard Clarkson, in his dissertation, "The Evolution from Conception to Production of the Dramas of William Inge," offers a three-page comparison of the two plays and concludes:

> The over-all effect of the two plays is different, but the differences are not very profound. Inge originally was concerned with the effect on a collection of females who had become unaccustomed to the presence of males, of a temporary masculine intrusion. *Summer Brave* does present this better than *Picnic,* and *Summer Brave* is altogether a more credible play; but it is less sensational and probably less theatrical [82].

Clarkson leaves his argument short of exploring the implications of the changes. Ralph F. Voss, in his 1989 biography, *A Life of William Inge*, traces the interesting history of the growth of the scripts but takes little note of the differences in the texts. He does offer, however, perceptive and pertinent analysis of Inge's life and work in general. Voss's claim that "Inge's dominant theme is acceptance, making the best one can of one's situation" (253), sheds light on the appeal to Inge of the original ending, in which Madge makes the best of her situation by accepting herself. R. Baird Shuman's analysis, from his revised edition of *William Inge*, strikes a similar note:

> In his four major successes—*Come Back, Little Sheba*; *Picnic*; *Bus Stop*; and *The Dark at the Top of the Stairs*—Inge carries the audience through the moment of crisis, and his final curtain falls on a note of hope and fulfillment, however faint. Except for Madge in the stage version of *Picnic*, this hope and fulfillment come as a result of the protagonists' acceptance of life as it is, followed by an adjustment to what is clearly inevitable and a willingness to face life on less romantic terms than before [2].

In light of this analysis, it is surprising that Shuman does not pursue the importance of Madge's decision in *Summer Brave* to stay, a revision which, in Shuman's line of thought, would have brought the play closer to the others, by offering a vision of hope and fulfillment through self-acceptance.

Inge's difficulty with Madge's decision to step off the porch in pursuit of her dream may be seen in Logan's recounting of the hard negotiations that resulted in this ending. Here we see Inge's convictions about the original ending and his fight to maintain a belief in the promise of staying home in the face of those pushing for the popular vision of moving. As the first production of *Picnic* was being developed, Logan felt that the major difficulty with the play was the last act, "which consisted of complete frustration for everyone." The focus of his concern was Madge's decision to stay home, where her scandalous actions with Hal would lead her to become, in Logan's words, the "town pump." Logan was convinced that this was an ending that "would leave the audience as unhappy as it did me" (347). Lawrence Langner, who was producing the play for the Theatre Guild, was also concerned about the negative third act. But Inge, according to Logan, "was afraid of being slick, of pandering to the public with a 'happy ending'" (347–48).

After a reading, Inge asked Nedda, Logan's wife, what she thought of the play. Logan remembers the following conversation:

> She answered just as bluntly, "I loved it with all my heart, every minute of it, until the end, and then I just hated it. I hated the way those two were separated after having my hopes encouraged. I was disappointed and frustrated."
> [Inge responded,] "But we can't just have a 'corny' happy ending."
> I [Logan] jumped in with, "It wouldn't be corny or happy. If Madge left with Hal, a worthless braggart with no money and no real job, it would ultimately be a disaster. Oh, they'd have a bit of sex all right, but no security and not the decent life she and her mother had dreamed of. She'd obviously end up where her mother is, deserted by her man, saddled with brats and destitute. It would be grim history repeating itself. Is that happy? Is that corny?"
> I could see Bill suddenly flush and stand up. He said, "What if Madge appeared at the door with a suitcase, wearing a flowery chiffon dress, tall six-inch heels, and a picture hat? She says, 'Mom, I'm going to Tulsa.' Her mother groans and begs her to stay, holding her, pleading with her, but Madge cannot be deterred. She pulls away from Flo—breaks the umbilical cord—and walks slowly and inevitably toward the bus station—while her mother collapses sobbing on the steps" [351–52].

Inge agreed to write such an ending, but when he appeared at a rehearsal four days later, he had not been able to write it—Madge had still not left home. Logan persisted and Inge got "very angry. '*All right*, I'll write it,' he said. 'But *I want you to know I don't approve*.' He turned sharply from me and left" (Logan 352).

The act of leaving in *Picnic*, an ending about which Inge felt embittered toward Logan up to the final days of his life (Inge, "William Inge: The Last" 21), represents Madge's desperate hope of escape and subsequent embrace of the promise of moving. But because such a move would undoubtedly end in a ruined life (as Logan pointed out), *Picnic* is about the failure of the promise of moving—a promise which plays a significant part in American thinking.

The importance of movement to Americans is noted by James Oliver Robertson in *American Myth, American Reality*:

> Movement is the magic which keeps expectations high in America.... Movement fuels the belief in unlimited opportunity and ultimate success. Movement—physical, geographical movement—is the symbol of social and economic mobility. It is also the symbol of progress, of independence, and of individual freedom all wrapped up in one [242].

Thomas P. Adler, in *Mirror on the Stage*, calls the promise of movement the "myth of spatial dislocation as guarantee of freedom" (37). In his later years, a period of intense disappointment and loneliness, Inge became acutely aware of the myth. But this awareness was not new. From his very early conceptions of *Picnic*, he was writing the story of a child's refusal to engage in the promise in the first place and of the resultant peace she must find in the choice not to move. Madge's nature, described in the earliest version of the play, *Front Porch* (present in an undated typescript in the Inge Collection at Independence Community College in Independence, Kansas), is "a simple one, frustrated only temporarily by the conflicting desires for security and romance" (*Front Porch* Description of Characters). These desires pull her in opposite directions, into the home or out to the world. In *Picnic*, Madge leaves the security of home in search of romance in the world. In *Summer Brave*, on the other hand, Madge finds romance in security and opts to stay home. Madge's story in its various versions is about the dilemma of leaving or staying home. However, by metaphorical extension—Inge treats the home as a psychic landscape—Madge's story is more importantly about escaping or accepting oneself. It is on this level that the endings of *Picnic* and *Summer Brave* take on particular significance.

A look at a number of strategies in three of Inge's earliest manuscript versions prior to *Picnic*, and a detailed exploration of the differences between the 1953 production of *Picnic* (using the 1955 Dramatists Play Service version rather than the 1953 and Random House edition as the most representative of the changes on which Logan insisted)[1] and the subsequent 1962 *Summer Brave* will reveal the inception and development of significant themes and forces that support Madge's decision to stay, as well as the source of Inge's reticence to change the ending for Logan. An additional version prior to *Picnic* is the 1952 *Summer Brave*, a version that the playwright, in his own words, took "out of my files and began to rework ..., just for my own satisfaction (SB 4), implying that it was the major source of the 1962 text of *Summer Brave*. What Inge may have been referring to as "his own satisfaction" was Madge's decision to stay home and the concomitant peace she finds in a reconciliation with self, what for Inge was a deeply personal, revealing, and final statement of acceptance. In this essay I will pass over a discussion of the 1952 *Summer Brave* and offer, rather, a detailed look at the 1962 *Summer Brave*, which Inge subtitled (on its cover) "The rewritten and final version of the romantic comedy *Picnic*," as it relates to its sources in the three earliest manuscripts and in the 1953 production of *Picnic*.

This is the chronology of the various versions:

Front Porch (*FP*), 1946. An undated typescript. A production was planned for 1946, but *Front Porch* was not produced until February 1948 in St. Louis (Shuman 11), after which Inge decided to put aside work on this script.

The Man in Boots (*MB*), May 16, 1949. Typescript. In this version, Inge worked on the character of Hal and added the train sounds as an important presence in the play.

Front Porch revised (*FPr*), 1951. Typescript. Inge resumed work on *Front Porch* in the summer of 1950.

Summer Brave (*SBe*), 1952. Typescript. Inge considered this his final version; it was produced in Hyde Park, New York, in 1952 (Shuman 11).

Picnic (*P*), 1953. Before *Summer Brave* opened on Broadway in February 1953, director Joshua Logan convinced Inge to change the title and make "substantive changes in the script" (Shuman 11). This is the text published by Dramatists Play Service in 1955.

Summer Brave (*SB*), 1962. Written after the success of both the stage film versions of *Picnic*, this is the text of the 1962 Dramatists Play Service edition.

* * *

In speaking of his early work on *Picnic*, Inge remembered "the feeling of a summer evening, the women sitting on their front porches, the feeling of peace, their delight in their small talk" (Inge, "William Inge Talks" 66). He said of the initial conception:

> One of the many titles I considered for my new play was "Women in Summer." No one else seemed to like the title much so I forgot it, but I rather liked it, though perhaps not as much as the present title, because it recalled something to me: a memory of women, all sorts of women—beautiful, bitter, harsh, loving, young, old, frustrated, happy—sitting on a front porch on a summer evening. There was something in that atmosphere, something I wanted to re-create, and that is how "Picnic" got under way [Inge, "'Picnic' of Women"].

Inge's choice of a front porch for the setting of his story is significant—both as a reflection of an important cultural phenomenon, and as a dramatic vehicle. Sue Bridwell Beckham, in a sociological study, "The American Front

Porch: Women's Liminal Space," notes a correspondence between the front porch as a transitional space and women during transitional periods in which they are "neither children nor adults" (72). She writes:

> There, betwixt and between absolute private and absolute public, relationships that would be impossible elsewhere can flourish for however brief a time—and they can be spontaneous. Thus, bashful and protected youth in the first flush of intimacy are free to experiment with new relationships; thus, caste and class can be suspended and commonality explored; thus the boundary between friend and stranger breaks down; thus, the powerless are empowered ... [75].

All of the social interactions Beckham points out here are clearly seen in Inge's work on *Picnic*. Through the empowering qualities of the space, Inge's "peaceful" front porch setting becomes infused with dramatic tension—tension that results directly from its being a middle space, "betwixt and between."

Characters most associated with this middle space find themselves, not surprisingly, in the throes of a dilemma. Tom Scanlan, in *Family, Drama, and American Dreams*, notes that "American drama plays its dilemmas again and again," dilemmas that are encompassed in an overriding theme, "the struggle to leave and the longing to stay" (180). This theme is certainly not new to dramatic literature and is played out in a variety of interior and exterior settings. The front porch, however, with its specific spatial orientation involving direct access to both interior and exterior, offers a setting in which this theme can be played out in particularly vivid terms (see Fisher).

The fundamental tension in all the versions of *Picnic* is between staying, which pulls the character into the house, and leaving, which leads the character off the porch. It is the porch's opening to the world which makes the dilemma particularly pressing. With his or her back to the front door, a character uses the front porch as a domestic vantage point—overlooking the open space beyond—from which he or she may contemplate leaving the home and family behind in pursuit of some imagined future. Additionally, characters may be on the porch and yearn not so much to get off the porch as to get out of the town, as though the edge of the porch may act as a symbolic reminder of the limits of the town. By the same token, a move off the porch can imply either a move away from home and hometown as it does in *Picnic* or a choice to stay as it does in all other versions. Hence, while many tensions in the various versions of *Picnic* are very clearly set up along the axis between the interior and exterior of the house, a further and corresponding conflict is set up between the hometown and the world.

One of the earliest extant versions of this story is the undated typescript, written sometime in the 1940s, titled *Front Porch*. The setting for *Front Porch* is simply the front porch of a rather large frame house somewhere in the Mid-west, in a small town. In the center of the porch is a swing, and around the porch is a low railing. A couple of steps lead down center. It is late summer and greenery still abounds. There is a vine growing up a lattice by the porch, magazines, maybe a small table with ashtrays, for the family has lived on the porch throughout the warm months ... [*FP* (1–1)].

This setting, in which the action focuses on the front porch, exists in all versions except *Picnic* where, in Jo Mielziner's design for the Logan production, the front porch shares the stage space equally with a neighbor's back porch. *Front Porch* clearly sets up a relationship between the porch and the areas beyond that operates in more subtle ways in later versions.

Inge explains in an Author's Note to this first version of *Front Porch* that he tried to "assimilate the pace, the rhythm, mood, and situations of every day, small town life and make them dramatic. The events in themselves are not at all unusual, and can seem dramatic only by contrast with the slow, casual mood and rhythm in which they occur. In a production of the play, the first thing the actors and director should feel is that they have all the time in the world" (*FP* Author's Note). Inge sets up the action of the play to remain essentially static. The porch railings reinforce a sense of entrapment. It is the parent figure attached to the house that feels the least impetus to move. Flo's opening lines indicate how much the front porch defines the parameters of her life:

> Well, I suppose I'll sit here again, all day, just like I do every other day, from morning 'til sunset. Here you all are getting ready to go someplace, everybody but me. I haven't been off this front porch all summer long, and here it is Labor Day, almost autumn [*FP* 1.1].

And in the closing moments of the play she reconciles herself to sitting on the porch. "Looks like that's what I was intended to do," she says (*FP* 3.28). The porch is the place on which not much out of the ordinary occurs. By extension, the town itself has much the same quality. A number of specifics in Inge's portrayal of the town remain consistent throughout the versions. Madge works in a dime store, a place where exciting things "don't happen" (*P* 11). There is a school, a country club, bowling teams, and a Bible class at the Baptist Church. The food at the hotel is decidedly inferior, even though "they serve it to you nice, with honest-to-goodness napkins" (*P* 36). A single movie theater provides the main source of entertainment in the town. On the whole Inge portrays both the front porch and small town as essentially ordinary and undynamic.

Rosemary, the boarder at the Owens house, serves as the most vocal, but not the only, mouthpiece against the town's provincialism. At times, she feels as trapped by the porch as she is by the town. In the earlier version of *Front Porch*, Rosemary walks dreamily around the porch complaining, "I wish I was in Kansas City tonight.... There'd be something doing there.... Never anything to do in this little burg" (*FP* 2.20). She calls it a "dull town" (*FP* 2.18) and a "hick town" (*FP* 2.19). When asked what she did one night, her answer is, "We went to the movies, what else is there to do?" (*FP* 3.5). Rosemary is not the only character who feels the difference between the town and the great world beyond. Millie Owens sits on the porch and, based on her reading, fantasizes about life beyond the town. In *The Man in Boots*, her excitement about the world clearly shows: "I just love New York, places like El Morocco and the Stork Club where all the famous people go. New York is the most stimulating, most cosmopolitan city in the world now. That's what *Life* magazine said— Marlene Dietrich likes to go there and so does Tallulah Bankhead...." She goes on to explain that New York has shows every night, Kansas City only two or three a year, and in this town they don't get any: "Only movies and you know how disappointing Hollywood is; they only put out commercial junk. I don't care for California at all. I much prefer New York ... San Francisco is nice. It's very cosmopolitan. And they have lots of fine restaurants, to [*sic*] and places like the Top O' the Mark and in Los Angeles there's Ciro's and the Mocambo...." When the listener is impressed how much Millie gets around, her answer is "Oh, I've never been to those places. I've just read about them" (*MIB* 2.11–12). Madge, Millie's sister, also finds her life in town to be lacking worldly excitement. Madge is the prettiest girl in town. She seems destined to marry Alan, the richest boy in town. But Madge finds little excitement in the relationship and finds herself yearning for action, adventure, and change. Women sit on the porch and fantasize about life beyond the town, while complaining about the town in which they live.

The women's hopes rest in a man who will take them off the porch, out of the town, and into the world. Inge sets up the porch as a female space and the area off the porch as a male space. This basic scenographic and dramatic strategy holds true through all versions of the play. Throughout the earlier version of *Front Porch*, the women sitting on the porch follow cars with their eyes, dream of men or their dream place, and crane their necks to catch a glimpse of the excitement in the street. Flo in particular is yearning to "get out someplace" (*FP* 1.9). The women's talk turns to places in the world that they would like to visit, such as San Francisco or Canada, and in rare cases, cities where they have been, such as Detroit. The talk of the world beyond increases the sense of the women's entrapment and isolation on the porch. Inevitably the women end up talking about men. Helen Potts mentions that she'd "always look across the street to see Clark Gable" (*FP* 1.8). From the vantage point of the front porch, a scene in which not much happens, the women imagine an exciting, romantic, fantasy world of men.

However, when a real man actually appears, the women find themselves strangely protective of their space. Inge was fascinated, after having written the first scene of *Front Porch*, "to find how protectively feminine it was, how the women seemed to have created a world of their own, a world in which they seemed to be pretending men did not exist" (Inge, "*Picnic*: From" 33). If the man's appearance is a surprise, the women respond with suspicion. As they are chatting, "suddenly A MAN appears on the porch and they become immediately quiet, regarding him a little suspiciously" (*FP* 1.11). It is a delivery boy and, feeling uncomfortable, he quickly leaves. Mrs. Potts admits that "the only man I ever see is the postman. Men are like creatures of another planet" (*FP* 1.16). In the revised *Front Porch*, a boy from town solicits Madge in front of the porch. A worried Flo looks down from the porch and asks, "Everything alright down there?" (*FPr* 1.35). Men can be met with more than a suspicious stare. In most versions, Millie acts as the guard of the house. In *Picnic*, when Bomber, the newsboy, comes by the house, he tries to attract the attention of Madge up in her room but is met with the protective actions of Millie. In *Picnic*, as Madge and Millie greet Hal for the first time in the yard, Flo comes out the front door to warn him: "Young man, this is my house and these are my daughters" (*P* 10). Millie, leaving the porch to get a look at Hal working in the yard, is immediately called back by her mother. When the women are caught unprepared for the sudden appearance of a man, they often run inside the house to hide. The women may fantasize about men and the world, but when a real man appears, the women often find themselves fearful of the intrusion.

On the other hand, the arrival of an expected date can create much welcome excitement. Inge clearly sets up a growing tension between the women on the porch and the approaching men beyond the porch. In the earlier version of *Front Porch*, when Howard finally drives up, the women become excited. Flo and Helen "almost unconsciously, start tidying themselves up. Rosemary has out her compact making whatever improvements she can" (*FP* 2.8). Rosemary tries hard to appear relaxed. In over a page of dialogue, the women comment on Howard's clothes, and try to discern whether or not he has been drinking. The tension builds through the scene, and the image is one of caged animals getting more excited with the slow approach of a human.

The scene of Hal's and Alan's arrival in this earlier version of *Front Porch* is worth presenting in full in order to show how Inge sets up the relationship between the interior and the exterior, female and male spaces:

(Millie comes zooming out the door)
MILLIE: Mom, haven't they come yet.
HOWARD: You look like a movie star.

> MILLIE: She's [Madge] the one looks like a movie star. I keep wanting to go. (She sits but twists uncomfortably and keeps watching the street constantly expecting the boys) Madge told me I should stay upstairs until they get here, and not be waiting for them on the front porch like I was looking for them. (Jubilantly) Here they come, Mom, here they come.
> FLO: Here who comes?
> MILLIE: (Getting up and holding her mother's arm) Yes, Mom. Here they are. Oh, mom.
> FLO: Now just sit down and act like you had some sense.
> MRS. POTTS: (Looking out) I don't see any Sir Galahads anywhere.
> MILLIE: Oh, Mrs. Potts.
> ROSEMARY: Is that your boy friend, Millie, the one in the tan sport coat?
> MILLIE: Yes, that's him. Isn't he divine? Oh, darn it, where's Madge? Should I run inside, Mom?
> FLO: Go wherever you like. Might as well stay here now that you're here.
> MILLIE: Oh, look, they're coming up the walk now.
> FLO: What did you expect them to do? Honk the horn and have you come out there? Now, sit down, Millie, and act like you had some sense. I'm getting real ashamed of you.
> MILLIE: (sitting) All right.
> ROSEMARY: He is a real nice looking boy, Millie.
> (There are a few moments silence while those on stage anticipate the arrival of the two boys. Millie is merely tense. The other women start again to fix themselves up in any little way they can, and they seem to acquire rather fixed smiles with which to greet the boys. Then Hal and Alan set foot on the front porch.) [*FP* 2.10–2.14].

The sense of this marvelously comic scene remains in later versions. In *Picnic*, whenever the sound of an approaching car is heard offstage, the women on the porch scurry into activity. As Alan drives up in his car for his first appearance, Millie calls out to him and runs inside to get her bathing suit. When Rosemary hears the sound of Howard's car, she "*moves excitedly to* R. *edge of steps*" crying "It's him! It's him!" (*P* 38).

Men, in one way or another, throw the women off balance by their actual appearance at the porch. A similar dynamic arises as the train, an important link with the world, comes to town. The train brings with it the possibility of upsetting the equilibrium of the women. The train is the source of both excitement and threat. This image first appears in *The Man in Boots*: "The morning train sounds in the distance. Its long whistle sounds happy and promising of adventure. All stop automatically and listen" (*MIB* 1.7b). Madge, who "seems to be listening with her very soul," says that the train "always sounds sort of exciting" (*MIB* 1.7b). Millie imagines famous people from far-off places, such as Morocco, getting off, and that "then it starts off to go somewhere else … to New York or Paris or Casablanca" (*MIB* 1.7b). In the revised version of *Front*

Porch, the train whistle sounds at the station and Madge listens with a far away look in her dreamy eyes:

> I love to listen to the train come in. When I hear the train come in, 1 like to think some famous person is getting off, just by accident maybe, that maybe President Roosevelt or the King of England or Greta Garbo is stopping between trains on their way somewhere else. (... Madge still listens to the train which now starts off, sounding a screeching whistle at the edge of town.) It's at the limits now. It always sounds its whistle like that when it gets beyond the limits, like it wanted to be free [*FPr* 1.5].

Sitting on the porch's limits, the threshold defined by the steps, Madge imagines the train at the town's limits.

In *Picnic*, the train is a commanding presence, and the train whistle, in the words of Inge, is "*a happy, promising sound*" (*P* 7). Madge listens intently to the sound of the train in the distance, in another variation of the scene:

> MADGE: Whenever I hear that train coming into town, I always get a feeling of excitement ... in here (*Hugging her stomach.*)
> MILLIE: Whenever I hear it, I tell myself some day I'm going to get on that train and I'm going to go to New York.
> FLO: That train only goes as far as Tulsa.
> MILLIE: Well, in Tulsa I could catch another train.
> MADGE: I always wonder, maybe some wonderful person is getting off here, just by accident, and he'll come into the dime store for something and see me behind the counter, and he'll study me very strangely and then decide I'm just the person they're looking for in Washington to carry on an important job in the Espionage Department (*She puts towel over face below eyes.*). Or maybe he wants me for some great medical experiment!
> FLO: Those things don't happen in dime stores [*P* 11].

Because the sound of the train engages the emotions and draws the girls out beyond the realm of rational discernment into the land of fantasy, Flo is always dubious of their responses and finds herself, as the parent, making an opposing claim by pointing out the reality behind the fantasy. In *The Man in Boots*, when Millie suggests that the train could be going "to New York or Paris or Casablanca," Flo reminds her that the train "just goes as far as Oklahoma City." Millie pursues the point: "But when you just listen to it and don't stop to think, it could be going anywhere." Flo answers, "Then always stop to think before you get on it" (*MIB* 1.7b).

Flo's parental advice has further implications. Inge provides the train, which moves in and out of the town carrying Hal, with powerful sexual imagery in a number of versions, bringing together the images of town, front porch, and self. In the revised *Front Porch*, Hal and Madge are seen highlighted in an area of the stage representing a grassy mound. Hal forces Madge to the ground as the stage directions read: "Now the train is at the city limits. It cuts loose with a shrill screech of its whistle like a cry of sudden pain. Curtain" (*FPr* 1.2.45). In *The Man in Boots*, after their evening together, Hal is on the train. As Flo tells Madge to come back in the house, the train is heard at the station:

> MADGE: In a minute, Mother. (Flora goes inside. Madge sits and listens to the train. Its bell is clanging, then it starts working up the power to leave. Its engine chugs gradually up to an overpowering roar. It sounds like an enormous beast in heat. Then it starts off picking up speed along the way, until it has achieved distance from the town. Then it emits one shrill, piercing screech of its whistle ... a sound of release and freedom. Then Madge quietly gets up and goes inside.) [*MIB* 3.2.8].

The sexual act, represented symbolically by the moving train, will in time become a distant memory as Madge carries on her life in the town. Hal's affair with Madge parallels the train's journey through the town's limits. Hal enters on the train, steps on the porch, enters the house, steals Madge away, violates her personal limits, and leaves town. She is left changed by the meeting.

Hal's power over the women comes from his being both a Hollywood figure and the epitome of a world that promises sexual excitement, physical thrills, and romance. In Hollywood, he received a screen test and had lots of pictures taken with his shirt off, was raped by two women, was a diving champion on the West Coast, has parachuted, and skin dived off of Catalina. Hal's associations as a movie hero and fantasy figure were part of Inge's conception from the start. In earlier versions he was like a slick sheik (*FP* 1. 26), Errol Flynn's double (*FPr* 1.28), and a Star performer (*SBe* 2.14). He is the answer to Rosemary's desire to see "flesh and blood actors" in town (*FP* 2.1.17), and he, like Madge, looks like a movie star (*FP* 1.34).

Although Hal has an effect on all the women, he upsets the equilibrium of the town most by seducing Madge. Inge struggled with how to portray the outcome of this event. One key to the outcome is based on Inge's dramaturgical strategy in defining the two opposing claims, the home/hometown and the world beyond. His strategy is clear from the early versions of the play and manifests itself in significant differences in the texts of *Picnic* and *Summer Brave*.

As we have already seen, two fundamental opposing claims have been present in the conception of this story from the beginning: the security of the home and town versus the excitement offered beyond, a static reality versus an active image. The forces of stasis, and one might even say, inertia, have always been stronger even though the world, through Hal, may provide momentary relief. In *The Man in Boots*, Mrs. Potts describes the situation simply:

she calls Hal "a romantic stranger." She goes on: "Town is full of strangers. Nice strangers and bad strangers ... that come and stay awhile ... and make everything gay for a while ... and then go away again, leaving everything just as it was before." Flo, ever suspicious, quietly responds, "I hope so" (*MIB* 1.18). In all versions except *Picnic*, Inge took pains to establish the town and home rhythms before introducing the upsetting, dangerous figure of Hal. In *Picnic*, Hal opens the play even before the people in the Owens household are introduced. This has the effect of strengthening the claims in his direction and diminishing the opposing claims of the home. In *Summer Brave*, Inge brings back the long introduction: five and a half pages of dialogue are in place before Hal even appears.

In *Summer Brave*, the establishment of the town is accompanied with a marked diminution of the importance of the train whistle. The whistle is still a *"happy, promising sound"* (*SB* 7) but it no longer provides that constant reminder that the great world beyond is accessible and beckoning. The train is heard at the opening of the play but no one pays any attention to it; it is not a means by which characters fantasize about the world.

Once this vehicle of access to the world is diminished, Inge brings the notions of change and fantasy into play in the town itself, strengthening the claims of home. As the town is more fully drawn in a variety of ways, we begin to see how a character may find what he or she wants without the necessity of leaving. Possibilities for movement and change in the town can certainly be found in all versions. For instance, in *Picnic* and *Summer Brave*, the work available in town is described in movement terms. Howard advises Hal that "it's a good business town. A young man can go far" (*P* 42). These possibilities, however, are compounded in *Summer Brave*. The importance of the picnic differs significantly in *Picnic* and *Summer Brave*. In *Picnic*, Mrs. Potts suggests that, "we plan picnics just to give ourselves an excuse ... to let something thrilling and romantic happen to us" (*P* 38). For Flo, the picnic is one of the few opportunities to get a man, to "walk out of a shanty like this and live in a palace with a doting husband who'll spend his life making her happy" (*P* 12). If Madge were to marry Alan, she tells her, she would have "charge accounts at all the stores—automobiles—trips. You'd be invited by all his friends to parties in their homes and at the country club" (*P* 12). The picnic provides the opportunity for outward and upward mobility, a chance to leave home for a better life in the world. In *Picnic*, Flo is pushing Madge upward and the picnic is the setting in which that change becomes possible. On the other hand, in *Summer Brave*, the picnic is not simply a vehicle to lead to change; it is valuable because it is itself a change. Mrs. Potts reflects:

Why is it more fun to fix your supper at home and take it out to the park and eat it, than it is to stay home and eat it? It's the change. We all like a change. And if we had to go on a picnic every night, we'd be so tired of picnics we could die [*SB* 54].

The picnic is not the only vehicle for change. Mrs. Potts is thrilled when Hal moves the big chiffonier in the front room of her house back into her mother's room (*SB* 19). With this change in detail, Inge suggests that people need not go beyond the town to experience change; it can be found by simply moving events or material possessions in their everyday lives.

In addition to the town offering the possibility of change, the town begins to take on fantastic qualities normally associated with the world. At the opening of *Summer Brave*, in a scene that is a correlative to Hal's physical exploits in the world, Bomber and Beano provide "*an exhibitionistic display of gymnastics. They turn summersaults and walk on their hands with almost professional grace*" (*SB* 8). This scene brings to the town a touch of the fantastic and the unexpected and tends to tone down the differences between the town and the world. Characters in town are compared with movie stars. In both plays, when Millie dresses up, she looks like Betty Grable or Lana Turner (Mrs. Potts can't remember which) (*SB* 36). This type of reference is extended in *Summer Brave*. Alan has an inferiority complex like Elizabeth Taylor (*SB* 12), and Irma tells of seeing shows in New York where she met Helen Hayes, who was "sweet! Just as natural as you and I" (*SB* 27). Millie even calls the people in town "characters." This melding of clearly defined opposites—common townsfolk and worldly figures—tends to diminish a townsperson's need to move.

As Inge begins to provide the town with more worldly attributes in *Summer Brave*, he correspondingly changes and expands Hal's sentiment, expressed in *Picnic*, that he is tired of moving and would like to settle down. In *Picnic*, when the men from town suggest to Hal that he might wish to engage in the town's activities, the suggestion is met with a frown. In *Summer Brave*, Hal claims that he plans "to join clubs and go to church and do all those things" (*SB* 42).

The town becomes a fantasy kingdom in Hal's eyes. Inge even suggests that Hal is a "Prince Charming looking for his kingdom" (*SB* 50). Although it is clear that Hal is probably incapable of staying, the town is seen, nevertheless, from the vantage point of one who is forever restless and would stop his wandering, if only he were able. At one point, Hal, sitting on the steps, "*leans back, stretches onto the porch and gives in to dreamy reflection. All seems well in his life at the moment, and he can safely phantasize [sic] the future.*" "You know," he says, "there comes a time in every man's life, when he's gotta settle down. I guess I've kicked around long enough. A little town like this, this is the place to settle down in, where life is quiet and easygoing, and people are ... well, people are sincere" (*SB* 43). His presence on the front porch makes this scene particularly striking. The townsfolk sit on the porch and dream of moving beyond the town; Hal sits on it and dreams of finding a home. A bit later another fantasy comes on: "You know, I wish I had more time to read. That's what I'm gonna do when I settle down. I'm gonna read all the better books, and listen to all the better music, like symphonies. A man owes it to himself" (*SB* 43).

Not only does the town take on fantasy dimensions in *Summer Brave*, but life in the world, promised in the escape with Hal, is painted in devastatingly real strokes, which effectively shatter Madge's fantasy of a life with Hal. Flo warns Madge:

> Listen to me, girl. Listen to *me*. I got things to say. There's true love in this life ... and there's something else, excitement and heart throbs and thrills. All of them vanish after a few years, maybe after a few days. Then you hate yourself for having been such a fool, to let yourself be tricked, to have given up your entire life and the years that lie ahead ... because one night ... something happened that made the blood trickle up your spine ... that made your heart beat like a gong inside a cavern ... that made you feel all of a sudden ... like you'd found the whole reason for being born [*SB* 62].

Madge answers Flo's warning: "He ... he *needs* me." Flo is quick to respond: "Yes, he needs you. He needs you to stay home and fry potatoes and wash his underwear while he's at the pool hall. He needs you to forgive him when he spends all his wages on booze. He needs you to lie to when other women call the house and want to know where he is" (*SB* 63). This reality is even graphically suggested in the revised *Front Porch*. Here Inge juxtaposes the porch scene in which Madge is dealing with Hal having left, with a scene of Hal "at the [railroad] crossing, making a new conquest with whom he walks toward the train, arm and [*sic*] arm" (*FPr* 3.1.13)

In *Summer Brave*, Flo's warnings are not graphically portrayed as in *Front Porch* but nonetheless Madge takes them to heart. When Hal appears the morning after their evening together, Madge insists upon talking with him:

(*There is an awkward silence between Madge and Hal.*)
MADGE: We wouldn't be happy together.
HAL: I don't see why not.
MADGE: Things like that don't last.
HAL: (*Sounding rather naive.*) Don't they?
MADGE: You make love to lots of girls.
HAL: ... A few.
MADGE: Just like you made love to me last night.
HAL: Not like last night, baby. Last night was ... (*He gropes for a word.*) inspired.

> MADGE: I'm not so conceited as to think I'm so much different from the others.
> HAL: You're a woman, baby, an honest-to-God woman. And there aren't many such creatures left.
> MADGE: (*shyly*) Silly!
> HAL: (*Hoping to reseduce her, he jumps impulsively to her side and tries to get her in his arms.*) Baby, let's go through with our plan. You throw some things in a bag and we can hitchhike to Tulsa. Yah, we can make it in a couple of hours. Then I can get a job, and we'll get a furnished room somewhere, and there'll be just the two of us, all cozy together, and....
> MADGE: (*His appeal is powerful. It takes all her character to resist.*) No. [*SB* 65].

Madge is trying to put their brief meeting into a sensible perspective; the reference to "her character" is an important and noticeable addition in this version. A few pages after this scene, however, Hal continues to pursue Madge. He "*takes her forcefully in his arms and kisses her.*" Hal claims, "I'm a poor bastard, baby. A guy's gotta claim the things in life that're his. When you hear that train whistle and know I'm on it, your sweet little heart's gonna be busted. And maybe it'll serve you right, cause you love me, God damn it! You love me, you love, you love me!" (*SB* 68). This speech is different from its counterpart in *Picnic* in which Hal claims to love her: "I feel like a freak to say this, but— I love you!" (*P* 71). This is a significant change. In *Picnic*, Hal, as the representative of the world, implies that the world will love her by providing the sense of security she would need to enter it. In *Summer Brave*, this is not implied. Rather, Hal claims something that Madge can deny.

For the moment, however, Hal's begging deeply affects her, and Madge weakens. As Hal lets her go, she drops in a heap "*crying uncontrollably*" (*SB* 68). When she hears the train begin to go she claims to feel "like everything inside me was going with it" (*SB* 68). Madge goes inside the house, but at this point in *Summer Brave* a major transformation occurs. Six pages after entering the house, Madge "*comes out looking very solemn, ready to start for work*" (*SB* 74). She walks out not with suitcase in hand but with the intent to stay. What has happened in order to make her decision to stay viable? Part of Inge's strategy, as we have already seen, entails bringing visions of change into the essentially unchanging, static nature of the town, thereby making the choice to move not so inviting. In *Summer Brave*, Inge takes this further by suggesting that Madge is able to change while at the same time, paradoxically, remaining the same. This condition comes about as a result of particular qualities of her beauty and Inge's conception of Madge as a cinematic phenomenon. As such, Madge need not move beyond herself or the town to get what she wants.

Madge both thrives on and is troubled by her beauty. She studies her face, puts on make-up and perfumes, powders her body, and wears beautiful dresses and sandals which show her painted toenails. She constantly applies instruments of beauty—perfume, make-up, etc.—designed to deny or cover up change. She seems to be successful in escaping the ravaging effects of change. By Mrs. Potts's account, Madge is getting prettier every day (*SB* 20). Yet when Flo asks Madge, early in *Summer Brave*, why she is wearing Rosemary's perfume rather than her own, she answers, "I want a change" (*SB* 36). Madge is troubled by her unchanging beauty and the way that people view her. Ever since her childhood, when her father used to carry her around on his shoulders for all the neighborhood to see, she has been aware of herself as the focus of attention. Recently she had been voted Queen of Neewollah, where she had to sit through the big coronation ceremony until they put the crown on her head (*SB* 51 and *P* 29). The passive nature of these experiences worries her. In similar scenes occurring in both *Picnic* and *Summer Brave*, she asks her mother, "what good is it to be pretty? Whether it just means that you stand around for people to *tell* you how pretty you are?" Flo answers, "Pretty things like sunsets ... and flowers ... and rubies ... and pretty girls, too ... they're like billboards telling us life is good.... Living can be hard and folks can get pretty discouraged, but when we see something beautiful it all seems worth while." Madge answers, "That's just fine, but where do I come in?" further explaining, "Maybe I get tired of being looked at" (*SB* 33–34).

Madge's beauty, in other words, comes from her essence as an unchanging image. Alan views her as unreal. "Every morning I wake up," he says, "and pinch myself to see if I'm dreaming.... She'll disappear. She isn't real.... I don't care if you're real or not. I love you" (*SB* 11). At the end of *Summer Brave*, Flo tells Madge to tell Alan a lie about being with Hal. "He'll believe you," she says, "because he wants to believe you" (*SB* 63). She is an image, like a star on the screen, into which Alan projects his fantasies. Through all versions, Madge is compared with a movie star. In the earlier version of *Front Porch*, Millie says that Madge looks like one. And the morning after her affair with Hal, she acts mysterious "like something out of a Joan Crawford movie" (*FP* 3.4). In *Summer Brave*, the newsboy "*in a moment's phantasy [sic]*" exclaims: "Gee, she's pretty as movie stars" (*SB* 61). Beano, who delivers the milk, says "I seen her ridin' around in Seymour's big Cadillac, makin' out like she's a movie star" (*SB* 8). This line is a significant change from Bomber's line in *Picnic*: "I seen you riding around in his Cadillac like you was a Duchess" (*P* 9). She is often the focus of attention. Her final scene with Hal, which "*all the neighbors are on their porches watching*," was something new to the town: "*The spectators have never had such excitement*" (*P* 68).

Inge reconciles Madge's being passive and unchanging with her need to be a moving, changing human being by portraying her within a cinematic paradox: a moving picture, an action projected within the confines of a stationary picture frame. Madge's status as a movie star is given theatrical representation in the framed image of her in her bedroom window. As the lights go on in Madge's bedroom, the image is clearly that of a movie star on the screen. Inge turns the movie image around: not only is the world beyond the porch seen as a movie image, but the window reveals a movie reality within the depths of the house. This screen image appears for the first time in an extended scene in *The Man in Boots*. The scene in *Picnic* has been truncated to only half a page, whereas in *Summer Brave* it has been extended back out to eleven pages. As Madge dresses, all seven characters on the stage are able to view her on the 'screen.'" In *Picnic*, Millie even wonders why Madge doesn't charge admission (*P* 47). In the window, on the screen, Madge is aloof, beyond touching. Howard says to himself, "Bevans, old boy, you can look at that all you want but you couldn't touch it with a ten-foot pole" (*SB* 45).

Another screen image is suggested in the final moments of the play. At the end of *Summer Brave*, after Madge has decided not to go with Hal, the boys come by wanting to drive her to school. She opts for walking and the car full of boys drives along beside her. As the boys look at her from the car, Madge, enclosed by the window frame, becomes another moving picture. In the last lines of the play we hear the boys calling Madge, "Hey gorgeous! Where you goin? Where you goin?"(*SB* 77). The answer is in a cinematic paradox that allows her to move while staying within the frame. Madge needs no suitcase. A beautiful movie image, she is able to experience mobility while staying at home. Inge takes this further: he fills out the image of Madge by providing her with a sense of peace that gives the image its real power.

Leaving, as Madge does in *Picnic*, is very much the simpler and more predictable choice. It is the typical Hollywood version of the happy ending, and, as Voss points out, in keeping with the romantic resolutions that mid–1950s audiences liked to see (154). But, as Flo voices for the first time in *Summer Brave*, "if you expect happy endings anywhere outside the movies, you're fooled" (*SB* 73). It must be remembered here that both Inge and Logan realized that such an ending, although appearing happy on the surface, would inevitably end in disaster for Madge. In *Summer Brave*, Madge does not fool herself by buying into the false promise of mobility. Instead she discovers what it takes to stay in one place. And what it takes is not necessarily "pretty" in the conventional Hollywood sense.

Inge expresses his aversion to the conventional Hollywood sense of prettiness through Millie, one of the clear author voices in the play. At the end of *Summer Brave*, Millie says: "I say phooey on all this 'pretty' business. I'm gonna be a great writer and a writer doesn't have to be pretty ... I don't care what anyone thinks in this town. When I graduate from college, I'm going to New York; and I'm gonna write novels that'll shock people right out of their senses." When Flo asks, "What could *you* write a novel about?" Millie answers, "*You'll find out*" (*SB* 74). Millie (and Inge) will eventually write about the town, of course, but more particularly about Madge.

Throughout the versions of the play, Inge was attempting to view Madge with a complexity that was simplified in Logan's vision of the story. Madge may see herself as one of the pretty pictures of Hollywood stars that are on her bedroom wall, but equally important is Inge's insight that Madge's choice to stay has a beauty of another sort. The beauty which Inge is concerned with involves a complexity more akin to the pictures of women by Picasso that adorn the walls of Millie's bedroom. Millie maintains that pictures do not have to be pretty. Inge puts Madge together with Millie's sense of beauty in a startling image. When Madge became Queen of Neewollah, the *Kansas City Star* ran a color picture of her in the "Sunday Magazine." She says it was pretty hard for her to get conceited over that though because in the printing, the "color got blurred and they printed my mouth right in the middle of my forehead" (*P* 29). This is an inadvertent Picasso-esque version of Madge and what Picasso recognized as the "truth ... revealed only through disconcerting discoveries" (Jaffe 11). The discovered truth in the play is Madge's sexuality, which, in a real departure from *Picnic* is openly proclaimed in *Summer Brave*. The boys write "*MADGE LIKES GUYS*" on the doorstep of the front porch (*SB* 61), thereby effecting a reconciliation of interior and exterior by labeling what is inside the house and proclaiming the truth to the world. Millie will write about it and reveal a Madge who has come to terms with herself—a Madge at home, finally, with her sexuality. (Inge never publically admitted his homosexuality. As Kathrene Casebolt, a designer of an early Inge production of explained: "He didn't approve of it [his homosexuality] himself ... in his own mind he was truly not at peace" [qtd. in Voss 80]).

It is not surprising that what Inge has in mind, for one who looks out from the porch and sees an opportunity to be at home with herself, may not be happiness but something far more difficult to achieve. The word "peace" appears several times in *Summer Brave*. And at the end of the play Flo throws at Madge, disparagingly, "Back to your job at the dimestore, selling chocolate drops and honey bars to all the riffraf in town" (*SB* 74). Madge answers "*peacefully*" that she likes her job all right (*SB* 75). At the end of the play, Madge exits to work "*with a sort of peaceful equanimity*" (*SB* 77).

She refuses the insistent offers for a ride from the boys and insists upon walking. The full meaning of this choice can be discovered in an extended scene in the earlier version of *Front Porch*. At the end of that play, seeing that Madge is feeling bad about her sexual encounter, Flo asks her, "What do you think you are, a harlot?" Madge's answer is clear. "With quick defense," she responds, "No!" Flo warns her not to condemn herself, "acting as if that's what you considered yourself. Did you ever fall down on the street and think you'd have to spend your life there?" She says you just get up and are more careful next time (*FP* 3.20). At the end of the play the following scene ensues:

> FLO: Do you ... feel ... like walking now?
> MADGE: (Smiles) Yes, I'll walk the whole way. (She leaves.)
> MILLIE: What's she talking about? She always walks to work.
> FLO: This morning ... she thought ... she might not [*FP* 27–28].

In *Summer Brave*, as Madge walks, she does so comfortable in the knowledge of who she is.

Her decision to stay in town is a decision to stay at home, and to be at home with herself. Throughout the versions, Inge draws clear connections between the house and the women. Inge intends both a general anthropomorphic reading of the house and, specifically, a reading of the house as Madge. What is implied in the later versions we see very clearly in theatrical terms in *The Man in Boots*. Mrs. Potts has been cleaning her house in case a surprise visitor appears: "I've lived there so long I'm beginning to feel like a turtle in his shell ... if the house is dirty, *I* feel dirty, and if anything happens to the house, it happens to me, because my house is all I've got in this world, my house is *me*" (*MIB* 1.7a). Later in the play, Buck, who is the Hal character in this version, steps inside the house to use the bathroom. At this point, Mrs. Potts thinks she hears a sound from her house and she fears a robber. The stage empties as everyone goes to check out her house. Buck comes out onto the porch and waits in shadows (*MIB* 1.19). When Madge steps onto the porch from inside, a long scene between the two ensues, during which Hal's courtship of Madge on the porch is juxtaposed with offstage dialogue about a robber trying to break into Mrs. Potts's house. At the end of the play Helen realizes that there was probably no one trying to get into her house, that it was all in her imagination. She has forgotten that the house is old now with worn carpets, loose wall paper, and curtains yellow with age. "There's nothing," she says, "in my house anyone would want, nothing anybody could harm." Madge comes out onto the porch and occupies herself freshening up, putting on rouge and lipstick, adjusting her hair as Mrs. Potts speaks:

> ... but I always forget that. I always remember my house when it was new, when John and I first moved into it. It was so pretty then. The woodwork and the paint all smelled so fresh, and the curtains were crisp and colorful ... and my lovely plum colored sofa was so comfortable and inviting ... (Madge puts her

compact in her purse and starts walking off. She walks straight, facing the world not at all defensively. There is a relaxed smile on her face. She takes her time, not to be disturbed) ... [*MIB* 3.2.14].

Madge is able to step off the porch and head into her hometown in peace as she has come to terms with the home that is herself. From the nostalgic, static atmosphere of the earlier version of *Front Porch*, through the drama of escape and flight in *Picnic*, and back to the peace of *Summer Brave*, Inge struggled with the dilemma of staying or leaving home. With the final ending, Inge moves the home from a place of entrapment to a place of comfort, in which the self is openly acknowledged to the world. It is here that Madge—and Inge—can find peace.

Madge joins a host of others in American drama who, given the option to stay or leave, find themselves heading inexorably inward: Lavinia in Eugene O'Neill's *Mourning Becomes Electra* desperately attempts to throw herself into the arms of a man who will take her away but discovers that there is no escape. Realizing that she can only find the release she seeks by turning inward, Lavinia, in a dramatic final gesture, turns on the porch, or grand portico, and heads inside the house to confront her past and herself. Tom in Tennessee Williams's *The Glass Menagerie* makes a desperate attempt to escape his family and find adventure and peace in the world. He soon learns, however, that in the landscape of the mind there is no escape, and he finds himself forever returning home. Eugene, in Ketti Frings's stage adaptation of Thomas Wolfe's novel *Look Homeward, Angel*, leaves home to pursue his romantic visions of the world but only in the knowledge that, as his brother warns him, "The world is nowhere, no one, Gene. You are your world" (276). Madge, in *Summer Brave*, realizes that in the landscape of the body, the home she calls her own, there similarly is no escape. She discovers that she is her world. In *Summer Brave*, Inge places Hal and Madge in sharp contrast. Against Hal's desperate need to keep moving, we see Madge's peace of staying. By the conclusion of *Summer Brave*, Madge lets Hal go and thus refuses to believe in the promise of mobility. In the end, the need to move out, to escape, is overpowered by a reconciliation with self.

In his final interview, Inge concedes that in *Picnic*, Logan "got the ending he wanted" but he goes on to say "I published my own version, you know, *Summer Brave*. The ending in that is the way I wanted it" (Inge, "William Inge: The Last" 21). Inge committed suicide soon after this interview. He did not, however, as Logan suggests, "kill his favorite child before killing himself." Nor was this return to the original ending "one of the saddest moves in a pitiful life" (Logan 356). Audrey Wood suggests that the enduring popularity of *Picnic* versus the relative obscurity of *Summer Brave* attests to the wrongness of

Inge's move. It is time we look at these judgments with fresh eyes. Quite to the contrary, with the courageous reinstatement of the final ending in *Summer Brave*, Inge has left us with a choice well worth experiencing: a triumphant vision of affirmation, acceptance, and peace.

NOTE

1. See David Richman's "The Two Texts of *Picnic*" in this collection for a detailed examination of the differences between these two texts.

WORKS CITED

Adler, Thomas P. *Mirror on the Stage: The Pulitzer Plays as an Approach to American Drama*. West Lafayette, IN: Purdue University Press, 1987. Print.
Beckham, Sue Bridwell. "The American Front Porch: Women's Liminal Space." *Making the American Home: Middle-Class Women and Domestic Material Culture 1840–1940*. Ed. Marilyn Ferris Motz and Pat Browne. Bowling Green, OH: Bowling Green State University Popular Press, 1988. 69–89. Print.
Clarkson, Philip Bayard. "The Evolution from Conception to Production of the Dramas of William Inge." Diss. Stanford University, 1963. Print.
Fisher, Kerk. "The Front Porch in Modern American Drama: The Promise of Mobility in O'Neill, Williams, and Inge." Diss. University of Georgia, 1989. Print.
Frings, Ketti. *Look Homeward, Angel. Best American Plays. Fifth Series 1958–1963*. Ed. John Gassner. New York: Crown, 1963. 237–76. Print.
Inge, William. *Front Porch* [*FP*]. TS. N.d. William Inge Collection, Independence Community College, Independence, KS.
———. *Front Porch* [*FPr*]. TS. 1951. William Inge Collection, Independence Community College, Independence, KS.
———. *The Man in Boots* [*MIB*]. TS. May 16, 1949. William Inge Collection, Independence Community College, Independence, KS.
———. *Picnic* [*P*]. New York: Dramatists Play Service, 1955. Print.
———. "*Picnic*: From 'Front Porch' to Broadway." *Theatre Arts* Apr. 1954: 32–33. Print.
———. "'Picnic': Of Women." *New York Times* 15 Feb. 1953, sec. 2: 3. Print.
———. *Summer Brave* [*SBe*]. TS. 1952. William Inge Collection, Independence Community College, Independence, KS.
———. *Summer Brave* [*SB*]. New York: Dramatists Play Service, 1962. Print.
———. "William Inge: The Last Interview." Interview by Lloyd Steele. *Los Angeles Free Press* 22 June 1973: 18–22. Print.
———. "William Inge Talks About *Picnic*." Interview by Naomi Barko. *Theatre Arts* July 1953: 66–67. Print.
Jaffe, Hans L. C. *Picasso*. New York: Abrams, 1983. Print.
Logan, Joshua. *Josh: My Up and Down, In and Out Life*. New York: Delacorte, 1976. Print.
Robertson, James Oliver. *American Myth, American Reality*. New York: Hill and Wang, 1980. Print.

Scanlan, Tom. *Family, Drama, and American Dreams*. Westport, CT: Greenwood, 1978. Print.
Shuman, R. Baird. *William Inge*. Rev. ed. Boston: Twayne, 1989. Print.
Voss, Ralph F. *A Life of William Inge: The Strains of Triumph*. Lawrence: University Press of Kansas, 1989. Print.

Robert Brustein's "Men-Taming Women of William Inge": A Re-Examination
Ralph F. Voss

The demolition of William Inge's critical reputation began in November of 1958 with Robert Brustein's "The Men-Taming Women of William Inge" in that month's issue of *Harper's Magazine*. Earlier in the decade, Inge had been widely considered, with Tennessee Williams and Arthur Miller, one of America's top three post–World War II playwrights, a writer who had invested the quiet lives of ordinary-seeming Midwestern Americans with a rich dramatic texture of conflict and place. Somewhat miraculously, all of his four Broadway plays up to 1958 had also experienced neither commercial failure nor significant critical severity, a good fortune that neither Williams nor Miller could claim. In retrospect, it might have been to Inge's personal advantage had he experienced scathing criticism before 1958. As it was, the unsuspecting Pulitzer Prize winner (for *Picnic* in 1953), who had cooperated with *Harper's* in supplying a good photograph of himself for that issue's cover, was personally devastated by Brustein's remarks.

"Stand high a long enough time, your lightning will come," Inge's friend and fellow playwright William Gibson was later to write about Brustein's article. Gibson went on to recall that after the article appeared the stricken Inge called Brustein from Gibson's home, and wept on the phone (Gibson). Brustein's article "cut a knife into Bill like you wouldn't imagine," said Inge's longtime friend and secretary John Connolly (Connolly). Another Inge friend, actress Barbara Baxley, remembered a meeting in her apartment in which Inge, Tennessee Williams, and Elia Kazan decided (against Baxley's urging) not to make a formal, written response to Brustein (Baxley).

That choice not to respond to Brustein was probably wise, given the odd symbiosis of playwrights and critics, but more than half a century after its publication and 40 years after Inge's suicide, Brustein's article can be seen as the turning point in Inge's overall critical reputation and, as a result, given the extraordinary linkage between Inge's self-esteem and his critical reputation, a major turning point in his life as well.

That Inge was so ill-equipped to withstand tough criticism was not well-known in 1958, when, if anything, he was widely seen as a can't-miss writing phenomenon whose works generated success not only as plays on the stages of Broadway but also as films on theater screens around the country. The author of *Come Back, Little Sheba, Picnic, Bus Stop*, and *The Dark at the Top of the Stairs* had been widely profiled as a quiet man who had a modest background, primarily as a schoolteacher, until his writing talent was discovered by Tennessee Williams at the very time Williams himself was on the verge of success. Inge had shielded from the 1950s glare of publicity all but the expected surface details of his life—his Kansas background (upon which he obviously drew for his work), his prior teaching and writing experience (the latter, ironically, including a stint as a wartime substitute critic for the *St. Louis Star-Times*), his bachelorhood, his discovery by Williams, the evolution of his plays, and the like.

Very few people knew in 1958 what later biographical work on Inge has brought to light (McClure, Shuman, Voss, *A Life*): that Inge was a recovering alcoholic who was also undergoing constant psychiatric therapy; and, even more significantly, that he was also an extremely closeted and painfully self-condemning homosexual whose unexpected writing success after age 30 had probably saved him from suicide. The popularity of his work had been an important new spark of life. Inge's writing was the one aspect of his life about which he could feel true pride, a fact which left him uncommonly vulnerable when, beginning with Brustein, adverse and often personally harsh criticism of his work began to appear almost routinely.

That vulnerability and its general consequences, however, are not to the immediate point here. One can now find, elsewhere, details about Inge's subsequent reactions to extremely negative criticism of all three of his Broadway plays after *Dark*: *A Loss of Roses* (1959), *Natural Affection* (1963), and *Where's Daddy?* (1966). Inge won an Academy Award for the original screenplay of *Splendor in the Grass* (1961), a very popular film that most print critics nonetheless disliked. His only other experiences with screenplays, *All Fall Down*, a 1962 adaptation of James Leo Herlihy's novel; and *Bus Riley's Back in Town*, a 1965 scenario based on his original one-act play by that name, both ended in disappointment. *All Fall Down* was generally neglected despite reasonably good reviews, and Inge's *Bus Riley* script was changed so radically by the filmmakers that he had his name expunged from the credits. Some critics liked Inge's work on *All Fall Down*, and some praised his judgment in disavowing *Bus Riley's Back in Town*, but for the most part Inge never knew critical success again after Brustein's ambush in *Harper's*.

Clearly, criticism is to be expected if one is to be as conspicuously accomplished as was William Inge. And just as clearly, it would be a mistake to blame harsh criticism for all of William Inge's pain. He was far too complex an individual with far too many problems to indict one cause so simplistically. Moreover, greater playwrights have suffered comparable, if not worse, criticism; they have simply been more thick-skinned than Inge.

What makes Brustein's criticism so important is that it was the first to assess all of Inge's work up to that time so negatively, the first to characterize it all as limited to "domestic romance" (Brustein, "Men-Taming" 53) intended to endorse marriage and family at the expense of male freedom, and one of the first to insist that it was mostly imitative of the work of Inge's friend, Tennessee Williams. There had been some earlier, similar rumblings about individual plays, most notably by Eric Bentley, but Brustein was the first to offer a synthesized perspective on what was to be the sum of Inge's successful Broadway career, and that perspective proved highly influential. After Brustein, several other significant critics—among them, at different times, Kenneth Tynan, Gerald Weales, Wilfrid Sheed, and Stanley Kauffmann ("The Theater")—joined in the general condemnation as if they had seen the error of their ways. As Inge's newer efforts appeared, more critics found more about his work to dislike. Brustein himself contributed increasingly personal and disdainful appraisals after the debuts of *Roses* and *Natural Affection*. Though he kept writing, turning out plays, film and television scenarios—even, near the end of his life, two novels—Inge's critical reputation never recovered. Brustein's initial article was twice anthologized near the end of Inge's career (once by Brustein himself in *Seasons of Discontent* [1965], and once by Alvin B. Kernan, in his edited volume, *The Modern Theatre: A Collection of Critical Essays* [1967]).

Given the Brustein article's significance in Inge's life and to Inge's critical reputation, it seems appropriate to study it closely again in Inge's centennial year, to criticize the criticism, so to speak, and see if the perspectives possible through time and other criticism make possible any important changes. Several years ago, I began some exploration in this direction, suggesting in a paper at the 1986 William Inge Festival that in criticizing Inge for seeming to endorse marriage and family values, Brustein may have unwittingly hit upon a truth: that, as a deeply ashamed and closeted homosexual for whom, personally, conventional marriage and family were always out of the question, Inge presented such relationships in a hopeful light at the ends of many of his popular plays *because he wanted to believe in the viability of such relationships*. That is, given his heritage and sexuality, along with his lifelong refusal or inability to live as a mate with another person (male or female), Inge's intensely realistic understanding of the difficulties in such relationships nonetheless did not completely overwhelm his hope that they might somehow work for at least some people, for he saw no other means for the survival of family values (Voss, "Robert Brustein's"). I repeated this idea in my biography of Inge, and there also very briefly argued that Brustein's thesis required considerable misinterpretation of what I think Inge actually wrote (Voss, *A Life* 180–85).

Before I fully elaborate Brustein's misinterpretation of Inge's plays below and suggest reasons for it, I want to note that I have not been alone in re-examining Brustein's criticism. There have been at least three other very thoughtful and original assessments of Brustein's criticism. One of these, Janet Juhnke's "Inge's Women: Robert Brustein and the Feminine Mystique," appeared in an excellent special edition of *Kansas Quarterly* that was dedicated to Inge and his works. The other two occur as parts of a larger mosaic of Inge criticism to be found in unpublished dissertations: Jane Lange Courant's "The Drama of William Inge: A Critical Reassessment" and Therese Jones's "An Individual Peace: The Work and Life of William Inge." My debts to these three scholars will be apparent as I proceed.

II.

"William Inge's star is now firmly fixed in the small but brilliant constellation of America's top dramatists," began Brustein, who himself was characterized under the article's title as "[a] fast-rising young drama critic" ("Men-Taming" 52). Having thus begun, Brustein hastened to the business of firmly fixing his own star in the small but brilliant constellation of America's top critics. He immediately undercut his opening compliment of Inge by declaring his puzzlement that Inge should be so highly regarded "[c]onsidering the modesty—one is tempted to say the mediocrity—of his work." A possible explanation for his success, Brustein ventured, was that "Inge is regarded as Broadway's first authentic Midwestern playwright," one who "seems to have restored to Midwesterners their privilege to be as traumatized by life as any other Americans represented on Broadway," and has thus dispelled the "homogenized" Broadway image of that region popularized by Rodgers and Hammerstein in *Oklahoma!* and Meredith Willson in *The Music Man* (52).

Most observers would probably have agreed with Brustein on this point, but Brustein's real purpose was to disprove it with a "closer look" (52) at Inge's work, which seems to reveal Inge as a "spokesman for a matriarchal America" (57), and which "reveals that beneath the naturalistic dirt and cobwebs lies a view of man as blandly nerveless as that held by Rodgers and Hammerstein— and more sinister since it robs the individual of his aspiration, his heroism, and even his manhood" (52). Few readers in 1958 were likely to have noted or questioned the powerful masculine prejudice of that passage ("man" is Brustein's subject, and apparently only males can be aspiring or heroic individuals; the worst robbery of all is of one's "manhood"); it is couched in the "universal masculine" view that prevailed in those times. But it also betrays an attitude about "manhood" that precludes any serious possibility that women will, or can, be viewed favorably.

Each play, Brustein asserted, is a "preachy" (54) endorsement of family life and love in which the women tame the freedom and spirit of the leading men *via* a kind of symbolic emasculation:

> ... Inge's basic plot line revolves around a heroine threatened either with violence or sexual aggression by a rambunctious male. Both terrified and attracted by him, she tries to escape his influence until she learns that, despite his apparent confidence, he is riddled with doubts, loneliness, and need. Once he has confessed this, he loses his ogre quality and the woman is able to domesticate him without difficulty [53–54].

That curious passage seems to present violence, sexual aggression, rambunctiousness, and phony confidence among males as positives. Conversely, males who confess normal human weaknesses (doubts, loneliness, needs, all seen as negatives) are—shudder!—*domesticated*, apparently the worst negative of all, to be equated with castration.

Anyone familiar with Inge's four plays up to that time can see the carefully selected surface details that prompt Brustein's analysis and seem to give it validity. Doc Delaney, the usually subdued husband, becomes briefly "rambunctious" in *Sheba* when he gets drunk and threatens violence in the play's biggest, most pivotal, scene. Hal Carter's virile sexuality is a looming presence in the minds of all the women in *Picnic*, and it ultimately helps trigger the most significant dramatic action. Bo Decker is a classic ignorant "hunk" in cowboy getup in *Bus Stop*, and his noisy pursuit of Cherie, the heroine, is futile until he learns a quieter, more respectful approach, again after climactic scenes. Finally, in *Dark*, Rubin Flood, the rough-hewn traveling (in more ways than one) husband, returns to his wife and family after he realizes that by himself he is unequal to the challenges of the changing times. With the possible exception of Doc, all of these Inge leading men assert their freedom and spirit in different ways, and all eventually betray doubts, loneliness, and needs that drive them into the arms of women. Such a summary of selected surface details provides evidence for Brustein's central criticism. Such a summary might also make someone who does not know the works well think Inge's big plays are, indeed, audience-pleasing "love triumphs over all" bits of fluff that ringingly endorse stereotypical notions of love, marriage, and family. (Not for one minute, but there is yet more to be noted about Brustein's view.)

Having established that the "surface theme" of Inge's work is "that people find salvation from fear, need, and insecurity only through the fulfillment of domestic love" (54), Brustein proceeds to detect the deeper "sinister" theme wherein Inge's men are emasculated. In this deeper theme,

> marriage demands, in return for its spiritual consolations, a sacrifice of the hero's image (which is the American folk image) of maleness. He must give up his aggressiveness, his promiscuity, his bravado, his contempt for soft virtues, and his narcissistic pride in his body and attainments, and admit that he is lost in the world and needs help [56].

Inge's men, in other words, lose the very essence of their manhood when they are "tamed" by Inge's women. (We will leave alone any questions regarding just how ideal this aggressive, promiscuous, bragging, heroic male "image" really is.)

The two great charges, then, that Brustein leveled against Inge's four plays were (1) the plays are "she-dramas" that are "preachy" endorsements of conventional love and marriage (and thus capitulations to popular 1950s tastes); and (2) the major male characters lose their manliness into the bargain because they are "tamed" by the major female characters. A close look at the plays, however, provides ample evidence for the dismissal of those charges.

III.

First, *Sheba*: Just how "man-taming" is Lola Delaney, the primary female character? She was rejected by her stern father after becoming pregnant by Doc while she was unmarried (she never saw her father again) (*4 Plays* 14). She is totally dependent upon Doc (who forbids her to take an outside job) for all her needs, both emotional and material. At the play's beginning she is lonely, unkempt, and forever calling her lost little dog, Sheba, who, it becomes clear, is the symbol of her lost youth and beauty. She fills her days with nervous chatter to anyone she can corner to listen, and she vicariously escapes her forlorn existence by listening to exotic radio shows and spying on the amorous developments between the boarder Marie and Marie's boyfriend Turk. Above all, she tries to do nothing that might make her alcoholic husband, Doc, want to get drunk again—even though it becomes apparent that her frequent talk about Doc's problem causes him considerable discomfort that Lola doesn't detect (*4 Plays* 9–10).

Much of Lola's nervous chatter provides us with the exposition we need: Doc was raised by an exacting mother to whom he was quite close; Doc had to drop out of medical school and marry Lola when she became pregnant, settling instead for chiropractic; Lola's father rejected her when this happened; the couple had to use inadequate medical assistance and lost their baby girl along with the chances of having more children; Lola's beauty and self-esteem have badly eroded—all this adding to the disappointments and frustrations that drove Doc to the bottle and Lola into whimpering ineffectually. When Marie comes to live with the Delaneys, Doc has been dry for a year and daily struggles to maintain his sobriety, despite no real changes in the circumstances of his disappointments.

The play's dramatic action is forced when Doc, who has unwisely come to view Marie as the daughter they lost, imagines a high, virginal ideal for Marie that she honestly (and wholly unmaliciously) does not meet. Doc learns that Marie, who is engaged to an absent young man, is having sex with Turk, an athletic schoolmate. Moreover, Lola seems to approve of this affair, which she considers wonderfully romantic. The knowledge destroys Doc's fragile equilibrium and he gets roaring drunk, precipitating a scene in which he gets a hatchet and threatens to "hack" the fat off Lola. He also swears he'll find Marie and Turk and "chop" the former and "fix" (i.e., castrate) the latter. Fortunately, he passes out before he realizes any of these threats (*4 Plays* 57).

After Doc is hauled away to the drunk tank by his friend from A.A., Marie announces that she is leaving to marry Bruce, her fiancé (Turk has been just a fling). Lola is once again rejected by her father, leaving her nowhere to go (62–64). The stage is therefore set for Doc's return and their reconciliation, which is not based at all on Lola's "taming" of Doc, but upon their mutual need for each other. They both face a future that is far from rosy; after all, Doc has had a bad slip, and though he is doubtless wiser regarding his idealization of Marie, in terms of his alcoholism he has fought his way back only to the place he was a year before the play begins. Lola has decided, thanks to her interpretation of a symbolic dream, that she will no longer call after her lost dog/beauty, Sheba. With no alternatives before her, she has cleaned the house and renewed her commitment to being as good a wife as she can for Doc. But she faces no other major changes in her daily life—so there is no strong reason to believe that the frowzy, lonely, daydreaming escapism will not return, or that she will find lasting means of raising her self-esteem (65–69). There is no way a serious reader or theatergoer can claim this is a "happiness ever after" ending. Brustein simply had to misinterpret the play to make his thesis work, primarily by focusing more on Doc as somehow "tamed" than on Lola—but the play clearly belongs to Lola.

Brustein's focus on Doc was a tenuous strategy in any case, for Doc is far from "the American folk image of maleness." The qualities Brustein lists when describing this folk image just do not fit Doc: *aggressiveness, promiscuity, bravado, contempt for soft virtues, narcissistic pride in his body and attainments* ("Men-Taming" 56; emphasis added). If Doc has been "tamed," the taming took place before the play, and Lola did not play the biggest part in the taming.

So, returning to the question of just how "man-taming" Lola is, Janet Juhnke offers this withering summary:

> Meet a forty-year-old housewife who is bored and lonely, who worries about becoming "old and fat and sloppy," who in fact cannot get up enough strength to fix her own breakfast (let alone her husband's) in the morning, who mopes around the house all day longing for her lost pet doggie. See her take advice from a neighbor with seven children and an immaculate house: "Being busy is being happy." Rejoice in her growing contentment as she cleans the house, polishes the silver, puts together an elegant dinner [all of which Lola does in preparation for helping Marie entertain her fiancé], and forgives her backsliding alcoholic husband. Finally, watch her accept the death of her pet dog, turn to her husband (whom she calls "Daddy") as her new pet, and open the bright new day of her life with the final words, "I'll fix your eggs" [105].

Juhnke persuasively discerns misogyny in Brustein's criticism, to the effect that it is ultimately not the *men* who are "tamed," but the *women* instead, who apparently must (in Brustein's view) conform to the "feminine mystique" defined and decried by Betty Friedan in her pivotal 1963 book by that name. Lola, Juhnke points out, could be "Case Study 1 in Friedan's description of the effects of the feminine mystique: infantilization, boredom, passivity, dependence, emptiness" (105). Certainly, Lola seems shaped and controlled by a male-dominated, stereotypical view of a woman's role: wife, mother (even she believes her inability to have more children is a strike against her), cook, housekeeper (she condemns herself because she is lax in such matters), and so on. Suffice it to say that Lola is no man-tamer.

Nor is Marie. Turk sacrifices none of his maleness in his relationship with Marie. He is the sort of brassy male Brustein describes, but Marie and Turk have sex because it is what they both want, and neither attaches any additional significance to the fact. Rather, it is Doc and Lola—especially Doc—who find Marie's and Turk's relationship extraordinary, bringing to it the attitudes and values that profoundly affected their own relationship. Doc's values can cause him to label both Lola and Marie "a couple of sluts" (*4 Plays* 56), and though it is clear from his threat to "fix" Turk that Doc considers Turk no better than a tomcat, it is also clear that he does not hold Turk as accountable as Lola or Marie. Courant and Jones both note that several critics of the play—not including, however, Brustein—seem perfectly willing to agree that Marie is a slut, while saying nothing at all judgmental about Turk's behavior. In this they perceive the infamous "double-standard," and they are doubtless right; after all, one of the "qualities" of the "American folk image of maleness," according to Brustein, is promiscuity. But in distinguishing between someone ideal for a sexual fling (Turk) and someone she considers ideal for marriage (Bruce), Marie does no more than many men do (Courant 220–23; and Jones 106–13).

Picnic also presents problems if we are to see the men, particularly the leading man, Hal Carter, as being "tamed" by the women in the play. Hal fits Brustein's description in some key ways: he is an aggressive, muscular, handsome braggart, and he is sexually attractive to women. But in important dramatic action we learn that Hal's overt behavior is largely a cover for his insecurities. Hal, we find, came from a broken home, and though his onetime athletic prowess won him a college scholarship, he left without finishing school and his life has been a series of misadventures (*4 Plays* 91–94). He has come to the little Kansas town in desperation; he has had enough of aimless drifting and he hopes his wealthy former college friend, Alan Seymour, can help him. "I gotta get someplace in this world, Seymour," he tells Alan; "I *got* to" (95). In other words, Hal *wants* a steady, productive job, *wants* a regular home, *wants* to settle down—all characteristics of "domestication"—*before* he meets any of the women in town. That Hal has no realistic conception of what his wants might actually mean (e.g., he seems to think he ought to start work at the top) is beside the point here; he is willing at the play's outset to sacrifice most of his "American folk image of maleness," but Brustein missed that. He also seems to have missed the ending of the play, in which Hal leaves town with no hope of staying and settling into a "tamed" existence.

But from its inception as *Front Porch*, first performed at the Galveston Island Little Theatre in 1948, to its "rewritten and final version" as *Summer Brave* in 1962, Inge intended *Picnic* to be a play about women (see Voss, *A Life*, especially 122, 129–35). The real force of the play is generated not by Hal but by the women, primarily the widowed mother, Flo Owens; her beautiful daughter, Madge; and their boarder, the spinster teacher Rosemary Sydney. Plot-wise, the most important women are Madge and Rosemary.

Madge is the most beautiful girl in town, and is engaged to Alan, son of the town's richest man. But she is not happy; in important exposition in Act 1 we learn that she daydreams about what life is like elsewhere, that there is no excitement and no lovemaking in her relationship with Alan, and that she seriously questions the value of her spectacular good looks. Flo nonetheless thinks Madge is in an enviable position, being so beautiful and being engaged to the wealthy Alan. In Flo's scheme of things, a woman's beauty vanishes soon enough, and men are generally unreliable, as her own experience with the girls' father has convinced her. (As might be expected, Flo is instantly wary of Hal.) As far as Flo is concerned, Alan and his wealth and the security it represents are to be grabbed (*4 Plays* 79–85).

Madge, however, suffers under the worshipful attentions of Alan, who clearly has trouble believing she is real (let alone believing that she cares for him). The lack of genuine feeling between Madge and Alan is manifest in a scene at the end of Act 1 when Alan proposes that the night of the picnic the two sneak away, not—as one might sensibly suppose—for sex, but because, as Alan tells Madge, "I want to see if you look *real* [Inge's italics] in the moonlight." Madge admonishes Alan not to say such a thing, and his response to that is even more obtuse: "I don't care if you're real or not. You're the prettiest girl I ever saw." And he is not listening when Madge replies, "Just the same, I'm real." At this critical point Hal drives up in Alan's car and, in Inge's stage directions, calls "*lustily*" for Alan, who is to leave with him to make picnic preparations (101). This scene quietly prefigures events to come; Inge's groundwork makes the attraction between Madge and Hal inevitable.

Still, the restraints and inhibitions Flo has carefully imparted to Madge, along with the general social and moral atmosphere of the town, might have kept Madge and Hal apart were it not for the teacher Rosemary's provocative role. Rosemary is possibly the most memorable secondary character Inge ever created. Certainly, she is one strong reason for the comparisons between Inge and Tennessee Williams, for she is a shriller, harsher, though saner emotional relative of Williams's unforgettable Blanche DuBois. Inge carefully prepares us for Rosemary's provocative scenes by presenting her as an aging schoolteacher whose desperate loneliness and sexual frustration are easily evident behind her garrulous and opinionated exterior. She is as intrigued by Hal as Mrs. Potts, the neighbor who first gives Hal odd jobs to do, but she would never admit it (see *4 Plays* 85–89, 107, and 112). Rosemary is regularly courted by Howard Bevans, an over-forty businessman from a nearby smaller town, and though Rosemary talks as though she's not at all serious about Howard— "I don't have time for any of 'em when they start gettin' serious on me" (85)— it is clear that her desperation would be far greater without him. Howard, a generally conservative man who is already far more subdued than Brustein's "rambunctious male," escorts Rosemary to the picnic, where in the early evening, as the dance begins, he shares his bottle of liquor with her, Hal, and— unwisely—Millie, Madge's younger sister, who is Hal's date. As the climactic scene approaches, everyone is in the mood to dance, and the drinkers have shed some of their inhibitions. Rosemary dances with Howard, but he is not very good at it. Hal dances with Millie (who this special evening has been briefly transformed from tomboy into lovely young woman), but she cannot seem to keep from trying to lead.

Thus the scene is set for Madge's joining Hal on the dance floor, where the two move gracefully and rhythmically together, their fingers snapping, their dance, in Inge's words, having "*something of the nature of a primitive rite that would mate the young couple*" (120). This sensuous dance to "Moonglow," which became an enormous hit song after the release of the 1956 film, confirms the attraction between Madge and Hal, and more importantly makes both Millie and Rosemary jealous. Rosemary, desiring to dance with Hal, aggressively grabs him: "Now it's his turn to dance with me," she says; "I may be an old-maid schoolteacher, but I can keep up with you. Ride 'em cowboy!" (121).

Hal, as politely as possible, declines, but Rosemary still clings to him and tells him (in a speech that Brustein quotes in its entirety):

> ... You remind me of one of those ancient statues. There was one in the school library until last year. He was a Roman gladiator. All he had on was a shield. (*She gives a bawdy laugh*).... All we girls felt insulted, havin' to walk past that statue every time we went to the library. We got up a petition and made the principal do something about it. (*She laughs hilariously during her narration*) You know what he did? He got the school janitor to fix things right. He got a chisel and made that statue decent. (*Another bawdy laugh*) Lord, those ancient people were depraved [121].

Though the castration imagery is unmistakable, also unmistakable in this context is Rosemary's physical fascination with Hal. She would not want him "fixed" like the statue anytime soon.

Clinging to Hal's shirt, Rosemary pleads with him to dance, but again he refuses. Howard then tries to persuade her: "He wants to dance with Madge, Rosemary. Let 'em alone. They're *young people*" (122). Howard's is not a wise choice of words. Reminded now that she is older than she would like to admit, feeling humiliated at Hal's rejection of her, Rosemary launches into a vicious verbal attack on Hal, gathering self-righteous momentum from the fact that Millie has become sick from the alcohol, for which Flo blames Hal:

> Oh, he'd have fed her [Millie] whiskey and taken his pleasure with the child and then skedaddled! .... (*Back at Hal*) You been stomping around here in those boots like you owned the place, thinking every woman you saw was gonna fall madly in love. But here's one woman didn't pay you any mind [123].

Howard tries to explain what *really* happened to Flo, but Rosemary continues her assault on Hal:

> You think just 'cause you're a man, you can walk in here and make off with whatever you like. You think just 'cause you're young you can push other people aside

and not pay them any mind. You think just 'cause you're strong you can show your muscles and nobody'll know what a pitiful specimen you are. But you won't stay young forever, didja ever thinka that? What'll become of you then? You'll end your life in the gutter and it'll serve you right, 'cause the gutter's where you came from and the gutter's where you belong [123–24].

This stinging attack humiliates both Hal and Rosemary. It does not "tame" anyone. The eruption of events causes Alan to take the sick Millie home with Flo tending to her, leaving Howard and Rosemary and Hal and Madge behind.

"What made me do it, Howard?" asks the crushed Rosemary. "What made me act that way?" Reminding Rosemary that men have feelings the same as women, Howard then tries to smooth things with Hal. But Rosemary's desire to escape the unhappy scene quickly persuades Howard away: "This is my last night of vacation and I want to have a good time," says Rosemary; "I want to drive into the sunset!" They take their leave, and now Madge is alone with Hal, who was supposed to drive the other car back to the Owens home behind Alan (125).

Madge also tries to console Hal, who is convinced that he deserved Rosemary's attack. "I'm a bum," Hal insists to Madge. "She [Rosemary] saw through me like a goddamn X-ray machine." Madge is not convinced. She refers to Hal's wonderful dancing and his desire to make changes in his life. He counters by telling her that at 14 he spent a year in reform school for stealing a motorcycle. When he got out, his mother did not want him back. "Well—that's the Hal Carter story," he says; "but no one's ever going to make a movie of it." Proud that Hal has shared his pain with her, glad to be treated as an emotional equal rather than some exquisite doll, Madge impulsively kisses Hal. "Baby!" responds Hal, "What'd you do?" Madge is not sure what she has done; she remembers that they are supposed to go back to the Owens home, but something powerful has happened to prevent that. Picking her up in his arms, Hal carries her toward the car, declaring, "We're not goin' on no goddamn picnic" (126–27).

The dance scene and its aftermath force the denouement of the play. Rosemary and Howard return to the Owens home later and Inge makes it clear that they have had sex. In one of the most powerful scenes Inge ever wrote, Rosemary begs Howard to marry her. Without actually saying he will, Howard finally gets away by promising he will return in the morning. Hal and Madge then return, and, again, it is clear that they have had sex. Though Madge and Hal both know that they have broken rigid codes and hurt those about whom they care, the chemistry between them is simply too strong to be denied (128–33).

When Howard returns the next morning, Rosemary has already told everyone in the Owens home (as well as some of her teaching colleagues) that he is coming to marry her. Howard is surprised—and at first reluctant—but he agrees, a cooperation that would help to make him fit Brustein's thesis if only he were not already so distant from the "American folk image of maleness" that Brustein describes. Moreover, he understands Rosemary's vulnerability now, and he knows that Rosemary has been deeply humbled and humiliated by the events of the previous night. He finds quick rationales that he mentions to Alan (who has come to see Madge)—"A man's gotta settle down some time.... And folks'd rather do business with a married man!" (139). Rosemary and Howard's future hardly seems one including, in Brustein's words, "salvation from fear, need, and insecurity ... through the fulfillment of domestic love" ("Men-Taming" 54). With work and perseverance, however, they might have a durable marriage. As for the notion of Rosemary's "taming" the already very gentle Howard, one need only examine again the scene in which she begs him to marry her (129–31).

Hal appears in the play's denouement because he wants at least to tell Madge goodbye before he jumps a freight train to Tulsa. Hal is on the run because Alan and his father have sent the police after him, ostensibly for stealing Alan's car (not his girl). Hal and Madge speak while everyone else is distracted by the noisy congratulations of Howard and Rosemary. Alan spots Hal and intervenes, but Hal quickly subdues him and ignores Flo's orders to leave because he is not finished talking to Madge. When Madge admits she cares for him, Hal allays her concerns that he has made love to other girls. "Not like last night, baby," he says; "Last night was ... (*gropes for the word*) inspired." When he tells her she is a "real, live woman," he tells her what she has long wanted to hear. He pleads with her to come with him, but the police siren signals that he must flee (140–43).

In both the popular stage/screen versions and in *Summer Brave*, Hal catches the train, alone. He has not been tamed; he has been humiliated and run out of town, and we have no strong reason to believe the future holds any real change for him. After a protracted battle with Broadway (and later, film) director Joshua Logan, Inge changed the ending of *Picnic* so that Madge packed her bags and followed Hal to Tulsa for whatever uncertain future she might be able to share with him (Voss, *A Life* 126–35). Such an ending pleased 1950s audiences, but not the less optimistic Inge. In the "*rewritten and final version*" (Inge, *Summer Brave* [1]), *Summer Brave*, a wiser Madge stays in town to adjust however she needs to her circumstances. In both endings, however, Madge has not "tamed" Hal, even though she does emerge as more independent, one who will no longer stand for Alan's unrealistic attitudes or Flo's overcautious admonitions. Thus, Madge and Rosemary, the two most important women in *Picnic*, are not "men-taming." Brustein said that each of Inge's plays "reads a little like *The Taming of the Shrew* in reverse" ("Men-Taming" 56), but with *Sheba* and *Picnic*, it is difficult to see how. The same is true of *Bus Stop* and *The Dark at the Top of the Stairs*.

Bus Stop, Inge's third hit, offers only one important female character to evaluate as a "man-tamer." This is Cherie, the "chanteuse" whom the leading man, the cowboy, Bo Decker, has abducted from Kansas City. The other two women in the play are Grace, the hardnosed proprietor of the bus stop, and Elma, the very naive young waitress. Grace is not interested in any permanent relationship with a man; in very early dialogue, as she and Elma prepare for the arrival of the bus in the snowstorm, we learn that Grace does not miss her husband, who has apparently long ago left her, because "I got just as lonesome when he was here. He wasn't much company, 'cept when we were makin' love. But makin' love is *one* thing, and bein' lonesome is another" (*4 Plays* 155). Later, Grace reinforces her philosophy by inviting Carl, the bus driver, up to her apartment for sex while the bus is stranded, but when he leaves there is no reason to think that their liaison has resulted in anything more than passing pleasure (203–04). She also locks Virgil Blessing, Bo's older male friend, out of the bus stop at the close of the play (219); Grace is not only not interested in "taming" a man, but she is not interested, period. As for Elma, she is still in high school, and spends most of the play being fascinated by the interplay of Bo and Cherie, and by Dr. Lyman, an eloquent and elderly drunk who appears to have a fetish about young girls, and who makes a date with Elma for the symphony in Topeka, a date he later breaks after a bout of self-recognition and remorse (212). Elma is also no man-tamer.

Cherie, however, is the only major Inge female in the four plays that Brustein trashed who might have serious "man-taming" credentials, if only because the brash and swaggering Bo so clearly *needs* taming and so clearly is made more tame in the course of the play. Cherie is a Kansas City nightclub singer of dubious talent and meager education whose training has been imitating radio and film performers. She has begun to suspect that her career is limited. She has had considerable sexual experience with men, and attracted to Bo because he quieted the noisy nightclub while she was singing "That Old Black Magic," and, as she tells Elma: "I'd never seen a cowboy before. Oh, I'd seen 'em in movies, a course, but never in the *flesh*.... Anyway, he's so darn healthy-lookin', I don't mind admittin' I was attracted, right from the start.... But it was only what you might call a *sexual* attraction" (*4 Plays* 184).

But Bo had never before experienced intercourse (in fact, it was one of the goals of his trip to the rodeo in Kansas City), and now he behaves as though

Cherie is his fiancée, and he has forced her to accompany him on the bus back to his Montana ranch, there to marry. His rowdy, bullying behavior does not derive from maliciousness, but rather from brute ignorance. He just does not understand that he is behaving badly, and he often does not understand or heed the advice of his older, father-figure companion, Virgil, who constantly tries to smooth things out between Bo and the several people he offends.

No one could really doubt that the couple would eventually get together; *Bus Stop* is the only romantic comedy Inge ever wrote, and when Cherie explains to Elma what she wants in a man, it is only a question of how Bo will somehow meet her criteria:

> I want a guy I can look up to and respect, but I don't want one that'll browbeat me. And I want a guy who can be sweet to me but I don't wanta be treated like a baby. I ... 1 just gotta feel that ... whoever I marry ... has some real regard for me, apart from all the lovin' and sex. Know what I mean? [187].

Cherie, however, is unable, on her own, to convince Bo to change. After asking Will Masters, the sheriff, to protect her, Cherie tells Bo that she does not want to continue the trip with him and that she does not want to marry him (174–75). When he repeatedly refuses to believe her, she says, "If I was a man, I'd beat the living daylights out of ya, and thass what some man's gonna do some day, and when it happens, I hope I'm there to *see*" (197).

That is precisely what it takes. A few moments later, when again Bo physically grabs Cherie to force her against her wishes, Sheriff Will Masters intervenes and administers the first thorough whipping Bo has ever experienced in a fistfight. It is Will, not Cherie, who then offers consoling philosophy to Bo, and who persuades Bo to apologize to Cherie (204–05). Once Bo apologizes, Cherie forgives him; soon she tries to explain to him that, because of her prior sexual experience, she isn't the "kinda gal you thought I was." A bit later Bo tells Cherie she was his first sexual experience (she already knew this, but is charmed by his admission), and asks to kiss her goodbye. The kiss is long and tender, and after a bit more stage action Bo tells Cherie he is "virgin enough fer the two of us," and "I like ya like ya are.... So 1 don't care how ya got that way." Proclaiming that is "the sweetest, tenderest thing that was ever said to me," Cherie soon agrees to go to Montana with Bo after all (206–15).

Cherie might be said to have "tamed" Bo in the sense that she did not change her criteria for returning the love of a man; Bo indeed must calm down and show respect for her. Still, without the beating administered by Will Masters and the near-constant advisings and urgings of Virgil, it is doubtful that Bo would ever have changed his approach to her. That Bo has been forced to behave himself is unmistakable; but in matters not directly involving Cherie, he is still a very brash cowboy when he gets back on the bus with her for Montana, leaving behind his friend and mentor, Virgil, who explains to Bo that his companionship is no longer needed. If Cherie is a man-tamer, it is only in a limited way, and only with the considerable help of Will and Virgil. If Bo and Cherie are headed for matrimony, it does not promise to be of the domestic-bliss-evermore variety.

Brustein ignored the very strong counterpoint to the Bo-Cherie story in *Bus Stop*: the fact that none of the other characters finds any sort of happy resolution—domestic or otherwise. Grace, Carl, and Will continue as before, their lives not notably affected. In presenting Grace and Carl's guiltless assignation, Inge seems quietly to challenge 1950s notions of propriety, just as he did with the Marie-Turk affair in *Sheba*. Elma has learned from Cherie that the "show biz" life in Kansas City can be rather tawdry, and she has learned from Dr. Lyman that eloquence can be misleading; but she is still very young and the important experiences of her life still lie before her. Dr. Lyman continues to ride the bus and to drink; his dissolution is not quite complete, but at least he has not committed any new indiscretions with Elma. His situation is more pathetic than Virgil's, for Virgil is not a drunk and is fully aware and philosophically prepared to deal with the fact that his life has just changed dramatically. It is almost as though the trade-off for the happy Bo-Cherie resolution had to be the lack of such a resolution for all other characters.

In the autobiographical *The Dark at the Top of the Stairs*, Inge's last Broadway hit, the most important man is Rubin Flood, a traveling harness salesman who cares very much about his family, even though he married his wife, Cora, because she was pregnant. Despite Cora's near-constant urging that he find a job that would keep him in their oil-booming little Oklahoma town, Rubin prefers the restless life of the road (and occasional affairs with other women) to a settled existence. It is the early 1920s, and psychologically, Rubin is only a slight remove from the rugged earlier frontier days; moreover, deep inside he fears the future in a changing world of increasing mechanization. In fact, the increasing popularity of automobiles and tractors puts him out of work near the beginning of the play; people just do not need harnesses as they once did.

There is in Rubin quite a bit of "the American folk image of maleness"; he is ruggedly handsome and jealous of his freedom of the road; though not exactly promiscuous, he is sexually active beyond the bounds of his marriage to Cora; he is stubbornly proud and considers it important to project a strong "provider/protector" image. He thinks that Cora has spoiled their daughter Reenie and especially their boy Sonny, who is daily taunted as a "sissy" by the other boys. Predictably, Rubin thinks Sonny should learn to get tough and "beat the tar outa the other boys" (*4 Plays* 227). Rubin is exasperated that

Sonny is not receptive to his offer to teach him self-defense, and resentful that Cora is so protective of Sonny that, while disapproving of his offer to teach the boy to fight, she still expects him to do something about Sonny's problems. As the play develops, an oedipal bond between Sonny and Cora becomes apparent—yet another problem between Cora and Rubin. Clearly, the couple have stereotypical communication and understanding difficulties. And true to Brustein's description, at the beginning of the play Rubin would never want to acknowledge his fears to Cora. He does not even want to tell her that he has lost his job, for he does not want to seem weak and he does not want to worry Cora.

A crisis develops, however, because Cora (who still does not know that Rubin has lost his job) buys an expensive dress for Reenie to wear on a "blind" date to an upcoming party. The party is being hosted by the daughter of a newly oil-wealthy couple, and Cora hopes that the date and the dress will help bring Reenie out of her extreme shyness. Though Cora has plans to pay for the dress a little at a time out of her modest budget, Rubin finds out about the purchase and it precipitates a great argument that begins about money but quickly proceeds to Cora's accusations of Rubin's neglect and infidelity. Rubin swears he will leave, and Cora tells him to go ahead; she taunts him that Mavis Pruitt, one of his lady friends, is waiting for him in Ponca City. Rubin then threatens to strike Cora, and when she dares him to, he does. He then stalks out of the house, vowing, "I'll go to Ponca City, and drink booze and take Mavis to the movies, and raise every kind of hell I can think of. T'hell with you!" (242–48).

As these events transpire in the first act of the play, the audience can already anticipate that Rubin will return, and that there will be a reconciliation. That is exactly what happens. But before one can casually assume that such a reconciliation equals a "taming" of Rubin by Cora, it is important to examine what happens to Cora and the children while Rubin is gone. For one thing, Cora learns in Act 2 that she and the children cannot leave the little town and go to Oklahoma City to live with her sister and brother-in-law, Lottie and Morris Lacey (276). Cora and the children, then, have nowhere else to go. For another, and more important thing, Cora also learns that contrary to what she has always thought, Lottie and Morris do not have a happy and fulfilling marriage—in fact, it is just the opposite (277–80). These revelations cause Cora to reassess her situation and realize that, on the whole, her marriage is not as bad as she thought. When Lottie changes her mind and tells Cora that she and the children can come to Oklahoma City to live after all, Cora has already changed *her* mind: "I'm going to work this out for myself, Lottie" (282). In other words, circumstances have already gone a long way toward "taming" *Cora*. She begins to realize that she probably *has* been too protective of her children, likely as a reaction to Rubin's frequent absence. She also decides that she is not angry with Rubin; even though he hit her, as she tells Reenie, "I was defying him to do it." She unsuccessfully tries to telephone him, and we know that he will be welcome when he returns (284).

Other events affect the Floods at this time. Reenie's "blind" date is with Sammy Goldenbaum, a Jewish boy who is neglected by his mother, a famous movie actress. In Sammy's brief appearance in the Flood living room he impresses everyone with his kindness and sensitivity. However, we learn early in Act 3 that the shy Reenie spent most of her time at the party cowering in the ladies' room because no boys had "cut in" while she and Sammy danced. Her absence caused Reenie to miss the *real* reason Sammy left the party early without her (she had thought he had left to avoid seeing her again): he had been told to leave the country club, the site of the party, because he was a Jew. This latest in what Inge makes clear is a long line of rejection causes Sammy to flee and commit suicide. When Reenie learns this and learns that Sammy had been asking for her before he left, she realizes that he might have thought she, like the country club, was rejecting him. Cora tells Reenie her shyness is selfish and Reenie begins to understand her need to overcome it (290–94). Cora also tells Sonny he must not "come crawling into my bed anymore," thus beginning to sever the oedipal tie which hampers her son and also complicates her relationship with Rubin (289).

Thus we have been well prepared for Rubin's return in Act 3. When he returns, Rubin tells Cora that he has lost his harness-selling job but has prospects for a new traveling job selling oilfield equipment. After overcoming her surprise at Rubin's revealing the lost job, Cora begins to complain because the new job would also involve traveling. This very nearly sets Rubin's temper off again:

> God damn! I come home here t'apologize to you for hittin' ya. I been feelin' all week like the meanest critter alive, because I took a sock at a woman.... I walked in here to *beg* ya to forgive me. Now I feel like doin' it all over again.... All these years we been married, ya never once really admitted to yourself what kinda man I am. No, ya keep talkin' to me like I was the kinda man you think I *oughta* be.... Don't you know who I am? [296–97].

Rubin goes on to say that he does not feel he can give of himself to his family unless he is providing well for them, and that demands the better income he receives from traveling sales. He expresses doubts about the new job, selling oilfield equipment—about which he knows nothing—to men he also does not know. "I'm scared," he admits (298). Therefore, circumstances have also gone a long way toward "taming" Rubin—much more than Cora has "tamed" him.

Cora has never seen this vulnerable side of Rubin, who then apologizes for hitting her and tells her he loves her. Cora admits her love for Rubin as well, and it is clear that these moments of lucid and honest communication have reconciled them, though, as Rubin still insists, "Just don't get the idea you can rearrange *me* like ya do the house, whenever ya wanta put it in order" (299). (Nor does he make any apology or promise regarding his extramarital affairs.) Reconciliation with the children then quickly follows, and the play ends with Reenie going to the library, Sonny going to the movies, and Cora going up the stairs where Rubin waits for her "*in the warm light at the top*" (304).

To see Cora Flood as a man-tamer is to ignore the circumstances not only of her distress, but also of Rubin's. Social and economic forces beyond their control go a long way toward "taming" them both—and the fact that Rubin still refuses to avoid traveling jobs, still refuses to be "rearranged" like furniture, makes it clear that any "taming" of him has been only partial—and mostly voluntary. Cora and Rubin have improved their communication and have a better understanding of each other, but they will still have to work to keep their marriage durable.

IV.

Are the women in Inge's top four plays of the 1950s "men-taming"? Are these plays "preachy" endorsements of marriage and family? Not really, as I hope I have shown. To see them in that light requires distortion not only of the women's roles, but also the roles of the principal male characters and the thematic thrust of each drama itself. Such distortion, it would appear, was necessary for the "fast-rising young drama critic," Robert Brustein, to make his case and hence, help make his name.

As for Brustein's dislike of Inge's plays as "she-dramas" in which "if not the leading then certainly the pivotal (and most insightfully created) role" belongs to a woman ("Men-Taming" 53), one wonders what can possibly be so bad about that. What would Brustein have said if he were assessing *Antigone* or *Lysistrata*? Or any number of great plays that centrally feature women? "She-drama" seems to be one of those vapid labels, like "chick flick," that Brustein uses to raise a phony issue. Similar questions might be asked regarding Brustein's dislike of plays depicting the complex strains of family life resolved, however tenuously or painfully. What on earth is *Oedipus Rex*? If prominently featuring a family working out its problems for good or ill makes for bad drama, how did *The Glass Menagerie* and *Long Day's Journey into Night* manage to be so good?

Brustein's charge that Inge was imitative of Tennessee Williams is also problematical; why should a few surface similarities be necessarily imitative? And if some slight imitation exists, why is it necessarily detrimental? Jane Lange Courant has put some of the longtime Inge-Williams comparisons to rest, I think. Noting that most critical detractors of those two playwrights were men, Courant says that the Inge-Williams "connection, in the male critical world, seems to derive from their mutual interest in female characters and their acknowledgment that this half of the population also had sexual drives" (36). Such interest and acknowledgment, Courant implies elsewhere, was rather unsettling to the male critical establishment of the time.

I think much responsibility for Brustein's misinterpretations can be attributed simply to his desire for a critical reputation. Eloquent bashing of a heretofore widely praised playwright's work is a promising way to avoid getting overlooked on a critical bandwagon, especially if you are good enough to develop your argument around a selective and exclusive modicum of insight and lucky enough to get your handiwork published in a conspicuous national magazine like *Harper's*. It has been done plenty of times. Brustein did not exactly come out of nowhere with his article, but suffice it to say he did not remain a professor at Columbia. And let me hasten to add that, Inge's pain aside, I do not think Brustein is a villain for having seized his opportunity in 1958. What happened *after* 1958 in widespread criticism of Inge (including Brustein's) however, may be another matter.

Wide critical reception of the plays *A Loss of Roses*, *Natural Affection*, and *Where's Daddy?* went from generally stinging to personally vicious. The film *Splendor in the Grass*, for all its box-office success, was savaged by most print critics. Gerald Weales found Inge's cameo role as the Reverend Whiteman in *Splendor* emblematic of his entire career to date:

> No actor and with no part to act, Inge can only look out sadly from large and liquid eyes at a world in which good intentions are of no consequence and where all of us must settle for second best. The same eyes have been looking at the same world in all of Inge's plays, beginning with the first and best, *Come Back, Little Sheba* [43].

When *Natural Affection* opened on Broadway, Brustein called it "a monstrous chimera proceeding from a heat-oppressed brain," denigrating Inge, "formerly the sweetheart of the old ladies in the mezzanine," for what he considered the new play's sensationalism ("Theater" 29). Richard Watts, Jr., accused Inge of deliberate sensationalism in *Natural Affection*, trying to keep up with Williams and Edward Albee. About *Where's Daddy?* Walter Kerr wrote, "I don't care where daddy is, where's William Inge?" Many more instances of such criticism could be given, but suffice it to say that after Brustein's "Men-Taming Women," the overall critical picture of Inge's work was bleak, and it was never to change while Inge lived and wrote.

The perspective of time brings us some additional and interesting observations. Among them is the fact that over 60 years after *Sheba*'s Broadway debut, Inge's four plays have all had an enduring popularity with audiences in theaters throughout the country. They have often been successfully revived in New York (*Picnic* as recently as 2013). *Splendor in the Grass* remains a popular story, and was refilmed for television. Time and popular tastes have made what critics of the late 1950s and 1960s had to say about Inge's work far less important than the plays, which endure.

Moreover, as the aforementioned special issue of *Kansas Quarterly* attests, scholars have continued to find fresh meanings in Inge's work. Certainly, Janet Juhnke, Jane Lange Courant, and Therese Jones are among those who have mined rich post–Brustein veins of Inge criticism. Reflecting on Inge's rough treatment by Brustein and many of the critics mentioned here, Courant suggests that "perhaps the most significant reasons for such deprecation of Inge's drama were deep and unconscious prejudices that contemporary critics shared with their society" (5). By such prejudices, Courant clarifies elsewhere, she means homophobia, "fears about the encroaching power of women" (5), and notions of what was appropriate for the stage at that time (25).

Jones agrees that homophobia may account for some of the negative attitudes toward Inge, and Williams as well. Both Courant and Jones note Stanley Kauffmann's controversial 1966 piece in the *New York Times*, which held that:

> Because three of the most successful American playwrights of the last twenty years are (reputed) homosexuals, and because their plays often treat of women and marriage, therefore ... postwar American drama represents a badly distorted picture of American women, marriage, and society in general [("Homosexual")].

Kauffmann seemed to think that homosexuals could know nothing about women, marriage, and families. He claimed that these playwrights were not to blame, for they had no choice but to masquerade, but he decries the "*disguised* homosexual influence." The unnamed playwrights, most readers (including Inge himself) assumed, were Williams, Albee, and Inge. "That Kauffmann man," Inge wrote to his friend Ned Rorem, "seems out to get us all."

That his argument would deny gay playwrights' creative imaginations did not seem to cross Kauffmann's mind. It is as though Kauffmann could not believe that a gay male playwright might actually know something about a married heterosexual male (or female, for that matter). One might just as well trot out the old argument that you cannot write about soldiers and war unless you've been one and in one (take *that*, Stephen Crane); or, to put a slightly different, more recent twist on the same canard, you can't play an oriental on stage unless you are one. Perhaps, then, the frequent claim of Inge imitating Williams was not based so much on the occasional surface similarities between their works as it was upon the deeper, necessarily unstated indictment of the two as homosexuals. Perhaps homophobia *was* a factor in the later extreme, personal criticism Inge suffered.

Courant and Jones also agree that Inge, far from affirming stereotypical male and female roles, was instead critical of such roles. Jones contends that many of Inge's plays "caused discomfort for critics and reviewers not because they were written by a gay male but by a radical feminist" (96). Courant credits Inge with foreseeing that sexual stereotypes and roles "would become one of the most significant issues of the years to come" (20). Courant, in particular, discerns in Inge's work—including that after the famous four plays of the 1950s—an "early warning system" which shows the "suppression of individual fulfillment in an increasingly mechanized society, and its corollary, sexual oppression" (38). In other words, Courant sees what might be called "The men- and women-taming world of William Inge," a world that works and reworks popular myths and conventions and "links him to more recent American playwrights, such as Edward Albee and Sam Shepard":

> Like Albee and Shepard, the Kansas playwright expressed his vision in the colloquial, cliché-ridden speech of characters distorted by false goals and fed by illusions produced by a technologically sophisticated culture. Although he spoke in the quieter, more modulated tone of romantic realism, he, too, investigated the dark side of a vanishing American Dream [49].

I think Courant is right. Far from Brustein's idea of "men-taming women" in Inge's major successful plays of the 1950s (including the 1961 screenplay, *Splendor in the Grass*), those works instead show human beings of both genders struggling in their environment to survive, to endure, to seek whatever triumphs they can find in their lives—not as battling genders so much as souls seeking meaning and purpose.

Until recently, William Inge was almost always mentioned in surveys or histories of American drama as having enjoyed, in Courant's words, a "contemporary overestimation of his work" (9). That reputation can be traced to Robert Brustein more than any other single critic. But Inge's work has outlived its severest criticism, and in more recent years serious, scholarly criticism (as differentiated here from after-performance reviews of local revivals of various of Inge's plays) has examined Inge's work in a variety of ways. Such criticism includes Susan Koprince's "Childless Women in the Plays of William Inge" and JoAllen Bradham's "Reprising *The Glass Menagerie*: William Inge's *My Son Is a Splendid Driver.*" Elsewhere, Georges-Michel Sarotte removed the "homosexual disguise" that Kauffmann found so troubling in Inge's work and found richer subtextual meanings in "William Inge: 'Homosexual Spite' in Action," a chapter in Sarotte's book, *Like a Brother, Like a Lover: Male Homosexuality in the American Novel and Theatre from Herman Melville to James Baldwin*. Jeff Johnson explored similar themes in his book, *William Inge and the Subversion of Gender*. And Steven Dansky begins his 2012 essay "Of Beefcake and Beauty Queens" with the undeniably true statement that "as the 2013 centenary of William Inge's birth approaches, his plays continue to be produced, even as some critics consider his work creaky, dated, and beyond resuscitation" (13). Precisely. The plays are the things, and I think Mrs. Monroe D. North said it best long ago. In a letter to the editor in an *Harper's* issue subsequent to the one containing Brustein's article, Mrs. North, dismissing Brustein's critique, wrote, "How could I ever have enjoyed the four plays so much?" (4).

WORKS CITED

Baxley, Barbara. Personal interview. 5 June 1986.
Bentley, Eric. "Pity the Dumb Ox." Rev. of *Picnic*, by William Inge. *New Republic* 16 Mar. 1953: 22–23. Print.
Bradham, JoAllen. "Reprising *The Glass Menagerie*: William Inge's *My Son Is a Splendid Driver*." *American Drama* 11.1 (2002): 58–72. Print.
Brustein, Robert. "The Men-Taming Women of William Inge." *Harper's* Nov. 1958: 52–57. Print.
_____. *Seasons of Discontent: Dramatic Opinions, 1959–1965*. New York: Simon and Schuster, 1965. Print.
_____. "Theater: The Anti-Establishment." Rev. of *Natural Affection*, by William Inge. *New Republic* 23 Feb. 1963: 28–29.
_____. "Theater: *A Loss of Roses*." Rev. of *A Loss of Roses*, by William Inge. *New Republic* 21 Dec. 1959: 23. Print.
Connolly, John. Personal interview. 7 Dec. 1986.
Courant, Jane Lange. "The Drama of William Inge: A Critical Reassessment." Diss. University of California, Berkeley, 1990. Print.
Dansky, Steven F. "Of Beefcakes and Beauty Queens." *Gay and Lesbian Review* 19.3 (2012): 13–16. Print.
Gibson, William. "For Bill Inge." *New York Times* 24 July 1973: 35. Print.
Inge, William. *4 Plays by William Inge* [*Come Back, Little Sheba*; *Picnic*; *Bus Stop*; *The Dark at the Top of the Stairs*]. New York: Random House, 1958. Print.
_____. Letter to Ned Rorem. MS. 7 Feb. 1966. William Inge Collection. Independence Community College, Independence, KS.
_____. *Splendor in the Grass* [screenplay]. *Men and Women*. Ed. Richard A. Maynard. New York: Scholastic, 1974. 12–74. Print.
_____. *Summer Brave and Eleven Short Plays*. New York: Random House, 1962. Print.
Johnson, Jeff. *William Inge and the Subversion of Gender*. Jefferson, NC: McFarland, 2005. Print.

Jones, Therese. "An Individual Peace: The Work and Life of William Inge." Diss. University of Colorado, Boulder, 1990. Print.

Juhnke, Janet. "Inge's Women: Robert Brustein and the Feminine Mystique." *Kansas Quarterly* 18.4 (1986): 103–12. Print.

Kauffmann, Stanley. "Homosexual Drama and Its Disguises." *New York Times* 23 Jan. 1966, sec. 2: 1. Print.

―――. "The Theater: Inge's 'Where's Daddy?'" Rev. of *Where's Daddy?*, by William Inge. *New York Times*, 3 Mar. 1966: 27. Print.

Kernan, Alvin B., ed. *The Modern Theater: A Collection of Critical Essays*. Englewood Cliffs, NJ: Prentice-Hall, 1967. Print.

Kerr, Walter. "Kerr's Review of 'Where's Daddy?'" Rev. of *Where's Daddy?*, by William Inge. *New York Herald Tribune*, 3 Mar. 1966: 10. Print.

Koprince, Susan. "Childless Women in the Plays of William Inge." *Midwest Quarterly* 41.3 (2000): 251–63.

McClure, Arthur F. *Memories of Splendor: The Midwestern World of William Inge*. Topeka: Kansas State Historical Soc., 1989. Print.

North, Mrs. Monroe D. Letter. *Harper's* January 1959: 4. Print.

Sarotte, Georges-Michel. "William Inge: 'Homosexual Sprite' in Action." *Like a Brother, Like a Lover: Male Homosexuality in the American Novel and Theatre from Herman Melville to James Baldwin*. Trans. Richard Miller. New York: Anchor/Doubleday, 1978. 121–33. Print.

Sheed, Wilfrid. "The Stage: Two for the Hacksaw." Rev. of *Where's Daddy?*, by William Inge. *Commonweal* 8 Apr. 1966: 82–83. Print.

Shuman, R. Baird. *William Inge*. Rev. ed. Boston: Twayne, 1989. Print.

Splendor in the Grass. Dir. Joshua Logan. Perf. Natalie Wood and Warren Beatty. Warner, 1961. Film.

Tynan, Kenneth. "The Theatre: Roses and Thorns." Rev. of *A Loss of Roses*, by William Inge. New *Yorker* 12 Dec. 1959: 99–100. Print.

Voss, Ralph F. *A Life of William Inge: The Strains of Triumph*. Lawrence, KS: University Press of Kansas, 1989. Print.

―――. "Robert Brustein's 'The Men-Taming Women of William Inge': Half Right, but All Wrong." William Inge Festival. Independence Community College, Independence, KS, 14 Apr. 1986. Lecture.

Watts, Richard, Jr. Review of *Natural Affection*, by William Inge. *New York Theatre Critics' Reviews* 24.1 (1963): 384. Print.

Weales, Gerald. "In the Grass, Alas." Rev. of *Splendor in the Grass*, by William Inge. *Reporter* 23 Nov. 1961: 43. Print.

Structures of Violence: Gender Roles in Inge's Plays
Linda Wagner-Martin

Rubin Flood says it to Cora in *The Dark at the Top of the Stairs*:

All right. If you're so determined to think it, then go ahead. I admit, in some ways I din wanna marry nobody. Can't ya understand how a man feels, givin' up his freedom? [*4 Plays* 273].

Marriage to Inge's male characters is more than making a choice among women; it is also losing the freedom that means the masculine. In an Inge play, any loss of the masculine often evokes violence, and the usually unexpected episodes of violence startle both the audience and the characters. The timing for these revelatory bouts of anger is one of the most expert things about Inge's dramatic structures: it is as if we never know these reticent, seemingly impassive male characters until their lives—and their monumental frustrations—bring them to physical action.

In *The Dark at the Top of the Stairs,* the first episode of unexpected violence is Rubin's hitting Cora. Near the end of the first act, when their domestic argument has turned to invective and insult, his blow sounds from offstage, sending his wife reeling into the parlor where the two children are watching. The blow points the action, makes a somewhat rambling scene take shape, and leaves the audience, for a time, in sympathy with Cora. Successive scenes shake that sympathy, however, though subtly and without Rubin's presence. Instead, the long-defeated Morris, Cora's brother-in-law, acts as surrogate male, and reminds the audience of the forceful qualities Rubin possesses. The real progression of the play is toward the suicide of the Jewish adolescent, Sammy Goldenbaum, whose death occurs at least partly because of the selfishness of the social code Cora and her daughter Reenie try to represent. A kind of quasi-emasculation leads to the end of Sammy's life, abandoned by a mother too busy with her own existence to care about her child's. His choice of suicide contrasts vividly with Rubin's choice—to apologize and return, after the loss of his job. The sexual reconciliation between Rubin and Cora creates the satisfying ending of the play in which, as well, the sexual tensions between Reenie and her younger brother Sonny are also dissolved in a more mature acceptance of each other's identity.

In *Come Back, Little Sheba,* Doc's threat to harm Lola with the hatchet serves a similar function. Through the play, Lola is seen as the inept, childlike wife, mourning for the Sheba-dog, which has become her child. Doc seems to care for her, and her involvement in young Marie's romances seems harmless, to a point, though hardly a full-time adult occupation. Doc's eventual anger at Lola's complicity in Marie's affairs appears somewhat irrational—until the full story of his life, his life with Lola, and his anger at their marriage is told. When Doc gets drunk after almost a year of sobriety, his rage at his entrapment into marriage to Lola, because of her (eventually miscarried) pregnancy, motivates his terrible verbal abuse of Lola, who pleads, "Doc, don't say any more ... I'd rather you hit me with an ax, Doc ... I can't stand to hear you talk like that" (*4 Plays* 57). Though Doc does chase her with the hatchet before he loses consciousness, his debilitating invective has already done its damage.

In *Bus Stop,* the violence is the fight between Sheriff Will and the overzealous cowboy Bo. The physical action catalyzes the milling characters, brings each of the women to her own realization of what love means, and focuses for each of the men their incapacity for romantic involvement. In *Picnic,* the physical violence—suggested from the first moment of Hal's appearance—remains offstage, but the verbal interchanges (Hal's "We're not goin' on no goddamn picnic" [*4 Plays* 127] as he carries her off to have sex and Madge's wish never to see him again afterwards [133]) are poignant closings to their respective scenes. In *A Loss of Roses,* Lila's suicide attempt brings the important dialogue between Helen Baird and her confused son Kenny to its necessary climax, and in *Natural Affection,* the abandoned son's fatal vengeance on the drunk woman, a substitute for his mother, illumines the action of the entire play before it.

Each Inge play has a violent moment as its turning point, yet the milieu of each seems boringly repressive. The lives of the Flood, Owens, and Baird families, as well as those of most of the assorted characters in *Sheba, Bus Stop,* and *Natural Affection,* are outwardly so placid they could put an audience to sleep. That is part of Inge's aesthetic for his drama: the lives of most characters are the quiet desperation of which Thoreau spoke, and that only a sudden, surprising spark can transform the calm surface of that disguising unreality into the genuine.

The genuine for Inge is the sexual. Instead of drawing the sexual as Eugene O'Neill did, however, so that it becomes the center of a male-female struggle that dominates the play, Inge creates a largely matriarchal world, a housebound culture in which the men who demanded place in O'Neill's plays must here struggle for even a niche. In *The Dark at the Top of the Stairs,* Cora arranges life as she wants it, and her fanaticism about her clean floors is so oppressive that Rubin enters their home in stockinged feet to make his dramatic apology for hitting her. The restaurant that is the setting for *Bus Stop* belongs to Grace, and everyone involved in the play is trespassing on both her property and her set of judgmental morals. The true extent of her power is clear in the closing scene when she is tired and leaves Virgil Blessing no choice but to wait outside for the next bus. The ironic use of her name—*Grace*—with no surname and that of *Virgil Blessing*—who does guide Bo to a blessed union, and provides some sanity for the other bus passengers throughout the night—shows Inge working hard to contrast Virgil's self-abnegation with Grace's self-centered lust. Rather than herself being a guiding presence, Grace is absent throughout much of the play.

Picnic, similarly, is set in a space dominated by two matriarchies—the Owens household of mother and two daughters, and that of the Pottses, Helen (whose marriage was annulled the day it occurred) and her ailing mother. Even the sub-plot of the play deals with the lives of three "old-maid" (*4 Plays* 85) schoolteachers, "professional women" who lead their own quietly desperate existences. The only stage space not dominated by these matriarchies is the "*narrow passageway*" (75) of yard between them—which is where Hal Carter makes his initial appearances. Hal is at his best in the open yard, swimming with Millie, on the open boxcar.

Even in *Come Back, Little Sheba*, although it seems as if Doc is in control of the household, once Lola begins to clean the house, he feels both out of place and out of control. Rather than being pleased that she has cleaned house, he is unsettled by that act. In fact, psychologically, it is Doc's seeing Turk coming out of "his" house early one morning—a scene that forces him to realize that Marie is sexually active—that leads to his relapse.

In *A Loss of Roses*, Helen Baird's home is the setting, and the initial dramatic controversy occurs over who—Helen's son Kenny or her drifting friend Lila—will occupy the second bedroom. Much of the conflict hinges on control of the household, and Kenny's role of surrogate for his dead father is by far the most interesting characterization in this heavily Freudian play. In *Natural Affection*, these themes of household control and sexual alignment are carried to extremes. Sue Barker, a modern career woman, not only pays all the expenses for the apartment in which she and her lover Bernie live; but much of the action of the play depends on Sue and Bernie's financial dominance. Power within the couple's relationship is disrupted when Sue's son, Donnie, comes to live with them. Set entirely within the apartment, except for a few scenes in the hall which deal with the sexual exploits of Claire Brinkman, a young neighbor, the play details the course of Donnie Barker's emotional life. The tragedy of his life is that he has been forced to move from one kind of incarceration to another (orphanage to work farm to apartment, where the frustration of his mother's final rejection maddens him). Immediately after Sue rejects Donnie to follow her lover, Donnie kills a strange drunken woman in Sue's apartment, behind the sofa, and then *"goes to the refrigerator and drinks from a carton of milk"* (*Natural Affection* 115). It is the most ironic reversal possible of Sue's fond recollection of nursing her son at her breast.

What is most interesting about Inge's structures and settings is that it at first seems, in every play, as if he is writing about women and their daughters—or at least about the primary bond of the matriarchy, mother and child. Many of the younger women in Inge's plays are learning to be women—Madge and Milly in *Picnic*; Marie in *Come Back, Little Sheba*; Elma in *Bus Stop*; Reenie and Flirt in *The Dark at the Top of the Stairs*. Claire in *Natural Affection* pretends to be learning from Sue, while Lila in *Roses* leans on Helen in many ways, and uses her as a confessor figure near the end of their relationship. If the primary teaching model is not the actual mother, then these daughter figures learn from another older woman (Mrs. Potts, Cora's sister Lottie, Grace). When a reader thinks of Inge, it is to remember dominant women characters.

Even in these plays which seem to be "about" women, however, women's actions—like their lives—are only supporting events. The kernel of life, of decisive action, in each Inge play is the behavior of a male character—Doc (and Turk), Bernie, Hal, Rubin, Bo, Carl, Dr. Lyman, Kenny. Male action is the catalyst for all character growth and change. That action may cause trouble, which the women's acts try to nullify. It may be precipitous, in that the past may be revealed or the future anticipated. It may be disastrous, in that the lives of all characters are changed irreparably. In contrast to the truly decisive acts by male characters, the kind of day-to-day activity Inge's women players partake of serves only as chorus. Women characters and their same-sex relationships provide background, context, milieu. They gain our sympathy, at least momentarily; but finally they seem sentimental—weak-willed, passive, or wrong. Inge's women characters could not, in themselves, carry any play. They are nothing without the sexual tension that Inge creates so consistently.

In most of Inge's plays, women are seed-bearers. They exist to be filled and fulfilled. Men are drawn to them through sexual attraction, whatever their other qualities; and Inge's men remain loyal to these early-loved women no matter what their later conditions. His men are loyal, dedicated, brusquely tender. When they war, it is never *with* a woman so much as it is with their own lost identity as a free, dominant male.

Usually, men and women are bound together through overpowering sexual attraction. Most of Inge's women characters have married because they were pregnant: Cora and Rubin had dated for only two weeks; Doc and Lola found that she was pregnant and cut short Doc's medical education so that they could marry. Sue in *Natural Affection* had Donnie without any help from his father, who "turned white as a sheet when he found out a kid was on the way" (16). Sexual attraction prompts such action as Madge leaving with her suitcase to follow Hal, knowing that her life will be one of chance and probably betrayal—not to mention poverty. As Dr. Lyman says from his years of searching for love, "two people, *really* in love, must give up something of them*selves*.... That is the gift that men are afraid to make" (*4 Plays* 189).

In Inge's plays, however, men do make that gift—repeatedly. Rubin returns to Cora, gladly. Bo feels lucky to have Cherie marry him, despite her sexual experience. Doc pleads forgiveness from Lola: "Honey, don't ever leave me. *Please* don't ever leave me. If you do, they'd have to keep me down at that place all the time. I don't know what I said to you or what I did. I can't remember hardly anything. But please forgive me ... please ... please.... And I'll try to make everything up" (*4 Plays*, 67). Doc's unexpected reliance on Lola mirrors Inge's plot in *Natural Affection* when Donnie pleads to stay with his mother instead of returning to the work farm. That Sue refuses him, as Lola does not refuse Doc, makes the later play much grimmer. In *Natural Affection*, complete with its ironic title, Inge leaves behind the world of reconciliation and moves to increasingly bleak scenes in which human beings have lost their right to their humanity.

In his best-known plays, however—*Come Back, Little Sheba*; *Picnic*; *Bus Stop*; and *The Dark at the Top of the Stairs*—men and women, drawn to each other through sexual charisma, remain joined throughout life. The dynamic of sexual response is given its mystery and its promise; Inge seems to believe that the attraction of physical impulse can lead to lives of fruition, despite the then-prevalent social conventions that criticized the passions of both sexuality and violence. In his use of key episodes of violent behavior throughout his work, Inge links sexuality and violence in ways that modern psychologists would approve, and also shows them as catalytic in interactions among characters. As Lottie tells Cora in *The Dark at the Top of the Stairs*, "I wish to God someone *loved* me enough to hit me. You and Rubin fight. Oh, God I'd like a good fight. Anything'd be better than this *nothing*" (*4 Plays* 279).

Or so Inge seemed to believe. And contrary to our more sophisticated insights into abusive relationships today, after viewing an Inge play, we believe as he did. We believe, somehow, at the end of *Picnic*, that Madge is better off going after Hal than she is waiting for Alan's proposal of marriage. We are caught in the spell of Inge's belief, worked out so clearly in his dramatic characterization. We almost believe Cherie is better off with Bo, and that Grace is better off with Carl as a lover than without him, although she already doubts his availability. We almost believe Rosemary is better off married to Howard, although her scene of entreaty is hard to believe. (It is also hard to forget.) So long as Inge couples the sexually powerful with his scenes of violence, we can believe his underlying themes.

When he sets those themes in opposition, however, as he does in *Natural Affection* and to a certain extent at the ending of *The Dark at the Top of the Stairs*, they war a little and distract us from the primary theme of male-female sexuality. (Rubin and Cora's reconciliation is overshadowed by Sammy's suicide, no matter how hard Inge works at making their relationship primary.) But as Inge said in his introduction to *4 Plays*, "I have been most concerned with dramatizing something of the dynamism I myself find in human motivations and behavior. I regard a play as a composition rather than a story, as a distillation of life rather than a narration of it" (vii).

Inge gives the theater drama that looks conventional. It has dramatic question, a plot that builds and changes shape, resolution. But it has more than the simple direction that such a plot outline suggests because Inge's own view of the action that comprises a plot is relatively complex. As he said about *Bus Stop*, it has "less real story than any play that ever survived on Broadway. I meant it only as a composite picture of varying kinds of love, ranging from the innocent to the depraved.... I was trying to prove that a play's merits can exist, not in the dramatization of one soul-satisfying event, but in the over-all pattern and texture of the play. I insisted that the audience be just as interested in what happened to all the characters as they were in Bo and Cherie" (*4 Plays* viii).

In some ways, Inge's comment here applies to all his plays, because each is a composite picture of varying kinds of love and of the male and female characters involved in those sexual alignments—even those that are not acknowledged to be primarily sexual, such as parent-child relationships. Because Inge could convey his dramatic vision with such passion, even with violence, we more modern viewers and readers can lay aside our objections to his exclusively heterosexual definition of love, and marvel at the insight and power of so much of his work. Inge was able to use his own ambivalence about matriarchal power (especially, in his later plays, that of mothers' power over sons), combine it with his conviction that sexual response was the major human emotion, and create drama that convincingly echoed life. No theater audience can ask for more.

Works Cited

Inge, William. *4 Plays by William Inge* [*Come Back, Little Sheba*; *Picnic*; *Bus Stop*; *The Dark at the Top of the Stairs*]. New York: Random House House, 1958. Print.
_____. *A Loss of Roses.* New York: Random House, 1960. Print
_____. *Natural Affection.* New York: Random House, 1962. Print.

Inge and the Empty Stage
Susan Koprince

One of William Inge's most effective theatrical devices is the use of an empty stage—not a stage that is bare of scenery—but one that is briefly empty of actors and actresses. The device itself is not unique to Inge. Many playwrights, including Chekhov, Ibsen, O'Neill, Miller, and Williams, have occasionally made use of an empty stage, particularly at the beginning of their dramas. But perhaps no writer has employed the device more frequently or more adroitly than Inge. Of Inge's four major plays, three actually begin with a view of an empty stage. During a pause of several seconds the audience sees no characters and no action. In the fourth play, *Bus Stop*, Inge uses the same technique to conclude his drama: the characters depart, one by one, and "*the curtain comes down on an empty stage*" (*Four Plays* 219). Why was Inge attracted to this curious dramatic device? And what purposes does it serve in his theater?

The primary effect of an empty stage—in any play—is that it calls immediate attention to the setting. If the stage is empty when the curtain rises, we, the audience, are not yet focused on the story or the characters; we are simply conscious of the "stage picture" in front of us. As playwright Thomas Kilroy explains, "the stage space itself is the first stimulant to the curiosity of an audience. What is this place? Why are we here? Why are we being shown this?" (Foreword ix). For a few moments the audience is free to examine the dramatic scene and to become aware of its symbolic import. Chekhov uses an empty stage at the opening of *The Cherry Orchard* to suggest a connection between Madame Ranevskaya's country estate and the blossoming cherry trees beyond it. And Miller, in *Death of a Salesman*, begins his drama on an empty stage so that we might sense the grim reality of Willy Loman's fragile-looking house, as well as the "*air of dream*" (A. Miller 11) which clings to it.

In Inge's major works the empty stage serves to introduce us to the setting that Inge knew best: small-town America. When the curtain rises, Inge brings us into an everyday home—into a commonplace living room, kitchen, or front yard—"creat[ing] stage pictures of the most ordinary sort" (J. Miller 26). Sometimes the impression is rather cheerless. In *Come Back, Little Sheba* we find ourselves in a drab Midwestern house which is "*extremely cluttered and even dirty*" (*Four Plays* 5). The sofa is littered, the woodwork is "*dark and grimy*" (5), and dirty dishes from the previous night are piled on the kitchen table. Since there is a pause before the action of the play begins, the audience is able to familiarize itself with this slovenly scene and to speculate about the people who inhabit it. In the words of the play's original director, Daniel Mann, "the space [is] telling a story" (Mann 17).

Inge also uses an empty stage at the opening of his next play, *Picnic*, but here he calls attention to a cheerier, more natural setting. As Inge explained, he wanted to move beyond the "gloomy household" of *Sheba* and write a drama "that took place in the sunshine, filling it with all the variety I could find of character, mood, pathos and humor" (qtd. in McIlrath 50). Set in the yards and on the front porches of two humble Midwestern houses, *Picnic* creates an image of innocence and bucolic simplicity, evoking "an idyllic vision of small-town life that is ... suggestive of Currier and Ives and Norman Rockwell" (Wentworth 59). On the "*empty, sunlit stage*" we view not only the modest houses with their "*tidy appearance*" and clean yards (note the contrast with the disordered scene of *Sheba*), but we see a green landscape in the background and a panorama of the town in the distance, "*including a grain elevator, a railway station, a great silo and a church steeple, all blessed from above by a high sky of innocent blue*" (*Four Plays* 75). Encouraging the audience to focus on this sunny outdoor setting, Inge implies from the start that *Picnic* will deal with bright, natural emotions, with youthful passions, yearnings, and dreams.

At the beginning of still another drama, *The Dark at the Top of the Stairs*, Inge calls further attention to his setting by prolonging the device of the empty stage. The play's first two characters, Rubin and Cora Flood, speak offstage for a short time before the audience actually sees them. Such a technique draws the audience quickly into Inge's small-town world, making us feel that we are virtually sitting in the Floods' living room, overhearing a domestic conversation. On the empty stage we see a spacious middle-class home with pleasant Victorian furnishings—"*one of those square, frame houses built earlier in the century, that stand secure as blocks, symbols of respectability and material comfort.*" But the offstage voices prompt us to focus on a more ominous area of the setting: the darkened upstairs hallway in the Floods' home. Immediately accentuated on the empty stage, this shadowy space functions as Inge's unifying symbol in the play. The "dark at the top of the stairs," we discover, represents simple human fears—the fear of loneliness, of failure, of change, and especially of the unknown. As Inge explains in his stage directions, "*We are conscious of this area throughout the play, as though it holds some possible threat to the characters*" (*Four Plays* 225).

Besides emphasizing elements of a play's setting, the empty stage serves another key purpose: it gives certain characters an important entrance. During the course of a drama, many characters may enter and exit the scene, but one of the most prominent entrances is the first one, especially if it is an entrance onto an empty stage. When Willy Loman arrives on the empty stage at the beginning of *Death of a Salesman*, when Eben Cabot comes onto the scene in O'Neill's *Desire Under the Elms*, or when Nora Helmer opens the door and enters her drawing room in Ibsen's *A Doll's House*, the audience immediately senses that this is a major dramatic figure. In Inge's works certain characters are likewise granted special significance by being the first to appear on an empty stage. But curiously, these are not the playwright's central *dramatis personae*. Instead, such characters tend to introduce—or prepare us for the arrival of—Inge's real protagonists. This technique—usually called "building an entrance"—can also be seen "in the arrangement of curtain calls, where minor characters come out first and warm the audience for the appearance of the stars" (Dean and Carra 138–40).

At the opening of *Come Back, Little Sheba*, it is the disillusioned chiropractor, Doc Delaney, who first enters the Delaneys' cluttered, dirty kitchen. Busying himself with domestic chores, Doc lights the stove, fills the dishpan, washes a frying pan, and begins to make breakfast for himself. Doc's appearance of "*neat cleanliness*" (*Four Plays* 7) stands in sharp contrast to his untidy surroundings; and indeed, we quickly learn that it is Doc's wife, Lola, who is to blame for the careless housekeeping. As Marie, the student boarder, tells him,

> Dr. Delaney, you're so nice to your wife, and you're so nice to me, as a matter of fact, you're so nice to everyone. I hope my husband is as nice as you are. Most husbands would never think of getting their own breakfast [6].

Doc's arrival on the empty stage thus serves not only as a means of self-introduction, but as a way of introducing the play's central character, Lola Delaney—of revealing her slatternly habits even before she makes an appearance in the play, and of building toward Lola's dramatic entrance.

In *Picnic*, the first character to arrive on the empty stage is Flo Owens's neighbor, Helen Potts—"*a merry, dumpy little woman close to sixty*" (*Four Plays* 75). Although Helen Potts is a secondary figure in the play, she fulfills a crucial function during this opening scene: she introduces the protagonist, Hal Carter, to the audience in a thoroughly sympathetic manner. Coming down the steps of her back porch, she waits for Hal, the handsome vagabond for whom she has just made a large breakfast. "Now, stop being embarrassed because you asked for breakfast," she tells him. "We all have misfortune part of the time" (76). As R. Baird Shuman has noted, it is the "incurable romantic," Helen Potts, who discovers Hal and who invites him into her house "because he represents all that she has missed in life" (36). Her admiration for the young man, which foreshadows Madge Owens's affection, tends to dispose the audience in Hal's favor from the start, preparing us to sympathize with the handsome stranger even when he encounters hostility from other characters.

In *The Dark at the Top of the Stairs*, it is the robust traveling salesman, Rubin Flood, who appears on the empty stage before anyone else. He comes down the stairs carrying a suitcase for a business trip, and says, "I gotta look good for my customers." Rubin's arrival on the empty stage allows the audience to appreciate his physical attractiveness (he is "*dressed in Western clothes—a big Stetson, boots, narrow trousers, colorful shirt and string tie*" [*Four Plays* 226]), but more importantly, it prepares us for the appearance of the play's major character, Cora Flood. As we soon discover, Cora resents her husband's itinerant job, believing that Rubin doesn't spend nearly enough time with the children and her. "I envy women who have their husbands with them all the time," complains Cora. "I never have anyone to take me any place. I live like a widow" (227). Rubin's solitary entrance onto the empty stage (which is really part of another exit, another leave-taking) gives the audience its first hint of the man's aloofness from his own family, and hence induces us to sympathize with Cora's loneliness and frustration.

Inge highlights Doc Delaney, Helen Potts, and Rubin Flood on empty stages not only to prepare the audience for the arrival of his protagonists but also to suggest the role of these secondary characters as *raisonneurs*. To a large extent, the three characters serve as William Inge's mouthpieces. Their lives are admittedly far from perfect. Doc is a deeply disappointed man and an alcoholic; Helen Potts is a lonely woman who is enslaved to her elderly, querulous mother; and Rubin is a frustrated harness salesman who recognizes that his trade is a thing of the past. Nevertheless, it is these characters who tend to voice the primary words of wisdom in their plays. They are *raisonneurs* who not only participate in the dramatic action, but who comment on it in a sensible manner.

Doc Delaney, in *Come Back, Little Sheba*, becomes a *raisonneur* when he tells his wife, Lola, "We should never feel bad about what's past. What's in the past can't be helped. You ... you've got to forget it and live for the present…. We gotta keep on living, don't we?" (*Four Plays* 33–34). Likewise, in *Picnic*, Helen Potts assumes the *raisonneur* role when she advises Flo Owens to let

Madge make her own decisions, especially about the man Madge wants to marry—Hal Carter. "You don't love someone 'cause he's perfect, Flo" (*Four Plays* 147). And after Madge's final departure, when Flo regrets not having told her daughter "so many things," Helen Potts simply advises, "let her learn them for herself, Flo" (148). Even Rubin Flood, in *The Dark at the Top of the Stairs*, becomes a mouthpiece for the playwright when he argues that a man needs respect and personal freedom. "Don't you realize," he says to a nagging Cora,

> [that] you can't talk to a man like that? Don't you realize that every time you talk that way, I just gotta go out and raise more hell, just to prove to myself I'm a free man? Don't you know that when you talk to a man like that, you're not givin' him credit for havin' any brains, or any guts, or a spine, or ... or a few other body parts that are pretty important, too? [*Four Plays* 296-97].

By initially spotlighting Doc Delaney, Helen Potts, and Rubin Flood on empty stages, Inge in effect urges us to take special notice of these *raisonneurs* and to appreciate the common sense of their remarks.

Not only does the empty stage give significance to any first character in a play, but it often reinforces what happens during a drama. In *The Cherry Orchard*, our original view of Madame Ranevskaya's estate (on the empty stage) is contrasted with our final view, in which the abandoned house has been stripped of its furnishings, and the previously blossoming cherry orchard is being cut down. The loss of the estate—and of the old aristocratic order it represents—is thus made poignantly visible on stage. Similarly, in *A Doll's House*, Nora's initial entrance onto the empty stage (when she arrives in her drawing room with a Christmas tree and in a mood of holiday good cheer) is contrasted with the heroine's dramatic exit at the end of the play, when she leaves her husband and children—perhaps for good—and slams the door shut behind her. Like Chekhov and Ibsen, Inge opens the curtain on an empty stage in order to emphasize his initial dramatic situation, and to contrast it with the very different situation at the end of the play.

One can observe this effect especially in *Come Back, Little Sheba* and in *The Dark at the Top of the Stairs*. In *Sheba*, the beginning scene of clutter on the empty stage clearly points to a marriage in turmoil. We soon realize that the lives of Doc and Lola Delaney are in shambles, much like their slovenly house. Lola is middle-aged, childless, and desperately unfulfilled (as her fantasies and her plaintive calls to her lost dog, Little Sheba, reveal); and she seems incapable of making a real home for herself and her husband. Doc Delaney's life is in similar disarray. Trapped years ago into marriage, and never able to achieve his dream of becoming a "real" doctor, Doc has escaped from his disillusionment through alcohol, and, more recently, through an unhealthy infatuation with their student boarder, Marie.

During the climactic scene of the play, in which Doc actually threatens Lola's life with a hatchet, the physical setting becomes even more disordered than it was when the stage was empty, reflecting the now violent turmoil in the Delaneys' lives. According to Inge, "*the remains of last night's dinner clutter the table in the living room. The candles have guttered down to stubs amid the dirty dinner plates, and the lilacs in the centerpiece have wilted*" (*Four Plays* 54). Sprawled on the sofa, Lola magnifies this sense of disorder, for her hair is uncombed, her dress is wrinkled, and one of her stockings falls loosely around her ankle. When Doc appears on the scene, he is completely different from the quiet, tolerant man that we met on the empty stage at the start of the play. Drunken and abusive, Doc increases the physical wreckage of the Delaneys' home—jerking the tablecloth off the table and sending the dishes crashing to the floor—before making his violent attempt on Lola's life.

At the end of *Come Back, Little Sheba*, however, a certain order is restored, both literally and symbolically, to the home of Doc and Lola Delaney. Not only does Doc return from his stay at the City Hospital in a thoroughly repentant mood, but Lola is willing to forgive her husband, to make breakfast for him, and to focus her attention on the present, instead of on the past. Given this apparent growth in the couple's relationship, it is appropriate that the Delaneys' house has finally been tidied up considerably, so that it bears little resemblance to the cluttered, dirty scene we viewed on the empty stage at the start of the play. Determined at last to create a genuine home for herself and her husband, Lola tells Doc, "You see I've got the place all cleaned up just the way you like it" (67).

The empty stage setting at the beginning of *The Dark at the Top of the Stairs* likewise reinforces the changes that have occurred by the play's end. In the opening scene, as noted earlier, Rubin Flood is preparing to leave on a business trip and the upstairs hallway of his home is enveloped in darkness. Cora's fears about her marriage, their children's fears about growing up, and Rubin's own fears about the future (about his ability to support his family and adjust to a rapidly changing world) are all reflected in this looming darkness. The darkness of the Floods' upstairs hallway becomes even more ominous in Act Two of Inge's drama. Rubin has abruptly left his family after a stormy argument with his wife, and Cora does not know if her husband will ever come back—or if she and the children will be able to manage without him. Ten-year-old Sonny Flood, who is too immature and too attached to his mother to be the new "man of the house," is especially afraid of the darkness that awaits him at bedtime at the top of the stairs. "You can't see what's in front of you," he explains to Cora. "And it might be something awful." Comforting her son,

Cora takes Sonny by the hand, and *"they start up the stairs to face the darkness hovering there like an omen" (Four Plays* 283).

By the end of the play, however, the upstairs hallway of the Floods' home is bathed in a new light. Rubin has returned home to reconcile with Cora; their daughter, Reenie, has overcome some of her painful shyness; and Sonny Flood has achieved a certain amount of independence from his mother. Anxious to celebrate his own homecoming, Rubin calls romantically to his wife, and *"Cora, like a shy maiden, starts up the stairs, where we see Rubin's naked feet standing in the warm light at the top."* "I'm coming, Rubin," Cora says, as the play closes. "I'm coming" (304). By stressing darkness (and separation) on the original empty stage and then light (and reunion) at the end of the play, Inge implies that his characters have finally begun to conquer their innermost fears, to come together as a family, and, in the case of Rubin and Cora, to enjoy a more fulfilling marriage (Shuman 21).

Thus far, we have examined how William Inge employs the device of the empty stage at the *beginning* of his plays. Indeed, most dramatists who adopt the technique do so at the opening of a production or at the opening of an act. But perhaps Inge's most memorable empty stage is found at the conclusion of *Bus Stop*, where the playwright uses it not only to punctuate the exits of his characters, but to express one of his most significant themes: human loneliness and isolation. Here the outer emptiness of the stage mirrors the inner emptiness of Inge's characters—an emptiness that threatens to consume them. As Thomas Kilroy has suggested, "there is nothing as desolate as an empty stage. It is an intense model of all desert places unwarmed by human presence" ("Theatrical" 91).

At the close of *The Cherry Orchard*—a play which Inge admired, and which conceivably influenced the ending of *Bus Stop* (Inge, "'Cherry Orchard'")—the principal characters depart from Madame Ranevskaya's house, one by one, until the stage is totally deserted. We hear the sounds of doors being locked, of carriages driving off, and of an axe striking a tree in the cherry orchard. Chekhov's use of the empty stage renders the departure of the family more dramatic and adds poignancy to the predicament of old Firs, the servant who has inadvertently been left behind. As J. L. Styan points out, "this ancient man, who seems to symbolize the history of the cherry orchard in his person ... [is] abandoned like the house" itself (336).

At the end of *Bus Stop*, Inge employs an empty stage in much the same manner in order to punctuate the exits of his characters. Like Chekhov's players, Inge's *dramatis personae* depart, one by one, until the stage is left dark and deserted. But in *Bus Stop* there are *two* characters who are left behind: Virgil Blessing, the good-natured cowboy who has suddenly lost the only "family" that he has in the world: his young sidekick, Bo Decker; and Grace, the proprietress of this dingy café, who admits that when she locks up the restaurant at night, she sometimes gets "kind of a sick feelin', 'cause I sure don't look forward to walkin' up those stairs and lettin' myself into an empty apartment" (*Four Plays* 155). When Virgil realizes that he is utterly alone and has no place to stay for the rest of the night, Grace remarks sympathetically, "Then I'm sorry, mister, but you're just left out in the cold" (219). Quietly exiting (and assuming the role of *raisonneur*), Virgil murmurs to himself, "Well ... that's what happens to some people" (219).

This is the last line of *Bus Stop*, but the action is not quite completed. Grace locks the doors (remember that in *The Cherry Orchard* we also heard the sound of doors being locked), turns off the lights, and "*casts her eyes tiredly*" over the restaurant. "*One senses her aloneness*," says Inge. Then Grace sighs, goes out the door, and "*the curtain comes down on an empty stage*" (219). Much like Chekhov, therefore, Inge uses an empty stage at the end of his play in order to urge the audience to reflect on the final lines of the drama (about Virgil's sad predicament) and on the last piece of stage business (the locking up of the restaurant for the night). Like Chekhov, he connects the emptiness on the stage with the emptiness of his characters' lives.

The setting of *Bus Stop* is itself a perfect image of isolation and loneliness. Grace's street-corner café has been temporarily cut off from the outside world by a raging snowstorm which has forced the bus's passengers to seek shelter within its walls. Furthermore, in its role as a small-town Kansas bus stop, the restaurant has witnessed the comings and goings of a variety of drifters and solitary human beings. These include Cherie, a flashy but untalented night club singer; Bo Decker, a brash, naïve cowboy; and Dr. Gerald Lyman, a cynical and dissipated professor. By the end of the drama, after most of the characters have departed, the bus stop becomes an even lonelier setting, with just Virgil Blessing and Grace remaining on stage—then only Grace—and at the final curtain—no one at all.

J. L. Styan, in his analysis of *The Cherry Orchard*, has spoken of the effect of the empty stage on the audience, both at the beginning and at the end of Chekhov's play:

> With the half-light, [Madame Ranevskaya's] house seems half deserted: in due course it will be peopled, and at that time the audience will seem to people it too. At the beginning, we *are* the empty house waiting to be inhabited. At the end, the stage will look like this again, and again we shall seem to be the house that has been abandoned [249].

Although *Bus Stop* is a very different play, it can be argued that Inge finally achieves a dramatic effect similar to that of Chekhov; for after Inge's characters have all departed, only the audience remains behind, locked into that desolate small-town restaurant. Engulfed in darkness, and confronted with a bare stage, we feel the emptiness of Inge's provincial setting, as well as the haunting loneliness of his characters. Until the final curtain releases us, in fact, we *are* the abandoned bus stop itself.

According to Harold Clurman, who directed the original production of *Bus Stop*, William Inge is "our dramatist of the ordinary.... His writing is bare but suggestive. At times it touches the rim of poetry, and the right actors can transport it into that realm" (qtd. in Teachout 73). Such a poetic quality derives not only from Inge's simple, homespun dialogue but also from his artful stagecraft—particularly his evocative use of an empty stage. In his four major plays Inge employs the empty stage to draw the audience into the world of the Midwestern small town—creating a *mise-en-scène* that reflects rural simplicity as well as the "quiet desperation" of his characters (Krasner 57). In *Bus Stop*, especially, Inge manages to "touch the rim of poetry"—creating one last effect, one lingering emotion in his audience. Closing his play with the image of a dark and deserted stage, Inge invites us, as he finally does in all of his dramas, to share in the tragic "aloneness" of his characters, to feel their rootlessness, their emptiness—to sympathize with those people who, like Grace, or like the kind-hearted Virgil, are ultimately "left out in the cold."

Works Cited

Dean, Alexander, and Lawrence Carra. *Fundamentals of Play Directing*. 3rd ed. New York: Holt, 1974. Print.
Inge, William. "'Cherry Orchard': An Expert Blend of Humor and Pathos." Rev. of *The Cherry Orchard*, by Anton Chekhov. *St. Louis Star-Times* 24 Oct. 1944: 8. Print.
_____. *Four Plays [Come Back, Little Sheba; Picnic; Bus Stop; The Dark at the Top of the Stairs]*. 1958. New York: Grove, 1979. Print.
Kilroy, Thomas. Foreword. *Staging Thought: Essays on Irish Theatre, Scholarship, and Practice*. Ed. Rhona Trench. Oxford, UK: Lang, 2012. xix–xx. Print.
_____. "Theatrical Text and Literary Text." *The Achievement of Brian Friel*. Ed. Alan J. Peacock. Gerards Cross, UK: Smythe, 1993. 91–102. Print.
Krasner, David. *American Drama 1945–2000*. Malden, MA: Blackwell, 2006. Print.
McIlrath, Patricia. "William Inge, Great Voice of the Heart of America." *Kansas Quarterly* 18.4 (1986): 45–53. Print.
Mann, Daniel. "An Interview with Daniel Mann (The Director of Inge's First Success and His First Failure)." Interview by Michael Wood. *Kansas Quarterly* 18.4 (1986): 7–22. Print.
Miller, Arthur. *Death of a Salesman*. New York: Viking, 1949. Print.
Miller, Jordan Y. "William Inge: Last of the Realists?" *Kansas Quarterly* 2.2 (1970): 17–26. Print.

Shuman, R. Baird. *William Inge*. Rev. ed. Boston: Twayne, 1989. Print.
Styan, J. L. *Chekhov in Performance*. Cambridge, UK: Cambridge University Press, 1971. Print.
Teachout, Terry. "Come Back, William Inge: A Half-Forgotten Playwright Gets the Revival He Deserves." Rev. of *Come Back, Little Sheba*, by William Inge. *Commentary* Apr. 2009: 71–74. Print.
Wentworth, Michael. "At Home in the '50s: Cultural Nostalgia and William Inge's *Picnic*." *Midwestern Miscellany* 30.[1] (2002): 56–71. Print.

Life with Father in Four Inge Plays
Robert A. Martin

Life with Father, a comedy by Howard Lindsay and Russel Crouse, opened on November 8, 1939, at the Empire Theatre in New York City. When it closed seven and one-half years later in 1946, it had been performed 3,224 times. The play became the prototype comedy that featured a slightly eccentric, but loveable father who finds his way through domestic complications without any perceivable major crises in his unquestioned role as the head of his equally eccentric family. The problems are small; maids quit constantly because father is too unpredictable, dominating his Madison Avenue brownstone by interfering with nearly everything that his complacent wife and four young sons happen to be doing at any given moment. His authority is unquestionable; his wisdom unimpeachable; his meddling intolerable—but Father is father. During a weak moment during a visit from the family minister, father admits that he has never been baptized, which sets in motion a small domestic tiff that can only be resolved when he, believing that his wife is dying, agrees to the baptism. As he departs for church, he tells his family, realizing that he has been tricked by his quite healthy wife, "I'm going to be baptized, damn it!" (Lindsay and Crouse 1049).

Perhaps because the Depression was still fresh in the American psyche and perhaps because World War II began shortly after its premiere and continued through its seven and one-half years on Broadway, the play's late-nineteenth-century setting evoked the audience's nostalgia and sentiment for an earlier, less stressful era, devoid of larger issues of death and survival. But the long life of the play established a permanent image—of the family, of fathers, of mothers, and of their children—that continued to reverberate through countless versions of television and film sit-coms such as *Father Knows Best*, *All in the Family*, and *The Brady Bunch*.

What was not very apparent in the late 1940s, however, was that father had gradually become someone else in the plays that emerged immediately after World War II. He became not the father who knew best, but the father who did not understand what had happened to himself and his family. He became Joe Keller in *All My Sons* (1947) and Willy Loman in *Death of a Salesman* (1949), fathers of a different dream whose emotional commitments to the well-being of their families lead them to compulsive acts of anti-social behavior, suicide, and a mistaken belief in the Madison Avenue precepts of material success and personal popularity. Or they appeared inferentially in a photograph as in Tennessee Williams's *The Glass Menagerie* (1945), "*gallantly smiling, ... as if to say, 'I will be smiling forever'*" (22). He became in the post–World War II theater the absent father who fell in love with long distance and Big Daddy in *Cat on a Hot Tin Roof* (1955), neither of whom precisely corresponds to the image that most of us believe goes with *our* fathers, in *our* lives, or in *our* families. And as that theater became more and more bold in its presentations, more and more direct in probing the psychological origins of social and emotional malfunctions, the worlds depicted within the plays—comedies as well as tragedies—became noticeably darker. With the production of Eugene O'Neill's *Long Day's Journey into Night* (1956), the image of the father as distant, removed, and disillusioned, caught between the family he cannot understand and the dreams he cannot fulfill, became the epitome of the family to which we all secretly and with sorrow return in memory with "*deep pity and understanding and forgiveness*" (O'Neill [7]), as O'Neill wrote in his dedication of the play to his third wife, Carlotta. In this family drama context of the 1940s and 1950s, William Inge suddenly came to his maturity as a dramatist of middle America, of small towns, large aspirations, and broken families.

As Ralph F. Voss has shown in his *A Life of William Inge*, Inge's early interest in drama and participation in high school and college theater productions clearly point to the background of a dramatist. Beginning in 1937, Inge taught drama for five years at Stephens College for Women in Columbia, Missouri, and in 1937 wrote his Master's thesis on "David Belasco and the Age of Photographic Realism in the American Theatre" at the George Peabody College for Teachers. From 1943 to 1946, he was the music, art, book, and drama critic for the *St. Louis Star-Times*, during which period he reviewed two professional productions of *Life with Father*, one on November 15, 1943, in which he noted that the play "still proves enjoyable," and the second one year later on November 21, 1944, in which he wrote that *Life with Father* "keeps its freshness." From 1946 to 1949, Inge once again returned to the classroom as an instructor in English at Washington University in St. Louis. By the time he interviewed Tennessee Williams as a local celebrity-playwright in St. Louis in November

1944, Inge had probably already decided to try his hand at writing plays. Traveling to Chicago in January 1945 at Williams's invitation, he saw *The Glass Menagerie* and was so impressed by the performance that he confided to Williams, "being a successful playwright was what he most wanted in the world for himself" (Williams, Introduction ix). Inge later recalled that after the Chicago trip, "I went back to St. Louis and felt, 'Well, I've got to write a play'" (Shuman 22).

Like Williams, Inge was the son of a rough-speaking traveling salesman with whom he felt neither comfortable nor compatible. Given his father's absence during the week, Inge felt closer to his mother and older brother, who were responsible for the daily matters of discipline and household organization. R. Baird Shuman has commented that *The Dark at the Top of the Stairs*, "while not completely autobiographical, represents the author's coming to grips with many of the fundamental psychological problems which faced him during adolescence and early adulthood" (19). With this background in mind, I propose to approach the father theme in Inge's plays as one way of discovering both the thematic configurations and the psychological motivations that inform the present of the characters' lives in terms of their pasts. In *Come Back, Little Sheba*, *Picnic*, *Bus Stop*, and *The Dark at the Top of the Stairs*, the father is either dead, missing, alienated from his family, or is so infrequently at home that his actual presence creates disruption and conflict among the entire family.

In thus approaching the plays through the father theme, it is necessary to examine three levels of relationships—text, context, and sub-text. An actress playing Lola in *Come Back, Little Sheba*, as one example, would need to understand why Lola alternates between addressing her husband as "Doc" and "Daddy," and why he sometimes addresses her almost entirely as "Baby." Is it simple affection or the hint of a more complicated relationship that lies beneath the linguistic surface of their domestic bantering? It is something of both, but overall Inge provides a clue in the way such shifts occur. When Lola switches from "Doc" to "Daddy," they have switched the subject of their conversation to (a) his alcoholism, (b) their past life, (c) her appearance, or (d) his hostility toward her or Turk as in the following exchange:

> LOLA: .... When I think of the way you used to drink, always getting into fights, we had so much trouble. I was so scared! I never knew what was going to happen.
> DOC: That was a long time ago, Baby.
> LOLA: I know it, Daddy. I know how you're going to be when you come home now [*4 Plays* 9].

As Doc is leaving, after verbally attacking Turk for his attentions to Marie, the context changes rapidly when he asks Lola:

> DOC: .... Wanta walk to the office with me?
> LOLA: I look too terrible, Daddy. I ain't even dressed.
> DOC: Kiss Daddy goodbye.
> LOLA: ... 'Bye, 'bye, Daddy. If you get hungry, come home and I'll have something for you [11].

The obvious pattern in this exchange is one of Lola responding to Doc as a daughter might to her father. Although critics have often taken Doc's anger at Turk as his sublimated passion for his eighteen-year-old boarder, Marie, the sub-text of *Sheba* suggests that Doc is actually playing the role of Marie's father more than her would-be lover. Inge reinforces the thematic relationship further when Marie tells Lola, "Really, Mrs. Delaney, you and Doc have been so nice to me.... You've been like a father and mother to me. I appreciate it" (12). And as Inge gradually darkens the plot, the role Doc is playing does indeed shift to that of an outraged father as much as a disappointed lover. Doc, a rich boy who had to marry Lola, is in a compulsive way repeating his earlier life by trying to prevent Marie from being ruined even as he and Lola ruined each other earlier at the same age. Lola recognizes the parallel and the danger of the past repeating itself as she tells Marie:

> I used to be pretty, something like you.... I was Beauty Queen of the senior class in high school. My dad was awful strict though.... Daddy would never let me go out with boys much. Just because I was pretty.
> He was afraid all the boys would get the wrong idea—*you* know. I never had any fun at all until I met Doc.
> MARIE: Sometimes I'm glad I didn't know my father. Mom always let me do pretty much as I please....
> LOLA: Doc was the first boy my dad ever let me go out with. We got married that spring.
> MARIE: You must have been married awful young.
> LOLA: Oh, yes. Eighteen.
> MARIE: That must have made your father really mad.
> LOLA: Yes, it did. I never went home after that, but my mother comes down here from Green Valley to visit me sometimes [14].

Marie, who is "sometimes" glad she didn't know her father, is set off against Lola whose mother comes to visit her "sometimes." In both cases the "sometimes" suggests that there are other times when both Marie and Lola wish their relationships with their fathers could have been better, closer, more familiar. As Marie and Turk become more involved sexually, Doc's anger becomes noticeably related to Lola's description of the intimacies developing in their home between the younger couple. Recognizing herself in Marie, and sensing Doc's increasing agitation, Lola finally returns to her past when she asks Doc:

> LOLA: .... Are you sorry you married me, Doc?
> DOC: Of course not.
> LOLA: I mean are you sorry you *had* to marry me?
> DOC: ... We were never going to talk about that, Baby.
> ....
> LOLA: ... I wish the baby had lived, Doc.... If we'd had the baby she'd be a young girl now, then maybe you'd have *saved* your money, Doc, and she could be going to college—like Marie [32–33].

Doc, a reformed alcoholic who inherited $25,000 and drank it all away, has no parents living, and is forced to relive his wasted youth by watching Marie—a younger version of Lola and the daughter he might have had—move into a dangerous relationship with Turk. When the parallels become too exact, when Doc can no longer play himself as the younger lover of Lola versus the protective father of Marie, he falls off the wagon, gets drunk, becomes violent with Lola, and ends up in the alcohol ward of the local hospital, thereby removing himself from both conflicts with Marie in the present and his own mistakes in the past. Although Inge chose to remove Marie from the conflict by marriage (Act 2, Scene 3), he returns our attention to the Lola-Doc focus and the Doc-Daddy implications by the classic expedient of a phone call and having Lola ask for sanctuary with her parents since Doc has threatened to kill her.

> LOLA: ... Hello. Hello, Mom. It's Lola, Mom. How are you? Mom, Doc's sick again. Do you think Dad would let me come home for a while? I'm awfully unhappy, Mom. Do you think ... just till I made up my mind? ... All right. No, I guess it wouldn't do any good for you to come here ... I ... I'll let you know what I decide to do. That's all, Mom. Thanks. Tell Daddy hello [63–64].

Rejected once again by a father-daddy who once loved her enough to forbid her to go out with boys because she was too pretty, her pathetic "Tell Daddy hello" is as close as Lola will ever come to her father in the eighteen years since her marriage to Doc. Her dream sequence of the athletic contest between Turk, Doc, and her father helps the audience to pull Inge's interwoven and Freudian plot together nicely as all themes and conflicts become symbolic.

> LOLA: .... Marie and I were going to the Olympics back in our old high school stadium. There were thousands of people there. There was Turk out in the center of the field throwing the javelin. Every time he threw it, the crowd would roar ... and you know who the man in charge was? It was my father. Isn't that funny? ... But Turk kept changing into someone else all the time. And then my father disqualified him. So he had to sit on the sidelines ... and guess who took his place, Daddy? You! You came trotting out there on the field just a big as you please ... [68].

One need not be a psychiatrist to see the Freudian implications of Lola's dream. She returns to her youth and home with Marie (a younger version of herself who has never known a father) to watch an athletic contest filled with phallic images of javelins in which Turk (a younger Doc chasing Marie-Lola, who changes into someone else) is thrown out of the game by Lola's father, even as he has thrown her out of his protection and family. Lola and Marie (a younger Lola and Doc's surrogate daughter) watch with delight as Doc replaces Turk as Marie's protector-father and surrogate lover. Lola's dream, in brief, symbolizes all the forces of rejection in her life as she sees her lost dog, Little Sheba, lying dead in the middle of the playing field and concludes that Little Sheba (her past, their dead daughter, her desire for love, acceptance, and a family) will not come back, nor will she ever get beyond that loss except by calling Doc "Daddy." Doc, whose dream of medical school has long since died along with his daughter and Little Sheba, consoles Lola for all their lost dreams with an allusion to the title of the play: "Not much point in it, Baby. I guess she's gone for good" (69).

John Gassner once remarked of *Sheba* that unlike Tennessee Williams in *The Glass Menagerie*, "Mr. Inge resolutely allowed the facts of a constricted, essentially small-town life to speak for themselves, without the accessory machinery of narrations, flashbacks, and symbolism.... *Come Back, Little Sheba* brings a large if quietly dispensed compassion to bear upon ordinary lives" (252). In *Picnic*, however, Inge relied less on "ordinary lives" than may have been apparent to Gassner. The main plot line evolves around the disruption brought into a family in a small Kansas town with the arrival of Hal Carter, who is seeking a fresh start in life by reestablishing his college friendship with his former roommate, Alan Seymour, the son of the wealthiest man in town. Hal is a drifter, down on his luck, a handsome, former athlete who meets Alan's girlfriend, Madge Owens. Madge lives with her mother, Flo, and younger sister, Millie. Flo has been a widow for ten years, and has some hope that Madge, the prettiest girl in town, will marry Alan and enjoy a better life than she has. Inge describes Flo as "*a rather impatient little woman who has worked hard for ten years or more to serve as both father and mother to her girls*" (*4 Plays* 78). It is again the classic Inge family, slightly reorganized, who must of necessity get on in life without a father-protector. As Hal and Madge begin to develop a serious attraction for each other, Inge unobtrusively reveals the tensions and the love that existed when Madge's father was alive:

> FLO: You were the first born. Your father thought the sun rose and set in you. He used to carry you on his shoulder for all the neighborhood to see. But things were different when Millie came.
> MADGE: How?

FLO: They were just different. Your father wasn't home much. The night Millie was born he was with a bunch of his wild friends at the roadhouse.
MADGE: I loved Dad.
FLO: (*A little bitterly*) Oh, everyone loved your father [83].

Madge and Millie are slightly different versions of Marie in *Sheba*, with Madge at eighteen and the favorite child retaining a more distinct image of her father than Millie at sixteen who never mentions her father at all, and apparently cannot remember him. Hal's father is also dead, but his memories, grounded in the more recent past, contain scenes of marital disharmony between his parents also. To Flo, "a woman is weak to begin with, I suppose, and sometimes—her love for him makes her feel—almost helpless. And maybe she fights him—'cause her love makes her seem so dependent" (83–84). To Hal, however, it is less a matter of love than of economics. And here Inge is careful to establish the similarities in family and fathers between Madge and Hal. His father, Hal tells Alan, "went on his last bender, the police scraped him up off the sidewalk. He died in jail.... The old lady wouldn't even come across with the dough for the funeral. They had to bury him in Pauper's Row" (94). Hal's account of his father's death reveals the same character traits for both his father and Madge's. Both were inclined to prefer the company of drinking companions over that of the home and family. Both Madge and Hal nevertheless have a vague sense of loss and affection for their dead fathers. For Hal, his sole legacy from his father is the boots he wears and which, as he tells Rosemary, represent his father's inheritance and philosophy: "He said, 'Son, the man of the house needs a pair of boots 'cause he's gotta do a lot of kickin'.... He says, 'Son, there'll be times when the only thing you got to be proud of is the fact you're a man. So wear your boots so people can hear you comin', and keep your fists doubled up so they'll know you mean business when you get there'" (111).

Oddly enough, Rosemary, the spinster schoolteacher who is a boarder at Flo's house, is also a not-so-successful product of a father-dominated home. In an echo of Lola's speech to Marie in *Sheba*, Rosemary tells Howard, her reluctant suitor, "I had boys callin' me all the time. But if my father had ever caught me showing off in front of the window [as she thinks Madge is doing] he'd have tanned me with a razor strap. (*Takes a drink*) 'Cause I was brought up strict by a God-fearing man" (117). Rosemary's father sounds suspiciously like Lola's except that Rosemary at 40 is frantically trying to find a husband, whereas Flo—who is about the same age—quite clearly wants only a wealthy husband for Madge to offset her life of raising two children with limited emotional and financial resources. But it is, finally, the wheel come full circle when Alan's father threatens Hal with arrest and jail. When the police attempt to arrest him, Hal has to leave town following his alcoholic excess at the picnic. Flo also wants him out of the way and threatens "to call the police and have you put where you belong" (142), at which point Hal sees himself mirrored in his father's image. Only after Hal has left on a passing freight train does Mrs. Potts (Flo's next door neighbor) enter carrying Hal's boots to announce, "The police found these on the river bank" (144), and to add a coda of sorts to Hal's presence in their lives for a brief time of regeneration:

> .... He walked through the door and suddenly everything was different. He clomped through the tiny rooms like he was still in the great outdoors, he talked in a booming voice that shook the ceiling. Everything he did reminded me there was a man in the house, and it seemed good [145].

The pointed references to Madge and Hal's dead fathers in *Picnic* are consistently juxtaposed with those of the love-starved Rosemary at 40 and with Alan's domineering father, who plans to send him on a fishing trip to Michigan. The absence, then, of a father for both Hal and Madge suggests loss—the loss of a father, who, even though long dead, as Flo reminds us, "wasn't home much" (83). And here Flo's final words to Mrs. Potts at the end of *Picnic* suggest the father's abdication of responsibility, metaphorically if not literally, when she says, "She's so young. There are so many things I meant to tell her, and never got around to it" (148). And if *Picnic* has aspirations dramatically to examine the lives of those who live on the far side of the American Dream, it equally aspires to an examination of present lives and loves disrupted by the necessity to overcome a family disaster not entirely of the younger generation's making. Inge allows Lola to keep looking for Little Sheba with the same degree of persuasion that allows Madge to board the bus for Tulsa in spite of the failed homes from which both she and Hal have come. Taken thematically, Inge's approach to his plays most certainly derives from his own unresolved feelings toward his father, with a considerable portion also deriving from his romanticized view of the advantages of married love, a home, and family. Gerald Weales has commented that "Rosemary, in *Picnic*, has some of Lola's virtues as a character; although she is solidly based on the stereotype of the old-maid schoolteacher. Inge's conception of her as comic allows him more easily to bring the submerged pathos into the open, makes her more touching than the romanticized Hal and Madge" (45).

With Lola and Rosemary as forerunners, in *Bus Stop* Inge turned to a full concentration on comic characters and a comic situation. In his third Broadway success, Inge used one of the oldest plot devices in literature—that of a group of travelers on a journey (as in *The Canterbury Tales* or in the film *Stagecoach*) who run into problems that must be resolved before the journey can continue or who agree to tolerate the problem during the journey. The plot is somewhat incongruous, if not mildly outrageous dramatically. But in 1955, with McCarthyism and the Korean War as a background, it was perfectly suited as a new twist on an old tale. Cherie is being pursued (or abducted) by a young cowboy, Bo, who wants to take her to his ranch in Montana and marry her. A storm delays the bus in *"a small Kansas town about thirty miles west of Kansas City"* (*4 Plays* 153), where Cherie seeks help to get away from Bo. In today's society, she would undoubtedly be a feminist and have him arrested for sexual harassment; in 1955 his pursuit against her wishes was material for high comedy, both on stage and in the film. Seemingly, the exploration of character and situation that Inge achieved in his first two plays would contain less dramatic potential in a group of four bus passengers and the driver waiting out a blizzard at one o'clock in the morning. But as Inge gradually brings one and then another character into focus, the plot and action gradually yield to a sub-text of nearly hidden references to missing or dead fathers. It is again Inge's secret weapon; people are the way they are because somewhere in the past they have lost a father.

The curtain is barely up when Grace, about 40, the owner of the restaurant, asks her young helper, Elma (*"a big-eyed girl still in high school"* [153]), if her folks are going to be worried because she has to work late to keep the restaurant open during the storm. Elma replies, "No—Daddy said, before I left home, he bet this'd happen.... Nights like this, I'm glad I have a home to go to" (154). As a rare character in Inge's plays who comes from a still intact family, Elma stands in contrast to Cherie, who has no home or family, and to Grace, who is another casualty of the divorce wars.

> ELMA: Where's your husband now, Grace?
> GRACE: How should I know?
> ELMA: Don't you miss him?
> GRACE: No! [154].

Similar to the father in *The Glass Menagerie*, Grace's husband apparently also fell in love with long distance or another woman. In either case, the context of broken family relationships is immediately and forcefully established in *Bus Stop*, and it remains only for Cherie to reveal that she too is alone in the world:

> CHERIE: .... I lived 'bout a hundred miles from there [Joplin, Missouri], in River Gulch, a l'il town in the Ozarks. I lived there till the floods come, three years ago this spring, and washed us all away.
> ELMA: Gee, that's too bad.
> CHERIE: I dunno where a of my folks are now.... We all just separated when the floods come ... [166].

Cherie, like Hal in *Picnic*, has no home, no family, and is on the move to some rather vague destination; she is, nevertheless, presented as a comic character with determination and fortitude. She asks for protection from Will Masters, the town sheriff, against Bo's unwanted attentions. He becomes, in dramatic terms, her surrogate father, since she has no one else to turn to. Bo is accompanied by his older friend, Virgil, who we learn has been "lookin' after me since I was ten," after his parents died (184–85). Virgil is, in effect, the only father Bo has ever really had, and throughout the play advises him on how to behave and how to deal with Cherie romantically. He stands in relation to Bo as Doc does to Marie in *Sheba*, the only father figure either of them has known.

In addition to Cherie, Bo, and Virgil, Dr. Lyman, the fourth passenger, is the strangest character Inge ever put on the stage. Dr. Lyman has been run out of several towns for molesting young girls; he is immediately attracted to Elma, the waitress. He and Elma share an interest in Shakespeare and poetry. He proposes that they meet in Topeka to attend a concert, but decides that his compulsion to molest young girls is in conflict with his fatherly feelings for her innocence. "Just think of me," he tells her, "as a fatherly old fool, will you? And not be troubled if I take such rapturous delight in your sweetness, and youth, and innocence? For these are qualities I seek to warm my heart as I seek a fire to warm my hands" (189). Dr. Lyman chooses to resolve his conflict between sexual attraction and fatherly interest in Elma by the same method that Doc removed himself from his conflict over Marie—by getting drunk to the point of passing out (201).

With the sheriff as surrogate father-protector for Cherie, with Virgil as surrogate father for Bo, and with Dr. Lyman's mixed father-molester feelings for Elma, Inge has created a cast of characters with displaced family relationships that are exceeded only by Cherie's missing parents and Grace's missing husband. By the end of *Bus Stop*, the sheriff has fought (and beaten) Bo over Cherie, Dr. Lyman has cancelled his trip to Topeka with Elma, Virgil has decided not to go on to Montana since Cherie has decided to marry Bo after all, and one has the sense that with Grace and Carl (the bus driver) forming an alliance, all's well that ends well. New families are forming, the homeless and the lonely are reasonably settled, and—except for Dr. Lyman and Virgil—the storm has passed. As he is about to board the bus, Dr. Lyman says goodbye to Elma:

> .... Goodbye, my dear! You were the loveliest Juliet since Miss Jane Cowl.
> ELMA: Thank you, Dr. Lyman. I feel it's been an honor to know you. You're the smartest man I've ever met.
> DR. LYMAN: The smartest?
> ELMA: Really you are.
> DR. LYMAN: Oh, yes. I'm terribly smart. Wouldn't it have been nice ... to be intelligent? [213].

Robert Brustein, in attempting to discern a pattern in Inge's plays, has commented that the excitement over Inge's plays in the 1950s may be explained by his being regarded as "Broadway's first authentic Midwestern playwright" (83–84), and that

> Inge follows Williams in writing she-dramas, in giving to women if not the leading then certainly the pivotal (and most insightfully created) role in his work. Inge, however, concentrates more on the pathos of the woman's suffering and—unlike Williams—permits this suffering to issue in triumph. Although the central issue is a struggle between man and woman, the woman's victory does not necessarily mean the man's defeat. Rather he capitulates, giving himself up to the woman's power to comfort and provide his life with affirmative meaning. Thus Inge's plays end—like most romances—in marriage or reconciliation [86].

While it is not necessary to disagree with Brustein's analysis of Inge's general patterns, it seems clear that behind the "pathos of the women's suffering" in *Sheba, Picnic, Bus Stop,* and *The Dark at the Top of the Stairs* lies not so much "a struggle between men and women" per se, but a struggle to overcome the rejection of self and family by fathers (past or present) who are dead, missing, alienated from their families, or infrequently at home. In much the same way that O'Neill's *Long Day's Journey into Night,* Williams's *The Glass Menagerie* and *Cat on a Hot Tin Roof,* and Miller's *All My Sons* and *Death of a Salesman* have generally similar dramatic struggles between fathers and sons, *The Dark at the Top of the Stairs* also descends dramatically and psychologically from *Oedipus Rex*. A standard and compelling representative of the American Dream, the salesman in Inge's play represents not only a way of life, but a period of transition from one era to another in the American marketplace. Rubin Flood, a road salesman, is gone from Monday to Friday; when he returns, he brings disruption into his own household in a small town near Oklahoma City in the early 1920s.

Rubin is a harness salesman in an era that produced the automobile in record numbers. As the play opens, he is about to leave for a week on the road. His wife, Cora, tells him he is needed and wanted at home:

> CORA: (*With a trace of self-pity*) I envy women who have their husbands with them all the time. I never have anyone to take me any place. I live like a widow.
> RUBIN: What do you want me to do? Give up my job and stay home here to pleasure you every day?
> CORA: ... Rubin! Don't say that.
> RUBIN: Jesus Christ, ya talk like a man had nothin' else to do but stay home and entertain you.
> CORA: Rubin! It's not just myself I'm thinking of. It's the children. We have a daughter sixteen years old now. Do you realize that? Yes, Reenie's sixteen. And Sonny's ten. Sometimes they act like they didn't have a father [227].

By opening the play with a scene of discord and the effect of Rubin's absence on the children, Inge has all the elements in place for complications leading to a domestic crisis. Rubin does not want to stay home; Cora does not want him to be away; the children do not know him and act as if they have no father. Sonny is apparently happier when Rubin is gone, and is overly attached to Cora with early symptoms of an oedipal complex beginning to emerge. Reenie, much like Madge in *Picnic*, loves Rubin, but is rarely given the opportunity to express her affection. To Cora, Rubin's extended absences are harming Reenie's personality. She tells Rubin, "She's got no confidence at all. And I don't know how to give her any, but you could. Her eyes light up like candles every time you go near her" (227). But Rubin, a former cowboy who likes the freedom his life as a traveling salesman holds for him, won't change his habits, preferring to leave the daily problems of household and children to Cora.

In this semi-autobiographical play, Inge was attempting to resolve several problems remaining from his youth. Like Rubin, his father was a salesman who was rarely home during the week. Inge frequently told his friends that he was terrified of his father and had always feared being around him.[1] Echoes of earlier Inge plays reverberate in several places. When Cora and Rubin were married, her father had a stroke. We learn that Cora had become pregnant within two weeks after meeting Rubin, which suggests the Doc-Lola complication with a shorter time span. Cora's sister Lottie and her husband, Morris, are childless and call each other "Daddy" and "Mama." Reenie attends a dance with Sammy, the son of a minor movie actress who never has time to see him. When Sammy tries to explain to Lottie that he is at school so much because his mother is busy, Lottie asks: "Where's your father?"

SAMMY: Oh, I never knew him.
LOTTIE: You never knew your father?
SAMMY: No. You see, he died before I was born. My mother has been married ... a few times since then. But I never met any of her husbands ... [265].

When Sammy commits suicide by jumping out of a window, his mother arranges for his funeral to be held without her since she obviously does not wish to acknowledge in death what she has so carefully denied in life. Doc and Lola, Hal and Marie, Bo and Cherie, and Sammy are all Inge prototypes, spiritual Ishmaels adrift in the small towns of the Midwest. For Inge, the model of that small town was Independence, Kansas, where he grew up in the 1920s and 1930s.[2]

The Flood family lives in two worlds—one with father and one without father. When Cora buys Reenie a new dress for the dance, the first question Reenie asks is one of conspiratorial necessity: "Is Daddy gone, Mom? CORA

Yes, he's gone. The coast is clear." And a few lines later Reenie asks: "Is Dad going to be awfully mad, Mom?" (235). With an atmosphere of secrecy and subterfuge, Inge prepares the audience for difficulty. When Rubin does return home unexpectedly, the dress purchase sets off a violent quarrel that culminates with Rubin striking Cora and leaving the house vowing never to return. Sonny, who has heard the argument, is glad his father is gone, and looks forward to a possible move to Oklahoma City. Reenie, however, sides with Rubin, and is concerned only with her father's departure: "Did he mean it about not coming back? Oh, Mom, why did you have to say those things to him?" (248). And here Inge makes it clear that Reenie, like Lola and Madge, will always be "Daddy's girl" no matter what the circumstances. Unlike Flo in *Picnic*, Cora is not forced to raise her children alone, but the fathers in both plays have similar characteristics and could have originated from the same prototype of Inge's terror of his father.

When Rubin returns home after losing his job as a harness salesman, he announces that he wants to try selling oil equipment—another job as a road salesman. Cora, however, wants him to remain closer to home for their children's sakes:

> CORA: All I'm asking is for you to give them something of *yourself*.
> RUBIN: God damn it! What have *I* got to give 'em? In this day and age, what's a man like me got to give? With the whole world so all-fired crazy about makin' money, how can *any* man, unless he's got a million stuck in his pocket, feel he's got anything else to give that's very important? [297].

Although Rubin is trying to be a good father to his children, he is of another time and place psychologically. As he tells Cora, "When I was a boy, there wasn't much more to this town than a post office. I on'y had six years a schoolin' cause that's all the Old Man thought I'd ever need" (298). But even as Inge partially exonerates Rubin for his failures as a father, he leaves little doubt in the audience's mind that Rubin and Sonny will never understand each other: Rubin "*looks at his son as though realizing sadly the breach between them. With a feeling of failure, he puts a warm hand on* SONNY'S *shoulder*" (301).

Inge once said that *The Dark at the Top of the Stairs* represented "my first cautious attempt to look at the past, with an effort to find order and experiences that were once too close to be seen clearly" (qtd. in Shuman 19). In approaching Inge's plays through the father figures, I do not intend to suggest that they represent a dominant theme in the individual plays; but in some way, perhaps understood only by the playwright, they serve to prepare the characters to face life with the memory of a father as an unfinished chapter in their pasts. In the three plays preceding *Dark*, there are entirely too many fathers to be coincidental in the characters' backgrounds—some quite remote—who are nevertheless brought into their conversations as essential reference points. Not until *Dark* did Inge, like O'Neill, have the distance and the objectivity to face his dead at last and write the play that had haunted him all of his life. And, also in the O'Neill vein, he wrote it with "deep pity and understanding and forgiveness" (O'Neill [7]).

Writing *The Dark at the Top of the Stairs*, however, did not entirely resolve Inge's ambiguous feelings toward his father. In a one-act play titled *The Love Death*, written sometime between 1968 and 1970 but unproduced and unpublished until 2009, Inge has a character named Byron Todd, a writer "*dressed ... in a luxurious silk Japanese robe and gold sandals*" and "*colorful pajamas*," telephone his mother from his apartment in New York City. That Inge's father was still a presence in his dramatic memory is clearly reflected in the following excerpt.

> I guess that's all, Mama. But remember that I love you.... No. I won't talk to Daddy. If you bring Daddy to the 'phone, I'll hang up. I never *could* talk to Daddy, because he never had anything on his mind but oil well supplies. But tell him I forgive him for his neglect of me. Tell him, I hold no resentments now whatever. I used to, I admit, but no more. I'm above those resentments now. I realize Daddy raised me the best he knew how. For many years, I held a deep grievance against him because I felt he didn't *understand* me, but now I realize we have no right to *expect* to be understood. Maybe one finds it in the next life. I hope so. Anyway, don't think I hold grudges against any of you. I know you didn't *mean* any of the cruel little ways you treated me when I was a child. I want you to know, I forgive you all ... [*Complex Evening* 10].

Notes

1. During the William Inge Festival, April 4–7, 1987, held at Independence Community College, Independence, Kansas, Luther Inge told me that his father, William Inge's older brother, actually enforced the family discipline in the absence of the father, but at the mother's direction. As the youngest of five children, Inge was afraid of his older brother also, according to Mr. Inge.

2. Inge's maternal grandfather was a harness salesman and his maternal great-grandfather was a harness maker. Inge's father and his uncle were both road salesmen for a dry goods company.

Works Cited

Brustein, Robert. *Seasons of Discontent*. New York: Simon and Schuster, 1967. Print.
Gassner, John, ed. *Best American Plays, 1945–1951*. New York: Crown, 1952. Print.
Inge, William. *A Complex Evening: Six Short Plays by William Inge*. Independence, KS: Independence Community College/On Stage Press, 2009. Print.
_____. *4 Plays by William Inge* [*Come Back, Little Sheba*; *Picnic*; *Bus Stop*; *The Dark at the Top of the Stairs*]. New York: Random House, 1958. Print.

———. Rev. of *Life with Father*, by Howard Lindsay and Russel Crouse. *St. Louis Star-Times* 15 Nov. 1943: 4. Print.

———. Rev. of *Life with Father*, by Howard Lindsay and Russel Crouse. *St. Louis Star-Times* 21 Nov. 1944: 17. Print.

Lindsay, Howard, and Russel Crouse. "Life with Father." *Sixteen Famous American Plays*. Ed. Bennett Cerf and Van H. Cartmell. New York: Random House, 1941. 979–1049. Print.

O'Neill, Eugene. *Long Day's Journey into Night*. New Haven: Yale University Press, 1955. Print.

Shuman, R. Baird. *William Inge*. New York: Twayne, 1965. Print.

Voss, Ralph F. *A Life of William Inge: The Strains of Triumph*. Lawrence: University Press of Kansas, 1989. Print.

Weales, Gerald. *American Drama Since World War II*. New York: Harcourt, 1962. Print.

Williams, Tennessee. *The Glass Menagerie*. 1945. New York: New Directions, 1970. Print.

———. Introduction. *The Dark at the Top of the Stairs*. New York: Random House, 1958. vii–ix. Print.

"Going Next Door": Placing Inge
Barry Gross

It became fashionable in the 1980s to deride William Inge. Reviewing the Broadway production of *Summer Brave* in *The New Yorker*, Brendan Gill dismissed Inge as a "sentimental fantasist" who is finally and fairly "slipping away from us into the shadowy country of [Booth] Tarkington and James Whitcomb Riley" (122). John Simon thought that the only value in an off-Broadway revival of *Come Back, Little Sheba* was to "alert those not yet aware of it to how little it takes to achieve privileged status in the American theatre."

Yet Inge's five 1950s plays ran on Broadway for 1638 performances (*Come Back, Little Sheba*—190; *Picnic*—477; *Bus Stop*—478; *The Dark at the Top of the Stairs*—468; and *A Loss of Roses*—25). Tennessee Williams also had five plays on Broadway in the 1950s, but his ran for 1503 performances and his audience was not consistent (*The Rose Tattoo*—306; *Camino Real*—60; *Cat on a Hot Tin Roof*—694; *Orpheus Descending*—68; *Sweet Bird of Youth*—375).

Inge's four consecutive hit dramas ran for 1613 performances, a record surpassed only by Williams in the 1940s (*The Glass Menagerie*—561; *You Touched Me!*—109; *A Streetcar Named Desire*—855; *Summer and Smoke*—100, for a total of 1625). Inge's three biggest consecutive hits—*Picnic, Bus Stop*, and *Dark*—ran for 1423 performances, a record also surpassed only by Williams (*Glass, Touched*, and *Streetcar* for 1525 performances).

But no one until Neil Simon, not even Williams, ever had three consecutive dramas run on Broadway for as many as 450 performances each as Inge did. No one except William Inge ever had three consecutive dramas run on Broadway for as many as 400 performances each. For as many as 350 performances each. For as many as 300 performances each. For as many as 250 performances each. For as many as 200 performances each.

Eugene O'Neill was more prolific—in the 1920s alone 17 O'Neill plays opened in New York—but his plays had greater impacts on critics and other dramatists than on audiences. Those seventeen plays ran for about 2000 performances and more than half of them played at small off-Broadway houses, which means that far fewer people saw O'Neill's 17 plays in the 1920s than saw Inge's five plays in the 1950s (O'Neill's only big hit in the 1920s was *Strange Interlude*, which, banned in Boston, was already a sensation when it arrived in New York). His family comedy *Ah, Wilderness!* found an audience in the troubled 1930s and *Long Day's Journey into Night* and *A Touch of the Poet*—naturalistic, straightforward family dramas both—were successful in the 1950s.

Elmer Rice's Broadway career spanned 40 years—his first play opened in 1919, his last in 1959. He had four plays on Broadway in the 1920s, including his two best, *The Adding Machine* and *Street Scene* (*Street Scene* ran for 601 performances, the kind of run no serious American play—much less a tragedy—had previously attained). In the 1930s Rice's only commercial success was *Counsellor-at-Law*, a well-made melodrama; his most distinctive work in the 1930s came in four fervently anti-fascist plays—*We the People, Judgment Day, Between Two Worlds,* and *American Landscape*—three of which, so urgent was Rice's response to the political problems of the period, opened in the 1934–35 season alone. He continued writing and getting produced—four plays in the 1940s, four more in the 1950s—but only one, a comedy—*Dream Girl*—succeeded.

Maxwell Anderson's Broadway career spanned thirty years. He had eight plays on Broadway in the 1930s—including his best known play, *Winterset*—and eight in the 1940s, but only one ran for as many as 300 performances. His longest running play, his last, *The Bad Seed*, an adaptation of William March's Gothic chiller about a child who kills, reflected none of the social and spiritual concerns of his history plays (*Elizabeth the Queen, Mary of Scotland, Valley Forge, Journey to Jerusalem, Anne of the Thousand Days,* and *Barefoot in Athens*) or his political plays (*Both Your Houses, Winterset, Key Largo, Candle in the Wind, The Eve of St. Mark, Storm Operation,* and *What Price Glory?*).

Sidney Howard and Sidney Kingsley were competent craftsmen of serious plays. Howard's *They Knew What They Wanted* is, except for Rice's *Street Scene*, the only American drama of the 1920s which can be put on the same shelf as O'Neill's plays but his only commercial success was his dramatization of Sinclair Lewis's domestic novel *Dodsworth*. Kingsley wrote two important naturalistic plays of social criticism in the 1930s, *Men in White* and *Dead End* (*Dead End* had an extraordinary run of 687 performances), and had one commercial success in the 1940s, the melodrama *Detective Story*.

Most of Philip Barry's and S. N. Behrman's seriocomic social plays about the well-to-do were failures. Barry's only hit was *The Philadelphia Story*; 16 of his 20 plays failed to run for 200 performances, eight failed to run for 100. Behrman's biggest success, *Jacobowsky and the Colonel*, was an adaptation about the unlikely friendship between a Polish Jew and a renegade German on the run from the Nazis and was totally unlike anything else he wrote.

Robert E. Sherwood wrote a successful sophisticated comedy in the 1920s—*The Road to Rome*—and another in the early 1930s—*Reunion in Vienna*—and then, like Rice and Anderson, got caught up in the politics of the period. In four successive and successful plays—*The Petrified Forest, Idiot's Delight, Abe Lincoln in Illinois*, and *There Shall Be No Night*—Sherwood portrayed ordinary people learning to resist, battle, and triumph over various kinds of fascism.

Thornton Wilder's *Our Town* in the late 1930s and *The Skin of Our Teeth* in the early 1940s also extolled traditional values and old verities in the face of catastrophe and death. Their sub-texts, like those of Sherwood's plays, were not lost on Broadway audiences: both plays, even the difficult *Skin of Our Teeth*, were warmly received.

Lillian Hellman achieved a huge success with her first play, *The Children's Hour*, which ran for 691 performances, and had five more Broadway hits—*The Little Foxes*—410; *Watch on the Rhine*—378; *Another Part of the Forest*—182; *The Searching Wind*—318; and *Toys in the Attic*—556. Only Williams has had more dramas run for 300 performances on Broadway—six—and there is a family resemblance: except for her anti-fascist plays (*Rhine, Wind*), Hellman's plays, similarly marked by murder and mayhem, madness, and miscegenation, were almost as titillating as Williams's. The failure of *The Autumn Garden* in the 1950s had less to do with its defects than with what Broadway audiences had come to expect from a Hellman play—*The Autumn Garden* was quiet, Chekhovian.

Williams is the American dramatist with whom Inge is most often compared. They were friends from 1945 on when Inge, a drama critic in St. Louis, interviewed Williams for a hometown-boy-makes-good story after the success of *The Glass Menagerie*. They were contemporaries—from the 1944–45 season through the 1962–63 season there was never a year when a Williams play or an Inge play wasn't running on Broadway. Inge dedicated *The Dark at the Top of the Stairs* to Williams, and Williams wrote the introduction when the play was published. But after *The Glass Menagerie*, Williams's characters are, increasingly, the perpetrators or the victims of the mental and emotional warfare, the sexual and physical violence, that Inge's characters assiduously avoid. Williams's plays become battle grounds and boxing rings—combat zones—whereas in Inge's kitchens and living rooms, bus stops and back yards, voices, much less fists, are rarely raised. Not that Inge's plays lack psychological conflict or sexual tension—on the contrary—but they are never as nakedly admitted as they are in *Summer and Smoke* and *The Rose Tattoo*, are never allowed to erupt as they do in *A Streetcar Named Desire* and *Cat on a Hot Tin Roof*, *Orpheus Descending* and *Sweet Bird of Youth*.

The contemporary to whom Inge bears a closer resemblance is Arthur Miller. Like Inge's and unlike Williams's, Miller's world is middle class and the people who populate it are, like Inge's and unlike Williams's, ordinary. The kitchen in *Come Back, Little Sheba* is not unlike the kitchen in *Death of a Salesman*, the back yard in *Picnic* is not unlike the back yard in *All My Sons*, the living room in *The Dark at the Top of the Stairs* is not unlike the living room in *A View from the Bridge*. The difference is that Miller does not like the middle-class world or the people who populate it, and Inge does. Miller's plays are structured like legal briefs: Miller, prosecuting attorney, arraigns and indicts; Miller, the jury, convicts; Miller, the judge, sentences. It is no accident that *All My Sons* and *Death of a Salesman*, *An Enemy of the People*, and *The Crucible*, *A View from the Bridge* and *Incident at Vichy*, *After the Fall*, and *The Price* deal with legal matters, prominently feature lawyers and officers of the law, and have so many courtroom scenes. It is also why, *Death of a Salesman* and *The Price* excepted, Miller's plays have been so unloved, why Broadway audiences have not found Miller company they choose to keep: they are, for the most part, the very people he is badgering and hectoring, shaking his fingers and fists at. How many people want to spend an evening—want to spend the money to spend the evening—being lectured at and disapproved of?

I think the American playwright whose work and career Inge's most closely resembles is, despite some very obvious differences, Clifford Odets. Odets was New York, Jewish, and 1930s; Inge was Kansas, WASP, and 1950s. But alone among American dramatists, Odets and Inge liked the ordinary people they wrote about, respected, even admired, them and the middle-class worlds they populated. *Awake and Sing!*, *Paradise Lost*, and *Rocket to the Moon* are domestic dramas primarily, paeans, really, to bourgeois inclinations and aspirations. Odets is not angry at his characters as Miller is, he is angry at the twist of fate—the Depression—that has sabotaged their dreams, dreams Miller dismisses and condemns as petty and corrupt but with which Odets identifies and sympathizes. Even his strike play, *Waiting for Lefty*, is interrupted—and enriched and deepened—by domestic scenes. Only *Golden Boy*, which ends with the death of the hero—is a Miller play, a cautionary tale in which Odets wags his finger accusingly à la Miller and intones, "See! I told you this would happen if you were bad!" Odets's five-year grip on Broadway audiences—1934–35: *Awake and Sing!* and *Waiting for Lefty*; 1935–36: *Paradise Lost*; 1936–37:

Golden Boy; 1938–39: *Rocket to the Moon*—is matched only by Inge's in the 1950s, and for similar reasons.

Although Inge was "dubious" about Harold Clurman's directing *Bus Stop*—Clurman had directed Odets's plays for The Group Theatre in the 1930s, and Inge "didn't see how [Clurman], the most metropolitan man [Inge] knew, could bring understanding to the play's rural types," but Clurman "understood them perfectly"(*4 Plays* x). I think he understood them so well because he had directed Odets and realized that Inge, like Odets, "was the dramatist of the ordinary," that Inge's "touch," like Odets's, "was popular," not popular in the sense of commercial (necessarily) but popular in the sense of populist. Which is why "serious critics," as Clurman termed them, never took Inge seriously—they thought his plays "sentimental, facile" (Clurman 92)—and why my teachers at the Bronx High School of Science and the City College of New York scorned Inge as middlebrow—bourgeois, superficial—and why my parents—high school graduates only, middle class and middlebrow—did take Inge seriously and did not scorn him.

I, however—an English major!—following in the giant steps of my teachers and not the timid tiptoes of my parents—knew I should not like Inge, knew that to like Inge—or admit to liking Inge—would have betrayed a weakness in me, that same smallness of spirit and undernourished imagination that he was accused of, an incipient—hereditary!—superficiality I was supposed to be overcoming, supposed to be getting myself educated out of. So I learned to pronounce his name with a wrinkle of my nose and a disdainful curl of my lips—William I-i-i-nge—anticipating by more than twenty years John Updike's sneering narrator in *Bech: A Book* who calls—labels—Bech's first novel "a minor classic of the fifties, along with *Picnic*, *The Search for Bridey Murphy*, and the sayings of John Foster Dulles" (149).

I was not alone. In his freshman year of college Alexander Portnoy,

> struggling to make [his] father understand—[and] it seemed that it was either [his] father's understanding or his life—tore the subscription blank out of one of those intellectual journals [he] had [him]self just begun to discover in the college library, filled in his [father's] name and address, and sent off an anonymous gift subscription. But when [he] sullenly came home at Christmastime to visit and condemn, the *Partisan Review* was nowhere to be found. *Collier's*, *Hygeia*, *Look*, but where was his *Partisan Review*? Thrown out unopened—[Portnoy] thought in [his] arrogance and heartbreak—discarded unread, considered junk-mail by this schmuck, this moron, this Philistine father of mine! [8].

Inge was their *Collier's*, *Hygeia*, and *Look*; Miller and Williams were my *Partisan Review*.

In Miller's plays ordinary people live ordinary lives until something compels them to do something extraordinary; the kitchens and living rooms and back yards of the middle class, Miller insisted, could be the locale of momentous acts—and should be (remember, this is Miller we are talking about). His middle-class audience is supposed to leave the theater radicalized, ready to return to those kitchens and living rooms and back yards they live in and overthrow them. In Williams's plays the people are extraordinary to begin with and they find themselves in increasingly extraordinary situations. At the ends of Miller's plays, Joe Keller and Willy Loman, John Proctor and Eddie Carbone are all suicides; and at the conclusions of Williams's plays, Blanche is raped and institutionalized, Alma picks up strangers, and unspeakable things happen to Val in *Orpheus Descending* and Chance in *Sweet Bird of Youth*. My bourgeois parents could only shake their heads and echo hopelessly conventional Tesman's observation when his wife Hedda shoots herself, "But people don't do such things!"

Miller's and Williams's people do the things people like my parents and their relatives and friends did not do. Inge's people do not do such things, and his plays end "happily." At the end of *Come Back, Little Sheba*, the wife resigns herself to her childlessness and her husband does not strike her with a hatchet but instead promises to stop drinking and to stop blaming her for his failures. (John Simon says that "if ever a happy ending was unpersuasive, this is it," and Inge admitted that he could see why "[s]ome reviewers felt ... that Doc's unexpected outburst of drunken violence revealed a deeper inner conflict than the rest of the play in its presentation of him had prepared for" ["Schizophrenic" 22] or that the ending justified.) In *Picnic* the spinster schoolteacher marries the druggist and the beauty queen runs off with the drifter (Inge admitted that the ending of *Picnic* did not fulfill his "original intentions," that he "wrote what some considered a fortuitous ending in order to have a finished play go into rehearsal" [Preface (ix)]). In *Bus Stop* the virgin cowboy and the nightclub "chanteuse" head for marital bliss at the ranch and the lecherous professor leaves the young waitress's virginity intact. In *The Dark at the Top of the Stairs* the sexually repressed wife ejects her ten-year-old son from her bed and welcomes back into it her sexually aggressive husband.

Inge was not—as serious critics like Robert Brustein, my teachers, and I alleged—too shallow to recognize and confront ambiguity and complexity, too timid to follow unpleasant facts and conditions to inevitable conclusions. Rather, as Harold Clurman understood, Inge was "ameliorative" (91). When Brustein used that same term in his famous attack on Inge in *Harper's*— "Despite its flirtation with the 'dangerous' subjects of modern American drama (sex and violence), Inge's drama is in the end ameliorative, and this fact accounts for his present-day popularity" (57)—it was an accusation, but all ameliorative means is to make or become better and meliorism as a doctrine claims only that the world might be made better by human effort. Inge wanted his plays to end on that note of hope, but hope he considered earned.

His plays begin with the "unnatural quiet" he remembered from his Kansas boyhood just before a tornado struck. It "wasn't a dull or monotonous quiet" but an intense, portentous quiet—"just an occasional breath of breeze to suggest a hidden restlessness that had to break. No one could interpret this atmosphere, but people in the community felt that something was going to happen" ("Schizophrenic" 23). My parents were people in Inge's community—they could tell that something was going to happen, something was going to break. And it did: the tornado always touched down, but it was never as destructive as it might have been; it did not do great or permanent damage; there were no fatalities. Inge's characters survive the tornado and achieve, as a result of its having touched down, what he called a "painful stab of insight," come "to a new realization, after their near catastrophe, of their need for each other; coming perhaps to some shadowy realization of a possible new life" ("Schizophrenic" 23). Near catastrophes, stabs of insight, shadowy realizations (perhaps), possible new lives—Inge's language and expectations are tentative, hesitant, qualified not because he was facile and sentimental but because he was realistic, unsentimental, not because he was timid but because he was tough.

In *The Dark at the Top of the Stairs*, Inge's last hit, there is a fatality: the insecure part–Jewish boy, rejected by his mother and pained by anti–Semitism, commits suicide. It happens offstage and between acts, and he is not a member of the family the play is about—his death, sacrificial, shocks the Floods into living and Inge admitted that he drew "a little on Christian theology to show something of the uniting effect human suffering can bring into our lives" (*4 Plays* ix), but it is a death nevertheless, Inge's first death, and it signaled the beginning of the end of Inge's popularity. Inge's last play of the 1950s—and first failure—*A Loss of Roses* does not end with a death but the play is more severe, much harsher than his previous plays, and the parting of mother and son at the end is not ameliorative. *Natural Affection*, Inge's first play of the 1960s and a commercial disaster, is populated with the same ordinary people who populated his previous plays—a boy both over-protected and rejected by his mother, a sexually starved and aggressive woman, a virile and vulgar stud, a henpecked husband, a repressed deviant—but this time the mother's rejection of her son for the stud drives the boy into a frenzy and he murders the lady next door who makes a pass at him.

It was the 1960s and Inge thought he could express the anger and pain he had so tightly controlled and contained in the 1950s because the "newspapers were so full of violence that the morning headlines were an assault upon one's breakfast digestion," with "outbreaks of the most bizarre and irrational killings and acts of desperation," especially by juveniles who, Inge thought, were "the only people free to react to a changing world with the animal hostility all of us felt but were cautious enough not to display" (*Natural Affection* viii).

ALL of us? All of US? Not my parents, or their relatives, or their friends. He lost his audience—that audience that was, in the 1950s, his and his alone, mostly middle-class Jews from Brooklyn and the Bronx and Queens who filled most of the seats in Broadway theaters in the 1950s, and who comprised most of the approximately 1,138,400 people who saw the 477 performances of *Picnic*, the 478 performances of *Bus Stop*, and the 468 performances of *The Dark at the Top of the Stairs* (the Music Box seats nearly a thousand and I am figuring on an 80 percent occupancy), all of whom continued, even in the violent and desperate, bizarre and irrational 1960s, to avoid or avert tornadoes, to control whatever intense restlessness, whatever animal hostility—my parents? intense restlessness? Max and Dotty? animal hostility?—they might have felt, not out of cowardice but out of common sense, a need to survive, out of a commitment to live what Inge so memorably called possible lives, all those people he spoke for when, at the beginning of his career, he defended his characters in *Come Back, Little Sheba* against charges that they were too small, too ordinary:

> Certainly, poor Doc and Lola could never begin to measure up to the proportions of tragic heroes. As people, Doc and Lola may point to vaster tragedies in the social background behind them, but I was concerned only with Doc and Lola themselves. I found them lovable, weak, warm-hearted, foolish, naive, a little pretentious, and only occasionally brave. Except for bravery, though on a full-time basis, these are not the characteristics that usually make up a tragic hero. We do not necessarily love Hamlet, or even Willy Loman ... nor do we sympathize with them; rather we understand the forces which would destroy them and are deeply moved by their inability to overcome them. Their tragedy lies not in the fact that they perish, but that they *must* perish; and the world, although it has not been able to sustain them, still will feel their loss. Doc and Lola are people the world was never aware of, but the world's ignorance doesn't make them any the more or less interesting and likable as human beings ["Schizophrenic" 23].

My parents, and their relatives, and their friends, sensed that Inge accepted and admired them, however weak and foolish, naive and pretentious and insufficiently brave they were, liked them and found them interesting, even if the world ignored them. And respected them: asked at the beginning of his career to express his notion of the playwright's "mission," Inge, with uncharacteristic vehemence, attacked those colleagues who wrote plays primarily "to shock, to teach, to preach at" audiences and said he "hate[d] a play" that told him what to think:

> If a man tells us he has a mission in his work, we immediately discredit him with arbitrary pretensions of nobleness and righteousness that make us a little wary. A playwright with a mission, we fear, is going to preach at us, rant at us, argue with us, turning the whole playgoing experience into the category of *duty* and the theatre itself into a meeting hall....
>
> Just as we resent a newspaper reporter who "slants" the news to bring his readers to his own point of view, so do we resent, and rightfully, a playwright (or any writer) who uses his medium as a means of persuasion; and this is what having "a mission" too often implies. A good play brings some illumination to life. It may expose the playwright's thoughts and feelings, and even his prejudices and worst limitations. Still, he never asks his audience to take sides with him. He lets them make their own decisions. He takes it for granted that his audience comes to the theatre not to be told something but to find out something for themselves ["More on the Playwright's Mission"].

He forgot that, I think, in the 1960s, but in the 1950s what Harold Clurman said about him was true: there was "very little synthetic in what [Inge] had to say" because he "really knew and felt his people," "was kin to them" (92). He really knew and felt his audience too, was kin to them, those middle-class New York Jews so different, it would seem, from him and his people. Tennessee Williams compared going to an Inge play to

> going next door to call on a well-liked neighbor. There is warmth and courtesy in their reception. There is an atmosphere of serenity in his presence, there is understanding in it, and the kindness of wisdom and the wisdom of kindness. They enter and take comfortable seats by the fireside without anxiety, for there is no air of recent or incipient disorder on the premises. No blood-stained ax has been kicked under the sofa. If the lady of the house is absent, she has really gone to baby-sit for her sister, her corpse is not stuffed hastily back of the coalbin. If the TV is turned on it will not break into the panicky report of unidentified aircraft of strange design over the rooftops. In other words, [you] are given to believe that nothing at all disturbing or indecorous is going to happen to them in the course of their visit [vii].

But after presenting "the genial surface of common American life," Williams observed, Inge, "this nice, well-bred next-door neighbor," begins "to uncover a world within a world," does not rip "but quietly drop[s] the veil that keeps you from seeing yourself as you are" and "in such a way that you are not offended or startled.... It's just what you are.... Inge tells you, in his quiet, gently modulated voice ... don't be ashamed of it, but see it and know it and make whatever corrections you feel able to make, and they are bound to be good ones" (vii–viii).

Works Cited

Brustein, Robert. "The Men-Taming Women of William Inge." *Harper's* Nov. 1958: 52–57. Print.

Clurman, Harold. "Theatre." Rev. of *Overnight*, by William Inge. *Nation* 3 Aug. 1974: 91–93. Print.
Gill, Brendan. "The Theatre: Of Kingship and Other Miseries." Rev. of *Summer Brave*, by William Inge. *New Yorker* 3 Nov. 1975: 121–22. Print.
Inge, William. *4 Plays by William Inge* [*Come Back, Little Sheba*; *Picnic*; *Bus Stop*; *The Dark at the Top of the Stairs*]. New York: Random House, 1958. Print.
———. *A Loss of Roses*. New York: Random House, 1960. Print.
———. "More on the Playwright's Mission." *Theatre Arts* Aug. 1958: 19. Print.
———. *Natural Affection*. New York: Random House, 1963. Print.
———. Preface. *Summer Brave and Eleven Short Plays*. New York: Random House, 1962. [ix]–[x].
———. "The Schizophrenic Wonder." *Theatre Arts* May 1950: 22–23. Print.
Roth, Philip. *Portnoy's Complaint*. 1969. New York: Bantam, 1970. Print.
Simon, John. "The Ashcan School." Rev. of *Come Back, Little Sheba*, by William Inge. *New York Magazine* 23 July 1984: 56. Print.
Updike, John. *Bech: A Book*. 1970. New York: Fawcett, 1971. Print.
Williams, Tennessee. Introduction. *The Dark at the Top of the Stairs*. New York: Random House, 1958. vii–ix. Print.

Another Kansan in the Land of Oz: Inge as Screenwriter
Thomas P. Adler

1. "Writing for Film"

When William Inge won the Academy Award for Best Original Screenplay of 1961 for *Splendor in the Grass*, he was the first American playwright of any note to be so honored. Prior to that movie's premiere, in an essay entitled "Writing for Film," he considered some of the distinctions between the two forms, theater and cinema, as artistic media, as well as the different approaches that authors for each must take. Inge, who believed that movie scripts were, indeed, "an art medium" (7), liked writing films, he tells us, for basically two reasons: first, "because they are a mass medium" that has provided "more good entertainment over the past decade than the theatre" has for its audiences; and second, because they are primarily "visual" and he deems himself by intention "not essentially literary" (5) in his most satisfying works (though he can hardly be called as visual a dramatist as others among his contemporaries, especially Tennessee Williams). While some observers, myself included, might want to soften Inge's claim that theater is basically an "audio-literary" mode of expression and "only secondarily a visual medium" with the caveat that drama at its best has always functioned as an almost symbiotic mix of verbal and visual signs, his point that theater, unlike film, privileges dialogue and can even exist on occasion without "physicalized action" (1)—radio drama would be an example—remains valid.

After producing four widely acclaimed and highly popular plays during the 1950s which left a few commentators almost convinced that he was of equal rank with Miller and Williams, and then experiencing a sudden reversal in critical fortune, Inge approached the turn to screenwriting with a sense of liberation. His exhilaration can be attributed, in part, to a release from an unnecessarily limiting and restrictive notion of theatrical form, since he seemed to equate the continued attraction of the type of realistic play he wrote with an absolute adherence to unity of place. Contrary to Inge's conviction, strict handling of theater space, that is, confinement to a single place at least within each act if not during an entire play, is not, we know, nearly so indispensable an element of stage realism as maintaining the absolute boundary between audience and actors. Fidelity to one place, to not moving spatially, may have generated greater "intensity" and "impact" ("Writing for Film" 3) in his work, yet it still limited free rein of the imagination. Film, however, rather than "confin[ing him] to the dimensions of the stage," freed him for the "mobile geography" (1) of the screen—albeit not without the need for increased "discipline of form" now that "unity of setting [was] destroyed" (4).

This ignoring of unity of place, rather than any more basic alterations in characters or thematic emphases, or even any increase in telling the story visually rather than through words, constitutes the main difference between Inge's plays on stage and screen. When *Come Back, Little Sheba*, assuredly the finest screen version of any Inge play, was adapted for film in 1952 with the screenplay by Ketti Frings, it was, in common parlance, "opened up" to include scenes at an AA meeting and in a hospital emergency room, just as the movie of *Picnic* (1956; screenplay by Daniel Taradash) was opened up through James Wong Howe's lovingly photographed long interlude at the picnic that was never seen on stage, or *The Dark at the Top of the Stairs* (1960; screenplay by Harriet Frank and Irving Ravitch) was freed to show rather than tell of the vicious anti–Semitism at the country club dance. Notable for Marilyn Monroe's performance, *Bus Stop* on screen (1956; screenplay by George Axelrod) pictured at some length Bo and Cherie's encounter and developing relationship before the play began; while *The Stripper* (1963; based on *A Loss of Roses*; screenplay by Meade Roberts) fulfills with a vengeance Inge's expressed wish that the final focus be on Lila, as it was expanded beyond the play's ending to show her plying her new trade. But in none of these five instances did Inge have an active involvement in the translation of play from stage to screen.

Of greater interest in any consideration of Inge as a creative artist, then, are the three instances—case studies, if you will—that find him actually writing directly for the cinema: first, the original script of *Splendor in the Grass*; next, the film adaptation of James Leo Herlihy's novel, *All Fall Down*; and, finally, Inge's screen treatment of his own one-act play, *Bus Riley's Back in Town*.

2. *Splendor in the Grass*

If Inge himself, when he turned from playwright to scriptwriter, was forced to deal with and solve an aesthetic problem having to do with the instantaneous movement in film from place to place as opposed to what he saw as the confining spatial conventions of the stage, the late adolescent hero and heroine of his first movie face a dilemma that also centers around freedom versus restriction—though theirs, because it is a moral one, is solved with much greater pain. But perhaps, then, moral quandaries never admit of as happy a solution as artistic problems. In *Splendor*, the central issue is how Bud Stamper and Deanie Loomis navigate the constraints that society (usually through parents) imposes upon them as regards sexuality; to follow these restrictions in their relationship with one another, this set of thou-shalt-nots, means to suffer, without any compensatory reward but with a good deal of self-loathing and repression and bitterness and defiance. The mores of the time shout "No," but no one can provide any rationale or positive reason that would explain or justify these—except fear of winding up in a family way. The young couple can only feel that they have been allowed less than has been held out or promised to them.

The exact details of the collaborative effort between Inge and stage and film director Elia Kazan that would result in the screenplay for *Splendor* remain murky. As he tells it in "Writing for Film," Inge came to realize that his story (based on some high school students in Independence, Kansas) was "too broad in scope for the stage," and so he took the "compilation of tight little scenes" and then "began to blend" them together by "identifying [himself] with the moving camera" that would record them on film "and to move with it, forgetting the pressure [he] had always felt before to keep [his] story located in one place. It was like learning to walk" (3). Afterwards, he "stripped the story down to a skeletal structure of dialogue" (2) that would permit images to tell as much of his story as possible. Kazan, however, has a quite different remembrance of how things were, which he has since recounted twice in print: in the extended interview that constitutes *Kazan on Kazan* he claims that the playwright sent him a "very rough first draft" manuscript that "beautifully provided ... the basic story and characters ... and then I wrote the script" (139); in *A Life*, Kazan bluntly reports that Inge "produced a novelette and I made it into a screenplay" (601). (Though his contribution went unrewarded at the time, Kazan feels that all was not wasted since the experience gave him "confidence" later for his own solo flights as novelist and screenwriter.)

If one of the distinctive characteristics of Inge as dramatist is his recurrent use of foil characters and subplots, this is carried over into the writing of *Splendor* by the many parallel situations and scenes that help to structure a film that not only moves from place to place but flows over a considerable period of time as well. Especially at the beginning this balanced, symmetrical arrangement is noticeable as Inge shows first the Loomis home and then the Stamper house; though of a different economic class (worker as opposed to owner/manager), both locales espouse much the same system of values, and each has a parent whose ideals or way of thinking limits their offspring: Mrs. Loomis's viewpoint that "no nice girl" would ever dream of desiring a boy and that a woman only submits to sex in marriage "in order to have children" but certainly "doesn't enjoy those things like a man does" (15–16) both robs Deanie of looking forward to sex with joy and makes her feel dirty for desiring it, while Ace Stamper's need as a failed athlete to have a son who will not "disappoint" his "hopes" (18) by doing anything other than go to Yale, take over the family business, and—unspoken—marry better than Deanie temporarily forces Bud into a way of life other than the immediate marriage to Deanie and the ranching he desires. Both parents are overly obsessed with money, both regard sex as a transaction rather than as an expression of affection, and each sequence ends with one of the young lovers looking wistfully at a picture of the other. Later, the film will crosscut again between the two houses on Christmas morning to show Deanie opening her expensive necklace from Bud and Bud unwrapping his handmade scarf from her.

Other parallel scenes include Deanie rejecting Bud's advances in the car, then later trying to lead him into a car, begging him to dominate her; the two scenes in high school English classrooms, the first discussing notions of medieval chivalry that idealized women, the second explicating Wordworth's "Ode on Intimations of Immortality"—a verse of which provides the film's title; Bud in the hospital suffering from pneumonia and Deanie in the hospital after her suicide attempt; Bud at Yale becoming involved with Angelina and Deanie in the metal institution meeting her future husband who, like Bud, is browbeaten by his father; the crosscutting between the Loomises and Ace Stamper on Black Monday listening to reports of the crash; the two suicides—Deanie's attempted one, and the aftermath of Ace's plunge from the window; and the two scenes at the ranch, the first of Bud and Deanie still together, "chaperoning" his disreputable sister Ginny on a date, the second of Deanie's visit to Bud, now married to Angelina and a father at the film's end.

Visually, almost from its opening moment, the movie is filled with water imagery, from the river and waterfall where Bud and Deanie's relationship is not consummated—but where Bud and Juanita's later is—and where Deanie will eventually attempt suicide, to the bathtub where Deanie becomes hysterical over being what her parents expect, "a lovely virginal creature who wouldn't think of being spoiled" (46). Water is thus symbolically associated with love and sex and death, but not with purification, since no easy salvation is ever won in this film. The downward spiral of Bud and Deanie's interrupted relationship follows—as R. Baird Shuman notes (89) in one of the few extended discussions available of an Inge film—the movement from prosperity to crash, with the Depression symbolic of an emotional and spiritual malaise, an analogy Inge had made explicit in *A Loss of Roses* (1959) through the voice of the tent-revival Evangelist, preaching "drought of the soul" and "deflation of the spirit" as "the worst Depression of all" (*Loss* 87).

Thematically, *Splendor* as a dual rite of passage may not have all the richness that Kazan attributes to it retrospectively, yet it does continue to speak of the need for children to forgive rather than blame their parents for flaws that are their own, and of American greed, represented by the "towering" phallic oil wells, despoiling the land. When Deanie glosses the lines from Wordsworth's "Ode," she explains that life is movement towards disillusionment, that "when we grow up ... we have to forget the ideals of youth" (43): if we trail clouds of former glory, the present and future will almost assuredly not confirm the promise of the past, but this must be recognized and moved beyond. Whether Bud would have been the great love of Deanie's life or not, clearly no one *else* can ever be; more importantly, Bud with his wife and child is now just "a man," not "a god" as Deanie hyperbolically deluded herself into believing he was. Yet it was abstract moral principles, held to unquestioningly, that kept them apart and never let them take the chance of finding out for themselves the truth of their love. In his autobiography, Kazan sees the bittersweet ending as growing out of Inge's experience, "full of what Bill had learned from his own life: that you have to accept limited happiness, because all happiness is limited, and that to expect perfection is the most neurotic thing of all; you must live with the sadness as well as with the joy" (*A Life* 605). The film moves visually from the fertile river of possibility to the dusty ground of reality. That the garden is somehow imperfect, and must be accepted as such, is an image that Inge would contribute to his next film project.

3. *All Fall Down*

Herlihy's novel (1960), on the surface the story of a rather unconventional triangle between two brothers and a somewhat mysterious older woman named Echo O'Brien is, as its narrative structure would indicate, more profitably seen as an examination of a young writer's coming of age through learning how to channel his considerable creative powers. Herlihy adopts a complex yet accessible structure (whose seams deliberately show) by shifting back and forth in time; by revealing his ending when the novel is barely a third of the way through; and by mixing omniscient narration with letters and extensive notebook entries—some of them containing interpolated metacritical advice to budding writers—all to show how sixteen-year-old Clinton Williams frees himself from his compulsion to transcribe people's lives, to get it all down. His addiction to his notebooks has become an obsession, a way to fight off the terror that "life was a thing that took place out of his presence" (Herlihy 42). His dependency on voyeurism and eavesdropping is every bit as destructive as his brother Berry-berry's need to dominate the women in his life, using violence, if necessary, to exert his power; these aberrations are, in fact, analogous. The novel proceeds toward a dual recognition: by Berry-berry "that there is life in other people than himself" and "that imagin[ing] contact with the livingness of another human being" ignites a salvific "wave of tenderness so profound that he yearned for its continuance" (262); and by Clint that the writer, rather than taking from other people by preying on their lives vicariously, must also channel his artistic gifts to nurture others emotionally. Life transcribed is simply stolen, not transformed by vision into art, and so is an abuse and violation of others. If the artist's gift is godlike, he must not employ it like some "invisible stranger" God who at whim "shook the high branches of all the apple trees in all the orchards of the world" (260) and blew all the children away.

Given the recent composition of both *Dark at the Top of the Stairs* (1957) and *A Loss of Roses* (1960), Inge may initially have been attracted to Herlihy's novel because of its oedipal overtones and portrayal of destructive mother love. He brings this element, aided by Angela Lansbury's performance, into even sharper relief in the screen adaptation; this focus may, indeed, have helped him to make several right choices, since it is undoubtedly for the better that Inge resists trying to render filmically the more abstract level of Herlihy's portrait-of-the-artist-as-a-young-man novel, foregrounding instead Clint's disillusionment over Berry-berry—which more easily lends itself to visual presentation. Clint comes to understand that his idealism was misplaced, that he had sentimentally romanticized the drifter/stud who must ultimately share in the culpability for Echo's death. In presenting the story chronologically, Inge, again wisely, chose to dramatize rather than narrate the notebook passages through voice overs; he retained, in fact, only three brief narrative segments, including one that opens the film, without totally sacrificing the viewer's awareness of the unhealthiness of Clint's obsession, since he is oftentimes seen scribbling things down. Furthermore, the fairly insistent use of point-of-view shots maintains some sense of seeing all this through an impressionable boy's eyes (Clint, however, undergoes no sexual initiation in the film as occurs near the beginning of the novel). Perhaps as an homage to that earlier Midwestern chronicler of Winesburg, the family's surname has become Willard rather than the Williams of Inge's source.

Inge's straightening out of the chronology places Berry-berry's involvement with Echo as the most recent in a sequence of encounters with older, golden women who find his blend of beauty and wildness irresistible. Echo, rebounding from the suicide of her alcoholic fiancé, toys with Clint and his adolescent infatuation in a patronizing way, telling him before she drives away, pregnant with Berry-berry's child, to a fatal crash in the rain, "Remember, Clint, you're still my guy." All that she asked from Berry-berry, who before had always been just out for "kicks," was the chance that he perhaps might break from his pattern and come to love her, a gamble that she knows she has lost; and so she allows him to go, saying, "You are as free as the day God made you." Clint's misplaced adulation and idolization of his brother is destroyed, however, not because Berry-berry rather than he himself "wins" Echo, but because Berry-berry's failure to love the pregnant Echo once he has won her is a continuation of his longstanding habit of abuse. Unlike Berry-berry's confession in the novel that he has misused and broken bonds with others, his tears in the film are more ambiguous, perhaps indicating only self-disgust rather than self-knowledge.

One brief scene in Herlihy's novel becomes the source for Inge's most significant additions in the film. In both, a volatile and deeply bitter Berry-berry breaks a manger scene in a store window Christmas display. Whereas in the book, his action is accompanied by a verbally explicit interpretation ("The attitudes of the little sculptures depicting the Holy Family so filled him with resentment against their heavy sentimentality that he was suddenly enraged. The longer he looked at it, the more he blamed his own desperate fix on this wicked myth of the Madonna, with all her smug purity, kneeling there, fondling the Infant" [173]), in the film the scene is wordless, with Berry-berry's eyes focusing on Mary and the Babe. The film then cuts to a sequence in a bar where Berry-berry beats the older woman who had picked him up as a traveling companion, and then cuts to a shot of the mantel in the Willard home, with a Christmas crèche next to an elaborately framed photo of the firstborn son. His mother Annabel moves the photograph adoringly to a table, where later it is seen enshrined, lit by candles. After word is received of Echo's death and Ralph calls his son "a real killer," Clint takes the photo, slams it to the ground, and stomps on it with his foot. In the film, unlike in Herlihy's novel, when Berry-berry first returns home, he adamantly refuses to kiss his mother full on the mouth (160). It is Annabel, however, who later arranges the meeting between her son and Echo, even though she comes to feel hurt and slighted that "the boy [she] love[d] love[d] somebody else." And yet, despite this, the frantic Annabel is ultimately seen pressing the smashed photo of Berry-berry to her bosom, crying: "I love him, d'ya hear. I love him. I don't care what he's done, I'll love him always and forever." The director John Frankenheimer has termed this a crucial scene, saying "we simply had to do [it].... Otherwise, the film would not have been valid" (Pratley 79). Though Orson Welles would downplay and even disparage similarly flabby psychologizing to establish motivation in *Citizen Kane* as really only "dollar-book Freud," for Inge—who might be called the chief practitioner of the "Freud on Broadway" school of playwriting during the 1950s—this explains the entire cycle of Berry-berry's actions.

Inge's other significant addition comes at the very end of the film with his introduction of the garden imagery that helps call the viewers' attention to the reversal of the Cain and Abel myth. When Berry-berry first takes Clint to his whorehouse in the country, they pass the apple trees in blossom, and he offers his younger brother an apple from the barrel that is "sweet as hell, but ya gotta look out for the worms." When Clint returns in the night to this orchard intent on killing Berry-berry after Echo's death, the apples are profuse; as he leaves the house the next morning, having committed no murder but defying Berry-berry's hatred for life with an exuberant "I like life," he walks back out through the garden of apple trees. The "good" son has not killed the evil brother, but much of his naiveté—though not his sexual innocence since he remains virginal—is left behind as he returns to his parents' far from idyllic household. The disillusionment of an Inge hero brings about a closer approach to reality: no one can escape corruption and knowledge of evil; the world is fallen, yet it can and must be lived in—though Inge never intimates here that it can be transcended, even by art. For Inge, art lacks the sacramental quality—and thus sustaining potentiality—that it has for Tennessee Williams.

4. *Bus Riley's Back in Town*

Other than its title and the barest thread of a woman trying to reestablish a relationship with a man returning home after some years away, the movie that opened in 1965 under the title *Bus Riley's Back in Town* bears no resemblance either to Inge's one-act play of the same name from the 1950s (published in 1962) or to the screenplay he wrote (ca. 1962) based on that work; in fact, Inge had his name removed from the credits before the premiere, and the group-effort script is now attributed to one Walter Gage. The original short play, notable for its careful modulation of atmosphere and tone, occurs in the bar of a mid–Texas hotel in a town that "really had it once" ("Bus Riley's" [one-act] 216) but has clearly seen better days; "one of the finest houses in town" has been, like the Stamper home in *Splendor*, turned into "a funeral parlor" (235). As the bartender depressedly remarks, "Things change" (235). Once, Jackie Loomis (the surname Inge gives to Deanie's family in *Splendor*) had been in love with the half-breed Bus Riley, thinking him "a *god*" (217) (as

Deanie does Bud). Daughter of a nouveau riche drunken oilman who "[l]ived like a lord" (218), she became pregnant and wanted to keep the baby, but her father, apparently jealous of her love for Bus, demanded she have an abortion; Jackie, again like Deanie, attempts suicide and spends time in a mental institution. Now when Bus, who has served a year in prison, arrives home "*wear-[ing] his Navy whites with splendor*" (225), Jackie dreams that their love can be renewed.

The embittered Bus, however, no longer wants anything "so corny" (233) as to be thought of as a god, nor does he want to think about times past; neither does he believe in falling in love anymore, since that is what "they put you in jail for" (239). At first, Jackie refuses to lower herself to being used by Bud as someone to "let off steam with, and then forget" (236), yet to the "*mocking accompaniment*" of the "*mean blues ... of a rasping trumpet*" (238) she returns willing to play his pick-up, agreeing not to speak of love anymore. Diminishment and disillusionment, settling for less—for the possible rather than the dreamt of—are the rules of the game, societally and in personal relationships as well. Inge seems to have had this short play much in mind when he wrote the script for *Splendor*, as the little details perhaps attest; in fact, *Splendor* seems a better and more faithful rendering of Inge's concerns and sentiments in *Bus Riley's Back in Town* than even the dramatist's own screen adaptation of it.

The small remnants of the one-act play that Inge retains are embedded in the filmscript beginning around two-thirds of the way through; these Inge has extended not only through additional (sub)plot lines involving new characters, but also by expanding and altering the exposition. Furthermore, what had originally been a single-set play is opened up by additional locations in New York (the Copacabana, where Bus is performing) and Houston (Jackie's music room and bedroom, a hotel lobby and penthouse suite, a patio, a concert auditorium, a diner, a hospital room, the zoo, and a cemetery where Bus's Mexican mother is buried). These changes work unintentionally toward diffusing the play's careful focus. What results remains more a play script than a screenplay, with sparse reference to visualizing the material and only rare suggestions of camera set-ups, usually close-ups (e.g., "Bus Riley's" [filmscript] 48). Finally, the main plot has been somewhat sanitized so as not to offend wider audiences at the time: no abortion has taken place, nor is the heroine any longer sexually forward or aggressive except in response to the male.

Jackie is now a single mother and piano teacher, counting Bus's slightly crippled younger brother as her prize pupil who needs to win the competition to prove himself to himself, to, as he says, "feel as though [he'd] justified [his] existence" (55) as the un-favored brother. The racial hatred and bigotry of her father that had prevented a marriage to Bus are now channeled into her brother-in-law. Bus, a smugly successful pop singer whose fear of failing to become a success has kept him selfish and always looking out for number one, seems even more than in the original like Bud from *Splendor* in his appeal to women. His father, whose awareness of the presence of a compassionate God still cannot substitute for the "human love" (22) essential to all but the saints, is literally drinking himself to death until redeemed by the understanding and forgiveness of a waitress whom he rather brutally forced to have sex. Jackie's motivation for her initial attraction to and continued love of the half-Mexican Bus comes out in a lengthy session on her analyst's couch in which she discourses rather artificially about the attraction that the forbidden dark object has for the overly protected "fair" maiden who "represented all the things in life that Bus felt deprived of" (29–30) and who wants to break free from her narrow experience and live all of life, especially the side that has been denied her.

Here, it is Bus, tentatively positioned before a "crucifixion" scene in the hospital corridor (62), who changes; although unable to forgive his father for his long-ago mistreatment of his mother, Bus is reconciled with his younger brother. Tired of a lifetime of "hating," somewhat like Clint in *All Fall Down*, Bus embraces life and "love" (68), turning away from the whores in the bar and taking the initiative in going up to Jackie's bedroom where she longingly awaits him, having "wanted [him] ... every night ... all these years" (68). Yet the movement here towards reconciliation and renewal is not as convincing—and consequently not as powerful—as the image of loss and disillusion, even degradation, in Inge's original play, or as the muted endings of *Splendor in the Grass* or *All Fall Down* are. The filmscript, at least in its manuscript state, remains word-bound rather than visually liberating, suggesting perhaps that Inge was quickly coming to find that the film medium could be just as restrictive as the stage if the material itself was overly familiar, falling into a narrowly repetitive mold which neither demanded nor inspired a creative re-visioning before it would be frozen on celluloid. Inge claims at the end of "Writing for Film" that the single "distinguishing characteristic of a real work of art is that we sense in it the pleasure (or fulfillment, if you must) that its creator experienced" (7). Though we might dispute whether the elation a creator finds in his or her work is sufficient in itself to raise craft to art, surely that essential ingredient of joy in creation, of being in the grip of something that absolutely cries out for expression, is sadly absent from Inge's filmscript of *Bus Riley's Back in Town*, in a way that it is not from either *All Fall Down*, with its refusal to hate the life dealt us, no matter what its unspoken side, or, more particularly, *Splendor in the Grass*, which must come very near to expressing Inge's own need to deal with a love that neither society nor family could sanction.

WORKS CITED

Bus Riley's Back in Town. Dir. Harvey Hart. Perf. Ann-Margret and Michael Parks. Universal, 1956. Film.

Bus Stop. Dir. Joshua Logan. Perf. Marilyn Monroe, Don Murray, and Eileen Heckart. Twentieth Century–Fox, 1956. Film.

Come Back, Little Sheba. Dir. Daniel Mann. Perf. Shirley Booth and Burt Lancaster. Paramount, 1952. Film.

The Dark at the Top of the Stairs. Dir. Delbert Mann. Perf. Robert Preston, Dorothy McGuire, and Angela Lansbury. Warner, 1960. Film.

Herlihy, James Leo. *All Fall Down*. New York: Dutton, 1960. Print.

Inge, William. *All Fall Down* [screenplay]. Dir. John Frankenheimer. Perf. Warren Beatty, Eva Marie Saint, and Karl Malden. M-G-M, 1962. Film.

———. *Bus Riley's Back in Town* [filmscript]. TS. William Inge Collection. Independence Community College, Independence, KS. Print.

———. "Bus Riley's Back in Town" [one-act play]. *Summer Brave and Eleven Short Plays*. New York: Random House, 1962. 213–39. Print.

———. *A Loss of Roses*. New York: Random House, 1960. Print.

———. *Splendor in the Grass* [screenplay]. *Men and Women*. Ed. Richard A. Maynard. New York: Scholastic, 1974. 12–74. Print.

———. "Writing for Film." TS. William Inge Collection. Independence Community College, Independence, KS.

Kazan, Elia. *A Life*. New York: Knopf, 1988. Print.

———. *Kazan on Kazan*. Ed. Michael Ciment. New York: Viking, 1974. Print.

Picnic. Dir. Joshua Logan. Perf. William Holden and Kim Novak. Columbia, 1955. Film.

Pratley, Gerald. *The Cinema of John Frankenheimer*. New York: Barnes, 1969. Print.

Shuman, R. Baird. *William Inge*. New York: Twayne, 1965. Print.

The Stripper. Dir. Franklin Schaffner. Perf. Joanne Woodward, Richard Beymer, and Gypsy Rose Lee. Twentieth Century Fox, 1963. Film.

Build-Up to *Natural Affection*
R. Baird Shuman

William Inge's *Natural Affection* opened on Broadway at the Booth Theatre on the last day of January 1963, more than a decade after its author brought his first play to Broadway and a little more than a decade before William Inge ended his life by inhaling carbon monoxide fumes in the garage of his home in southern California. The play can be read as both a cry for help from a sensitive artist who feared he was nearing the end of his artistic resources as well as a bleak commentary on what life has to offer and on the difficult choices it thrusts upon people.

Inge, long tortured by self-doubt, mood swings, and alcohol and drug dependency, suffered through most of the decade of the 1950s without permitting his growing emotional problems to interfere significantly with his writing. Although he was in extensive psychoanalysis during much of the decade in which he experienced his greatest dramatic triumphs, play followed play in an orderly procession from 1950 until 1957, one opening on Broadway about every two years.

Come Back, Little Sheba provided Inge with a more propitious beginning on Broadway than any major American playwright had enjoyed since Clifford Odets brought *Waiting for Lefty* (1935) and three of his other plays—*Awake and Sing!* (1935), *Till the Day I Die* (1935), and *Paradise Lost* (1935)—to Broadway. Inge, although he did not burst on the scene with Odets's dramatic profusion, followed *Sheba* two years later with *Picnic*, which won the Pulitzer Prize and several other major awards. Two years after *Picnic*, *Bus Stop* received high critical praise and was made into a successful film that starred Marilyn Monroe. Two years after that, as though following some preordained schedule, Inge brought *The Dark at the Top of the Stairs* to Broadway, where it generally evoked critical acclaim and popular plaudits.

The continuing success of Inge's plays, however, did not bring him the elation and inner satisfaction one might have expected such a well-received playwright would experience; with the production of each play, Inge's insecurities mounted. He was a regular patient of first one New York psychoanalyst and then a second between 1949 and the summer of 1956, after which he was forced to seek another arrangement (Voss 168). His friends, William Gibson, the playwright, and his wife Margaret Brenman-Gibson, who was associated with the Austen Riggs Center in Stockbridge, Massachusetts, urged Inge to seek help from Dr. Robert Knight, one of Dr. Brenman-Gibson's colleagues.

Inge's need for continuing psychiatric treatment was sufficient to warrant his renting a small apartment in Stockbridge, even though Dr. Knight treated him as an outpatient. Inge spent a great deal of time in that apartment for the next five or six years, although he still retained his apartment at the Dakota and, after 1958, at 45 Sutton Place South in New York City as his major residence. He found Stockbridge a good place to write, and he completed *Dark* during the time he stayed there. One might assume that he preferred his quite simple apartment in Stockbridge and the small-town life that staying there afforded him to his more elaborate, permanent digs in New York and to the hurly-burly of the city. Stockbridge, although in New England, must certainly have seemed closer to Inge's small-town Kansas roots than New York did.

External appearances suggested that Inge was riding the crest of a wave that would run along unchecked into some indeterminate future. In his own eyes, however, Inge was someone other than the successful playwright who had become the toast of Broadway. He was, rather, a creative artist growing ever more desperate to prove himself—mostly *to himself*—by accomplishing something he had failed to accomplish for almost a decade: to write an original script. He had shaped *Sheba* from one of his early, unpublished short stories. He created *Picnic* from his earlier play, *Front Porch* (written in 1946; produced in 1948 in St. Louis). He derived *Bus Stop* from his one-act play, *People in the Wind*, written sometime in the late 1940s.

Now, sequestered in Stockbridge, Inge was molding *Farther Off from Heaven* (written in 1945; produced in 1947 in Dallas) into *Dark*. The knowledge that he had not done anything in six or seven years that conformed to his own standard of genuine dramatic invention gnawed at him relentlessly and made him increasingly apprehensive. The nagging doubts and insecurities that seventeen years later led him to conclude that he could no longer write (Shuman [1989] ix–x; Inge, "William Inge" 19; Voss 267) were already becoming difficult for him to manage.

A turning point in Inge's life came when the November 1958 issue of *Harper's* reached the newsstands. Some would date his decline as an artist from that single event. The cover picture, a profile of Inge flanked by posters advertising his plays, seemed innocent enough. Within the cover was Robert Brustein's article, "The Men-Taming Women of William Inge." The thirty-one-year-old Brustein, bright, contentious, and ambitious, one year past his Ph.D., was then an assistant professor at Columbia University. He was not averse to drawing attention to himself even if he had to do it at the expense of someone as ill-equipped for combat as Inge.

Brustein's article, which contended that all Inge had done in nearly a decade in the theater was to endow "the commonplace with some depth" (57), reached the conclusion that Inge was a "fiddle with one string" (56). To many who read the article, Brustein was like a stray dog yapping at a tank, but in the long run, the stray dog prevailed not because it was right, necessarily, but because the tank was not up to withstanding the assault. What followed was to the detriment of William Inge personally and to American theater as well. Brustein's acrimony aroused all of Inge's insecurities; it left him wholly dispirited, emotionally paralyzed.

Much of the Brustein article, extremely well written and at times perceptive, is out of alignment. Brustein singled out Inge, seemingly because he had a need to attack a Broadway dramatist whose career was at its apogee, an American playwright who still seemed to be rising rather than falling into oblivion, as Williams at the time was beginning to do. Appearing in the prestigious *Harper's* gave Brustein's attack considerable weight and broad distribution. Inge realized this all too well and a few days after the piece appeared, he met in his Sutton Place apartment with three old friends, whose judgment he trusted—Tennessee Williams, Elia Kazan, and Barbara Baxley—to plot his strategy for dealing with Brustein. Inge, never a fighter, was utterly crushed by this first major attack of his work, and he took the criticism extremely personally, as well he might have, given the pervasive tone of the article. Although Baxley thought he should respond to the piece, Williams and Kazan persuaded him that he should not distinguish Brustein's charges by answering them; their opinion prevailed. Inge, who was at Stockbridge when he read the article, used the Gibsons' telephone to call Brustein (Gibson). During the telephone conversation, Inge broke down in tears, realizing how utterly incapable he was of jousting with Brustein at the level this rising critic had established for their combat.

The chief problem with the Brustein article is that it deals in half-truths and at times, as a result, it charges Inge with sins of which he was not guilty.[1] Brustein's greatest critical limitation in dealing with Inge was a big-city bias that prevented him from understanding in any depth what constitutes the small-town Midwest, the milieu fundamental to Inge's plays. If he found Inge dramatically banal, he placed the responsibility on Inge's doorstep, failing to acknowledge that what gave Inge's plays their verisimilitude was his depiction of the incredible banality of the lives his characters led. Inge's greatest asset—his ability to penetrate the routine existences of commonplace, sometimes boring people and to write effective drama from this penetration—came through in Brustein's assessment as a handicap for Inge rather than as the dramatic advantage it was.

Brustein's charge that Inge had written four plays with similar settings and broadly comparable situations was demonstrably true. This charge, however accurate it may have been, seemed a spurious basis on which to attack one of the nation's most gifted writers. To many who read the piece and responded to it at the time, Brustein seemed more self-serving than critically acute—and little has happened to dispel that notion. Inge's first four plays remain popular with audiences and receive favorable comment from critics and modern interpreters of drama.

The Brustein attack came at a critical time in Inge's artistic development. He was beginning to make headway in broadening the sphere within which he would work. *A Loss of Roses*, Inge's fifth Broadway play, was written from new material, and he considered it broader in scope than anything he had written previously. Random House was on the brink of publishing *4 Plays by William Inge*, and this gave him additional encouragement and reason for optimism. *Loss* was the straw to which Inge clung after the initial shock of Brustein's invective had subsided.

Unfortunately, *Loss* seemed jinxed from the beginning. Shirley Booth, cast in the lead as Helen Baird, demanded significant changes in the script, and Inge acceded to her demands, although he feared that he was weakening his play by doing so. Booth lasted through the Washington opening of *Loss*, but then suddenly withdrew from the cast because she thought the role of Lila Green, played by Carol Haney, overshadowed the Helen Baird role—and she was probably correct in this assertion. Betty Field was brought in quickly to replace Booth in the lead, and she had so little time to rehearse that she was not fully ready for the Broadway opening on November 28, 1959. Inge was distraught because he realized that he should not have brought *Loss* to Broadway in its present form, but it now seemed too late for him to turn back. He had put a great deal of his own money into the production, and to withdraw the play for further rehearsals and an opening after the Christmas holidays would have been financially devastating both to Inge and his backers.

Critical reaction to *A Loss of Roses* was more than simply negative; it was vindictive and often vitriolic. Inge, demolished by the tone of the criticism, left New York immediately to lick his wounds. He gravitated via Nashville and Florida to California where he delivered *Splendor in the Grass*, written mostly during the time he was in Florida. Its screenplay won Inge an Academy Award. As encouraging as this recognition was, however, Inge craved acceptance again on Broadway. Acceptance in Hollywood did not have the same meaning for him as a triumph in New York.

With his sights fixed on a victorious return to the New York theater world, Inge began work on a new play, *Natural Affection*. Like *A Loss of Roses*, it was an original script rather than a reworking of something he had written earlier, although seeds of the story are found in *Picnic*, where Hal Carter has a background not unlike that of Donnie Barker, and in *Dark*, where Sammy Goldbaum reveals a background that is also similar to Donnie's. As in *A Loss of Roses*, the central motivation in *Natural Affection* is the oedipal attraction a teen-aged boy, Donnie, feels for his mother, Sue Barker.

Sigmund Freud's early contention that all boys as they grow up pass through an oedipal stage in which they feel a sexual attraction to their mothers and a corresponding wish to kill their fathers was certainly well known to Inge after a dozen years in psychoanalysis. He had dealt quite openly with this theme as early as 1957 in *Dark*, where Sonny Flood's attachment to his mother is pronounced to the point that he cheers when the father and mother separate and is remorseful when they reconcile. Inge carried the theme much farther in *Loss* and farther still in *Natural Affection*. With his own mother's death in 1958, he felt freer to explore publicly themes he considered himself constrained from broaching openly while she was alive, able to see or read his plays.

In his introduction to *Natural Affection*, Inge discusses the violence in the play. He speaks of the ugliness of contemporary existence, a sentiment Sue Barker reiterates in her early lines, when she gets up in the morning, looks out the window, and comments on the ugliness of the scene below, a speech she repeats in almost identical words close to the end of the play (106). In his introduction, Inge tells of being unable to work in his apartment in New York City because of the racket being made across the street, where a fine old building is being torn down to make way for a modern monstrosity. He also tells of how he has given up reading world news, which he finds distressing, and now reads in his newspaper stories of teen-age violence like that which he recounts in *Affection*. He defends the psychological validity of having Donnie at the very end of the play commit the senseless murder of a woman he has never seen previously. Few could quarrel with the fact that such senselessly brutal acts do occur. That they can and do occur, however, is not really the issue. The question rather is this: In a play like *Natural Affection*, what artistic purpose does this violent act, from which playgoers and critics alike recoiled in horror as they watched the play, serve?

To answer that question, one must get to the heart of what Inge presents on both the conscious and unconscious levels on which the play operates. The basic conflict is oedipal. Donnie Barker at seventeen has spent three years on a work farm to which he has been sentenced for beating up a woman in Lincoln Park. The audience learns early that Donnie is capable of violence against women and also that he has had sexual experiences with women older than himself (13). The play's first scene also reveals that Sue Barker, now in her mid-thirties, is attractive and that she lives with Bernie Slovenk, a Cadillac salesman some years younger than she. Inge sets up an immediate conflict by having Donnie come to spend the Christmas holidays in the small apartment Sue and Bernie share. Sue asks Bernie to restrain himself sexually while Donnie is visiting, and Bernie is duly irritated by Sue's request. Sue does not yet know that Donnie has been given the opportunity to leave the work farm, which he wants urgently to do, if Sue will allow him to live with her.

Inge has Donnie arrive home when Sue is out shopping. His friend Gil, also from the work farm, is with him, and the conversation between them enables Inge to provide the audience with essential information in a graceful manner (26–33). During this scene, Donnie also wanders into his mother's bedroom and fondles her slip and panties, which she has left on a chair, suggesting that he has inherent sexual feelings for Sue or at least sexual curiosity about her. Soon after Sue gets home, she fuels the oedipal situation, which Donnie resists by pulling away from her when she wants to hold him close. She gives him Bernie's silk dressing robe to wear and allows him to wear Bernie's clothes when he goes out to shop for new clothing of his own (39). Unwittingly, she is at the unconscious level casting Donnie in the role of her lover, a man whom Donnie has not yet met but someone he will soon, in true oedipal fashion, want and need to have out of the way.

Further, Sue is also going to buy Donnie clothes as his Christmas gift; this is significant in view of the fact that she told Bernie early in the first scene that before he went to the work farm, Donnie "was shacking up with some old whore down on Division Street. She was buying him clothes. My Donnie! When he was only fourteen years old" (13). When Donnie asks Sue whether Bernie will mind that he is wearing his robe, Sue responds that he had better not mind because she bought it for him, again reinforcing the parallel of Donnie's earlier encounter with the woman on Division Street, someone probably close to Sue's age. As Donnie prepares for his bath, Sue catches a glimpse of his developing body and comments to him on how manly he is becoming (41).

Donnie and Bernie first meet under adverse circumstances. Bernie has just smashed a new Cadillac at the agency for which he works. The crash was with a woman driver and Bernie reveals an appalling male chauvinism in discussing the accident (46). His attitude toward women is somewhat contemptuous, and he reveals in the first scene his feelings of inadequacy because Sue is more successful than he (8). After the accident, Bernie turns to her as a child would to a mother, seeking consolation and nurture just as Donnie has turned to her immediately before to beg her to allow him to live with the two of them so that he won't have to return to the work farm. When Bernie comes home after his accident, he wants to relax in a bath, but Donnie has left the tub a mess, thereby heightening the tension between Bernie and Sue while simultaneously setting the scene for discord between Donnie and Bernie, who still have not met. Sue calms Bernie down and, rather than take his bath, he wants to take her to bed. This scene relates to the first scene, where abstaining from sex during Donnie's visit becomes an issue between the two of them. Sue thinks they should be chaste during Donnie's visit, a notion that does not sit well with Bernie.

Now Sue and Bernie are in the apartment by themselves. Bernie finally has Sue on the brink of acquiescing to his sexual advances when there is a knock at the door. It is Vince Brinkman, a neighbor from across the hall, an alcoholic who has sexual feelings for Bernie. This situation echoes in other Inge plays, like *Bus Stop*, in which one might construe Virgil's feelings for Bo to have a homoerotic base even though those feelings are not acted out. Similarly in *Picnic*, as Georges-Michel Sarotte has noted,[2] Alan Seymour has an underlying homoerotic attraction to Hal Carter. In both cases, as in the Vince Brinkman/Bernie Slovenk context, the surrogate father or older brother (mentor) figure is attracted to the younger man. Having heard that Bernie has been involved in an accident, Vince is now at his apartment door to inquire about his welfare and to bring him a bottle of English Leather after-shave lotion. He stays only long enough to make his inquiry, deliver his gift, and complain that the Internal Revenue Service is after him for additional taxes.

Vince is one of two autobiographical figures in the play, embodying the repressed homosexuality, alcoholism, and drug dependency with which Inge was then coping. Inge was also at this time being audited regularly by the Internal Revenue Service, so this allusion is straight from details of his life at that time. In a typical split that occurs when one writes autobiographical characters into plays, Inge also wrote Donnie as the young Inge who grappled with oedipal feelings that Inge began to understand more deeply as his psychoanalysis progressed. By this time he had a substantial technical understanding of Freudian psychology that he carried over into his writing.

When Vince leaves, Bernie and Sue smell the English Leather, and soon their libidinous mood has returned. They are about to go to bed, when Bernie asks Sue if she has locked the door. She has not, so she goes to lock it, and at that moment, Donnie, the other autobiographical character in the play, arrives, making the liaison between Sue and Bernie impossible. Vince can be read as having an unconscious jealousy for Bernie, Donnie as having a similar jealousy for Sue, and each is a party, though not by plan, to keeping Sue and Bernie from their sexual act. Sue reveals her feelings about Donnie's sexuality, however, in more overt ways. Before Donnie arrives for his Christmas visit, Bernie suggests to Sue that he might fix him up with a girl (13), but Sue vetoes the idea and a few lines later expresses her disgust at Donnie's having had his earlier encounter with the older woman on Division Street, showing by her intensity as much jealousy as maternal concern, the dividing line between the two being hard at times to discern.

At times, Sue is not unlike Inge's own mother, Maude Gibson Inge, a righteous, capable woman, sufficiently independent to run her family during her husband's week-long absences when he was away on his selling trips. Maude was puritanical to the point that—if Inge's mildly fictionalized account of her in *My Son Is a Splendid Driver* is accurate—she left her husband after their wedding night and tried to return to her mother, who persuaded her to be patient with her new husband and to return to him (Voss 6–7). Whether or not this account is factual, Maude Inge was Victorian in her outlook, and at times Sue speaks lines that could have come directly from Inge's mother. One such occurs when she is trying to convince Bernie to be chaste during Donnie's stay with them. Bernie objects to Sue's proposal, and she responds, "If I couldn't control myself for a few days, I'd be ashamed to admit it" (15). The only other time Sue uses the word *control* in the play occurs when Donnie has asked Sue about his real father. She tells him about how he ran away before Donnie's birth, and Donnie becomes enraged, saying that he hates him and that if he were there now, he would kill him (40–41). Sue tells him, "I don't like to see you lose control of yourself that way" (41) and suggests that he take a tranquilizer the doctor has prescribed to calm him. In this scene, the classic Freudian interpretation of the oedipal problem is obvious: the male child, jealous of the father's hold on the mother (even though in this case Donnie's real father is not present physically), harbors a death wish for the father. When Sue tells Donnie that she does not like his losing control, her words, particularly in the light of her earlier admonition to Bernie, have a psycho-sexual impact.

In the last scene of Act One, Bernie is upset because he has wrecked one of his agency's Cadillacs, but there is an undercurrent of his insecurity about and animosity toward Donnie, whom he has not yet met. Bernie wants a bath to relax his nerves, but Donnie has left the tub dirty. Bernie puts on the robe Donnie has worn and immediately complains because it smells of the disinfectant used at the work farm. The olefactory references are quite conscious. Bernie buys Sue a large bottle of jasmine perfume for Christmas; Vince gives Bernie a bottle of English Leather; Donnie, smelling of disinfectant, has the same institutional smell he had when he was in the orphanage as a child and Sue came to visit him smelling lusciously of perfume. Donnie would nuzzle into her neck where the smell of perfume was strongest; Sue went so far as to leave Donnie one of her handkerchiefs, whose corner she had soaked in perfume, and Donnie, then a mere child, kept it with him as a reminder of his mother (35–36).

Inge makes Bernie appear infantile and self-pitying in his dealings with Sue in the last scene of Act One. He thereby reinforces for the audience Sue's dilemma of being caught between two men she loves and of having to make a decision that will essentially eliminate one of them in their contest for her affections. Donnie, who expresses his hatred for his birth father, has every reason to want Bernie out of the way. Bernie is the obstacle to Donnie's staying home rather than returning to the work farm, and finally Donnie gains the upper hand by catching Bernie in the kitchen during a party kissing Claire Brinkman, Vince's wife, with whom he has been having a casual affair. In an attempt to discredit Bernie, he quickly reveals this information to Sue, and this revelation precipitates the ultimate clash between Bernie and Donnie. After Sue and Bernie quarrel, Sue, having demeaned (emasculated?) Bernie because he earns less than she, tells him to get out, thereby seeming to leave the way open for Donnie to live with her. Prior to this altercation, Sue and Bernie were to take the Brinkmans and Donnie to the Playboy Club. When Vince passes out, however, he is left at home to sleep off his drunkenness, and Bernie makes a point of saying that Claire has a new escort, Donnie. Claire makes a point of mentioning the age gap, but Donnie not only escorts Claire, but also teaches her how to do the twist (52), whose sexually suggestive gyrations recur in the play when Donnie twice plays at full volume a twist record he has bought and at the very end of the play when he puts that record on the turntable after he has committed a murder.

When they get home from the Playboy Club, it is Bernie, while Sue is out of the room, who makes a point of getting Donnie to take Claire to her apartment (99), knowing that she will go to bed with anything that moves and having—earlier in the play—set her up in an assignation with one of his friends (21). Having Donnie go off with Claire serves two purposes for Inge: first, it clears the apartment of people so that Bernie and Sue can have an argument in which Sue expresses her disgust at Claire for having pawed Donnie all night. This gives Bernie his opening to say that Donnie danced with Sue the whole evening and that he never took his eyes off her (100–01), again heightening the play's overpowering oedipal overtones. Also, Bernie reveals that Donnie is "across the hall banging Claire" (101). Actually, Donnie is not having sex with Claire, but Bernie's suggestion is almost more than Sue can bear. She moves toward the door to go and rescue him and, in the course of restraining her, Bernie accuses Sue of having "the hots for him yourself"(101).

The play's resolution comes quickly. Bernie has spent the night across the hall at the Brinkmans', where an orgy is taking place. He apparently distances himself from the orgy, but he returns to his and Sue's apartment on Christmas morning to get his things and leave, presumably forever. Donnie is elated. He has dispatched his surrogate father. Now he fantasizes about the things he and his mother can do together. He will get a job, he will take Sue on trips, he will take her to restaurants, and they will not have to move to a larger apartment, which was the one stumbling block to his staying at home rather than returning to the work farm (112). Sue, who up to this point has consistently been trying to get Donnie to show more affection, is now frightened and warns Donnie not to come so close to her. Apparently panicking because of the oedipal feelings she is now becoming aware of, she pushes Donnie aside and goes after Bernie. Donnie offers himself to fill the void that Bernie's leaving will create. He says that he will keep his mother company, but Sue cannot accept this offer.

Now in a panic of his own because he faces the almost certain possibility of having to return to the work farm, Donnie puts his arms around Sue, begging her to keep him. She struggles to free herself from his grasp and, in a fit of panic and frustration, she calls Donnie a worthless kid she never wanted, saying that she is not going to throw away her happiness for him (113–14). The instant these words are spoken, she tries to retract them, but it is too late for that. Donnie has been totally rejected, and he knows it. Just then, a besotted woman Donnie has never seen before comes from the Brinkmans' apartment into Sue's kitchen, grabs Donnie and kisses him full on the mouth. She tells him that she could go for someone like him. Donnie grabs a knife and pounces on the woman, stabbing her repeatedly, orgiastically. As the curtain falls, Donnie has turned from the dead woman and pours himself a glass of milk as the phonograph plays the twist record he has put on (115).

In Donnie's irrational act, Inge seemed to be venting a great deal of the anger with which he had lived since Brustein began an attack on him that was only the beginning of a great deal of critical condemnation. When Inge and I talked about the play, he seemed unable to realize that the reason for its failure was not that it was bad drama. Indeed, I tried to make him realize that the play actually had great strengths but that he had spent ninety-nine percent of it making the audience feel sympathy and eventually love for Donnie then had pulled the rug out from under it. When Inge argued that things like this happen regularly in real life, I could not offer any counter-argument except to say that audiences will not put up with this sort of extreme reversal, particularly when the bloody, violent act takes place before their very eyes. I tried to make him see that the Greeks got away with acts as bloody as this one by having the violence occur offstage and be reported by a messenger. I reminded him of how misused audiences of *Dark* had felt when he had Sammy Goldbaum, who was one of Donnie's dramatic prototypes, commit suicide. *Dark* was saved from a fate similar to that suffered by *Affection* only because the suicide occurred offstage, because Sammy was not a central character, and because the event took place in the middle of the play, not at the end of it.

I had the feeling in my conversations with Inge about *Natural Affection* that he was using the ending of the play to exorcise some of his own demons, that perhaps the victim of the stabbing represented for him the New York critics who had all but destroyed him by now. One line in *Natural Affection* can be construed as reflecting Inge's subconscious reaction to what the critics had done to him. The line occurs when Bernie tells Sue about his father, an alcoholic who would come home and beat his children. Sue asks Bernie if he cannot feel pity for him, and Bernie responds, "No. Ya don't feel pity for anyone in this life until he's through, washed up, had it. Ya don't feel pity till then. It's an insult if you do" (50). The critics had made Inge feel that he was washed up, and one of the things he feared most was pity. Certainly, Inge never again wrote anything as violent as *Natural Affection*. The autobiographical character and protagonist in his next play, *Where's Daddy?*, was relatively benign, representing possibly an Inge who was trying to prove to the world—and to himself—that he had mellowed.

For all its flaws, *Natural Affection* is a well-crafted play and perhaps deserves reconsideration. A production of it staged in Los Angeles in 1988 at the Zephyr Theatre, directed by Lorenzo DeStefano, minimized the stabbing scene by having it occur behind a sofa, out of sight of the audience. Even this solution is imperfect; possibly some director should omit that scene altogether and have the information reported as the curtain falls.

Notes

1. Valuable responses to Brustein's article are Juhnke's "Inge's Women: Robert Brustein and the Feminine Mystique" and Voss's essay in this collection.

2. In Sarotte's book, originally published by Flammarion in Paris in 1976 as *Comme un frère, comme un amant: l'homsexualité masculine dans le roman et le théâtre américains de Herman Melville à James Baldwin*, he identifies a number of homoerotic overtones in Inge's work and identifies his little-known one-act play, "The Boy in the

Basement," as central to an understanding of homoeroticism in Inge's writing. Sarotte points out the mentor relationships that exist for a number of the older men in Inge's plays who are identified closely with younger ones. See especially his chapter "William Inge: 'Homosexual Spite' in Action" (121–33).

Works Cited

Brustein, Robert. "The Men-Taming Women of William Inge." *Harper's* Nov. 1958: 52–57. Print.
Gibson, William. "For Bill Inge." *New York Times* 24 July 1973: 35. Print.
Inge, William. *Natural Affection*. New York: Random House, 1963. Print.
———. *My Son Is a Splendid Driver*. New York: Little, Brown, 1971. Print.
———. "William Inge: The Last Interview." Interview by Lloyd Steele. *Los Angeles Free Press* 22 June 1973: 18–22. Print.
Juhnke, Janet. "Inge's Women: Robert Brustein and the Feminine Mystique." *Kansas Quarterly* 18.4 (1986): 103–12. Print.
Sarotte, Georges-Michel. "William Inge: 'Homosexual Sprite' in Action." *Like a Brother, Like a Lover: Male Homosexuality in the American Novel and Theatre from Herman Melville to James Baldwin*. Trans. Richard Miller. New York: Anchor/Doubleday, 1978. 121–33. Print.
Shuman, R. Baird. *William Inge*. New York: Twayne, 1965. Print.
———. *William Inge*. Rev. ed. Boston: Twayne, 1989. Print.
Voss, Ralph F. *A Life of William Inge: The Strains of Triumph*. Lawrence: University Press of Kansas, 1989. Print.

Unnatural Affection: Sons and Mothers
Therese Jones

"There is not a woman in the world the possession of whom is as precious as that of the truths which she reveals to us by causing us to suffer."—Marcel Proust, *The Sweet Cheat Gone* [10]

Two years before his suicide in 1973, William Inge published his last work, a novel-memoir titled *My Son Is a Splendid Driver* (1971).[1] Just as Raymond Roussel's last work, *How I Wrote Certain of My Books*, provided Michel Foucault with an implement for unlocking the mysteries of the poet-dramatist's other texts, so too does *Driver* provide us with the kind of access to Inge's work and life that Foucault described in *Death and the Labyrinth*:

> By giving us a key at the last moment, this final text would be like a first retrospective of the works with a dual purpose: it opens the structure of certain texts closest to the surface, but indicates for these and the other works the need for a series of keys [7].

Inge's final text becomes both a means of understanding—or unlocking—the artist's own relationship to his work and of interpreting the dominant pattern of oedipal relationships throughout his drama—an "answer key" if you will. An examination of his unpublished manuscripts, a collection which includes the earliest fragment and the first completed version of another autobiographical work, *The Dark at the Top of the Stairs*, valorizes the novel-memoir as a key for recovering the origins of Inge's compulsive configuration of an oedipal triangle and his exhaustive exploration of how an unresolved oedipal conflict, unresolved because actively fostered by the mother, determines the sexual and social dysfunction of her son.

The writer's ambivalence towards his own mother—to whom he dedicated

My Son Is a Splendid Driver—is borne out in the novel-memoir as is his need to redeem himself for never measuring up to her standards of masculinity as did his older brother, aptly named Jule in the story:

> For a few moments, I stood there, a child in the woods. And then I became a man again, humbled and a little embarrassed to realize what an infantile love I still bore her. It was this very love that had made me miserable for so many years, and made me crave some unattainable prominence that would finally raise me above Jule in her esteem.... It was a love that had made me hate her ... [220].

Inge's end was an "unattainable prominence," the public's unequivocal admiration and unreserved acceptance that would simultaneously negate his mother's rejection of him and restore her unconditional love for him; his means was the transformational power of writing.[2] In this work and in the plays and stories in which fear of rejection is the controlling motivation of a male character, maternal rejection is the initial, terrifying punishment for the expression of sexual desire. In general, this is a mother who has created and sustained a close-binding, intimate relationship with her son and who either turns in horror from its incestuous energy or righteously condemns him for latent or overt homosexuality, a consequence of the mother-son dyad in the dramatic and fictional world of Inge who was influenced by the established opinion of the psychiatric industry regarding the etiology of homosexuality.[3]

The dynamic Inge presents is that the revelation of one's untoward sexual desires—either incestuous or homosexual desires—incites maternal rejection which prefigures cultural and societal rejection. Moreover, that initial rejection is rendered more poignant and more unjust by Inge's consistent portrayal of the mother as ultimately responsible for the son's unacceptable cathexes, female surrogates or male homosexuals. The novel-memoir and the successive versions of Inge's memory play present a compelling justification for a homosexual orientation. He constructs a persuasive argument that displaces responsibility onto the mother and absolves the son of guilt, a balance with which he could live: "I suppose [*The Dark at the Top of the Stairs*] represents my belated attempt to come to terms with the past, to rearrange its parts and make them balance..." (Frenz 131). Writing itself presented an ongoing opportunity for Inge to try to accept what his mother and his society deemed as aberration and insufficiency[4]: "He didn't approve of [his homosexuality] himself ... in his own mind he was truly not at peace" (Burgess 465) and presented as well an opportunity to fantasize possible responses to rejection, an imaginative process both compensatory and empowering.[5]

The central conflict of *My Son Is a Splendid Driver* is the painful coming of age of the narrator, Joey, who must adjust to life in a "nervous matriarchy" (6) and constantly suffer his mother's "belittling comparison" of him with his older brother (119). When describing the conditions of his own boyhood, Inge expressed feeling dominated and devirilized by his mother: "I thought at times that Mother made me a physical coward, because she was quite a high-strung woman.... She sapped my physical adventurousness and I felt held down.... It gave me a very early insight into neurotic women" (Inge, "The Dark" 62). Throughout his work, Inge privileges the parental role in child development, and he had almost unanimous medical support for the view that dominating women impaired the personality development of their sons. Psychiatric orthodoxy before 1973 displayed prominently in clinical works such as Irving Bieber's *Homosexuality: A Psychiatric Study* (1962) accounted for a homosexual adaptation as the "outcome of exposure to highly pathologic parent-child relationships and early life situation" (173).[6] From the outset of his novel-memoir, Inge hints at such a pathologic dimension to the relationship of the mother with her sons. Her "belittling comparison" fosters the narrator's deep-seated insecurity about his masculinity, "an uncertain thing at best" (136), an overwhelming sense of inadequacy, and nearly impenetrable defenses against intimacy: "And I know I felt frightened by my compulsion to be excluded from any personal relationship that threatened to be binding" (163).

To understand the significance of Inge's last attempt to transform himself through a novelistic record of his maturation, one needs to be aware of the value that he placed on psychoanalytic technique as remedy and Freudian psychology as a system of meaning. Inge extolled the virtues of psychoanalysis, designing much of his work to accord with Freudian theories of the psychosexual development of the male child: "Psychoanalysis seems to me to be the great learning experience that the Twentieth Century can provide ... all writers who have undergone analysis have been grateful for its broadening influence upon their insight" (Freeman 173–74); "[analysis] for me was a valuable experience"(Inge, "Playwright"). Ultimately, however, the insight into himself and others, enhanced and codified by an accessible formula for understanding how he came to be psychically and sexually, seemed not to provide Inge with either the control or the solace that he needed. At the height of his success in 1958, he again described the experience as valuable but also as alienating and disorienting:

> "When the analysis began to take hold, it was as though something had uprooted the foundations of my life and set them down somewhere else inside me in a new form.... It was like looking at life through another window in which you see faces at a different slant and don't quite recognize them for a while" [Inge, "The Dark" 63].

The occasion for these comments was the success of his then current play, *The Dark at the Top of the Stairs*. To date, it was the most autobiographical of his works and the first to focus directly on an oedipal situation.[7] *A Loss of Roses* and *Natural Affection* followed, also dramatizations of nearly pathological, explosive relationships between mothers and sons. That Inge's experience with psychoanalysis gave a shape and a focus to *Dark* is a viewpoint supported by R. Baird Shuman: "It was not until he had undergone extensive psychoanalytic treatment ... that he was able to achieve the deeper perspective which is evident in his finished product..." (19).

Inge's first full-length play was a version of *Dark at the Top of the Stairs* entitled *Farther Off from Heaven,* which Margo Jones produced in June 1947 (*4 Plays* ix). By his own account, Inge continued to work on the material for approximately six years (Frenz 131), through intense psychotherapy and at least one hospitalization. When he spoke about revising the play, he indicated that it was a process of looking backwards and inwards, of confronting the past and making sense of it—comments appropriate to the psychoanalytic process as well: "Part of the play is a resurrection of material I was working on about ten years ago, material that I was unable then to bring into focus ... at times, I felt almost haunted" (Inge, "Culled" 1, 3). "[*The Dark at the Top of the Stairs*] was when I really first tried to examine my past, to get certain things out into the open" (Inge, "William Inge: Last" 18).

What appears to be the earliest, certainly the least developed and structured extant version of the material is entitled "Memories of Green Summer." Inge neither completed nor dated this draft, but elements and characters that find their way into *Farther Off from Heaven* and *The Dark at the Top of the Stairs* seem to have their genesis here as he began to shape childhood memories into dramatic form. A comparison of all three versions indicates that what Inge was finally able to "bring into focus" was the complex dynamic of a mother-son dyad, that what he described as the process of "[getting] things out into the open" yielded the dramatic presentation of his own oedipal attachment and its probable consequences. Side by side, the different versions of the material present a kind of simplified chronicle or case history of a son's changing and increasingly complicated views of and feelings toward his mother.

In "Memories of Green Summer," Inge names the characters portraying himself and his siblings but affixes only the generic labels of Mother and Father to the parents. The choice establishes point of view; Sonny, Inge's childhood self, is at the center of the drama and will remain so throughout all revisions of the material. The words and actions of the parent characters are important primarily because of their impact on their children's lives. Signified by the absence of names, the parents are not developed characters but rather are idealized and sentimentalized types—fantasy figures who are selflessly protective, extravagantly affectionate, and completely accepting of their young son.

Inge sketches a maternal character most accurately described as a sexualized madonna, a fantasy that we recognize as common but that seems, nevertheless, uncommonly transparent here:

> Now a beautiful woman comes graciously down the stairs, wearing a flowing negligee. Her smile is like a blessing. She picks [Sonny] up in her arms and caresses him, smothering him with kisses.
> "You worry your Mommie when she doesn't know where you are. Now, you may run out to the kitchen and see what's left in the cookie jar" ["Memories" 1–5].

The father character is rendered just as fantastically. He not only permits his eight-year old son's infantile dependency but also defends the boy's timid, effeminate behavior, behavior which is antithetical to the father's traditional gender presentation—"The Father is a big ruggedly good looking man who exudes the outdoors ... a cigar in his mouth"—and behavior which provokes the aggressiveness of Sonny's peers toward him: "He's the youngest we got. There's nothin' wrong with our baby. He's gonna make people sit up and take notice one a these days" ("Memories" 3–5). Inge dramatized what amounts to a child's fantasy version of the oedipal triangle: gratification from mother rather than denial; complicity with father rather than rivalry; acceptance and empowerment rather than guilt and the threat of castration.

In the early scenes of the play, the father figure is essentially another mother figure who is completed by the child, prepared to satisfy its needs, and referring to the child as their baby.[8] However, the father changes radically in the space of a few pages, blaming the mother for misdirecting or retarding the boy's development so that Sonny will neither defend himself nor participate in traditional male activities like hunting: "His Mother's pampered him. He'll turn into a lounge lizard" ("Memories" 11). As Father becomes the source of authority, the feared and hated rival, or the signifier which demands that the subject be bound to gender, the mother becomes culpable for the child's failure to separate from her and be gendered "normally."

The next version of the material, *Farther Off from Heaven*, sees an end to fantasy and a beginning to the more realistic and more complex treatment of what would eventually become a successful play. Inge began to develop the conflict between Sonny and his mother, an oedipal power struggle. The family dynamic presented is what the psychiatric community had defined as the "classical pattern" of the triangular system most likely to produce a homosexual son: a close-binding, intimate mother paired with a detached, hostile father (Bayer 32). The opinion fell in line with Freud, who generalized about any number of factors "[favoring] inversion," such as intense attachment to the mother, the disappearance of the father, and "quarrels between the parents and unhappy marital relations" (561, 619). Emphasis on the triangular system ultimately led Bieber to conclude that a homosexual son becomes the "interactional focal point upon whom the most profound parental psychopathology [is] concentrated" (Bieber 310). The statement goes far in capturing the family dynamic that Inge most often dramatized.[9]

Although there is scant biographical evidence to prove conclusively that Inge was familiar with psychoanalytic theory per se during the writing of *Farther Off from Heaven*, his past and current life experience increases the likelihood that he was aware of contemporary psychoanalytic opinion on male homosexuality. He had already undergone treatment for mental problems; he was personally and professionally involved with Tennessee Williams, a homosexual whose own work was psychologically oriented; and though his sexual life was not open, it was active during these years.[10] This was a time when Inge seemed to be trying to understand and realize himself both artistically and sexually. Charles Burgess, examining the St. Louis years, also highlights a connection between relief from sexual restrictions and creative expression during the time when Inge was absorbed with material from childhood and adolescence (467). In his biography, Voss notes how the anonymity of the city "helped him both to indulge and to cloak his ... homosexual propensities" (78).

In *Farther Off from Heaven*, the mother character, now named Sarah, substitutes Sonny for her attractive and independent husband, a traveling salesman like Inge's own father. Resenting her financial dependence and sexual need, Sarah empowers herself by encouraging her son's dependency and growing rivalry with his father. Money becomes the currency of sublimated desire; Sarah uses money as a weapon against her husband, insinuating that he can neither provide materially for his children nor sexually for his wife, and as a measure of control with her son, compelling him to defer gratification until she permits. Inge also began to coalesce the symbolism of the play with the device of the dark at the top of the stairs which signifies the two repressed wishes of the oedipal complex: Sonny "hopes [his father] stays away" so that his mother will continue to accompany him upstairs to bed, indulging his fear of the dark (*Farther Off* I, 22).

There are two important differences between *Farther Off from Heaven* and *The Dark at the Top of the Stairs* that point to the impact of Inge's psychoanalytic experience on the revision of the material. The first is the change Inge made in the ending of *Dark at the Top of the Stairs*. In *Farther Off from Heaven*, the parents reconcile uneasily—there is too much sexual tension for complete domestic tranquility—but well. Possibly for the first time, they articulate childish fears and selfish motives. Sonny reacts petulantly to this reconciliation, sensing his parents' exclusive intimacy. However, when his father asks Sonny to fetch something from upstairs, he is able to overcome both jealousy and fear. The act marks a significant transition in Sonny's psychosexual development. He can break the intense neurotic attachment to his mother, identifying healthily with a male model, his father:

> Sonny gets up unwillingly. Walks slowly to the bottom of the stairs and looks up at the darkness beyond him. Sonny's great moment of victory is unwitnessed. He hesitates for a second, looks at [his father] with childish hate. Then rushes up the stairs.
> Here, Dad, I went upstairs and got your magazine. He can speak up like a man now. Dad, may I have fifteen cents to go to the movies tonight ... please? [*Farther Off* III, 28–29].

In *Dark at the Top of the Stairs*, Sonny's final action is not a positive, successful step towards fully realizing manhood, the construct embodied in the father who is traditionally masculine, sexually potent, and the real controller of family finances. "*With a heroic gesture of defiance*," Sonny hurls his piggy bank towards the fireplace, retrieving money his mother ordered him to save (*4 Plays* 303). While he may be breaking out of the dyadic relationship, his motivation appears negative and self-destructive. He is not acting but violently reacting: to his mother's desire to ascend the stairs to her husband, to his inability to replace the father, to his own desire for pleasure that Mother could have allowed but has forbidden. Forced to surrender his mother, Sonny moves toward autonomy but also aloneness—there is no father figure, no male model, either beside him or interacting with him: "*SONNY looks at [his mother] with accusing eyes.... CORA starts up the stairs ... stopping for one final look at her departing son. And SONNY, just before going out the door, stops for one final look at his mother, his face full of confused understanding*" (304).

The exchange of meaningful glances between mother and son and the uncertainty about Sonny's future—he is poised on a threshold—follow much more believably and coherently given the psychology of the characters, the structure of the play as a domestic drama, and a much more sophisticated and sure handling of an oedipal crisis. Gone are any remnants of the fantasy play that still informed the ending of *Farther Off from Heaven*. Inge's presentation of oedipal situations became more knowledgeable and more complex as he constantly experimented with the family dynamics and social conditions most conducive to the formulation of problematic attachments between mother and son and as he explored a variety of resultant behaviors in the male. However, his personal wish remained quite simple and fixed: to return once again to that threshold moment when he was neither forced to separate nor to understand completely. Just a few months before his death, Inge revealed that of any age, he would "rather be ten," Sonny's age in the play (Inge, "William Inge: Last" 21).

The second important change that Inge made in the revision process was the introduction of Sammy Goldbaum. In *Dark at the Top of the Stairs*, Sammy functions as Sonny's mirror image, enabling Inge to reinforce some effects and to suggest others from an oedipal attachment. There is a striking resemblance between the characters but also some distortion (age, background), as well as some reversal (Sammy's absent mother, Sonny's present mother). Both characters lack male role models: Sonny's father is away, and Sammy has never known his. Both characters privilege the relationship with mother over any other, and both are outcasts by virtue of their difference: Sonny is a "sissy," and Sammy is Jewish. Inge places responsibility on their respective mothers for their difference and hence, their alienation—an alienation that prefigures the social and cultural marginality of the homosexual and intensifies the ultimate maternal rejection.

According to Sammy, his mother is not "Jewish at all" (*4 Plays* 266) and has in effect abandoned him because of the demands of her career. Exaggerating maternal otherness in the relationship, Inge creates Sammy's mother as a stereotypically blond (266), beautiful, and larger-than-life "moving picture" actress (265) Her refusal to interact with her child in any characteristically maternal way and her overripe sexuality ("My mother has been married ... a few times" [265]) fuel the imagination and desire of her adoring son. Sammy's fantasy relationship with his real-life movie star mother mirrors Sonny's fantasy relationships with his scrapbook movie stars:

> My mother doesn't have a place for me, where she lives. She ... she just doesn't know what else to do with me. But you mustn't misunderstand about my mother. She's really a very lovely person. I guess every boy thinks his mother is very beautiful, but my mother really is.... One time we were together, though.... She let me take her to dinner and to a show and to a dance. Just like we were sweethearts. It was the most wonderful time I ever had [271].

The anti–Semitic persecution that Sammy encounters at the country club dance replays in the social arena his Gentile mother's abandonment and rejection, and he commits suicide.

Sammy and Sonny, even resembling one another in name, are narcissistically drawn together, and there is much homoerotic play between them, such as the game of "wild West rider" with Sonny astraddle the older boy (269). There is also the business of Sammy brandishing his sword and then handing it over to Sonny who lunges about, exclaiming how he wants "to show people" (267). His desire to exhibit something for Sammy inspires Sonny's spontaneous recitation of Hamlet's soliloquy, and his "To be or not to be" performance playfully formulates the question of his future sexual orientation. Inge establishes an undeniable link between Sonny's oedipal strivings and homosexual attraction to Sammy in this dramatization of a male seeking a partner who resembles himself and who will love him in the way he would have his mother love him (Bayer 24).

The playwright's experience in psychoanalysis provided both a means into the reservoir of memories and a method to organize and interpret them. He suggested that the composing process was an extension of the cathartic "talking cure," recovery through discovery of repressed traumas worked through by means of and within language: "[a play] may come out of memories or it may come out of one's desire to deal with experience. To get it down on paper. The writer, maybe, just feels he wants to be honest with himself in some way. To face something in an honest way" (Wager 115). Although Inge obsessively drew upon his own experience for plays and stories, he just as obsessively thwarted any direct connections in the public mind between his life and work. When asked about his almost exclusive focus on family life, Inge responded in typical discursive fashion, embedding information about the source of his material—childhood memories—and tentatively generalizing from experience as well as bias: "The American family does concern me. And I do have my childhood memories to draw upon. One might say that our greatest problems stem from the family" (Inge, "William Inge: Playwright" 53). His hesitation at disclosing biographical facts derived as much from a fear of rejection as a resistance to closure which would have deprived him of a past that he needed as the means of modifying his way of being, of actively engaging in the process of becoming, through language. Critics like Harold Clurman intuited Inge's relationship to his material and more significantly, his motive for repeatedly dramatizing disturbed mother-son relationships: "these plays reveal the sorrow, pain and protest which were always latent ... but which for a while he succeeded in tempering with ... perhaps too heavy a dependence on the therapeutic aspects of Freudian psychology" (91–92).

My Son Is a Splendid Driver is no exception to a dependence on Freudian psychology as Inge isolates the far-reaching effects of a disturbed family dynamic—what he calls an "ancient curse" (*Driver* 142). The title of the novel-memoir is the inscription of the psychological, emotional, and sexual configuration that is imprinted upon the narrator in childhood and that he compulsively replicates in adult relationships. Although it is his own story, the title neither directly refers to Joey nor is it something he says, subverting our expectation that the "I" narrator is the son so highly spoken of. Rather, it is his mother's line, the refrain that accompanies both hymns of praise for her older son and sighs of disappointment in her younger son who can never replace the lost Jule, dead at twenty-one[11]: "You're a good driver, Joey, but not as good as Jule. Jule was a *splendid* driver" (119). By using that line as the title, Inge directs our attention to the relationship between Mother and Jule and its impact on the narrator: the model for nearly ideal, adult male-female relations in the story of Inge's childhood is an oedipal relationship, one that the mother consistently demonstrates to be more fulfilling, more romantic, and less degrading than the inadequate and shameful union of the traditional conjugal couple.

That Jule, in Mother's estimation, is not merely a good or able driver but a splendid driver illustrates the romantic nature of the relationship. The line functions as the verbal token of an exclusive and intimate bond between mother and son, a bond created by circumstances (Jule's birth order, the father's absence, the mother's emotional neediness) and characterized by the pair's assumption of the conventional gender roles of romance. Jule eagerly plays the stalwart and chivalrous protector of Mother's frail and fluttering womanhood. His exaggerated masculinity only reinforces his knight-like gallantry, making him the *beau ideal* of his mother and the imposing rival of his younger brother.

Inge begins his story with a family trip to Colorado, showing how secure Jule's position as "man of the family" has become. The most vivid illustration is Jule's place in the family car—behind the wheel with Mother beside him; Joey, little sister, and Father ride in the back seat. The displacement of the legitimate father-husband by Jule who jealousy guards his position of power and favor is obvious, and equally obvious is Mother's collusion in the arrangement: "Jule drove the entire distance, all day, not allowing Father to relieve him. 'I always feel safe with Jule at the wheel,' Mother purred, sitting proudly beside him. 'Even when we're going fast'" (43).

As a narrating adult recreating his childhood, Joey is intellectually capable of speculation about the unusually intimate relationship between his brother and mother which figures as the center of the story: "I hate now to call their love 'unnatural' because it seemed to us all the most natural thing in the world. We all knew ... that Mother loved Jule more than any living creature, but we had never heard of Oedipus and never felt it necessary to give that love a name" (66). One question that the passage raises is when did it become necessary to name the particular kind of love featured here, limiting its possible significations and restricting it to predominantly negative connotations? For Inge, the time was this moment in his novel-memoir. As Marilyn Mitchell points out, this is the only explicit reference to oedipal love in his work (299). Although the narrator hates to call such love "unnatural," he does just that in the passage. Moreover, he presents it as such, reinforcing a general impression of abnormality (at the very least, unwholesomeness) and assigning specific responsibility to the mother who initiates and nurtures such a relationship. Luther

Inge, Jr., the only child of Inge's older brother, characterized his uncle's novelistic account of the family as a "story of hate" (L. Inge), uncannily choosing the same word as the narrator chose to express his aversion to labeling the relationship between Mother and Jule.

However, the most suggestive linkage comes within the text itself. The other instance in which the narrator expresses a reluctance to specify behavior (again, doing what he says he does not want to do by reporting how he hated or feared to do it) is his first adult sexual encounter with another male: "tentative, groping, unfulfilled experiences ... that I never had the courage to classify with any name" (*Driver* 138). Within the full account of the incident, the narrator represents his role as a passive one, behavior consistent in a section replete with denials: "I cannot say that I minded or felt repelled ..." (139). "I could not think that [he] was homosexual because he was thoroughly masculine.... I never asked myself if I was rejecting a love that I might need or enjoy. I never dared tell myself that ... any kind of sexual love could have existed between us. I'll never know whether it could have" (140–41). Inge goes to some length to ensure that the narrator appear innocent. However, the preferred method of denial—choosing not to encode some experience—is becoming a pattern in the text while the presence of absent names highlights a causal link between an oedipal relationship and a homosexual orientation.[12] By mentioning his reluctance to affix specific labels to the relationships between his mother and brother and between himself and his college friend, the narrator labels and connects them.

In addition, Inge styles the narrator's would-be lover in the fashion of Mother's love object and his rival: "[Bob Luther] often went to the campus wearing high laced boots and whipcord pants like Jule. He had been raised on a ranch in Colorado in the company of men ... [and] was good looking, strong and well made" (138). Continuing the play with "names," Inge uses his own older brother's, Luther, for the character. The decision to do so may be what prompted his nephew to call this a "story of hate." The brother's name is the last in the string of names that cannot be named, forming a code that is central to understanding the text: Oedipus, homosexuality, Luther. Inge places himself within and without a chain of signification, words which bind the subject to gender and to gender-oriented desire: within as the powerless subject defined by these signifiers and without as the artist arranging any number of signifiers to transform himself in the process of writing an autobiography.

The chain of words is imaged in the seating arrangements of the family car which present the Freudian schematization of the oedipal triangle. Joey is back-seated, a child trying to situate himself between a powerful male in the driver's seat and a beloved mother on the passenger side. The narrator's adult relationships throughout the text are similarly configured: erotic triangles composed of himself and attractive, hyper-masculine males and fragile, often neurotic females. Inevitably, Joey defers to his rival, and inevitably, the intimate bond between males becomes more significant to him than the outcome of the rivalry.

A suicide attempt initiates the process of psychotherapy, forcing the narrator to scrutinize and to re-evaluate his relationship with his mother. However, there remains a vestige of his breakdown: "a traumatic fear of driving an automobile.... So, for several years, I did not attempt to make this unconscious competition with the long-deceased Jule" (207). Biographical information supports Inge's own inability to drive; his personal secretary once described the playwright as phobic.[13]

To any reader of *My Son Is a Splendid Driver*, Inge's death in a car, the result of carbon monoxide poisoning, seems equally ironic and appropriate. As he himself said of suicide: "We always find reasons ... motivations we had previously overlooked" (*4 Plays* ix),[14] and the novel-memoir demands that we search. Inge's final act in the driver's seat of a car going nowhere was not an act of submission to his mother's, the psychiatric industry's, or society's judgment that he would never be a splendid driver, never be a man, but an act of defiance that he alone would write the ending to a story that he described in the prologue to *My Son Is a Splendid Driver* as "the life and the lives that I knew" (3).

Notes

1. Family members and scholars alike consider the novel-memoir to be an autobiographical text. In a taped interview with Luther Inge, Jr., Inge's nephew, he described *My Son Is a Splendid Driver*, as the "nearest of [William Inge's] work to being biographical, right down the line." In his 1989 biography, Ralph F. Voss classifies the work as "a largely factual memoir thinly garbed as fiction" (6).

2. Inge once described his sense of the connection between a playwright and his play in the Foreword to the 1958 Random House edition of his collected works: "the play contains something very vital to [the playwright], something of the very essence of his own life. If it is rejected, he can only feel that he is rejected too. Some part of him has been turned down, cast aside, even laughed at or scorned" (*4 Plays* vi).

In an autobiographical, unpublished play, *Many a Glorious Morning*, the playwright character reaffirms a complete identification between self and work: "If the public doesn't like my work, I hate myself, I walk down the street feeling like a member of some despised minority" (*Glorious Morning* 11). Because so many of his characters were projections of himself and so many of the dramatic situations based on his own experience, when Inge's worst fears came to pass and the public did reject his work, he felt rejected as well.

3. In his study, *Like a Brother, Like a Lover: Male Homosexuality in the American*

Novel and Theatre from Herman Melville to James Baldwin, Georges-Michel Sarotte isolates a dominant dynamic in Inge's published plays: devirilized father, domineering mother, and secretly homosexual son. Sarotte argues that Inge consciously and spitefully mirrored what a homoerotophobic psychiatric community had conjectured: that male homosexuality was a conditioned response to what Irving Bieber termed the double-bind, "maternal seductiveness-maternal sexual restriction" (Bieber 53). However, I question homosexual spite towards medical and social institutions as sufficient explanation for so many works on mother-son relationships. With the availability of the unpublished materials, I characterize Inge's focus on a mother-son dyad as compulsive.

4. In a personal interview, actress Shirley Knight said that "Inge's homosexuality is what destroyed him."

5. Although it is virtually impossible to organize chronologically the unpublished material, Inge appeared to be experimenting with more and more extreme situations to indicate the damage wrought by mothers and to depict the measures of defiance, escape, and revenge resorted to by their sons. In *A Loss of Roses*, Kenny steals personal items from women; in *Natural Affection*, Donnie murders a woman who resembles his mother; a character in an unpublished one-act play entitled "The Friends of Sir Galahad" assaults and rapes a young woman who expresses desire for him; a young man in another unpublished play, "Venus in Therapy," angrily flees his mother's condemnations, threats, and nagging only to crash his motorcycle and die; in *The Last Pad*, performed off-off Broadway in 1970, a homosexual character is convicted of murdering his mother and grandmother. In *My Son Is a Splendid Driver*, the narrator attempts suicide.

6. In *Homosexuality and American Psychiatry: The Politics of Diagnosis*, Ronald Bayer summarizes the theories, methods of treatment, and attitudes of the American psychiatric community up to 1973 when the American Psychiatric Association removed homosexuality from its official list of mental disorders. Bayer makes the point that, with few exceptions, psychiatrists proceeded from the assumption that heterosexuality was the normal end of psychosexual development, thus following that homosexuality was psychopathologic. However, there was disagreement about the conditions for the development of homosexuality and the success of therapeutic intervention.

7. In an interview, Loretta Watts, a childhood friend who remained close to Inge throughout most of his life, spoke about the biographical accuracy of *My Son Is a Splendid Driver* and also reported that Inge had revealed to her and her husband that *The Dark at the Top of the Stairs* was an autobiographical play. Also in an interview, Elia Kazan, the director of *Dark*, said that he did not discuss the autobiographical nature of *The Dark at the Top of the Stairs* with Inge until after directing it. He felt there was "a lot of pain in the play."

8. In a Lacanian model, the beginning of "Memories of Green Summer" would correspond more to a pre-oedipal stage, particularized by a primitive belief which Lacan terms the "Desire of the Mother." The child imagines itself as completing the mother's desire by satisfying her lack (in psychoanalysis, becoming the phallus for her), as the mother promptly satisfies the child's desire for her (Wright 108). Inge simply created two maternal figures in the opening pages.

9. Besides *My Son Is a Splendid Driver* and the versions of *The Dark at the Top of Stairs*, a partial list of published and unpublished works that dramatize dysfunctional

family situations with a mother-son relationship figuring prominently would include: *Come Back, Little Sheba, The Call*, "The Boy in the Basement," "Departure," *A Loss of Roses, Natural Affection*, "The Friends of Sir Galahad" or "Vic Burns," *The Last Pad*, and "Venus in Therapy."

10. In an interview, Inge's sister, Helene Inge Connell spoke about her brother's "difficulty with [homosexuality]" and her own uneasiness with his childhood transvestism. As far as I know, this is the only on-record discussion of Inge's homosexuality by a family member. She also commented about his activities during the St. Louis years, mentioning that she became specifically aware of his lifestyle during this time.

11. The cause of the character's death, blood poisoning from a shaving nick, is the same as that of Inge's own older brother, Luther.

12. In "The Beast in the Closet: James and the Writing of Homosexual Panic," Eve Sedgwick discusses an historical chain of "space-clearing negatives to void and ... to underline the possibility of male homosexual genitality." She compiles a list of the speakable terms in Christian tradition of homosexual possibility: "Unspeakable, Unmentionable, *nefandam libidinern*, 'that sin which should be neither named nor committed,' ... 'things fearful to name,' ... 'the Love that dare not speak its name'" (258).

13. In an interview, John Connolly spoke about Inge's acrophobia and claustrophobia which prevented him from driving or flying. And in another interview, Pat Hingle, who acted in both *The Dark at the Top of the Stairs* and *Splendor in the Grass*, described Inge as terrified of driving.

14. Many critics thought the suicide of Sammy Goldbaum was awkward and melodramatic. Inge defended his artistic decision by pointing out that suicide is always a shock yet always a possibility: "I never heard of a suicide that I expected" (*4 Plays* ix). Self-destruction was evidently never far from Inge's mind. He often mentioned suicide in letters as well as using it in many plays and stories. Besides the suicide in *Dark* and the attempted suicide in the novel-memoir, a writer character in an unpublished one-act, *The Love Death*, methodically ends his life, taking an overdose on stage. Another unpublished, one-act play, "The Killing," concerns a man too frightened to kill himself and who goads someone else into doing the job.

Inge did a number of treatments of a full-length drama, the working titles of which are mostly variations of *Out on the Outskirts of Town*, in which a character attempts suicide in his car. One of his most successful projects was the screenplay of James Leo Herlihy's novel, *All Fall Down*. There is a chilling moment in the film when the character played by Eva Marie Saint describes the way in which her lover took his own life in a car with carbon monoxide, exactly as Inge does some years later.

Finally, Inge explores fleeting fame in the one-act, "I'm a Star." The central character is an aging stage and screen actress who drinks and swallows pills to forget that she is no longer beautiful, young, and good box office: "I almost feel ... as if [people in the theatre and film industry] wonder why I just don't take an overdose of sleeping pills to keep them from being embarrassed" (11).

Works Cited

Bayer, Ronald. *Homosexuality and American Psychiatry: The Politics of Diagnosis*. Princeton: Princeton University Press, 1981. Print.

Bieber, Irving, et al. *Homosexuality: A Psychoanalytic Study*. New York: Basic Books, 1962. Print.
Burgess, Charles E. "An American Experience: William Inge in St. Louis 1943–1949." *Papers on Language and Literature* 12.4 (1976): 438–69. Print.
Clurman, Harold. *Lies Like Truth: Theatre Reviews and Essays*. New York: Macmillan, 1958. Print.
Connell, Helene Inge. Taped Interview. 7 Aug. 1981. William Inge Collection. Independence Community College, Independence, KS.
Connolly, John. Taped Interview. 13 Sept. 1981. William Inge Collection. Independence Community College, Independence, KS.
Foucault, Michel. *Death and the Labyrinth: The World of Raymond Roussel*. Trans. Charles Ruas. Berkeley: University of California Press, 1986. Print.
Freeman, Lucy, ed. *Celebrities on the Couch: Personal Adventures of Famous People in Psychoanalysis*. Los Angeles: Ravena, 1970. Print.
Frenz, Horst, ed. *American Playwrights on Drama*. New York: Hill and Wang, 1962. Print.
Freud, Sigmund. *The Basic Writings of Sigmund Freud*. Trans. and ed. A. A. Brill. New York: Random House, 1938. Print.
Hingle, Pat. Taped Interview. 18 Mar. 1975. William Inge Collection. Independence Community College, Independence, KS.
Inge, Luther, Jr. Taped Interview. 24 Oct. 1981. William Inge Collection. Independence Community College, Independence, KS.
Inge, William. *All Fall Down* [screenplay]. Dir. John Frankenheimer. Perf. Warren Beatty, Eva Marie Saint, and Karl Malden. M-G-M, 1962. Film.
_____. "The Boy in the Basement." *Summer Brave and Eleven Short Plays*. New York: Random House, 1962. 161–85. Print.
_____. "The Call." *Two Short Plays by William Inge*. New York: Dramatists Play Service, 1968. 3–19. Print.
_____. "Culled from an Author's Past." *New York Times* 1 Dec. 1957, sec. 2: 1, 3. Print.
_____. "The Dark at the Top of William Inge." Interview by Gilbert Millstein. *Esquire* Aug. 1958: 61–63. Print.
_____. "Departure." TS. N.d. William Inge Collection. Independence Community College, Independence, KS. Print.
_____. *Farther Off from Heaven*. MS. N.d. William Inge Collection, Kansas Collection. Kenneth Spencer Research Library, University of Kansas Libraries, Lawrence. Print.
_____. *4 Plays by William Inge* [*Come Back, Little Sheba*; *Picnic*; *Bus Stop*; *The Dark at the Top of the Stairs*]. New York: Random House, 1958. Print.
_____. "The Friends of Sir Galahad." TS. N.d. William Inge Collection. Independence Community College, Independence, KS. Print.
_____. "I'm a Star." MS. N.d. William Inge Collection, Kansas Collection. Kenneth Spencer Research Library, University of Kansas Libraries, Lawrence. Print.
_____. "The Killing." TS. N.d. William Inge Collection. Independence Community College, Independence, KS. Print.
_____. *The Last Pad*. TS. N.d. William Inge Collection. Independence Community College, Independence, KS. Print.
_____. *A Loss of Roses*. New York: Random House, 1960. Print.

―――. "The Love Death." *A Complex Evening: Six Short Plays by William Inge.* Independence, KS: Independence Community College/On Stage, 2009. [5]–10, 33–34, 45–46, 97–99. Print.

―――. *Many a Glorious Morning.* TS. N.d. The William Inge Collection. Independence Community College, Independence, Kansas. Print.

―――. "Memories of Green Summer." MS. N.d. Kansas Collection. William Inge Collection, Kansas Collection. Kenneth Spencer Research Library, University of Kansas Libraries, Lawrence. Print.

―――. *My Son Is a Splendid Driver.* Boston: Little, Brown, 1971. Print.

―――. *Natural Affection.* New York: Random House, 1963. Print.

―――. "Playwright at Turning Point: Inge Feeling Urge for 'Happy Plays.'" Interview by Barbara Maddux. *Washington Post* 22 Jan. 1963: A 14. Print.

―――. *Summer Brave and Eleven Short Plays.* New York: Random House, 1962. Print.

―――. "Venus in Therapy." TS. N.d. William Inge Collection. Independence Community College, Independence, KS. Print.

―――. "Vic Burns." TS. N.d. William Inge Collection. Independence Community College, Independence, KS.

―――. "William Inge: The Last Interview." Interview by Lloyd Steele. *Los Angeles Free Press* 22 June 1973: 18–22. Print.

―――. "William Inge—A Playwright in Transition: A Conversation with Digby Diehl." Interview with Digby Diehl. *Transatlantic Review* 26 (Fall 1967): 51–56. Print.

Kazan, Elia. Taped Interview. 17 Sept. 1981. William Inge Collection, Independence Community College, Independence, KS.

Knight, Shirley. Personal Interview. 11 Apr. 1988.

Mitchell, Marilyn. "William Inge." *American Imago* 35.3 (1978): 297–310. Print.

Proust, Marcel. *The Sweet Cheat Gone.* 1925. Trans. C. K. Scott Moncrief. New York: Boni, 1930. Print.

Roussel, Raymond, John Ashbery, and Trevor Winkfield. *How I Wrote Certain of My Books.* New York: SUN, 1977. Print.

Sarotte, Georges-Michel. "William Inge: 'Homosexual Sprite' in Action." *Like a Brother, Like a Lover: Male Homosexuality in the American Novel and Theatre from Herman Melville to James Baldwin.* Trans. Richard Miller. New York: Anchor/Doubleday, 1978. 121–33. Print.

Sedgwick, Eve Kosofsky. "The Beast in the Closet: James and the Writing of Homosexual Panic." *Speaking of Gender.* Ed. Elaine Showalter. New York: Routledge, 1989. 243–68. Print.

Shuman, R. Baird. *William Inge.* Rev. ed. Boston: Twayne, 1989. Print.

Voss, Ralph F. *A Life of William Inge: The Strains of Triumph.* Lawrence: University Press of Kansas, 1989. Print.

Wager, Walter, ed. *The Playwrights Speak.* New York: Delta, 1967. Print.

Watts, Loretta. Taped Interview. 17 Aug. 1981. William Inge Collection. Independence Community College, Independence, KS.

Wright, Elizabeth. *Psychoanalytic Criticism: Theory in Practice.* New York: Metheun, 1984. Print.

Reminiscences

Memories of Happier Times
Helene Inge Connell

William Motter Inge was the youngest of five children of Luther Clay Inge and Maude Sarah Gibson Inge. There was an older sister, Lucy, sixteen years old when he was born; an older brother, Luther Boy (Mother always called him Luther Boy—I guess because my father's name was Luther too), about fourteen; and yours truly, six years old at the time of his birth. A little girl, Irene, was three years old when she died. She was ill with just some child's illness and the doctor proscribed calomel—he always gave calomel for anything that was wrong with anyone—and one day Mother said the strawberries at that season were so good; they were just beautiful. Irene was begging for strawberries; so when the doctor came, the private nurse they had for her asked if she could have some and he told her that one or two wouldn't hurt her. So she gave her strawberries, but it seems that you shouldn't take anything acid if you're taking calomel and she died very shortly after that.

Bill was christened Billy when he was a baby. My mother wanted to call him William, I guess, but my older sister Lucy had a number of friends and Billy was a very popular name at the time and they all wanted him to be called Billy—so that's the way he was christened. He changed his name to William later on. Billy was born on May 3rd, 1913; and about all I remember about it was that my big sister Lucy took me to my Grandmother Inge's house just a block away and told me I had a new little brother and I was to stay with Grandmother for a day or two.

Mother always said that she felt as if she had raised two separate families because of the eight years between the first two and the last two children. Another reason she said that was because Billy and I were so different from Lucy and Luther. They were good-time folks more than Billy and me. They loved to go and they loved parties; they were always doing things, while Billy and I were more quiet and more the studious type, I guess you'd say. Luther loved to get in the car; he loved automobiles and he loved to drive fast. Dad would try to keep him from driving the car while he was gone but Luther would get it out without asking anyone. One night, my father had chained the wheel of the car to the floor in the garage, and Luther told Mother that he wanted to take the car out. She said, "You can't do it; it's chained to the floor." He said, "Hell, that won't stop me from getting that car out." And he got the car out too! Another time he came home and the top of the car—it was a Buick—had been burned off. One of the guys that he had with him was smoking cigarettes and had burned the top off. But Luther was also so good to Mother; he was very kind and thoughtful. That was the good side of him. His death was devastating to her. He had just been married a short while and he had a hickey, I guess you'd call it, on his lip. He was working in a clothing store at the time, and he picked that with a needle. That was during the war and the dyes in the clothing were so poisonous and he got infected and died of the strep infection [ed. note: for alternate version of this event, see Unnatural Affection essay, note 11].

Dad was a traveling salesman and he was gone most of the week and then he'd come home weekends. He was a very kind man but having five children he had to work pretty hard to keep us all in clothes and education and all. Mother loved her children. She hung on to all of us just as long as she could. I guess you'd say she was a feisty little thing at times, and she was quite a talker. I didn't learn to talk really until I got away from home because Mother was always talking and I had to remain quiet because children were seen and not heard in those days.

Billy was a handsome youngster—rather plump, towheaded, freckles across his nose, big blue eyes, and a rather decided lisp that was quite irresistible. One of our neighbors across the street, Mr. Wagstaff, liked to hear him talk with that lisp so much that he would give him a nickel every time he could persuade him to "speak a piece." Then Billy would recite the well-known verse "Mother calls me William, Daddy calls me Will, Sister calls me Willie, but the boys all call me Bill."

When he was old enough to go to the movies, he became quite a fan. Nearly everyone was in those days because that was the only entertainment, other than parties—and not everyone could give parties. We went to the movies every time we had a chance. In those days a fan letter to a movie star would bring a large 5 × 7 or 8 × 10 signed picture of that star, so Bill started writing for these and he received a great many. I remember he had pictures of Betty Compson, Gloria Swanson, Joan Crawford, Mary Pickford, Dolores Del Rio, Marguerite Clark, Conrad Nagle, Douglas Fairbanks, and Rudolph Valentino, to name a few. He started a collection of these photos and had twenty or thirty or more, some of which I still have. He entertained himself and anyone who was interested by going through them time and time again. He would sit on the floor and spread them out, one by one, enjoying them.

In 1922, we took a trip to California. It was for a Shrine convention; my father, of course, was a Shriner as were many of the men at that time in Independence—and several families went on this trip. The convention was in San Francisco, but when it was over we went down to Long Beach and rented an apartment there. We must have stayed there a month at least. Every day we would go down to the beach, of course, and we spent most of our time swimming and sunning. There was a pier with all kinds of entertainment, but Billy and I especially liked the dance halls because we had learned to dance at that time. Mother was always with us. They had good orchestras and in the afternoon it was really fun to go dancing. It must have been funny to see because I was tall and skinny and Billy was very short and plump at the time.

One day the whole bunch of us went to the Paramount Studios and we stood out in front hoping that we'd get to see some movie stars. Sure enough, it was payday and here they came in one at a time and we had our cameras ready and we asked them to stop and pose for us. Gloria Swanson wasn't a bit nice about posing; she just swished on in and got her money and left. There was Burt Lytell; we got a picture of him. And we went to the Fairbanks Studio where Doug Fairbanks was making one of his pictures where he swings around from one place to another. He was coming out of a castle down a ramp and Billy—we had crawled under a fence to get in—yelled at him, "Hello, Doug" and Fairbanks yelled back, "Hi, Bill"—so that pleased Billy very much.

Mother also let us take some art lessons; we took lessons in water coloring. I'll never forget a picture Bill did while he was taking lessons. It was a picture of a rose. William Inge the playwright was also William Inge the artist, and if he had chosen painting and sculpture as his profession, I think he could have made his name in the art world as well known as it now is in the world of the theater. When we were children, anything I could do, he could do better; so when I showed some talent and interest in drawing, Billy became interested also. He was especially good at figure drawing, and in his later years, after he came to California, he did several pieces of sculpture that he had cast in bronze that are really excellent. He collected paintings by well-known artists and had the ability or knowledge to spot paintings that were important—or would be someday.

I think Bill's interest in acting started when he was five or six years old. Both of us took elocution lessons from a very fine teacher, Mrs. Sanford, who had a collection of clever readings and monologues for all ages, some of them in dialect. I was the first to start taking these lessons and would, of course, practice memorizing my monologue for the week at night. Billy would be in the room listening; and he memorized it before I did. We found that he was entertaining his third grade class at school with my recitations. Needless to say, he then started taking lessons also, and the two youngest Inge kids were asked to recite at many of the clubs and parties in our town. We had Irish dialect and Negro dialect and it was great fun. A young lady by the name of Edna Oakes was giving private "lessons" about Shakespeare and Mother thought it would be nice for us to learn about him. We received a book of many of Shakespeare's plays written for children to understand; I kept that book for many years. It was an excellent way to introduce us to good literature when we were in the lower grades. I always thought Bill would go on the stage or in the movies as his interest in speaking and the theater continued in high school and college. I knew he would someday be important.

When we lived on 4th Street, we had a garage that at one time had been a barn. It could have been used for three cars but since we owned only one car, the extra apace was used for storage and for Billy's plays. He was maybe six or seven years old and he would get some of the kids in the neighborhood; they would dress up and he would make up some stories or poems for them to act out. They used an old sheet for a curtain and charged other kids in the neighborhood two pins or maybe a penny to see the plays. I didn't participate in any of these plays because I was six years older than he and didn't want to participate in that little kid's activity.

One day, Mother and I went to town to do some grocery shopping. When we got almost to our house, we saw this little old lady coming out of the side door. Mother said, "Who in the world has been visiting us? Who is that little old lady?" I looked but I didn't know who it was. As we got up closer, we saw it was Billy. We really hadn't recognized him from a short distance away. He had put wrinkles on his face with an eyebrow pencil; he had put on one of my grandmother's little old hats and a shawl around his shoulders. He had a cane and he was dressed just like a little old lady—so we took a picture of him.

Another night, when Billy was about five or six, Mother, Lucy, and I were sitting in front of the fire chatting and we weren't paying much attention to Bill and what he was doing. Pretty soon, we heard, "Mama, look at me!" We looked up and there he was, he had his head through the banister. He was about halfway up the stairway and the banister was such that it formed a little square right at the step. He had stuck his head through there. Mother said, "Get your head out of there"—but he couldn't do it; he couldn't pull his head out. It finally wound up that Mother went to the garage and got a saw and she had to saw through that banister and get his head out. I wonder if that banister is still there. I guess it is because she sawed in an inconspicuous place where it didn't show.

Billy was always interested in his big sister's dates and if I went to a party he sometimes waited up for me to hear all about it: Did I have a good time? With whom did I dance? Before our sister Lucy got married, Billy and I loved to go to her room when she was getting ready for a date and watch her fix her hair and put on her makeup.

Bill was an introvert, a quiet person with a soft, almost soothing voice. He disliked being in a crowd and avoided crowds whenever possible. In attending a play, movie, opera, or whatever, he had to have an aisle seat in the back row or he would not go in. He had all kinds of phobias. It took years of psychoanalysis before he could ride in an elevator, or live in a room or apartment above the second floor, or even be in a closed room. These fears must have been developing throughout his childhood, and although I do not recall that he was afraid of the dark, the young boy in his play *The Dark at the Top of the Stairs* makes me think that he was.

Most of the time Bill had a very even temper, but he could get very angry; and when he did, it was anything but pleasant. Throughout his adult life he was subject to spells of depression, brought on perhaps by a nervous breakdown when he finished his master's degree in college. From that time on he had spells of depression that grew worse and sometimes lasted for weeks or months.

I have been asked if Bill's plays were taken from real life. He told me once that a writer had to write about what he *knows* best. So some of the characters in his plays may resemble someone he has known at one time or another. Also, the plot may have been suggested by some happening he has seen, heard, or read about—some small event around which he weaves the story. When I first saw *Come Back, Little Sheba*, Lola was so much like my aunt, my mother's sister; she didn't have a dog, she had cats galore. But she was very slovenly; that's a horrible word to use about an aunt who was really a lot of fun too. She was a good sport, but she was a little careless in her dress and her housekeeping and her husband was a dentist whom she called Doc. There is a similarity, so much so that when I went home and found that Bill had given the folks the book, I wanted to hide so that Aunt Ellen wouldn't see it—because I thought she would be hurt. I shouldn't have worried because she was determined to see the play; so she and Doc hired a driver and went to Kansas City to see it. After it was over, she went backstage and told Shirley Booth, "You had my part in the play." She was thrilled about it; she just thought that was great.

In all Bill's plays, I can recognize characters that maybe somebody else wouldn't recognize. Mrs. Potts in *Picnic* was very much like Annie Watts, the woman next door to us. I was quite a bit like Reenie in *Dark at the Top of the Stairs* in the fact that I was shy and didn't like to talk to boys; I was shy around the male sex. Sonny was very much like Bill because of the movie star business and the fact that he wasn't too popular with the boys and the boys teased him some. And the schoolteachers in *Picnic*: Mother liked to have someone around since Dad was away so much, so she took in three teachers to room at our house. They didn't board there but they might as well have because every time Mother would bake bread or bake a cake they would come home from school and the smell of the cake or bread or whatever was so good that they wanted to have some of it and my mother would always let them cut into a cake or a loaf of bread. Sometimes she would have a nice Swiss steak for dinner and she'd invite them to stay for dinner if they wanted to, and they enjoyed that. The same three teachers lived with through my high school years and part of Bill's high school days; they must have been with us seven or eight years at least and it was just like one big happy family. It was kind of fun. But what is also true of Bill's plays is that people who can't recognize these characters the way I do may find that they had a friend that looked like or spoke like one of his characters—but, put together, it is all fiction.

Loving Memories of a Kindly Uncle
Luther C. Inge

The words that follow may perhaps be best described as those memories of a good and decent man whom I cherished very much. To me, he was an uncle, a near brother, and a lifelong friend both as a boy and as a man who later became one of the finest of playwrights and of whom I was always extremely proud.

William Motter Inge was born on May 3, 1913, and I, his nephew, was born on April 5, 1921. William, or Bill as I knew him best throughout his life, was the younger brother of my father, Luther C. Inge, who pre-deceased my birth. Because I lived for several years in my maternal grandparents' home across the street from the home of my paternal grandparents, Bill's home, I spent my early years running back and forth between the houses of these dear grandparents. I really had the best of two worlds.

Our close blood relationship caused me to regard Bill more as a brother than as an uncle since neither of us had a living brother. As a child I followed him around as one would an older brother. I always believed this feeling to be a mutual one and our relationship over the years tended to bear this out. Bill was always a caring person during his lifetime, but at times this characteristic did not appear to be one of his attributes. During his most successful years he sometimes wanted to be remote from relatives and friends alike. This was most often from professional necessity rather than his real desire. I know that his heart must have ached at times when he had to turn away from those whom he loved the most.

On many summer evenings when it was too hot to stay indoors, Bill would sit on the street-lighted curb by my mother's parents' home and tell ghost stories to the neighborhood kids more nearly my age. In looking back now, I can readily see when and where his theatrical talents were beginning to emerge. Significantly, he made up these stories as they were being told but that did not detract one bit from their thrilling nature. We kids considered him to be the best ghost story teller of the entire group collected under the street light. Perhaps this ability for on-the-spot development of such vivid stories was inherited by Bill from Great-Grandpa Inge who was an acknowledged master at telling of his experiences during the Indian Wars and of the "old West" as he had known and lived it. Grandpa had been a cavalryman with the 19th Kansas Volunteers under the command of Generals Sheridan and Custer and had been a member of the three-man party who sought out and rescued two white women captives of renegade Indians. Grandpa was a highly imaginative teller of marvelous stories and knew just how to capture children's interest and imagination.

Grandpa's stories usually were told to younger members of the family following one of those delicious fried chicken dinners for which my Grandmother Inge was famous. These Sunday dinners were usually attended by Great-Grandpa and Great-Grandmother Inge; Uncle Walter and Aunt Nona McVey, Grandfather Inge's sister, their sons, Lawrence and Walter, Jr.; Grandfather and Grandmother Inge, Helene, Bill and myself. On occasion, Aunt Helen Gibson Mooney, Grandmother Inge's sister, and her husband, Dr. Earl Mooney, would be the dinner guests.

During the same time period that Bill was the teller of ghost stories, he was also writing, producing, coaching, and acting in his own plays for the neighborhood kids in his parents' garage loft. The loft served Bill well as a "theater." By stretching sheets across ropes or wires stretched between supports, he had his "curtain." Not only sheets had to be stretched for these performances but also the neighborhood players' and viewers' imaginations had to be stretched so as to visualize stage "properties." But draw a crowd of the neighborhood kids he did!

It was only natural, I suppose, that these plays would follow the general plot of the comedies, mysteries, and love scenes he saw in the movies at the old Best and Beldorf theaters. All of us, at all ages, loved the wonderful "Shoot-'Em-Up" serial shows which were on the screen at the Best Theater every Saturday! Bill did quite well in adapting some of these movie plots into his garage-loft "productions."

Bill always acted as though he enjoyed the company of the neighborhood kids of both his age and mine. However, as time passed, there appeared to be a better defined line of demarcation between the age groups. While I was still a pre-teen, I came to realize that Bill, who was some eight years my senior, had "suddenly" discovered that girls were worthy of his interest and investigation!

This was all taking place while I still looked upon girls as those persons who only played with dolls and were always looking for boys to play "house" with them. Bill, on the other hand, was beginning to frequent the front porch of the neighboring Seymour family who, incidentally, had two very attractive daughters, Jeanne and Rosemary! He was also beginning to "run" with the older boys of the neighborhood such as Fred Aldred, an outstanding high school tennis player, and the Watts brothers, Phillip and Fred, to the exclusion of the "younger set."

During this time I began to notice a change in myself too. I was becoming more interested in the more "manly" sports of fishing and joining with my grandfathers while they hunted quail, pheasant, squirrel, and rabbits. Bill never took an interest in these sports and although always invited to go along he declined, as he had other interests and other older kids with whom to share his time.

Bill always had a keen eye for the prettiest girls especially those who were the better dancers but then this was a lifelong tendency he never lost. Many, many times Bill and his friends would roll up the carpet in the parlor of the Inge home and dance to the very latest music coming from the Edison record player. Oh, how they did enjoy themselves! I was too young to engage in these dances other than to observe. Still, Bill never ignored me and there were many occasions during his mid- and late-teen years when I went swimming with him at Riverside Park. And, although I did not care much for tennis, I did go with Bill to the park tennis courts and watch him and others more of his age playing this game which, in some ways, seemed to fascinate him. While Bill was far from being an outstanding tennis player he was an even worse swimmer. He could stay afloat and propel himself across the pool without taking on too much water. Although Bill's prowess at these sports was anything but exceptional in his younger years, swimming did provide him needed relaxation as he grew into full manhood.

Bill's years of garage loft plays were far behind him as he entered high school. The following few years were full of riches for Bill and he gloried in his opportunities to become a real actor on the high school's formal stage. Generally, Bill was a reasonably good student, but he excelled in those subjects he liked best, such as English, Literature, and—in particular—Drama.

Bill's departure for Kansas University in Lawrence left something of a void in my life as well as in the lives of his parents, my grandparents. Grandmother was the one most directly affected since she had been the one who got him off to school in the morning and was the first to greet him upon his return at the end of his afternoon classes and play practice. Grandfather, who rarely made much of a show of emotion, upon Bill's leaving had a tear or two in his eyes also. The departure of the remaining son was quite an event which impacted the entire family who must remain at home. Even the high school teachers who rented rooms at the grandparents' home missed Bill and his extemporaneous performances.

Neither was I about the old home as much, as I too was in school and went to my own home now in another part of town after my classes were finished for the day. But then there were the weekends when I very often took my grandmother out for a drive to Sycamore or Neodesha on sunny Sunday afternoons. I always suspected that she enjoyed getting out of the house more than the actual drive. Sometimes Grandfather would accompany us on these jaunts and we would stop to visit with Uncle Dave Vandeveer, brother of Great-Grandmother Inge, and a lady, whom we referred to as "Aunt Daisy." They lived on Uncle Dave's farm close by Neodesha and had an interesting farm lot filled with all kinds of farm animals, a subject of interest to all.

Unfortunately, Bill wasn't what Grandmother considered to be the best of drivers when he took her on short drives and implied as much to him when the occasion presented itself. In or out of his presence, Grandmother frequently compared my driving to that of my deceased father, with whom she would have driven to the ends of the Earth, to hear her tell the story. I gathered that her confidence in my father's driving came because he had done most of the driving on their auto trip to Colorado Springs years before. I doubt that Grandmother realized the impact her intended lighthearted criticism of his driving had on Bill but certainly he must have felt belittled to some degree. The evidence of this appears in Bill's novel, *My Son Was a Splendid Driver*. Jule, in the story, was my father, Luther, while Bill was cast as Joey. This story of Bill's was the closest to being a biography of their immediate family than any of his other plays or novels. I had "words" with Bill over parts of this novel that I disagreed with, disliked, and knew to be untrue. His defense was that it was a fictional story in its nature. We left the disagreement with that rather weak and unsatisfactory explanation.

On several weekends during Bill's stay at Kansas University, I drove with the grandparents to Lawrence to visit Helene and Bill. Helene's apartment, which she shared through the working week with another teacher, was too small to accommodate three extra people so I stayed in the Sigma Nu frat house with Bill. That experience for a high school student was like living in Heaven! And Bill was a great host too. On my first visit Bill drove me all around the campus describing the uses of the many buildings and showed me where he had his classes. Because these were weekend trips only, Bill couldn't take me into any of the classrooms but I always appreciated Bill's attempts to entertain me even though his time with me was limited as he had to have time with his mother and dad also.

Later, when Bill was attending Peabody College in Nashville, the grandparents chose not to drive there to visit Bill and Helene due to the great driving distance. However, when Bill was about to graduate from Peabody with his Masters degree, I drove the grandparents to attend the festivities. I recall one early morning before we had had breakfast, Bill and I were walking on campus toward the College and I lit a cigarette. Although Bill smoked cigarettes himself, he apparently never smoked before breakfast and he gave me the very dickens for doing so, stating that I would ruin my health! From then on during our visit he watched my cigarette consumption closely. The graduation ceremony was, in itself, something I had never seen before and was quite impressive although it was performed during the summer session and there were few graduating with Bill.

Bill was already well situated in his second teaching position at Stephens College for girls located in Columbia, Missouri, while I was trying to get through one year at Independence Junior College. Bill wrote to me once saying that it was sheer torture having to be so close to all of these beautiful girls yet could not (dared not) date a single one of them. I could not help but envy him the opportunity to see these "beauties" much less to date them!

I was unable to see Bill for some time after I left Independence in the summer of 1941 as he was tied down with teaching and in September of that year I enlisted in military service and almost immediately went to the west coast for training. While in the service for the next several years, I had little direct correspondence with Bill, a matter which I never fully understood but one about which I never asked him. I always felt that he was a bit embarrassed because he had been passed over (for what reason I never ascertained) by the draft.

Most of the information I obtained about Bill's whereabouts and activities during my military years came from Grandmother Inge; what wonderful letters that dear soul did write and she managed to keep me abreast of happenings throughout the family circle. In 1947 I entered Tulsa University in Tulsa, Oklahoma, and I again began to correspond frequently with Bill and heard from him regularly. He told me of many of his difficulties in obtaining acceptance of his plays and then when accepted, some of the problems and disappointments of a different nature that he encountered. Of course, I was having my problems too and neither of us could help or see the other much as we might have liked.

In 1959, when I was offered the opportunity to spend the following two years in Europe, my wife and I gladly accepted the offer. Bill was then living and working in New York City. We learned that we would embark via military air from McGuire Air Force Base, New Jersey, and so notified Bill. Imagine our complete surprise and delight to see Bill and his assistant, John Connolly, at the airport awaiting our arrival at the base to visit with us prior to our departure! This show of concern by Bill has been one of my life's most memorable surprises although how insignificant it may seem to others who were not involved. He was a very kind and considerate man.

In 1963, following our return to the United States from our European tour of duty and while situated in Cincinnati, Ohio, my wife and I adopted a fine two-day-old baby boy to be our son. Bill graciously became our son's godfather. Because of the work he was doing on the west coast, Bill was unable to attend the baptism of our newest Inge in person so his sister, my Aunt Helene, who lived fairly close by in Nashville, offered and did act for Bill as his proxy. This involvement by both Bill and Helene was very important to my wife and to me. We knew of no friend who could fulfill this ceremonial need as could these two delightful family participants.

Correspondence continued to flow occasionally between Bill and ourselves. I notified him in late 1965 that I was soon to be transferred to the Los Angeles area as my position had been abolished in Cincinnati. Bill's immediate response was to offer me temporary lodging with him in his Bel Air home until such a time as my wife could dispose of our home in Ohio and join me. Much as I wanted to accept his offer I had to decline as his home was too far away from what was to be my new office location near the Los Angeles International Airport. Prior to the arrival of my wife and son, Bill and I did manage to visit frequently and have dinner on Sunset Strip in one or the other of the fine dinner restaurants. During our eight-month stay in Los Angeles we visited often with Bill in his home. One evening, after we had invited him to our apartment for dinner, he had to decline and sent a gallon bottle of Scotch instead. That was typical of Bill, sending a gift when he could not fulfill an invitation.

Bill's gift giving was not limited to offerings for declined invitations. His Christmas and birthday gifts included such delightful and important (to us) gifts as pieces of Grandmother Inge's finest Chinaware which he knew full well we would treasure. These were articles that both he and I had grown up using when Grandmother had her fine family dinners. No newly purchased gifts could possibly have been of greater importance than these as each brought forth reminders to both Bill and me (as he mentioned in the notes he wrote to accompany the items) of our childhood when we were so much closer than was possible in our later years. For Bill to part with these treasures took a large measure of generosity on his part as he loved these things as he knew I did. Never did I ask him for a single one of these pieces, he just knew instinctively what I would appreciate and care for as he would.

Several times prior to his move to California, Bill wrote to me of his disenchantment with the eastern lifestyles and the frustrations he was having to cope with in New York and stated that he had always felt "out of place while living there." This was not surprising to me as I had always pictured him as a small-town boy who had gone to the Big City to make his mark in the world regardless of the tortures he must endure to do so. By this time, he was fed up with Big City life and wanted to seek out another, kinder, and more livable place where he could avoid the rigors of winter weather and other things he disliked about the east. By moving to the west he could better enjoy his remaining years of which, at that time, seemed to me to be many.

I could never have pictured Bill as an old man in his advanced years as we had seen Grandpa Inge, who lived into his nineties, nor of his Father, who as a very ill man, lived on into his later years in misery then died in his eighties. Bill just did not seem to fit well into that picture of an aged person. However depressed he was from time to time, I could never have anticipated his suicide. No one misses Bill more than I do. The deep-felt hurt caused by his untimely, self-destructive act will never cease for me.

Perhaps some of these thoughts passed through Bill's mind as he prepared to end his life. That we will never know.

Billy
Jeanne Seymour Mitcham

When I first met Billy Inge he was about 12 years old. I was a year older and a grade ahead of him in school. My parents, Pascal and May Seymour, had just bought a house at 316 Westminster Street in Independence, Kansas. Within a few days after moving in, my sister Rosemary and I and our tag-along little brother Joe made a thorough inspection of the new neighborhood. As we strolled by the Inge home, we struck up a conversation with Mrs. Inge, who was sitting in a swing on her front porch. She informed us about other children in the neighborhood. She said that her son, Billy, would be eager to meet us, although he was not at home just then. We liked the new neighborhood. It had a comfortable, friendly look about it. There were beautiful old elm trees along the street. The lawns in front of the pleasant houses were freshly mown and smelled like summer.

That summer was hotter than usual, even for Kansas. For days the air languished motionless; the heat and stillness seemed almost palpable. Cicadas set off a deafening prolonged whir. One afternoon, however, a sudden freakish breeze gusted around our house. Delighted, my sister and I rushed indoors to stir up a pitcher of iced lemonade. When we came out again, the magic breeze was gone, leaving the neighborhood even mere unbearable than before. Heat simmered up in invisible waves from the brick street; the motionless atmosphere settled over everything like a blanket. Although the branches of the elm trees filtered some sun-speckled spots of shade across the sidewalks, there was not enough to be of any real comfort to one elderly lady we saw approaching our house from about a block away.

Even from that distance, we could see that she appeared to be in danger of suffering a sunstroke. Elderly, feeble, slightly stooped, she was inching her way forward with uncertain, tottering steps. As a shield against the merciless sun, she was carrying a small ruffled parasol that bobbed and swayed above her prim bonnet. The hem of her long dress swished over the sidewalk with each faltering step. As she came closer, my sister and I were surprised to see that she wore a short, thread-bare cape over her narrow shoulders. Her hands were partially covered by a pair of ridiculous half-gloves that were several sizes too large. In spite of her apparent frailty, she chirped a cheery greeting in an amazingly young voice imitating a deep–South accent: "Greetin', l'il girls. Delectable weatha', ain't it."

By then, of course, we had realized that the old lady was neither old nor a lady, for the young boy's disguise disintegrated completely under the strain of trying to suppress his uncontrollable glee for having carried the charade as far as he had. After thanking us for the glass of cold lemonade that we gave to him, he informed us that he was our neighbor, Billy Inge, and that his mother had insisted that he come to get acquainted with the new girls in the neighborhood. This was only one in a series of surprise "get-ups" in which Billy later appeared at our house. He loved disguises and the appreciation of a receptive audience. In time, the disguises ceased and were replaced by a wonderful series of "back-yard" theatricals instigated by Billy. All of us immensely enjoyed being a part of those amateur productions, which Billy wrote, produced, cast, and acted in.

Billy's father was a traveling salesman who frequently was away from home on business trips. This left the Inge garage available for our use as a "back-yard" theater. It did not matter to us that audiences were few and far between. We simply reveled in the creative process. An empty theater in no way diminished our young enthusiasm. On a few occasions, we did manage to lure some of the neighbors to see our plays. They entered into the fun and did not seem to mind sitting on the crude up-ended wooden orange crates that we had found in an alley back of a local grocery store. All our props and equipment came to us from equally humble sources.

I think that our biggest "pay-to-see" effort was a play which Billy adapted from a movie he had seen. I think it was called "Twelve Bells." We passed around hand-bills in town that described the play as "a thrilling mystery that will baffle you and amuse you." On the day of the performance, Mr. Inge made an unscheduled return from a business trip. When he tried to park his car in his garage, he was certainly "baffled," but far from "amused." Apart from that one slight hitch, our efforts were charitably received by the recruited audience. They seemed especially pleased with Billy's spirited portrayal of an energetic detective whose power of ratiocination equaled that of Sherlock Holmes. My neighbor, Vivian Hiatt, did well as the leading lady. Unfortunately, my thespian brilliance was lost to the world in the role of a housemaid who wore a short organdy apron and bobbed in and out of one scene carrying a small silver tray.

Many, many other happy times were spent with Billy and other friends. We were innocents who found fun in such naïve activities as taking "time-about" making fudge in each other's kitchens. Mrs. Inge, a dear but frugal lady, liked to be called "Maudie," and Billy always volunteered to supply the vanilla flavoring.

A Sunday morning ritual in our house was a visit from Billy and his pal, Phil Watts. They came to read the funny papers in our newspaper, which they shuffled through hurriedly, leaving most of it scattered on the living room rug. My Dad, a man of reasonably standard orderliness, was infuriated by this Sunday-morning sacrilege. He would stomp out of the room muttering dire predictions under his breath concerning the probable after-life residence of "those two brats." Sometimes Billy would stay for dinner, especially when mother was serving fried chicken.

My friends and I enjoyed many activities that today would seem dull to most young people. It was fun to play croquet in the Watts's back yard after dark under a string of electric lights installed across the yard. Later, we liked to tell ghost stories. Sometimes Mrs. Watts would invite us in to dance to victrola music in her parlor. Billy was a good dancer, and he took considerable pride in knowing a variety of steps.

In high school my sister and I dated a lot. Billy was always interested in knowing who our dates were, where we were going, and what we planned to do. He greatly enjoyed that kind of social conversation. If he happened to be at our house on a night when one of us had a date, he would sit in the living room chatting away until a knock at the front door announced the arrival of the date. On that cue, he would rush through the house to make his hasty exit through the back door. In my school annual, he wrote: "...always I have to leave by the back door...."

Billy was quite sensitive. I recall how he would suffer if any of us, wittingly or unintentionally, excluded him. Most of all he could not abide rejection or deliberate unkindness. One time he tried-out for a place on the school cheer-leading team. Some students apparently thought that his efforts were funny or awkward, and they laughed long and loudly at him in public. This thoughtless unkindness hurt him deeply. It took a long time for him to get over it.

I was always proud of the way Billy strove for excellence, and in many fields of endeavor he earned the admiration of his teachers and classmates. He was an enthusiastic member of the school dramatic organization, called the Dee Dee Club. His work in the French club, "Le Cercle Francais" provided him with a useful knowledge of the language and a heightened awareness of

French literature. I especially cherish fond memories of his time on the staff of the school newspaper, "The Independent Student." I worked on the paper, too, and we had a lot of fun gathering news items together.

Billy had an interest in music. He was a member of the glee club, he enjoyed singing immensely, and on many occasions came to my house to join my sister and me when my Dad accompanied us on the piano.

Billy, also, was very talented in art. He could draw quite well. I remember a set of caricatures that he sketched. They were quite professional, I thought, and seemed to cut a bit deeper than the mere satirizing of surface peculiarities.

So many memories crowd around Billy in those days that I cannot begin to catalogue them. He was such an interesting, talented, and complex person. As I try to dredge up some of my recollections of him, one thought seems to stick in my mind. Over and beyond his later celebrity as an outstanding American dramatist, I see him as a very human, very true friend during those important formative years of our adolescence in Kansas. Once graduated from high school, each of us went our separate ways; but in those few years I think I learned something about friendship and human dignity from him.

In my senior year I broke up with my boyfriend. It was a trying experience for me. Young as he was, it was Billy who seemed to understand most. That year he wrote a little message—sentimental and perhaps somewhat trite—in my class annual, but I think it says something about Billy and his view of life:

> Dearest Jeanne: Whenever you need advice or comfort just let me know as I shall always be the truest of true friends. May Dan Cupid toss a petite arrow through your heart and someday you will know real love. Probably you do now. Who knows? Maybe and maybe not. Although love will always find a way, love is everlasting. True love is always found somewhere.

Billy, wherever you are—you were right.

My Teacher
William Stuckey

It was 1946 and I was just out of the army and enrolled at Washington University, a "street-car college" in the West End of St. Louis. Before the war I had gone to night school at St. Louis University, studying business. Now the government was footing the bill and I was free to study whatever I wished. I chose English with a minor in Journalism.

It is impossible to remember how one was at an earlier age; one always sees oneself, past or present, through that hall of mirrors which the mind (with the aid of vanity) contrives. I had kept track of some of the novels and plays I read in the army and as I look over the list—*Sartoris, Wild Palms, Sanctuary, Dubliners, The Hairy Ape, Desire Under the Elms, The Lesson of the Master, A Twist* [sic] *of the Screw*—I'd like to think I was more sophisticated than I was and that college, therefore, held few surprises for me. My judgment, however, tells me that despite what seems a fairly advanced reading list for a twenty-two-year-old, much of what I read settled on the top of my mind, like veneer, or evaporated without a trace. Most of the courses I took in English as an undergraduate were the standard fare of the time—composition, surveys, Shakespeare—more detailed (and sometimes more tedious) repetitions of what I had had in high school. In those days—at least at Washington University—courses in contemporary or even modern literature were almost nonexistent.

Almost, for me, because of a course in continental drama taught by a young instructor named William Inge. I had been an avid playgoer before the war and during my senior year in high school had taken a drama course taught by a Miss Charity Grace who later gave up a secure and well-paying position with the St. Louis public schools for a doubtful career as an actress in a traveling company. The plays I had read for her or had seen performed at the American Theater in St. Louis were traditional works—*Hamlet, Macbeth, The Rivals,*

The Admirable Crichton, Green Pastures, to name ones that come most readily to mind. In Inge's course I was confronted by very different kinds of plays, plays that shook one up in ways the familiar, tamer plays of high school hadn't: *Ghosts, Miss Julie, R.U.R.,* and *He Who Gets Slapped.* It was this latter play, especially, that for some reason made the greatest impression on me and I think it must have been Inge's own response to the play and to the kind of discussion he aroused. I have not reread *He Who Gets Slapped,* and so I am drawing on what may be an imperfect recollection. It was a play, we concluded, about the role of the artist in modern society, about his use as a whipping boy for the failures of that society. I can't say that I was drawn to that theme or even that I wholly accepted it, but what I took from the play and possibly from the course itself is what I now think of as a special quality of the modern sensibility.

My memory of Inge's physical appearance is vivid. He was young (compared with the rest of the faculty) and handsome in a haggard sort of way. Blond, receding hairline above the temples, with prominent eyes and a thin, drinker's mouth. I had seen a lot of mouths like that in the army. For some reason, I recall that he always wore khaki trousers, possibly because in those days we were always wondering who had been "in" and who hadn't. His khakis looked like authentic government issue. His jacket—black and white tweed—and tie—navy blue and knitted—were the standard academic garb. My memory of what he said in class, however, is totally nonexistent. He would come in, always a little late, open the book to the play that had been assigned, throw out a question and then lean against the blackboard, chain smoke, and let the discussion go on. I think there were people taking the course who knew him and perhaps talked to him outside class, and he depended on them to carry the ball, particularly over the heads of the fraternity boys and sorority girls who sometimes objected to what they considered the negative, antisocial cast of the discussion.

Inge was also absent on more than one occasion. My memory is that he was often absent, but that may be because it was a class I particularly enjoyed, and when the department secretary showed up to tell us that Mr. Inge would not be coming and that class was canceled, I was disappointed. Rumor had it that he suffered on these occasions from acute hangovers. But this was never confirmed.

There were a number of other temporary instructors in the English Department at Washington University in those post-war years, as there were at other colleges, taken on to handle the influx of ex-servicemen and women. One of these, a friend of Inge's, a tall, deep-voiced man, whose name I cannot recall, was later said to have been the inspiration for Doc in *Come Back, Little*

Sheba. I heard this a few years later, when I was at the University of Iowa, from someone who seemed to know a good deal more about Inge than I did. I hadn't known at the time I was in his class that he had written a play that was shortly to be produced by Margo Jones in Dallas (but then I hadn't heard of her either). I didn't even know that he was, or had been, drama critic for the *St. Louis Star-Times*. But there was a lot in those days I didn't know.

Shadows on Success
Audrey Wood

William Inge came into my life through Tennessee Williams. As I remember, Bill Inge was living in St. Louis, had met Tennessee there, came to Chicago to see Williams's first great success, *The Glass Menagerie*, and was so inspired by it that he decided to write a play himself. This was the beginning of the relationship. Actually, the first play that Bill ever gave to me—a play called *Farther Off from Heaven*—I didn't feel was ready for the Broadway theater, and being an honest person I rejected it. Despite this he was good enough to come back to me with *Come Back, Little Sheba*, which was the first play he had produced in New York. From a professional standpoint, it was of the utmost importance that a play like *Sheba* be the first play because it was a stronger play.

My early contact with him was all done through the United States Mail. He was working on a newspaper in St. Louis and during that period he did many rewrites, almost unasked; I remember writing him one day and saying "Hold. Enough. Let me get through reading what I'm reading before you start rewriting the play." He was unusually cooperative. Nobody was really even asking him to do all the things he was trying to do.

He eventually moved to New York and was in New York when we did *Sheba*, which was produced by the Theatre Guild. It opened in Wilmington, Delaware. None of the Guild came for about the first week, which was very fortunate because we were completely alone and did all the work that we thought had to be done without anybody telling us what to do—which with a first playwright is very fortunate. It was directed by Daniel Mann; it started his career. It was also the first really important starring role Shirley Booth ever had in the theater. She had been in plays for many years but this was the thing that really established her as a great actress.

But there was another, serious problem for us. It was Bill Inge's alcoholism, and it had surfaced in the past few days. I'd come to realize that when Bill was under tension, he, like his character Doc he'd so brilliantly created, resorted to the bottle. I'd already seen what liquor did to him. A warm and shy man, under its influence he became almost mute. Thus tranquilized, Bill would look at you and you could smile at him, but he had no conversation. You could take his hand and hold it, and he'd hold yours, but you got no verbal response. It was almost like dealing with a shadow, not a man. Come the morning of our opening night, and luckily there was a man with us, Paul Bigelow, who was working for the Theatre Guild, who was well aware of Bill's problems. Paul improvised a brilliant way to ensure that Bill did not wander off somewhere and go on an alcoholic binge. Early in the morning Paul managed to take all of Bill's clothing out of his hotel room and send them to the hotel tailor to be cleaned and pressed. Unable to leave his room, Bill stayed sober. When the curtain went up that night, he was in control of himself. When it came down, and the Wilmington audience applauded the cast, it was truly a happy time for all of us.

At the beginning of his career everything went extraordinarily well for Inge from a critical standpoint and from a box-office standpoint. The first play that didn't come off was *Natural Affection*, which I still think is one of his best plays; it starred Kim Stanley and Harry Guardino and was directed by Tony Richardson, the illustrious British director. That play was, unhappily, produced during a newspaper strike, which didn't help us very much. But after that his plays did not succeed and that's when he withdrew, left New York, and went to California to live. I think he enjoyed all his plays and had pride in them whether they succeeded or not, but on the other hand he was also hurt by the criticism. In our business it's very cruel because very often when you get to the top of a ladder they very much enjoy knocking you off the ladder, and that's really what happened to Bill. They got to the point where they decided that he was no longer the man they thought he was. And this was most unfortunate because he was still a very fine writer and would be for the rest of his life. He got terribly hurt and that's why he retreated.

He wrote about a certain section of America that no one else, perhaps, will ever write about as well again, in terms of the theater, and all of these works will endure.

Hampton Sundays
Horton Foote

I have only a vague memory of when I first heard the name of Bill Inge, but I'm sure it was in connection with having his play *Farther Off from Heaven* done at Margo Jones's theater in Dallas.

I was working with a theater group in Washington, D.C., at the time but returned to New York soon after to take over Robert Anderson's playwriting class at the American Theatre Wing. It was soon after that I learned that *Come Back, Little Sheba* was being produced by the Theatre Guild at their Westport Playhouse. Not many plays tried out there by the Guild were brought to New York and so when I heard that Bill's was to come to Broadway I was very impressed. I heard, too, that the playwright had great talent, and his play a welcome relief from the usual Broadway slickness.

I went to see *Come Back, Little Sheba* soon after it opened in New York and I was very taken with it, heartened, too, because it seemed to me the playwright was trying to find, and in most part succeeding, his own style, uncluttered by present Broadway conventions. I liked, too, the direction of Daniel Mann and was greatly moved by the performances of Shirley Booth and Sidney Blackmer.

The following year my play *The Chase* was produced and at one of the previews before the opening I was in the lobby between acts when a man I'd never seen before came up to me and said, "I'm Bill Inge." He was friendly and very supportive of my play and his speaking to me at the time meant a great deal. I don't remember seeing him again until the summer of 1953, but I heard a great deal about him through our mutual friend Kim Stanley. I must have seen him, too, during this time at a party or a friend's house, for somehow he knew (perhaps through Kim) that my family and I were spending the summer at East Hampton where I was working with Fred Coe on two television plays,

The Death of the Old Man and *Tears of My Sister*, and rewriting *The Trip to Bountiful* for a Westport tryout by Fred and the Theatre Guild. In any case, one Sunday morning, early, he appeared at our front door with a copy of the *New York Times*. He said he was spending the summer in Southampton and I invited him in and we talked a little and he settled down in a chair in our living room and read his *New York Times*, stopping every now and then to speak to my wife or me. It was then I became aware of his eyes. They were, I think in some ways, the saddest eyes I had ever seen on a human being—kind and friendly, too, but oh, so sad. He came back then, Sunday after Sunday, never calling to see if we'd be home, but just appearing at the front door with his *New York Times*.

On our first meeting in the lobby of the Playhouse Theatre he had seemed very animated and quite talkative, but on these Sundays he said little and seemed most unhappy. Struggling as I was at the time to make a living for my family as a writer, his sadness seemed inexplicable to me. For, with the financial and critical success of both *Come Back, Little Sheba* and *Picnic* he seemed to me the most fortunate of playwrights. I was puzzled, too, that when he talked it was always to question me about television. He seemed fascinated with it and the plays I had written for it, and he seemed anxious to try and write for it. Why in the world, I wondered, when he could write for the theater and make a living doing so, would he or anyone want to? I never told him that but answered his questions as best I could.

I left East Hampton before the summer was over to begin rehearsals for *The Trip to Bountiful* and though I must have told Bill of my leaving I have no memory of saying goodbye. I wonder now, if he arrived one Sunday at the East Hampton house only to find us gone.

I've often wondered, too, why he came those Sundays to sit in our living room to read his Sunday *Times* and then go home. The last time I saw him in California, many years later, I almost asked him. I regret now that I didn't.

My wife and I only stayed in New York for a few years after that summer and in those years I saw Bill only intermittently, mostly at parties at my house, or at friends' houses. He was always extremely friendly wherever we met and I was always kept in touch with what he was up to by Kim and other mutual friends.

It was many years before I was to visit with him alone again. I was in California working on a film and mighty unhappy about being away from the East. Again, I don't remember how Bill knew I was in California; my memory is that we ran into each other in a restaurant. However it was, he called me at my hotel and asked if I'd have dinner with him. He came for me in his car and we drove out to a restaurant in Malibu. And this time he talked—incessantly.

He was angry and bitter at Audrey Wood, his agent, at Hollywood and the New York theater. It was as if all the good things that had happened to him didn't matter. We were together about five hours ending up at his house. I left with a one-act play he had written and that, according to Bill, Audrey had not wanted to submit even to an off-off-Broadway theater.

He rang me the next morning to see if I had read the one-act play. I had and we talked about it and his plans to have it produced in California. We made plans to see each other again, but I left California soon after and we never did.

Inward Bound
Jerome Lawrence and *Robert E. Lee*

Every April, dramatists, contemporaries of William Inge, gather in his hometown of Independence, Kansas, to taste the air and sense the special quality in the atmosphere of the town and countryside where Bill Inge and his best plays and films were born.

Robert Anderson stated it most succinctly: "There are only two spots in the whole world which honor the birthplace of a playwright: Stratford-on-Avon and Independence, Kansas." Originally mothered by the remarkable Margaret Goheen, the annual William Inge Festival pays perfect honor to Inge by appreciating, understanding, and saluting the honorable profession of playwriting. Former winners of the annual "Lifetime Achievement in the Theatre Award" flock back to Kansas each year to pay tribute to their fellow craftsmen, to state their "Declaration of *Inter*dependence."

All around us in this "open sky" plains state we find the sources of Inge's most telling creations: the picnic grounds, the front porches, the faces of the neighbors, the staircase no longer dark at the top but enlightened by Bill's understanding memory. The physical as well as the mental scenery of this place enchants us: the fields stretching to blazing sunset horizons, the long-haired cattle grazing on both sides of the highway to Tulsa, Glencliff—the magnificent farm mansion where playwrights are housed and fed to the gills. When we described these rustic vistas to Garson Kanin, he said: "You want to know my kind of scenery? Times Square!" But Gar came to Independence. And kept coming back.

Is it true that the posh country club of this oil-rich boom town never admitted the Inge family to membership, though the teen-age Bill occasionally sneaked into dances "on a pass"? There is dramatic irony in this snub to the unwealthy lower middle-class of Independence, for the beautiful William Inge

Theatre is built on the very site of that original country club. It's probably just a legend, for legends gush like oil out of the rich earth of Kansas.

We were first introduced to Bill Inge by "The Texas Tornado," Margo Jones, in New York City during the remarkable spring of 1955. *Bus Stop* opened on March 2; Tennessee Williams's *Cat on a Hot Tin Roof* came to town three weeks later; and our *Inherit the Wind* blew into Broadway on April 21. All of these dramatists were Margo's "playwriting finds."

Of course, we knew how Margo had launched Bill's *Farther Off from Heaven* onto the stage of her tiny but discovery-rich theater at Dallas Fair Park. That was in early summer of 1948. Later the play grew up and became *The Dark at the Top of the Stairs*. But like Tenn's early plays and our *Inherit*, nobody on world-weary Broadway wanted to do it until Margo Jones "took a chance."

After her tragic too-early death, Williams, Inge, and Lawrence and Lee established the annual Margo Jones Award to producing-directors who, like Margo, "had the vision to contribute to the dramatic art with hitherto unproduced plays, that having been her ardent spirit and unremitting purpose."

Bill invited us to *Bus Stop* at the Music Box that happy Spring of mutual hits, and we invited him to *Inherit the Wind* four blocks downstream at the National. He told us he could come on one condition: he'd have to have the aisle-seat in the last row closest to the nearest exit. It didn't mean, he assured us, that he intended to "escape" from our play, it's just that he had terrible claustrophobia in a theater, not only with other writers' plays, but even at his own.

He also invited us for a "quick drink" once or twice to his Sutton Place South apartment, where we admired his Pulitzer Prize for *Picnic* displayed prominently on the wall where nobody could miss it. After he gave up New York for the West Coast, Lawyer L. Arnold Weissberger and Agent Milton Goldman bought that apartment, where it became *the* party place for theater personalities of three continents. To our knowledge, the loner Inge never had more than a dinner party for three the entire time he lived on Sutton Place South.

Our encounters with Inge on the West Coast are reported both vividly and accurately in Ralph F. Voss's fascinating book, *A Life of William Inge: The Strains of Triumph*. And we have repeated on tape, in greater detail, a number of those experiences to Dan Sullivan for his eagerly awaited biography of Inge. Mostly they concerned Bill's reading scripts aloud, playing all the parts (and damn well), at Lawrence's beach house in Malibu, and our heedless attempts to get him to change the title of *Where's Daddy?* and cut the violent ending of *Natural Affection*. We had admired his poetic titles, mainly *Come Back,*

Little Sheba and *Dark at the Top of the Stairs* and felt that Bill should dig back into the poetry barrel for another such, certainly a replacement for *Where's Daddy?* But Bill would have no part of it.

The Lee half of this team's close encounter with Inge-Whitehead-Clurman during the Phoenix tryout of *Natural Affection* has never been set down, however, in print or on tape. JL was in New York, teaching as "Master Playwright" at NYU and REL was pulling plays out of tyros as Adjunct Professor at UCLA. We had suggested to our old friend Bob Whitehead the excellent facility at Sombrero Playhouse, run by the enterprising Richard Charlton. Early in 1962, Whitehead took his company, directed by Harold Clurman (who had previously brought *Bus Stop* to dramatic and comedic life), to Sombrero, housed in the filthy-rich Phoenix suburb of Scottsdale. He found (to our later dismay, too) that audiences were bored with anything but total entertainment and amusement, and expected carbon-copies of New York hits, especially from Inge, such as *Picnic* or *Bus Stop*. So the assassination pistol was cocked for instant boredom.

Bob Whitehead invited REL to fly to Phoenix with his actress-wife Janet Waldo to have a "look-see" at the play: REL's California ranch-house was closer than JL's brownstone on East 50th in Manhattan. When the Lees arrived, Scottsdale was full of sunshine, but not inside the Sombrero Playhouse, where opening night was frigid February in Baffinland. The theater complex included a restaurant; after the first act, half the audience retreated to the bar and stayed there.

REL saw the failure-scarred Bill Inge walking around like a zombie, and proferred no advice, when he noted Bill was turning a deaf ear to both Clurman and Whitehead, refusing to change a comma. This was not arbitrary stubbornness on Bill's part. He had no choice. His plays were his. They demanded to be done as he conceived them, heard them, saw them inside his own head. Producer and director abandoned *Natural Affection*, which fared not much better in New York, even with Tony Richardson as director. A brilliant production in Hollywood in 1988, directed by Lorenzo DeStefano, revealed at last a viable play hidden under the scab of failure.

We tried to befriend Bill Inge in his too-early sunset years on the West Coast. But he was essentially inward-bound, and could never really partake of the potentials of collaboration—social or literary. But he knew always of our admiration and respect for his work, especially his ability to draw energy from his past, his roots, his growing up. And each year, as we come "home" to Bill's hometown of Independence, we're more aware of the widening plains of *his* independence, the splendor of his grass roots.

Counted Among His Friends
Robert Anderson

My first wife, Phyllis, who died in 1956, produced Bill's *Come Back, Little Sheba* for the Theatre Guild. He dedicated the play to her. It was a high moment in her life. She had trained to be a director at the Royal Academy in London and the Yale Drama School, but it was a poor time for women directors. There had been some idea that she might direct *Sheba*, but she stepped aside in favor of Danny Man, who did a superb job.

Phyllis deserved the dedication for many reasons, but perhaps most importantly for "landing" Shirley Booth to play Lola. Shirley loved the part but was reluctant to play it. Her husband had been ill, and she didn't want to be away from him and she didn't want to play such a sad play. She felt with her personal circumstances, it would depress her.

The Theatre Guild wanted to see the play in tryout at Lawrence Langner's summer theater in Westport, Connecticut. Phyllis said to Shirley, "Please do this play for this one week. If you don't this fine playwright may never be heard of." Shirley succumbed and as they say, the rest is.... The production launched Bill and "discovered" Shirley as a dramatic actress. She won the Tony for her performance, and I imagine it is the part for which she is best remembered.

For me one of the fascinating aspects of opening night was to watch something Shirley did. She was famous as a comedian. There is a great deal of comedy in *Sheba*. But early on, Shirley began to realize that the audience was laughing too much and that somehow they had to be led into the darker tones of the play. She began to kill her own laughs. What a strange lesson in acting.

I had read *Sheba* about the same time as Phyllis had read it. She was head of the Play Department at the Guild. I had written some notes on the play for Phyllis to give Bill if she wanted to and if Bill wanted to have them. (This was before my play *Tea and Sympathy*, but I was teaching playwriting at the American

Theatre Wing and writing extensively for radio and television, and had no hesitation in "analyzing" any script that fell into my hands!)

I don't think my notes on *Sheba* were in any way important to Bill, but soon after the play was produced, he came to me with a play that was to develop into *Picnic*. (It always amazed me to see how Bill kept going back to earlier plays to re-work them.) I again gave him some notes, and we talked. Then one day, at a meeting of the Dramatists Guild, he handed me the script and said he had done all he could do with it. Would I be interested in collaborating? I told him I felt that our "voices" and styles were too dissimilar, that I would be glad to continue to give him notes but I wasn't the collaborator he needed. Josh Logan as the eventual director of the play became that "collaborator."

Picnic was very successful, but Bill never stopped bitching about what Josh had done to the end of his play. One night in my apartment I teed off on him. He had won the Pulitzer Prize with the play. He had made a good deal of money with it. The Dramatists Guild contract gave him absolute control over his play. Nobody was allowed to change a word without his permission, etc., etc. So I thought he should shut up about it. Of course he didn't. He later brought out his own version of the play, *Summer Brave*.

My wives somehow had an affinity for Bill's plays. I was courting Teresa Wright in California when Kazan sent *Dark at the Top of the Stairs* to her. She flew east to confer with him, took the part, and my courtship continued for eighteen months, conveniently for me, in my hometown, New York.

In the early 1970s when I was President of the Dramatists Guild, Audrey Wood, who was Bill's agent and my agent, took me to lunch. She told me how depressed Bill was. He was now living in California. Nothing was going right for him. He felt worthless. Wasn't there some award the Dramatists Guild could give him that might help his self-esteem?

I brought up the subject at the next meeting. Bill had received all the awards available: the Pulitzer, Drama Critics, Tony, and in California, an Oscar for *Splendor in the Grass*. The Dramatists Guild has no award of its own to bestow. And none of us could come up with any half-way legitimate reason for establishing an award we could give Bill. More's the pity.

In Ralph Voss's splendid book on Bill, he writes that towards the end of his life, someone asked Bill about his friends. Who were his friends? Among the three or four he named, he mentioned me. I read this and was very sad. I hadn't seen Bill for many years. He had dropped out of our lives when Phyllis had become ill. We had never spent much time alone together, and then only to discuss his plays. And yet he counted me among his three or four friends.

Directing *Picnic*
Joshua Logan

I first met Bill Inge outside the dressing rooms at the Westport Playhouse where *Come Back, Little Sheba* was playing. It was before he came to New York. He looked very strange. He had had a very bad night I think. It was a well enough known fact that Bill drank a great deal in those days, and he had a pretty bad hangover. But he was charming, nice, gentle, when we liked his play, even nicer. And so not too long after that he called me up—I guess it was after I'd done *Mister Roberts*—and he said, "You have a lot of sunshine in your plays. The sun comes up in the plays."—I didn't quite know what he meant—"And therefore I would like you to consider this play that I am sending you." He sent me *Picnic*—or rather, *Front Porch*; it was called *Front Porch* at that time. I was very much taken by the people in the play and by the dialogue, but I felt that it had a rather sprawling way of being told: every time he wanted to introduce a new character he took them to another setting. There was one scene out in front of the hotel where a bunch of schoolteachers had their luncheon; and there was another where Hal got in a fight in front of a store. There were about five or six sets; it would have been a very expensive production. Not only that but somehow there was no time lapse taken care of. In other words, you would have just had to change the set and the audience would have had to wait in the darkness while they changed it and started the next scene. It would have slowed things down a great deal. I was very much against that and when I first talked to Bill I said, "Can't we find another setting for you?" He said, "I don't think so." But he said, "I'd be perfectly willing to talk about it." So we did. As a matter of fact, over a long period of time we talked a great deal and he would go back and write and he would suddenly appear at my house up in the country—because he had taken a house not too far away from me.

A funny thing happened once when Bill used to come to our house in the country. We lived in Stanford, and Bill used to come there early in the morning and just sit in the front waiting for us to wake up. One time he came and we had a very famous lady swimming in our pool. Her name was Greta Garbo. We had met her quite a few times through the man who was with her, George Schlee, a very good friend of ours. When Bill, not knowing who was there, came down to the pool, I said, "Oh Bill. Miss Garbo, this is Bill Inge." And she said, "How do you do?" or something like that. He turned and looked and then he went over and sat down and never said a word. He didn't come over closer; he just sat there. Finally we got up and left the pool and went on up to have lunch and had lunch; toward the end of lunch Bill appeared. I went over to him and I said, "Where have you been? What is the matter?" He said, "Well, when I met Miss Garbo, I felt that I just had to sit down and think that over. I've been thinking it over for quite a while. That is quite an experience. Do you realize what it means for me to meet her?" I certainly did because I was just as impressed as he was; but the fact that he had to go sit down was something very nice. He was a charming fellow, no question about it.

I think I must have said the moment we first discussed *Picnic*, "The ending is the most awful thing I have ever read in my life. You are led up to a point and suddenly you are let down. You are just absolutely kicked out of the door." But I didn't realize how strongly he felt about that because he was so passive and nice and agreeable to almost every other change. Finally I gave it up. I thought there would be no chance. He was nice, and he was gentle and fine, and it just was wonderfully written and yet it had no cohesiveness. It just couldn't hold together. But the Theatre Guild, that is Lawrence Langer and his wife Armina Marshall, did not give up on plays very easily. Finally Lawrence called me up and said, "I think you ought to do this play. Maybe it isn't perfect, but certainly the first two acts are much better than they were when we read them several months ago. And surely he will rewrite the last act when we are in rehearsal." So I reread it, and it was a better play than I had been reading anywhere else, so I said, "Yes, let's go ahead."

We went into rehearsal with a script; the first two acts were very much the way they are now. But in the third act everybody disappointed us. Howard never came back to see Rosemary. Alan left town for good and dropped Madge. Hal went off chased by the police and escaped on a freight train, and Madge walked down to the dime store where she worked with the boys riding past her in a jalopy and calling out rather lurid names for her indicating that they were all going to have her. It was really very disappointing. I thought, how am I ever going to do this play? I just don't believe in it. Fortunately Bill Inge came to our apartment for lunch the first day after the cast read the play aloud.

And, unfortunately for himself but very fortunately for the play, he asked my wife who had seen the reading what she thought of the play, and she said, "I loved every moment of it until they got separated. If those two people don't get together at the end I am not even going to go see it." At first he was kind of surprised that she had said that and then suddenly he stood up as though he were Madge and said, "Suppose Madge came out of the house with her big picture hat and her high-heeled shoes in a lovely summer dress with a little suitcase packed and said, 'Mom I'm going to Tulsa.'" We were both absolutely thrilled at the thought. And he said, "Then the mother runs after her and begs her not to do it and she just keeps on and she goes." I said, "Now I think it is going to be not only a wonderful play but a big hit." He said, "Well, I will go home and write it."

The next day I didn't see Bill until the end of the day; he came in and said, "Here it is."—and he handed me the scene. All it was now was a much longer version of the scene that he had written originally. They said, "Good-bye," and separated longer and slower; it was just endless. Rosemary and Howard still weren't going to get together. It was just too much disappointment. It was setting everyone up and then hitting them over the head. Then it got to be a passion with me. I said, "We've got to have that, Bill." He said, very, very angry at me, "I'll write it. But I don't like it." He did write it, it was very good, and we went on and we rehearsed it. I said, "If it isn't absolutely marvelous on the road, I'll listen to anything you say." He said, "I just don't want a happy ending, a wrapped-up, tied-with-a-blue-ribbon ending." I said, "It isn't all wrapped up. If she goes after that bum and he is on the top of a freight train, he is going to meet her in Tulsa and they are going to share a room while he is a bellhop. First of all, that is not very happy for most of our audience, certainly not the mothers. And also it is exactly the same thing that happened to Flo, her mother. She was deserted with her two little children and she has been working and taking in boarders and taking in washing ever since." But that never seemed to appease Bill. He still felt that this ending didn't have any basis in the play.

After the show opened I took my kids and headed down to Jamaica. And someone sent me a clipping saying that Bill Inge was going to publish *Picnic*. In the meantime it had gotten almost the best notices of the year. He announced that he was going to publish two endings, his ending and my ending; of course, "my" ending was still written by him. I got back as soon as I possibly could and I said, "Bill, you can't publish two endings if you are going to win the Pulitzer Prize, which you might do, and also the New York Drama Critics' Circle Award, which you might do. For God sake, don't do it if you want to get those prizes because they are very important to your family. When you die, it is going to mean an awful lot to have those two prizes." He didn't publish the two endings, but I'm sure he went home and growled and hit a few pillows or something.

It won the Pulitzer Prize and the Critics' Award and then sold for a huge amount to the movies, and became the biggest dramatic hit in years. But I kept hearing that Bill was saying, "I am going to put this play on with a different ending and they will really see what it is like." Well, he didn't get it on until after he was dead. It did open on Broadway as *Summer Brave*, and it lasted a few days, I think. I couldn't go to see it, it was too painful. I will never understand why Bill thought it was necessary to make it that unpleasant and unhappy. He was an artist and he certainly had a right to his opinion; but I don't know of any play that the public adored as much as they did *Picnic*; they just loved it.

Before we opened on Broadway, we toured *Picnic*; as a matter of fact if we hadn't had the out-of-town tour I don't think we could have made it into a success. When we came to Cleveland, I began to notice that the audience was very divided in their feelings; I didn't feel a unified reaction to anything. David Merrick came to see it and I asked him, "What do you think of the leading man?" David said, "I don't know; every time he comes on the stage I just bristle. I react very badly to him. He's showing off and bragging. I can't stand him." Then I heard a man in the audience say, "Some hero!" And it suddenly occurred to me, "My God, they feel that we don't know that he has got bad qualities." I thought if we could get some lines in the play that let the audience know that we knew he was an unattractive boy; but the characters that could say it had to be people that the audience believed. They would believe anything Paul Newman, who played Alan, would say; certainly the women would. So I took the lines that David Merrick had said, and the "some hero" kind of feeling and just put in about six or seven lines for Alan to say that spoke of Hal's past. I called Bill and I explained to him what had happened, and he said, "I see what you mean." I said, "Would it be all right for Alan to say this?"—and I read him the three or four lines. He said, "Fine, go ahead. Just let me know how it goes afterward."—because Bill for some reason couldn't bear to be around while the play was playing. That night we put those lines in and it was a smash. The audience understood where they stood.

Designing *Picnic*
Jo Mielziner

I met Bill Inge in 1950 when he was about 37 years old. At that time he had moved into the old Dakota on Central Park West in New York where I'd been living and had had my studio since about 1938. Inge was, to me, a very thoughtful, sensitive man. At our first meeting we talked theater only, not just my work on Broadway but his interests in production and playwriting and theater in general. I found him broad in his point of view, very sensitive, and I was curious about what our relations would be if we ever worked together.

I got a call shortly thereafter from Joshua Logan, the producer, who informed me that he had taken an option on a new manuscript by Inge. Bill's living quarters were on the second floor of the Dakota and we met several times in his digs to talk about the script of *Picnic*. He'd been very curious about my approach to designing this play, and I was primarily digging from him his feelings about the atmosphere of a small Kansas town, which was the subject of the background of the play. I found him very helpful because he was not dogmatic; at the same time he was open to ideas and he seemed to have great trust in his producer. The early discussion was primarily on background.

Then during the pre-rehearsal days we met a great deal with Bill and Josh Logan; they used to stop in on my ground floor studio in this same building where Bill lived. He was very interested in watching the early sketches, the models, and finally the final paintings for his play. In general, I had a feeling that Bill's confidence in Logan as director and in the excellent cast that Logan had put up with the author's approval eased his feelings in a way that I thought was quite unusual because my impression was that Bill could easily be thrown by lack of confidence in the materials around him. But he had complete confidence in his producer, and his concern as the playwright was not too evident. He was very excited and very pleased as the play got into dress rehearsals and, of course, the opening was excellent. As we all know, it finally proved to be not only a great success but a Pulitzer Prize winner.

Later on, Logan asked me to design the film for *Picnic* and I regretted that we didn't have personal contact with Inge at that time. I don't know why he wasn't out in Kansas then. Maybe he was tied up with other work, but he'd mentioned several towns in Kansas that I should visit, and he felt that these had the right atmosphere for the film, which I designed and eventually got an Oscar for. I saw Bill socially a few times after that, but I never had the pleasure of working with him on another production. I had great admiration for him both as a sensitive human being and as a fine craftsman.

On the Verge
N. Richard Nash

William Inge had a secret. It may have been a secret he himself didn't know he had. We were both living in New York during the run of each of our plays; his was *Picnic* at the Music Box Theatre; mine, *The Rainmaker* at the Cort. The two theaters are only a few blocks from one another. To add to the sense of propinquity, the part of Madge in Bill's play was being enacted by Janice Rule, who was soon to be my wife. Quite often, Bill and I met backstage at the Music Box. He knew that I admired his work full-heartedly, and he professed to like mine as well. But at that stage we were, I thought, just accidental acquaintances.

Then, for a number of weeks, I was in California. When I returned, the backstage doorman at the Cort gave me a note from Bill. It said, tersely, "Where ya been?" So I called him.

We would meet in Jan's dressing room or at the Cort. We walked a lot. He was an obsessive shopper and he had unpredictable taste. He bought raffish old magazines that would not cause the flicker of an eyelash nowadays but were considered erotic/pornographic in the fifties. He bought neckties he never wore. His favorite haunt was a pawn shop on Eighth Avenue. He would gaze at the windows, as enrapt as a child, then go indoors and purchase a nonfunctioning old Graflex camera or a pack of trick playing cards or a jeweled Turkish dagger. He had paid a lot of money for the dagger, and be was heartbroken when be faced the reality that its rubies had to be made of glass. When I tried to comfort him by saying rubies are always made of glass, he laughed in an inordinately loud voice.

Inordinate because he had one of the world's quietest voices. A sad and tentative voice. And frightened eyes. Excited as he was by Manhattan, it intimidated him. And I think he felt that way about the theater. Terrified. Even by his own success. It's been said, quite often, that he hated Josh Logan's work on *Picnic*. I don't think he hated it; I think it scared him. People were praising the dramatist for something he hadn't said; for being someone he couldn't be. He was accepting rewards under false pretenses.

One night we were standing at the back of the theater, watching a scene in the third act of *Picnic*. At a particularly touching moment, the audience laughed. It distressed him. He turned to me and said, "Why are they laughing at that?" It was as if he had said, "Why are they laughing at me?"

This question of inapposite laughter came up in connection with another scene in the play, quite a critical one. Logan had been complaining, before the play opened anywhere, that the original script had no love scene between the two leading characters, Madge and Hal. When no love scene was forthcoming, Josh created a "love dance," a slowed-down jitterbug, a sensuous foreplay of the two lovers. It was beautifully danced by Janice and Ralph Meeker.

One night. Bill asked: "Why don't they laugh at that?"

"Because they're moved by it."

"Are you?"

"Yes."

"Why?"

"Well ... it's not only erotic, it's full of yearning. They're lonely people." Then I added pedantically, "Besides, it's a love scene, and your play can't do without it."

"I hate it," he said. "It embarrasses me."

He felt outside it, deserted by it, and somewhat betrayed.

The question is: If Bill felt lost and alienated, if he felt callously misused by a heedlessly dancing heterosexual world, if he felt he did not belong in the theater, where did he feel he belonged? Not in the military academy he had taught in, not in the newspaper rooms where he'd been a mediocre journalist, not in Kansas. And if not in the theater—then nowhere, maybe. Perhaps, at the end, when he closed the garage doors, got in his car, and turned the motor on, he was on a journey to find somewhere.

He used to live at the Dakota, on Central Park West. I too lived on Central Park West, a few blocks to the north. We frequently, when the weather was good, walked homeward, along the park. When we arrived at his house, he nearly always paused and said, "I think I'll walk you up to your place." In addition to his forsaken need for companionship, I think there was something else he had to say, something he'd forgotten to mention. Or some secret he was about to impart. We would get to my place and we would pause. I'd think: Any minute now, he's going to tell me whatever it is he has held so privately to himself. But the moment would pass.

Finally, I dismissed the notion that there was any mystery of any kind. No secret: those moments were just the man's natural hesitancy about arrivals and departures.

A few years after *Picnic,* in a conversation with Tennessee Williams, the latter said, "I always thought Bill was on the verge of telling me some very intimate secret."

Perhaps he was. Perhaps we'll find it in his plays. In *Picnic,* maybe.

What Remains Behind
Richard H. Goldstone

> Though nothing can bring back the hour
> Of splendour in the grass, of glory in the flower;
> We will grieve not, rather find
> Strength in what remains behind....
> —*Wordsworth, "Ode: Intimations of Immortality"*

Bill Inge was the loneliest man I've ever known. The lines quoted above, which are from the poem Bill loved best of all, tell us something about that loneliness. By nature shy and withdrawn, he resisted being physically alone. He wanted a human presence near him, most particularly in the hours between midnight and dawn when inexplicable fears—those very fears that were ultimately to cost him his life—became most intense and most intolerable. But despite that need he lived an isolated existence. He had friends, but no friend, no wife, no mistress, no one with whom he could share his life, nor even a part of his life. It was the worlds of the imagination—literature and painting—that were his passions. And he clung to the memories of the life of his childhood and growing up, a life which he understood, without romanticizing it, as safe and uncomplicated. That world of the 1920s which provided him with the setting for a number of his plays stood in sharp contrast to the world of the decades following World War II which to him were full of insecurity and menace, irrationality, and horror. Only in one of his plays—one of his best, by the way—did he face the contemporary scene: that play, *Natural Affection,* confronts what have become the twin super-problems in American life today: the breaking-up of the family unit and teenage violence. But Inge's previous plays, *Come Back, Little Sheba, Picnic, Bus Stop, The Dark at the Top of the Stairs,* and *A Loss of Roses* are set not only deep in the heartland of America, away from the urban centers, but they take place at a time when middle-aged people spent evenings listening to the radio and young people mainly went to the movies.

But I have wanted this piece to be a recollection, my own memory of Bill Inge. And I don't want it to overstress the dark side of his nature, though I was always aware of the self-destructive element that lay deep beneath the surface of his genial and gentle personality.

I knew Inge best during the decade of the 1950s when he emerged from obscurity to become one of the most successful playwrights in America, a role he filled with considerably more courage and humility than most people realized. Very few knew that the William Inge who came to New York in 1950 to participate in the production of *Come Back, Little Sheba* had already conquered the alcoholism and despair which nearly destroyed him in the previous decade. His celebrity was dearly won, but it was something he never quite believed in anyhow.

When I first met Inge at the home of another writer, several months after the closing of *Sheba*, I was a young college instructor of English—as he had been only a few years before. He had resigned from Washington University in St. Louis when the Theatre Guild decided to produce *Sheba*. Despite the modest success of the production, Bill did not have any real financial security; he lived in a one-room apartment at the Dakota, husbanding his resources as he worked on his second play.

I told Inge something at that meeting that deeply gratified him: that I had lunched with a former Air Force associate, Thornton Wilder, the day after he had seen *Come Back, Little Sheba*; that Wilder had expressed great admiration for Inge's play, but that Wilder detected what he believed was an interesting but not an incapacitating flaw in it. "Nobody seems to have noticed," Wilder exclaimed with a roar of laughter, "that Inge's play is really about a couple of bona-fide saints whom he passes off simply as a childless middle-aged Midwest couple!" Inge smiled delightedly, neither confirming nor denying his agreement with the justice of Wilder's observation. But he was very happy that Wilder, for whom he had prodigious respect, took his work seriously. As a teacher and critic of literature, Inge was much more interested in the judgments of artists than in reviewers, even though it was the reviewers who sent people to the theater—or kept them away.

After that I met Inge from time to time and heard a little about his work in progress. I particularly recall a Christmas party in 1952. Even though he was fascinated by celebrity-peopled gatherings, Inge had retreated to the furthest corners of a bedroom which partygoers occasionally passed through en route to the bathroom. He was pleased to see me, pleased, that is, to have someone to talk to. We talked at length about his new play which he had titled *Picnic* and whose premiere was scheduled for February in Columbus, Ohio. Since I was teaching at the University of Kentucky and Columbus was accessible from Lexington, Inge invited me to the opening, an invitation he renewed some weeks later by phone on the day of the performance.

That evening in Columbus was the real beginning of our friendship. During the first intermission I told Inge that his play would receive both the Pulitzer and the Critics' prizes. "How can you tell, after only one act?" he asked incredulously. "I can tell," I responded with an authority for which there was no basis except that as a native New Yorker I had been seeing plays since the age of five. Moreover, the cast, though they were unknowns, were extremely gifted. They included Ralph Meeker, Janice Rule, Eileen Heckart, Kim Stanley, and Paul Newman, backed up by a group of solid Broadway veterans. When the final curtain came down I observed Inge huddled with producer Armina Marshall and director Joshua Logan. Not wanting to interrupt I drove back to Kentucky in the early hours and composed a letter in my head to Inge filled with minor comments, quibbles about a word here, a phrase there. I wrote it all out before I went to sleep and dispatched it without rereading it. I no longer remember what I wrote, and I most assuredly made no suggestion of any consequence. Nevertheless, a few days later I received a note from Inge full of thanks and urging me to visit him when I next came to New York. Moreover, on the night of the New York opening my phone rang at two a.m.: Inge thought I'd like to hear the *Times* and *Tribune* reviews confirming my earlier enthusiasm.

For the next ten years I was one of Bill's close friends, a status that meant less than it seemed. He had several close friends: Charlie Jackson, Saint-Subber, Elaine Stritch, William Goyen, Gore Vidal, James Leo Herlihy, and Tennessee Williams. But being a friend of Bill's consisted principally of being on a list of names whom he would call in the hope of snaring one or another for dinner and talk and then a movie. I never knew whether Bill called people alphabetically or according to a preferential rating system. After I returned to New York permanently in 1953, Bill called me frequently, usually on weekends when everyone else was out of the city. He had acquired a large Lincoln sedan, which he was reluctant to pilot in New York and its environs; I have many happy recollections of driving with him to East Hampton, Bucks County, the upper Hudson Valley, and to Brooklyn Heights. Riding in a car with Bill was a particular pleasure because not only did he like to talk about writers (Proust was his god) but he could recite from memory most of the great English lyric poems. Note that the titles of his television play *Glory in the Flower* and his film play, *Splendor in the Grass,* both come from the same lines of Wordsworth's "Ode: Intimations of Immortality."

Our drive to Brooklyn was occasioned by his wanting to show me a house in Columbia Heights that he wanted to buy. A five-story brownstone with windows on three sides and a commanding view of lower Manhattan. It was cheap at forty thousand. He was reluctant, however, to make a decision unless someone would be willing to live in the house, that is, to rent the self-contained basement apartment with an enormous garden leading down to the Esplanade. Once I expressed my willingness to be the tenant, Inge seemed determined to obtain the house. But when some weeks went by and I heard nothing further, I called to ask when I could start moving in. To my dismay he confessed that he had changed his mind, that he had rejected the opportunity to become a house-owner. "But why, Bill?" I asked. "Dick, I just can't move to Brooklyn. I just can't. Who would ever visit me there?" He was right. No one would have. When instead he moved to an apartment on Sutton Place, he was pretty much alone there.

I did live with Inge, as his houseguest, during the summer of 1960 when I was at loose ends having just finished my doctoral studies and he had rented a beach house in Quogue. I learned a great deal about Inge that summer that I had never understood before, for example, his work habits. I had known from the beginning that he was a conscientious craftsman. He had shown or read me four independent drafts, each completely revised, of *The Dark at the Top of the Stairs* before he turned it over to his director, Elia Kazan. But I had always assumed that Bill worked intensively on a play and when it was completed relaxed for weeks or months until he was ready to begin a new one. That summer sojourn showed me I was mistaken. His routine was to get up early, around six or six thirty. Every day he would type for about an hour before having breakfast. After breakfast he spent the remainder of the morning at the typewriter where he would work on one of several projects. Plays commanded his principal energies, but he worked on stories, memoirs, one-act plays, extended fiction, poems, and some highly therapeutic pornography (in 1960, Inge was a healthy man in his late forties who nevertheless led an existence of sexual continence). During those weeks in Quogue he was at work on an early draft of *Natural Affection* (when it was finally completed, it opened during a newspaper strike, and its unusual qualities went unobserved by the general public).

I also realized that Inge could not remain in the beach house at night unless someone else was there. One night I inadvertently locked myself out after he had gone to sleep; not wishing to wake him, I almost drove back to New York. Finally I solved the problem by calling him from a local diner. He was not at all annoyed by the inconvenience. In fact, he was greatly relieved that I had done so; for if he had wakened in the middle of the night and discovered that I had left, *he* would, he told me afterwards, have had to drive back to the city.

After the failure of *Natural Affection*, Inge sold his New York apartment and purchased a house in Hollywood where he lived until his death. With a continent between us, I saw him infrequently after he left the East. For a while he kept up connections by talking on the telephone on Sunday mornings, but neither of us felt at ease under those circumstances. Our last real meeting was in 1966 when I visited him at his Hollywood house. A small unpretentious house but beautifully located, well-landscaped and with a magnificent swimming pool, it would seem to have provided him with all the creature comforts a man could possibly want. But I realized during the day we spent together that, despite his expansive hospitality and his several plans about movie scripts, he was no more at ease in Hollywood than he had been in New York. What basically troubled him was not the fact that playgoers, moviegoers, and readers were no longer as interested in his work as they had been a decade earlier; the problem was the fact that he was still afraid of the dark at the top of the stairs. Nothing that was happening to him or to the world around him seemed to be bringing any light. Neither success nor neglect changed the circumstance that Inge was a desperately unhappy man. The gods had given him many gifts: perseverance, talent, discrimination, charm, even good looks and a fine voice. But they had withheld from him the means of coping with life's terrors though they gave him the courage to withstand them for sixty years. Bill had a lot of courage. As his friend Tennessee Williams observed in 1958, "the personal odyssey of Bill Inge ... is a drama as fine and admirable as any of the ones he has given ... to the American Theatre ... one in which the stairs rise from dark to light through something remarkable fine and gallant in his own nature."

A Softness That Never Toughened
William Gibson

I met Bill for the first time in 1948 and talked to him for the last time the night he killed himself; our friendship over the quarter-century between was light, but it spanned his years from the bad to the good to the bad. In the forties we were both novice playwrights in Kansas. Bill was a slim young man then, with an aristocratic nose and a shapely head, boyish, rather diffident, not happy, teaching at a girl's college in Missouri and reviewing theater and music for a St. Louis newspaper; he was worried that he was drinking too much. After we moved to Stockbridge he wrote my wife asking whether he could be interviewed at the Austen Riggs Center for therapy. A happier letter cancelled the request; he was having a play done at Westport called *Come Back, Little Sheba*. The play went on to New York, was a hit, and was followed over the years by *Picnic* and *Bus Stop*; and for a decade the critics called Bill one of our top three playwrights.

I was surprised thus to run into him one night in the Riggs workshop sawing a piece of wood; he was an in-patient. I never asked him why, but I knew his life was often a misery, and the only rock in it was his place in the theater. In that period he came to eat in the kitchen with our family on many a winter night, always a gentle guest and a pleasant talker, gossipy without malice; a speech mannerism was that he kept his voice light, only in his mouth—he never let into it the man who was deeper. He was a teetotaller now and getting fat instead. Discharged from Riggs, he rented a bachelor's apartment in town and stayed on for a year or two, wrote, read, bought paintings, wore a dark spot into our wallpaper back of a couch with the pomade on his thinning hair, talked of going back to Kansas to teach, and put deposits on houses he could never bring himself to buy; he went occasionally to New

York and checked in with us when he came back. It was a solitary and rootless life, these good years. The Sunday a half-page ad for his new play appeared in the *Times*—with his name featured in bold type over it, *The Dark at the Top of the Stairs*, the whole ad like an escutcheon of fame—he phoned and asked could he watch Perry Como on TV with us that night; he had nothing else to do, nobody to do it with.

I saw a lot of television that way. We never talked much technically about writing, our approaches to it were too dissimilar; but he was responsible for my turning a television script, *The Miracle Worker*, into a stage play—he recommended it warmly to a theater producer, who lunched me, and I began the stage version that week. Our other literary experience in common was when one night in a Great Barrington five-and-ten we bought two succulent gum erasers and congratulated ourselves on having advanced our careers so brilliantly.

The Dark was his fourth straight smash, something of a record among serious playwrights. "Stand high a long enough time, your lightning will come," wrote a poet, and the night Bill was hit I do not forget. A respected magazine was to run a long essay on his work, with Bill as their cover, and he had with pleasure supplied the photo for the honor; when he brought the issue to our kitchen he was trembling. The essay was by a clever young critic, making his name, and with cruel intelligence it flayed and dissected and buried every play, Bill's life-work. To crown it, Bill had called the critic to protest and wept on the phone.

It marked a turn in taste—whether critical, public, or Bill's own; he never had another hit. His work did change: over the next three flops, the real and simple folk of his Midwest settings turned into big-city neurotics, modern, super sexy, violent—thin fantasies. In between he wrote a movie script, won an Oscar, settled on the-coast, and wrote a couple more that were flops. When the movie jobs stopped, he taught writing at a college, not for the money, perhaps for the respect. Still writing plays, he couldn't get them produced now, they went begging; one of our top three playwrights had simply been liquidated. When the Berkshire Theatre Festival got under way he sent me a dozen new scripts, full-lengths and one-acts, which I didn't like but thought we should stage for him—we never had a producer who didn't detest them. One full-length was about a lonely man whose unexpected visitor is the beautiful wife who divorced him, passionate now to come back, and after a night of lovemaking he learns she has escaped from a madhouse. I read it as a parable of Bill and his audience. He wrote and published two novellas, which sank without a ripple, and in a letter he said that since his beloved theater didn't want him any more "I guess it's curtains for me." I didn't read that literally enough either.

On June 9th I found a message to call him back on the coast; it was "urgent." My wife was out of town, but when I spoke to Bill—his tongue was thick with sedation—his last question was the same as his first to her, twenty-five years earlier, could he come to Riggs? I said I'd make some calls and get back to him. It was a Saturday night and eight calls later I had no authoritative news, but a bed might be available some time next week; and at midnight I phoned Bill again to say I'd know more in the morning. I said I hoped he came, it would be good to see him, and he said yes and he appreciated all I'd done, and I said nonsense and asked was he alone, and he said his sister lived with him, and I asked was she there, and he said yes. I said the Berkshire Theatre Festival was doing *Summer Brave* and his voice lifted a bit with interest—the only time—to say yes, wasn't that nice. So I said I'd call in the morning, have a good night if possible.

He said, "What?"

"Have a good night."

He said, "All right."

In the morning I got more information, and with the three-hour difference waited for the sun to rise in California; when it did, it found him in his car in the garage, dead.

Little Sheba was a lost dog, like the hopes of boyhood, and there was softness in Bill that never toughened to adult business; it dreams back in his best plays to that lost world, hateful and lovely. But the dreams now were lost, too. That he wanted to come to Riggs was a final sigh to be whole; by now he was addicted to tranquillizers, trying to ease the pain. And he did.

Driving Inge
John Connolly

I met Bill through Glenway Wescott, a family friend. Glenway Wescott was an American author from Wisconsin. He introduced Bill to me at a time when a Marine Corps buddy of mine was coming to town with his fiancée and in order to impress them I asked Glenway to give a literary tea at his home on Park Avenue. He invited Sir Sacheverell Sitwell, Sir Osbert Sitwell, and Dame Edith Sitwell—the three Sitwells; she was the center of attention, to say the least. Marianne Moore, Katherine Anne Porter, and Auden were there—and Bill. Bill brought Shirley Booth, who was then in one of his productions and apparently an old friend. I must say it was an eye-opening event; even for the likes of Glenway it was rather exotic. Glenway was used to traveling with that kind of company. I wasn't, but I was impressed

In the six years that I worked for him as his assistant, Bill used to like to ride, not drive, but have me drive every conceivable place. He was, at the time, asking for, and I use this word advisedly, psychiatric counseling at Riggs Center in Stockbridge. Bill used to go up there and live off campus, as he would call it, at Mrs. Smith's boarding house on the main street in Stockbridge. Sometimes we would travel up and back in the same day; and that's a four-hour drive. I would do that round trip as many as five days a week. He would forget something or want something—or want me to stay there or not want me to stay there. In addition to that, we would drive to Florida two or three times a year, and eventually when we went to California I would make that trip three or four times a year.

Bill had both agoraphobia and claustrophobia. He couldn't stand airplanes. He had a fear of flying. He loved to be in a car. I think of him just sitting there rocking back and forth in a car for hours and hours on end without saying a word and then suddenly for the next hundred miles or so he wouldn't stop talking—ideas, plots, people—especially people from Independence, Kansas, where he grew up. He would tell me stories of all the things that he felt were important in people's lives, which is what his plays were all about: hopes, fears, ups, downs, the stuff that every single writer that has been worth anything has ever done. He would tell me whole plots of plays and stories. He would say, do you remember so and so and what's her name and such and such? Do you remember my cousin so and so and all these things that happened? The ideas were fantastic; they would be written down in his mind but not in reality. I would remind him of this several days or weeks later, and he would say, "Oh, I don't remember that in detail but remind me again sometime." He talked away more plays and stories than any man I've ever known. If I'd only had a tape recorder, the library of William Inge would be voluminous indeed.

He did go with me in an airplane the day after his mother died in Kansas. That was in the spring of 1958. I practically had to drag him. He said, "I've got to get there fast." Trains wouldn't do it, so he got onto a plane. It was a Super Constellation which at the time was the biggest plane they made and would have enough room for him to sort of breathe. He sat in an aisle seat in the First Class section, absolutely petrified. We landed in Kansas City—it was a non-stop flight—rented a car, and drove first to Lawrence and then to Independence. I remember him walking into his mother's house; and he turned, silhouetted against the window, and I thought he was going to cry, but the first thing he did was to stop and walk over to the mantel and stop the clock. He could not stand the ticking of a clock in any room that he was in. If it was someone's home, he left the room. If it was a hotel or a public room, he wouldn't stay. If it was his own or any place that he had control of, he would stop the clocks. He couldn't stand the ticking of it.

All the townspeople there were very sympathetic to Bill, wanting to come up to be family with him, and he just mumbled. When they left the room, he would then start saying who was who and what was what—as though it were almost, not a gossip column, but trying to give a background for all these various and sundry people he knew, trying to tie in people who were in certain plays of his that had been produced or in short stories he had written. I met all of those people that had meant so much to him, and I recognized all the people in his plays. And I would look and he would sort of grimly nod. I say grimly because his mother's death was very traumatic for him. I remember that we went to the funeral home. He saw his mother; he almost had to be carried out of there. I don't remember if he stayed for the funeral. I don't believe he did, because I remember driving back to Kansas City with him and putting him on a train.

The other time that he flew, he wanted to go to Dallas, where a play of his was being done. And we started out by car, and got as far as Tennessee, where his sister Helene lived. And he decided that he would take a plane from there to Dallas. He and seven pieces of luggage got on the plane. The plane took off and Bill and seven pieces of luggage got off in Little Rock, Arkansas—and he took a train from there. In the meantime I drove on to Dallas to meet him there, not knowing that I had passed him in the meantime.

* * *

Bill never wanted to have a home—although his delight in life was asking real estate agents to show him any number of places. He would time and again say, "I'm going back to Lawrence; I'm going back to Independence"—and he'd settle on Lawrence. We came several times, staying at the University of Kansas—the president at the time was a friend of his and would lend him the guest house—and he would get all excited about buying a house there. I think on two occasions we actually contacted real estate agents and set up appointments, one of which he kept and the other of which he didn't. We went and looked at several pieces of property. Eventually he settled on something that was an abandoned or almost abandoned stone house or barn that he wanted to redo. He never did anything about it. I think he resented all the slickness of New York and at one time felt that they looked down on him. It turned out that that wasn't it at all; he was just scared that he wouldn't fit in with all the people that he had tried to emulate.

His sexuality was sublimated. He put all of those feelings into his writing. The obvious thing people talk about is: Did he go cruising? Did he do this? Did he do that? I could tell you stories about various incidents, about people he knew—especially in Hollywood. We spent part of each year there for six years. The number of people who literally threw themselves at Bill Inge or wanted to call up and be a part of his life—I'm talking about the so-called leading men of his day! You'd simply have to look at any movie credits of the period, and you'd know who these people were. It didn't affect Bill. He would have them to dinner. He was more curious about how they handled their sexuality than he was in trying to participate or be with them in a sexual encounter. Bill's sexuality was voyeuristic more than most people would think. I don't mean watching somebody making love; it was in picking their brains about why they made love, to whom they made love—but without seeming to be too intrusive. Most people don't seem to realize that, in order to get the most information out of someone, sit back and be a good listener and people will pour out their hearts. Bill and Tennessee Williams were the greatest listeners of all time—except when we were alone and Bill would tell those endless stories. The minute people would get around him and talk to him about things, he would turn himself off to listen. He would ask one or two questions, just to feed that little spark of their memory. He would ingest it and digest it.

At one time, it was suggested that I was his lover, and I thought, oh boy, you really don't know Bill Inge. If I were, I'd be a rich man. Bill paid me a pittance to do things because I was interested in working for him because it was an astonishingly glamorous job. I did almost routine things—getting his notes ready, handling his day-to-day finances. He had lawyers and accountants, and I became a glorified errand boy. But everything I've done in my career has been because of it. I was interested in plays and films and in television; and I've not done badly. As a lighting designer, I've been nominated nine times for Emmys and I've won three.

* * *

In the summer of 1958, Bill and I drove to State College, Pennsylvania. A group of his one-act plays were to be done at a summer theater there, a small barn really. Barbara Baxley wanted to appear in them. Audrey Wood just wanted to see these plays to see if she had anything in the way of an electric prod to get Bill to do a full three-act play for Broadway. I remember Bill saying, "Barbara is coming this afternoon. We will go and meet her. She is coming with Audrey." Bill and I pulled up to this small, dusty airport and we sat in the car watching the sky for this plane to come. The door opened and out stepped onto the hastily pushed-up steps Barbara Baxley, looking like something out of Hollywood—with a turban streaming in the wind, standing like she expected photographers—and Audrey Wood looking stern, looking to see who was here. And off we went—Bill, Barbara, Audrey, and myself—to the local motel. Bill did the plays, and he did an interview for a man named Brustein, for *Harper's*. Bill was to be on the cover; the picture was taken there in the arena by a female photographer who was very good. And Robert Brustein tore Bill to shreds. Bill was so bitter about it and so angered by it; I never saw him as angry as that. The man, to make his reputation, tried to destroy Bill. It was so unfair, unwarranted, and certainly untrue.

* * *

Bill had very little to do with the films made from his plays. They always just took his property and sent it off to the Hollywood factory to be hammered out into whatever they wanted. Bill thought very little of most of their adaptations of his work. Once we were at a private screening of the film of *Dark at the Top of the Stairs*. He was so disappointed in it that he walked out—I went with him of course—in the middle of the film and refused to talk about it. One of the ones that he liked most was *Bus Stop*. He adored Marilyn Monroe. During the time that I knew him, they used to have dates. They would go off and just sit in a corner somewhere at friends' homes or restaurants and just simply talk. She was an astonishingly bright girl. All of that dumb blonde bit was a great put-on. Bill's interest in his films was so much that he decided that he couldn't stand anybody working on his films. He wanted to do one of his own; that is when he first started working on *Splendor in the Grass*.

Splendor in the Grass was done on four New York locations. The body of the work was done in Filmway Studios on 125th Street. The second location which was what I guess to Bill would be equivalent to the Riggs Center in Stockbridge was done on Long Island at a sanatorium. The third location, the settings of Natalie's (Deanie's) home and Warren's (Bud's) home, was on Staten Island where they found a neighborhood that resembled the 1920s. The fourth location was out on Long Island in Quogue—within not even three blocks of the ocean—and Kazan somehow managed to make it look like a Kansas prairie with corn and a windmill and oil wells.

Bill was more than pleased with *Splendor*. Warner Brothers was pleased with it tremendously but they wanted total control of it. The stipulation in the contract was that it was to run no more than two hours and three minutes. No one has ever been able to tell me why there was that stipulation, but it was two hours and fifteen minutes. To cut it they had to pare it down very severely. I was with Bill and Kazan; at the time the Johnson office or the Hays office, I don't know what it was called then, was the regulatory body of the screen's censorship board, where we went for a screening. The people that represented this were two men. One was a tough Mr. Hays or whatever his name was and the other was a Jesuit priest, who before the film began told me one of the dirtiest stories that I think I have ever heard. It made my ears cringe, so you can imagine this man was the salt of the earth. He was no stranger to the ways of life.

The film was run and there was much scratching of notes being written hastily in the dark. And the lights came up; well we've got problems. The problems turned out to be two tiny little bits in the film, one was Warren on the floor with Natalie, fully clothed—they were just wrestling around as two kids do—and Warren just happened to put his leg between Natalie's, rolling over. Disaster! Couldn't have that sort of thing! The other was a "nude scene," Natalie running from the bathroom—a rear view on a long lens at a great distance and slightly out of focus on purpose. End of the world! Off with their heads! Kazan said, "No way. We've cut this thing down, we don't want to cut it anymore. Those are very important, crucial things to the film." Bill echoed this and stated it in even stronger terms. Round and around they went. The upshot was they wouldn't release it unless those two offending sections of the film were cut. The film would then be released in Europe as it was but not with these two scenes in "pure" America.

When it received an Academy Award nomination, Bill decided to take a train from New York to Los Angeles; he always did. We went on the Twentieth-Century Limited—one of the great trains—to Chicago and then on to Los Angeles from Chicago. He always took four days. I refused to drive it in less than six. I don't enjoy driving great distances, especially that much by myself. I arrived exhausted and the first thing Bill said was, "You've got to go to New York to get my tuxedo and rent one for yourself; we have got to appear at the Oscars." I said, "Why me?" He said, "The studio wants me to take some young lady that I don't know and I simply refused. I will go with somebody that knows me. I refuse to go with somebody that doesn't know me." I said, "All right." So I flew back to New York, picked up his tuxedo, rented one for myself, and flew back to Los Angeles.

As a nominee, Bill was expected to sit way down on the aisle, as close to the stage as possible. To my knowledge, he never sat closer than the very last row on the aisle anytime we went to the theater. I saw everything from the last row on the aisle, be it movie, play, musical, whatever. But they insisted that Bill sit down there. Comes the big day. It was held in the Santa Monica Auditorium at the time. We walked down the aisle and were shown our seats, and Bill took one look at how far down it was, looked back up the aisle longingly, and sat down. Then he got up, came back, got up, came back. Then the show started and he said, "I can't stand it."—and he walked right out. When they announced his category and announced the winner, the camera panned, the stage manager looked over expectantly, shrugging his shoulders to me. I shrugged my shoulders back at him and pointed up the aisle; the camera swung up the aisle and there was Bill coming down in his usual stalwart steady pace—not running ever. The music played endlessly and finally Bill accepted it on stage. I didn't see him again until after the ceremony was over, because they whisked him backstage to do interviews and all of that. After the ceremony, I heard someone saying, "William Inge's car, please." And there was Bill standing at the front door, with the Oscar clutched tightly in his hand, with this fixed expression on his face. The first thing he said—between his teeth, not smiling, and with sort of half-closed eyes—was, "Open the trunk." I opened the trunk and very carefully put it in on top of a blanket. He got in the car and we went to I think it was the Beverly Wilshire Hotel where they were holding a big party. All the people that had received nominations were gathering at this big "do." The winners had brought their Oscars in triumphantly and smacked them down in the middle of these great tables, to be oohed and ahhed over by everybody. Not so Bill. He was fiercely proud, scared to death, and very, very shy.

That happened at a time that Bill was not that well known in Hollywood. People said, "Who is this William Inge?" So the flood gates of popular acclaim, if you'll pardon the corny expression, opened. Bill was wined and dined by everybody that you could ever imagine. Every hopeful that had ever crashed a gate pounded on the doors and windows—telegrams, telephone, mail. Bill wanted to get away from it all. He came back to New York and went up to Massachusetts several times, down to Florida, and then still these communications arrived. And so started the gradual change of Bill and his attitude towards a lot of things.

That kind of success cannot help but turn people's heads. It is one of the most heady things in the world. He was himself inside but everybody wanted to get him "hip," "with it." This is 1961, 1962, 1963. We were in a whole new age. Bill was afraid that he was going to be old-fashioned. He didn't know that his forte was his astonishing memory of things that he had fashioned out of his heart, out of his mind, out of his whole being. These are all corny phrases but they exactly tell you what Bill had in him—and his writing reflected it. I gradually began seeing all of these buzz words as we say today, catchphrases, the with-it generation, the up-to-date things, and it wasn't Bill. He was writing to please an audience rather than to please himself—which he had always done. His first four plays were from the heart; the ones that followed were from the craft. You can see the difference. The plays still have form and structure and technically they are better but they don't have that spark. And from then on things were never the same, and Bill felt it. And that is one of the great tragedies, that he didn't listen to himself; he listened to all the others that were telling him how to run his life.

Not too long before he died, I had been on my way back from Australia and had stopped in Los Angeles for a week to visit friends. I was shocked at seeing Bill. Helene was there and she just sort of looked at me as though: is there anything you can do? I know that is what she felt. Bill just looked drugged. He was so sedated that he wasn't anything like I had remembered him.

That Was Bill
Robert Whitehead

In the case of *Bus Stop*, Bill Inge brought the play to me and together we agreed to get Harold Clurman to direct it. Then the three of us sat down and started casting. We cast it quite quickly as I remember. Bill finished the play rather more quickly than almost any production I ever did. I think I read the play in October or November and we put it into rehearsal in late January or February, which is really rather quick.

Bill always wrote very carefully. He didn't hand you a first draft. When Bill handed you a play it was very much a finished play. He had reworked it himself. He was very economical in his use of language and his vision; he didn't hand you a play that needed forty minutes cut out of it—which is invariably the case. When Bill presented *Bus Stop* to me, that was the play. We went into rehearsal with that script; he didn't go back and rework it. When we were in rehearsals he did some slight changes, and we did some changes in the casting. Bill was like Harold Pinter in that respect; Pinter usually handed you a play and it was worked and reworked by him before anybody saw it, and he brought it down to such an economy of words and shapes that that is the way it was. Bill was like that. I think I read most of Bill's plays before they were produced and what arrived on the stage was almost exactly what I read.

We opened *Bus Stop* in Princeton, and then we went to Philadelphia. We got very badly received in Philadelphia. There was a feeling that the play was a sort of quiet conversation that was boring us all to death. We replaced a leading actor who played Bo Decker. Bill was aware that the character wasn't right. Albert Salmi came in in Philadelphia; in four days he came into the part. He was marvelously received and made a difference to the play. Again, Bill's plays had a certain psychological honesty about them and you couldn't put in just effective acting. It had to have that honesty, that simple truthfulness. When

Albert Salmi came in, it changed the quality of the play; it changed the character of the play. We had Kim Stanley, who was magnificent; she had been in *Picnic* and was later in *Natural Affection*. We came into New York and it was a huge success; I remember that opening night was just like a love affair with the audience.

Harold Clurman and I had done two or three plays before *Bus Stop* and we had a marvelous working relationship. I know that Bill was for Clurman directing *Bus Stop*, and I think that one of the reasons that Bill wanted me to do that play may have been because of the fact that I had a good working relationship with Harold. Bill and Harold and I were kind of a trio that almost automatically came together. Bill and I didn't sit around for several days wondering about who we wanted. We were quite clear about that.

The setting was done by Boris Aronson; it was a beautiful design, a lovely set. It was just right; it was exactly like Bill Inge. There was a poetic quality about it and there was a simplicity about it. There was an absolute truthfulness about it. Combine those, and that's really what Bill Inge's qualities as a writer were.

The last play Inge had on Broadway, *Where's Daddy?*, I co-produced. I did it in the summertime because we felt it had to be done then: let's try it and see how we feel about it. I worried about it, I must admit. That was in the summer of 1965. I was busy working at Lincoln Center at the time as a director of the theater there. Also my wife died that year, and I went away; I went over to England, and I made arrangements for Bill's play to be done in New York. We got another producer involved, Michael Wager. I went away and the play was done and I was listed as a co-producer. I think Bill was rather angry that I had gone away. He felt I had let him down, he told me later. On the other hand, he also understood that I had had a difficult time and I just had to get away and I wasn't in any mood to give myself to *Where's Daddy?* at that point. When I came back I think Bill was on the coast and I saw him several times then. And he told me that he was burned up with me but then we managed to solve our differences and we saw each other again quite often—though I didn't see him at the end of his life. I was not on the coast then. I was busy here and I didn't get out there for a year or two, and Bill died.

I did *Natural Affection* in Texas with Shelley Winters, directed by Harold Clurman, for two or three weeks, the winter before it was done eventually on Broadway with Kim Stanley. We felt it needed some further work and certain things done to it—and Bill agreed. Then Bill called me about four months later, and he said, "Bob, I just can't do that work. I don't feel like it and I just want the play the way it is. I think that is the way it should be done." I said, "Well, I don't want to do it the way it is. I think it is a mistake and I don't think you ought to do it that way." He said, "I don't want to do the rewrite. I agreed to it and I felt good about it but now I don't." So I said, "Well then maybe we should amicably separate." And that is what happened. He did it later, with Kim Stanley, and Tony Richardson directed it.

* * *

Bill's life never seemed to be in disarray. I know that he had a period of drinking which was a kind of terrible sickness for him. But about the time I met him he was on the wagon. I first met him when he did *Come Back, Little Sheba* and he was on the wagon completely. Although I think there was a tremendous conflict within him, his life always seemed to have shape. His apartment was very tidy and very well furnished and pleasantly looked after at all times. You never came into a place that was a shambles, and his house in California was utterly charming and attractive and everything in it was pleasant and well organized. And he planned in advance. He planned things very carefully. He had a very conservative quality about him as a human being. I don't mean intellectually, but as a human being. He had a quiet calm exterior and everything seemed quite reasonably in place. He was kind of an organized gentleman.

He had very charming manners and he seemed like a superior, educated, well-organized human being, even though one knew that he was having troubles and that it wasn't that easy. Those neuroses grew and developed in his life from the time that he was very young, right through his school and his days in the newspaper in St. Louis and on into his life as a playwright; whatever they were they were ingrained into Bill and they eventually destroyed him. But the outer manifestations of Bill were always well-dressed, well-mannered, and comfortably organized. The same goes for the shape of his plays in a way. The turmoil was inside the plays. His ability was to hone them down to what he finally really wanted and to use not three words where two would do. His sense of character, the logic of a character's conversation, the logic of a character's thought, that is to say the logic within the qualities of that human being that he was writing about, were very organized and complete. There were never wasted words with Bill.

He had thought his plays out carefully; they were very subtle actually. He never had a strong or melodramatic story line; there was an emotional development. They were rather quiet plays in a way, but they were very noisy inside finally—and very funny, of course. His sense of truth was extraordinary. He never attempted to go beyond what existed inside him as an artist; he kept within the realm of his own subjective life. He never went out beyond it and said, "Now I am going to embrace another kind of experience, a larger, more classic experience." He kept always to what was his truth; there was a modesty to his work and an absolute truthfulness. It was quite beautiful.

Writing for Bill was a very personal and subjective thing, which is why he was never really going to have a success trying to write movies—and it pained him terribly that he didn't. I remember that he once said to me, "I can't bear living out here in this atmosphere where success is so important." I think that, even though he had been a big theater writer with prizes behind him, he wanted to make that film money in some way, which is a human weakness. After the success of *Splendor in the Grass*, he went to Hollywood and he found that people were admiring him and wining and dining him but he wasn't getting millions of dollars of film money to write things. They'd say to Bill, "We've got a great story here and we want you to write it" and they had him trying to write about racing cars and everything; you know he wasn't going to come up with a marvelous movie about racing cars. That and the feeling that he wasn't being sought after constantly I think hurt him a lot. He would have been better off staying in New York.

There were times with Bill that people would see him and he would seem not to be there when he was. It was as if he would go into himself and would just get lost in some thought. I remember Charlie Jackson, who wrote *The Lost Weekend* and was quite close to Bill because they were both drinkers and in AA, telling me that Bill called him one night in desperation and said, "You've got to come over and see me, Charlie." Charlie said, "Gosh, it's three o'clock in the morning, Bill." But Bill insisted: "No, no, you've got to come over!" So Charlie struggled out of bed and came across town to Bill's apartment. When he got there, Bill came to the door and said, "Oh, what a surprise. Nice to see you, Charlie. Sit down. I'll be right with you." And then he made a one-hour phone call, came back, and said, "Charlie, I'd completely forgotten you were here."

Gestures of Love, Gestures of Despair
Jo Ann Mahan Kirchmaier

He loved art. He bought and sold art. He bought up and he bought down; he made money. I don't know that he ever lost any money on anything he bought. But then when he began to feel poor he began to sell off Modiglianis and Hoppers. When he moved to California he had an Edward Hopper that hung over his mantle. He had a wonderful collection and a wonderful knowledge of art. He really was an artist. I have a picture that he painted—he signed it Billy Inge and he was about eight—and someday when I'm feeling very generous I will give it to Independence Community College. It was of an Indian on a horse, a watercolor. It's just beautiful. He loved to do cartoons and he used to draw me paper dolls. I remember the paper dolls; they were the sexiest, curviest you ever saw in your life.

He also loved to sculpt—most of his sculpting was done at Riggs Sanitarium or places where they had lots of clay and you could sort of vent your frustration. But he did some very nice nudes. I don't know if he would have won any prizes, but he was an all-around artist. The way he decorated his house was elegant; he had elegant things; he had an eye. Obviously, he wrote very well, and he could draw; he could sculpt; he could do a little bit of everything. He was an artist, really, in every sense of the word. And he had an eye for what was good. He was buying things that nobody else would buy; but he said, "Hang onto this, it's going to be great." Bill enjoyed possessing things but he got tired of them and he'd get rid of them and he'd buy something else.

He didn't really take good care of his animals. When he died he had Toby, who was a little white Sealyham terrier, and he had had a black Scottie in St. Louis. He had another dog, too, that was sent to him in New York by Danny Mann, and he *detested* Danny Mann. This dog coming from Danny was just the last blow; he didn't pay any attention to that dog. The doorman would walk the dog or John Connolly, Bill's assistant, would walk the dog. It was a great big black standard poodle that he named Joker. Well, Bill called me one time and said that he had this *wonderful* dog and he just praised this dog to the skies, how wonderful he was and how worried he, Bill, was about him. He was going to go to California and would I mind taking care of the dog? I said certainly not. He said, "Well he's been spending weekends,"—the dog had—"at a rest place in the country where he can play with other dogs. To leave him for three, four weeks would be just terrible." So Bill and John drove to Perrysburg, Ohio, with the dog. Peter Kirchmaier, my husband, said, "Jo Ann, that dog is here to stay. Bill will never be back to get him." I said, "Oh, but of course he will because he loves him."

Well, that trip Bill said, "Jan"—he always called me Jan—"I'd like to buy you some clothes. Let's go downtown shopping." So we went down to the nicest dress shop, and he bought me a suit and a couple of dresses. And he said, "Now I want you to have some perfume." He loved the same kind of perfume my mother loved, Shalimar, and Bill wore Shalimar because my mother wore Shalimar. So he bought me some Shalimar. Then he said, "Let's go out and buy you a little record player." This was 31 years ago, and he spent $1,500 on a little record player for me. He told the man, "It's got to be delivered this afternoon; it's got to be set up. I want to see it going"; and he bought all these records, I think about 40 records, to go with it—all of Tchaikovsky, not any of the heavy stuff that he loved. He said, "You've got to have this, you've got to have this, you've got to have this"; and then he said, "And now, your teeth." He said, "I want you to go down and have them all capped; it's terrible—the Inges all have just terrible teeth. Just tell me how much it costs and I'll pay it." Well, John said later that he was feeling so guilty about this dog. Eventually, I got a letter from Bill: "Dear Jan, I'm sorry I missed you on the way back, but we were going the southern route and it was 500 miles out of our way." So I had the dog, and the dog was a terrible dog. It ate my alligator shoes; it ate my grandfather's little Shakespeare series. It was a *terrible* dog.

Billy really did want to have a dog and when he moved to California he could have one and he got Toby. He loved Toby, but he couldn't take care of him. He wanted to, but he was unable to. He had little doors cut in the big doors so the little dog could go out and Bill never had to do a thing; he had a maid so the maid fed the little dog. Toby would jump up and Billy would pat him; but Toby was a rotten little dog. He bit Bill. He bit Helene once and drew blood. As a matter of fact, Bill had to take "Enie" to the Emergency Room to get stitched up or cauterized or something. And he said, "We're going to have the dog destroyed." And Helene said, "No we're not, no we're not. He's just a wonderful little dog; it was my fault." But that little dog snapped at everybody—a mean, vicious little dog. And he also lifted his leg on everything in the house. Even with his little doggie door he just didn't bother to use it. There was an attachment but, as I said, Bill didn't feed him; occasionally he did.

* * *

He had a very wonderful relationship with an actress named Barbara Baxley and, amazingly, at one point he even considered marrying her but he didn't. She came to his funeral; she was the only woman—except for his mother and Helene and me —I think that he probably ever felt anything for. She understood him, but he couldn't commit himself to anything really. He really couldn't. In his last years when he wanted Helene to come, I think he was groping for something. I don't know that they found it. Intellectually they weren't alike at all. "Enie" was a sweet, lovely person, a little on the timid side.

In the last two years of his life he was in and out of sanitariums. We went so far as to bring him back to Topeka. I got him on an airplane to fly back to Kansas and I was allowed to give him a pill to calm his nerves, and I said to him "If..."—and we were weeping—I said, "Billy, if I ever thought you'd had a meaningful relationship in your life, I'd be happy," but I don't think he ever did.

Bill was a vain man, he really was. He was a good-looking young guy; he was handsome and he could get himself together and look like a million dollars. But in the end he'd lost his hair, he'd lost his teeth, he'd lost his looks, and he lost his life. I think that was a terribly brave thing he did. I just was amazed that he had done it the way he did. Taking sleeping pills would have been so easy for him; this had to have been hard.

His suicide didn't surprise Helene, it shocked her because he had been hiding Valium and we had been finding it and trying to keep it away from him. The only thing that he did in the last few months was he would jump in the pool every day, swim across it, swim back, get back in bed. Walk out in his underwear, jump in the pool and drink lots of milk with eggs in it for sustenance. He didn't drink alcohol because he couldn't get at it; we had it all locked up.

I don't know how Helene called the police. She got on the phone and she called the police and the sirens came up the hill. The houses were right on top of each other. You had neighbors next door, but it wasn't a neighborhood kind of community. Nobody—when the sirens came up the hill—even opened their doors. Here there were sirens under somebody else's bedroom, and nobody even came out. So Helene was really all by herself; she had to have discovered him. We had just moved into our new house and we did not have a phone. She had to call my dad, who waited until 8:30—she must have called him at 2:30 her time, which would have been 5:30 our time—because there wasn't anything I could do. I got on a plane and I was there at 5:00 that afternoon, their time. My stepbrother was here and he was going back to California so I just got on the plane with him.

I think Helene was numb. The house was full of people but I can't remember who was there. Her Presbyterian minister was there and that night everybody congregated and we sat in a circle and we discussed his death and why he had died. I don't think anybody resolved anything except that he wanted to die—he had wanted to die and he did.

It had to be in some way that he didn't bleed. That would have been most unattractive. He couldn't have slit his wrists. It would have been too messy. But, you know, the garages in California are crummy little garages. They're not built for winter weather and they're certainly not airtight and I just wonder how long it must have taken in a leaky garage.

Our only regret was he didn't take the dog with him. I laugh about that now but the little dog did love Bill, it really did. It was a devoted little dog. And when Bill would close the door at night and not let Toby in, that little dog would sleep right up tight by the door, and if Bill let him in, the dog slept right on the foot of Bill's bed. It might have been a very natural thing for Bill to—but I don't think Bill was thinking about anybody but Bill then. But I guess if you've never married, who do you think of? You think of self. And if you've never had a meaningful relationship with anybody or anything, I guess you think of self.

Waiting for Inge
Jack B. Wright

I believe it was my first year at the University of Kansas (1965) working on my Masters Degree, and I remember how excited I was to hear that William Inge was going to teach a playwriting class to graduate students. It was in the Fall semester and there were about 8 of us, some new and some older graduate students, who were all anticipating his arrival on campus. Dr. Lewin Goff, Director of Theatre, had invited Inge to teach the class and Inge had agreed to come back to KU. Dr. Goff had directed a production of *Picnic* some years before and he and Bill Inge had enjoyed the time they spent together. Goff was very excited on that first day of class to introduce Inge to all of us and I recall his saying something about the fact the Inge could not make the first week of classes but that he was looking forward to teaching the playwriting course and would be there the following week. The class met two days a week on a Tuesday-Thursday rotation, and since playwriting was not a specialty of Dr. Goff's, he simply dismissed the class telling us how much he was looking forward to Inge's visit. Dr. Goff was quite an accomplished director and he loved directing plays by William Inge.

The following Tuesday we all gathered in class to hear what Inge had to say about the art of playwriting. He had unfortunately been panned by the New York critics for his most recent production of *Where's Daddy?*, but that really didn't matter because we all were looking forward to sharing a class with the man who had written so many wonderful plays such as *Come Back, Little Sheba, Picnic, Bus Stop,* and *Dark at the Top of the Stairs*. I had read all but *Sheba* and quickly reread it before coming to class that next Tuesday. I had always wanted to direct an Inge play and as a first-year graduate student I was considering doing just that at my time at KU.

Dr. Goff was the first to arrive and he was preparing to introduce Mr.

Inge to all of us. He waited for a while—I think it was fifteen minutes or so—excused himself, and went off to see if Bill Inge had arrived. I believe we waited another thirty minutes or so when Dr. Goff finally returned to say that Bill Inge was unable to come but that we should be patient and show up again the following week. Now, my memory after all these years is a little faded, but I do recall that Inge did not come in that third week; and maybe even a fourth week went by without Inge being present. Our hopes were fading and Dr. Goff told us in one of those later meetings that Inge was very depressed after the recent New York reviews, and he was not sure if Mr. Inge would be coming at all. By this time we were all disappointed but continued to stay in class and talk about Inge's plays and how important they were to the American theater. We were all learning from sharing each others' perceptions and talking about his characters and his passion for Kansas stories.

In week five, I believe, we had come to class yet again in hopes that Inge might be there and sure enough, William Inge walked into our classroom, and stated that he was sorry about the delay but that he wanted to help us write plays and hoped that he might have something useful to say. And then a stunning thing happened; I will never forget it. Mr. Inge started to cry, very quietly; with tears rolling down his cheeks, he talked almost angrily about New York's circle of critics and how hurtful they were to him. They didn't appreciate his style, his subject matter, or the characters he had written. For what seemed like the entire class of two hours, he rambled on about how hard it was to be a writer and how, if there was anything else we could think of doing, we ought to do it. We were all stunned to say the least. After a while, he gathered himself and said, "But I am here to help you write plays, so let's get started. I want you to write a short play—a one-act—and bring it to me next week and we will talk about them." And so we all did. I can't recall now what he said about my one-act but as we all listened to the advice he gave each of us, I know we were all captivated. He was a different person for the remaining weeks of class—constructive and positive; with all of his criticism we each took to heart his passion for our individual writing. He found something in each play that showed promise. I was never passionate about my own skill or lack of it in playwriting, but this class taught me that a playwright should have my respect. He taught me that his heart was in all of the characters he created, and that RELATIONSHIPS were the most important element in a playwright's toolbox. I have never forgotten the importance of finding and defining "relationships" in the plays I have directed over the years. The impression he made on me was astonishing. To have witnessed his "pain" is to understand the compassion he wrote into so many of his characters. It was, without a doubt, the most inspiring class I have ever taken.

It was many years later that I learned that Inge had been hospitalized at the University Hospital in Kansas City and that they were treating his depression. That's why he was so late in joining us for that class in Playwriting.

The Stairs to Darkness
Philip Clarkson

My first conversation with William Inge was over a telephone. I was working on my doctorate at Stanford, and my wife and I attended a party with other graduate students. I was explaining that I wanted to write my thesis on where a playwright gets his ideas and what happens to his plays from conception to production. My problem was to find the playwright willing to share in the project with me. To my amazement, my host said he knew Bill Inge and would be glad to call him and see if he would help. He picked up a phone and next thing I knew I was talking to the man I considered the most successful American playwright of the 1950s. Bill listened to what I had on my mind; he promised nothing but agreed that if I would come to Phoenix, Arizona, he would be willing to discuss the possibilities with me. This was early in 1962, and his play *Natural Affection* was in tryout at the Sombrero Playhouse.

I first saw Bill Inge playing tennis at the Camelback Inn. From the plays I had seen and read, I somehow visualized their author as a small, gentle, studious Midwesterner; but my initial impression was of a large and gracious Teddy Bear. I was soon to discover that this was a Teddy Bear with a powerful mind and strong convictions. He was cautious in receiving me and made it clear that he had had some unhappy results from giving interviews. When I assured him that my project did not in any way involve an evaluation of his work or of him, that I was engaged in narrative not criticism, and that he would be welcome to see what I had written before any publication, he decided to go along with me. He agreed to a series of interviews in the afternoons. I had hoped he would let me tape-record them, but he refused to allow that. As a result, I hurried back to my motel after each session and transcribed my notes onto tape so that I could recreate our conversations as accurately as possible.

As the afternoons went on, Bill relaxed more and more. Originally I had prepared my questions with great care, but soon I discovered Bill taking an interest in the evolution of his work himself. He became more trusting, and I was able to let our conversations run their natural course. Bill obviously enjoyed introspection. Slowly he began to weave together what happened to him, the people and places he knew, with the people and places and events in his plays. As he did so, I began to realize how much better the plays were than I gave them credit for being. When I saw *Picnic* on Broadway (with no idea then that I would know the playwright), I thoroughly enjoyed the play, but I didn't take it very seriously as lasting literature. I greatly underestimated its quality. Inge has demonstrated a penetration into the characters and what moves them that continues to move us even in these very different times. I came to look forward to my meetings with him more and more as I came to know him better. He was not easy to know even though he talked so easily. No matter how personal some of the subject matter was, in my presence he always maintained a reserve and a dignity. I felt that we were becoming friends but that I must always be careful never to impose on that friendship.

After a couple of sessions, Bill invited me to go to the theater at night to watch the tryouts with him. Clurman was directing *Natural Affection* then and Shelley Winters was in the cast. We didn't sit in the audience area; we sat in the projection booth because Bill disliked crowds. He was also terribly nervous. It was then that I understood playwriting wasn't simply a profession with him—it was his way of life. Unlike some playwrights who take delight in seeing the realization of their efforts, for Bill the process was long and painful. His attention was riveted on the stage. He swung from high hopes to great fears. I remember his muttering about one poor member of the cast, "No emotions, just constipation." Night after night he went home and back to the drawing board. One night I was brash enough to complain that I thought the murder in *Natural Affection* was not properly motivated. He called me at the motel to be sure I was going a few nights later because the murder was taken out. The next night it was back in again.

Fortunately I was not brash enough to tell Bill what I really thought of the play. Because I was enthusiastic about everything Bill had produced up to then, I automatically assumed I would like *Natural Affection*. I was sad to discover I didn't and subsequently even sadder to find that the public, for the most part, didn't like it either. That doesn't mean I was right. There are Inge aficionados who regard it as his best play, and the day may still come when it is a big Broadway success. Nevertheless I wished then as I wish now that I could have displayed more enthusiasm for it.

I was able to generate a lot of real enthusiasm for Inge's next offering. He invited me to meet him in Los Angeles and attend a screening of *All Fall Down*.

I think that is a fine movie. I have seen it again on television recently, and my enthusiasm for it remains undiminished. What surprised me so much was that Bill cared for my approval. I had assumed that anyone with his extraordinary record of success would not concern himself with a student's view of his work. He knew criticism was no part of my thesis and that my comments would necessarily be casual. The trouble is he cared what I thought—he cared what everybody thought. Part of his greatness as an artist was his sensitivity to the thoughts of people around him, but this made him terribly vulnerable. It was only relatively late in our association that I understood how deep his need was for approval.

In 1963 I finished my thesis. I had examined carefully what Bill had said and written about his theater and what others had thought about it. I spent many hours finding out what he had thought when he was a critic. I felt I had come to know him professionally very well. I sent him a copy as I had promised, and I was glad that he was pleased with it and that he accepted it as essentially correct in fact. I left Stanford to teach at Ripon College in Wisconsin. Ripon had the happy tradition of establishing a theme for its Commencements and conferring honorary degrees upon those with special achievements in that field of endeavor. The spring of 1965 was designated as having the performing arts as its theme, and I proposed Bill's name to receive a Doctor of Literature degree. I knew that travel was difficult for Bill since he wouldn't fly; I knew that he was afraid of going to places he hadn't ever been to (he once put that in a letter to me.); I knew he didn't like crowds, and graduation exercises do involve numbers. Even so, Ripon is a small college in a small town. Other distinguished artists were going to share that weekend, and I thought Bill would be delighted with the atmosphere if I could only get him that far. He was pleased to be invited and happy at the offer of the degree. He said he'd come, and he did get as far as Salt Lake City when he lost heart, turned around, and went home. I felt so sad for him. He, in turn, was deeply concerned over whether he had caused me professional embarrassment. Fortunately there was no problem there. He always wanted the degree and Ripon always wanted to give it to him; but, though we discussed from time to time his coming to Ripon as a guest lecturer or as a visiting professor, he never got to the campus.

Bill had always been highly critical of dramatic criticism as it was published in Chicago. When he heard that Claudia Cassidy had retired from the *Chicago Tribune*, he decided that he would like to take on that job. Certainly he was wonderfully qualified to do that with his background as instructor, playwright, and critic, but I was surprised that he thought he would like such an assignment. Anyway, he asked for my help in approaching the *Tribune*, and through friends we reached the managing editor. He responded that new critics for music, drama, and film were already in place and that they would be glad to have Bill's application and resume on file in case there was an early opening. This curt response to a leading playwright confirmed Bill's assessment of dramatic criticism in Chicago. Bill explained what he wanted to accomplish when he wrote me on February 17, 1966, from the Hotel Algonquin in New York:

> I did think that I might be able to help build up theatre in Chicago if I held the post on the <u>Tribune</u>. Their rudeness baffles me. It is as though they held a personal grudge, and they don't even know me. I feel that Chicago newspapers have killed theatre there, and I said so once in print, blaming the Tribune and Claudia Cassidy, although I did not name her. The story made good-sized headlines in the Chicago papers about two years ago. Maybe they have not forgiven me. But I know I'm right. I've been fighting for a long time for a criticism that retains a respect for the theatre itself, even for a bad play, when it has to criticize. We have been treated so long with the contempt of spiritless, defeated men, suffering their own self-hate and projecting it onto the shows they review, men who long since have lost any ability to participate in any group experience, who always pronounce the negative aspects of a play first, neglecting to consider the good, or the potential for growth and development. Commercial theatre can not live any longer with this kind of treatment.... God knows, there is not much worth seeing on Broadway, but the few things that do come along with a little life and spirit, it seems to me should be applauded and encouraged.... I am so fed up with these men of intellect and no sensibility. They are the intellectual equivalent, I believe, of weight-lifters and musclemen who have developed a fine, impressive musculature that does not serve them in any useful way.... Well, it's all very depressing. I honestly believe that if we could keep critics out of the theatres for three or four years, we might have a chance to present a fresh, original drama for our audiences.
>
> I seem to be getting a lot off my chest while 1 wait here in my room to hear whether or not we give a show tonight. My own play is <u>not</u> avant-garde in any way, but it is the most articulate play I have ever written, and perhaps the funniest. It <u>could</u> be very successful. Clurman has done a good job directing, and the small, invited audiences we have played for in run-throughs have responded just as we hoped. But we still have not seen it before a big, ticket-buying audience. I don't expect to have much rewriting to do from now on, so I may return to California before the press opening. I'll be very glad to get out of New York and get home again.

Bill and I continued to correspond and to phone each other through the following years. He shared with me manuscripts of plays he was working on, some of which he allowed me to keep. Early in 1968 he asked me to be his Literary Executor and I agreed to accept the responsibility. In 1967, I was busy directing a college production of *King Lear*. In response to my writing Bill about it, he replied:

> I admire you for doing <u>Lear</u>. I'd much rather see an amateur or college production of Shakespeare than of Anouilh. And just appearing in a Shakespearian

production is a contribution to educational growth. Not that the contemporary playwrights are not that worthy, but I think that young people, if drama is to mean anything in education, must be able to find identification with what they are playing in. They must find their own reality in the theatre. And I think they're able to do this with very few contemporary plays. I suppose it's something like teaching painting. I'm sure that the best painters today are those who have an understanding of the "Old Masters." Certainly Pollack [sic] and deKooning, the greatest contemporary American artists, have this understanding. And I think that college students are better off doing Moliere, Shakespeare, even Ibsen, Shaw and O'Casey, and some of O'Neill, than today's very worldly and urbane playwrights. We can always find what is basic in plays of the past. We can not always do this in the present.

Nineteen sixty-nine proved to be the year in which we spent the most time together. I came to California for a year and settled down to redo my thesis in a form that I hoped would interest the public. Bill agreed to help me with it and to contribute an essay and an unpublished play to it. We had a verbal agreement that we would share royalties on it. My wife and I stayed in Carmel and urged Bill to join us there for a visit, but we were never able to persuade him. He was most hospitable to us. He served excellent drinks though he never took any alcohol in my presence. He did his best to train me to appreciate his very handsome collection of modern paintings. I even got along happily with his dog Toby, which seems to have been something of an accomplishment. One night Bill took me to the Brown Derby for dinner. He seemed to be glad for the recognition he received there. Though our times together always seemed pleasant and happy, I knew he was deeply dissatisfied with his world. I couldn't understand it. His home was beautiful. It was modest but with a gorgeous view of Los Angeles. He had ample means to live well. He was still turning out plays and had added novels to his career. He was teaching.

Back in Tempe, Arizona, when I first met him, I had taken him out to Arizona State to lecture to drama students there, and he taught well. Teaching was not new to him, and he was good at it, but it never seemed to give him much satisfaction. Sometimes I felt he deliberately evaded happiness. Even when he was involved in his most successful work, he worried and fretted and knew little of the delight most of us take in success. He and I enjoyed conversations about plays or movies we had seen, whose acting was good, and which directors knew their business; but when the conversation switched to fading friendships and destructive critics, the depth of his unhappiness became apparent. To help me with my book, Bill shared his journal with me, and this added a new dimension to my work. When I finished writing, Bill read the book and seemed pleased with it. I returned to teaching, and my wife tried to find a publisher for my latest effort. We never did find a publisher. Bill made some suggestions which we followed but with no success. Readers were uniformly kind and complimentary but always concluded that they were the wrong press for us. This didn't help Bill's morale. He was already convinced that he was unappreciated, and the book's failure to publish simply confirmed this view. In a letter to me in January 1971, Bill wrote that he felt completely rejected and concluded, "I don't think you'll find a publisher until I am dead. Only then have I a chance that my works, many of them unproduced and unpublished, can be looked at fairly."

Meanwhile, Bill had found another Literary Executor to replace me. He was right to do so. I was under contract to write a textbook. I became much more absorbed in teaching and administrative work, and I accepted a new appointment farther away from him in New York. I tried to stay in touch with him, but the phone calls grew fewer, and then the letters and phone calls stopped altogether. In late May of 1973, I wrote him with my new address and phone number in New York and another invitation to him to be a guest professor. I knew he wouldn't accept. I urged him to stay in touch and I concluded, "...but, if I don't hear from you, I shall continue to seek news of your career and to think of you as a gentleman and an artist." Those proved to be my last words to him. A few weeks later he chose to leave a world that he found unliveable.

The night we heard the news of Bill's death, my wife and I sat up late in front of the fireplace. We were burning manuscripts. Bill had made me promise that many of the manuscripts that were works in progress must be destroyed in the event of his death, and we were careful to designate which these were. I had written some years before with the comment, "...it is always painful to tear up evidence of how any play has grown to what it finally becomes. In this respect authors and scholars work at cross-purposes. The scholar, like the alchemist, is always trying to catch the process through which gold emerges; whereas the writer—though he may take pride in the diligence of his efforts—always wishes to reveal the final product as if it had sprung like Athena full-blown from one of Zeus's headaches." It takes quite a while to burn a manuscript, never mind a large number of them. It was a sad night. I was tempted to break my promise because I knew there was value to what I was burning. The critics may have been unkind to Bill in his later years—even as he thought unfair and brutal—but I knew there was still a broad appreciation of his wonderful talent among those who knew his work. His name was not only appearing in crossword puzzles; it was in the hearts of playgoers, students, and community theater lovers all over this country and other countries. I knew generations to come would take delight in his work. I had hoped he might accept this and live happily with the knowledge of it. When the last flames had consumed the last manuscript, I packed away the ones I was allowed to keep with the copies of our book. I wish Bill hadn't been so sensitive, so easily hurt; but perhaps without that sensitivity we would never have known his fine artistry. Whatever the case, I miss him not only as an artist but as a truly fine gentleman.

He Knew the Poetry of Life
Jack Garfein

The earliest memory I have of Bill is when he lived at the Dakota. I went up to his apartment one afternoon and we simply sat there and talked about people and life, but very little about theater. Bill sat very calmly and let me do all the talking. He was always fascinated. I always loved being with Bill because of his constant observation of human behavior. It wasn't an intellectual observation or analytical observation. Years later, I walked down the street with Bill and he suddenly made this sound; I said, "What is the matter Bill?" He said, "Did you see the way that mother yanked that child's arm?" What he observed went right through his being. Another time, we were sitting at the Brown Derby having lunch and this couple behind me in the next booth were arguing. Bill stopped and he looked at me and said, "Look at human emotion, isn't it astonishing? It is the most frightening thing in the world. Jack, there is nothing more frightening than human emotion." He said, "You should see that man's face as he is talking to that woman and that woman's response to him." Now whenever I am in a restaurant or a public place and I hear that kind of argument, I think of that moment with Bill. It was never simply something he observed and watched; he immediately permitted it to touch his own emotional experience and lived it at the moment. Harold Clurman described him brilliantly; he said, "What was so wonderful about Bill Inge was true about him in life as well as in his writings: he never went beyond his own feelings; and he never could be untrue to what was happening to him at the moment." Because of that, there is a sweetness, a modesty, and a tenderness in his characters and in his plays.

I worked on a number of plays of Bill's on the west coast. And he also taught at the Actors and Directors Lab. As a matter of fact, we have a whole series of tapes of one of his lectures, and we had them typed up as well. They are fascinating. He recalls his first meetings with Tennessee Williams and talks about his life with his family. What was wonderful about Bill was that whatever came up in class was the same as when he observed things in life; he always related it to something specific in his own life. It was never an abstraction or a generalized idea. He was a good teacher in the sense that he didn't pay much attention to structure; that is not what he was interested in. He always said that he didn't really want to teach because he didn't know how to teach; he would say to people when they asked him about learning to be a playwright or a screenwriter, "Act." He felt that the most valuable things he learned were from being an actor, even playing small parts.

I first invited him to teach at the Actors Studio on the west coast, and then he did it at the Actors and Directors Lab on a regular basis, on Saturday mornings. I was happy that he did it then because it got him out of his house and it got him involved with other writers. But he became so sensitive to everything that even if a young writer mistreated him or didn't sense what was going on within Bill, Bill was very hurt about it. It was as serious to him as if some terrible review of his work had come out. It got that way towards the end. He was super, super sensitive. When he went to the theater he wanted a seat in the last row so that he could leave. He was in such pain. He was totally exposed. He was totally raw and everything would affect him. All the layers of protection had gone

The one-act play, *The Call*, he wrote about the two men: a Shriner who comes to visit a man in New York; I did a reading of that play for Bill and a group of people. The loneliness in that play came out of his loneliness. There is a character who is unable to relate to things. He is unable to stay in this place, to fly on a plane, and all the things that Bill had difficulty doing towards the end. Someone asked Bill what he thought of the reading and he said that he felt that I had touched something in his subconscious that he wasn't aware of. The play came out of his loneliness. I knew the hurt. I knew what was going on and felt that all of this beauty was just being trampled on. So I sometimes, even like you would with a child, almost overcompensated in order to try to boost him or inspire him. And he accepted that. He liked it. He knew what I was doing. It meant to him that obviously I cared. One inscription that he wrote in a book to me said, "To Jack, who I hope is my friend"—or something like that.

During that period, everything you said to him went right to the quick. There was no shield of any kind. Because he was strong, no one could destroy him; he would take the pain. He would take it and hold it inside of him. I remember a young writer that Bill had helped got his play produced at the Mark Taper Forum; and he gave interviews in the *Times* in which he attacked

Bill Inge—because it was sort of fashionable. Bill read this attack in the papers and said to me, "Why did he do that to me? What did I do?" I said, "Bill, you know this guy is just trying to get his name in the paper. To attack you has become something that serves him. I know you think he is talented but I never thought he was; I think he is OK, and it doesn't matter." I think I even said, "Listen, long after he becomes a vague memory, your plays will be there. Who cares what he says? What does it matter?" But it mattered to him—and the irony was that Bill not only helped him in his work but I believe he had lent him money, a couple of hundred dollars.

Toward the end we had a very interesting relationship. I had said to him that any time he wanted to have dinner or wanted me to go out with him that I was available and he could call me. He said, "You've got your own life. What about if you have a date?" I had just been divorced, and I said, "Bill, I will cancel my date or bring my date along." I was purely selfish; I said, "I love being with you and talking to you." I did feel that he sort of demanded that you deal with real things. That was wonderful. And the fact that when you were with him you felt that you were with a sort of a phenomenon in human nature—someone you knew wasn't going to compromise his emotions or feelings. As a result of that, it was always joyous, that part of it. There was this openness and vulnerability there, this tremendous control and vision of life. He was someone who knew the poetry of life.

One of the sweetest things is that whenever we had dinner he wanted to eat delicatessen. I said to him one day, "Bill, I don't understand what is a boy like you from Kansas, whenever you eat dinner, doing in Jewish delis? It seems like your favorite restaurant. Is it your New York background?" He said, "No. When I left Kansas, my mother—who had probably never been out of Kansas—took me to the train and the last thing she said to me when I got on the train was, 'Now, Bill, you know whenever you get to New York or any of the cities and you need a good home-cooked meal, you just go to a Jewish deli and get it there. You'll get a nice warm home-cooked meal.'" He said, "How she knew that, where she picked that up, I don't know." But that was the last piece of advice she gave him when he left Kansas.

* * *

He once told me, "*Come Back, Little Sheba* wrote itself, but I learned my craft in *Picnic*. I did thirty drafts of it." When it came to working, he was very disciplined. As a matter of fact, even the scripts that he wrote towards the end he had his secretary come in, and they were typed properly and numbered and bound; he was very thorough as far as that aspect of his work went. He did feel that this last cycle of plays was the best that he had done and he particularly thought that the one about the couple watching television and throwing the baby down the chute was the best he'd ever written. I couldn't understand that. I remember I kept asking him, because it seemed so cruel and so dark and so unlike the things that he had done. He kept insisting that that was the play that was really the best, maybe because somehow he had controlled himself all of those years and just let it come out at the end. Maybe he felt it was the best in terms of revealing something, the dark side of himself. It is a couple that throws the baby into the garbage shoot while they are watching television; *Two Boobs* I think it is called.

The play of his that I did, the prison play, *Don't Go Gentle*, had a homosexual in it. When I read the play I felt that the character was too much like a queen and I didn't even want to do it. I called Bill and I said, "Look I just don't see the humanity of this character. I keep seeing him as a queen." He said, "Well he *is* a queen." I said, "Come on, Bill, I don't think that is what you would want on the stage. What I would like you to do is read the play to me so I can just hear you read it." So he read it and he started to read it like a queen. I said to him, "Bill, you are acting. Just read it straight." He said, "Well the character really is that." And I said, "No, I don't think you would write that. I don't think I want to do that." So at one point he lit a cigarette a certain way and put the script in his lap and picked up a drink and I said, "There, look at that, the way you did that, now what was all that?" He said, "Oh, it is elegance. It is Archie. He comes from a small town in America, but he dreams of refinement and elegance." And I said, "Well, now we are getting there." And that is what I finally worked on.

I guess the most vivid scene I had with Bill to do with his homosexuality was when we were up at my apartment one evening and he was sitting in a chair and he suddenly got very inwardly violent, I mean anger, a real anger and sort of pounded the arm of the chair. He said that he just hated his mother and his aunts for what they did to his father, that the way they treated him was what made him a homosexual—or contributed to it. He firmly believed that it was those relationships that made that happen for him. He mourned that, and he said that the worst mistake he ever made is when Barbara Baxley wanted to marry him and he didn't want to marry her. He referred to his aunts particularly as bitches, who had done that. I don't know where it came from. It was sort of an outburst. It just came out.

But it was interesting because you know right after he died we sat around in the room and everyone was supposed to talk about Bill and for a while no one mentioned the homosexuality and then someone did say, "Well, why don't we talk about that?" And I said, "You have to be careful about that with Bill." I said Bill was a romantic, and the reason that he had difficulty getting on in this world was because it was difficult for him to compromise and difficult for him not to live a certain kind of romantic love. I think that Bill was always in search of that. That was the most important thing to him. Then a young man who had lived in the building said, "I don't know, but I just want to add to what Jack said. I had lived here for a couple of years and one evening I saw Bill was very lonely and I went up and I sort of offered to go to bed with him. And he said, 'No thanks; I appreciate that.' And during the whole time I was here he never slept with me or made love or anything like that." This young man always had difficulty understanding what it was. I think that that was part of the struggle; Bill really had this desire for love, real love, and wouldn't compromise, and I think that is why he was so lonely and isolated because he wouldn't compromise like most of us would and accept something that was close to it. He couldn't do it.

At the very end I remember him saying he had run out of ideas. I've always felt that whatever the problems were, they were there before the success of the 1950s. I think that if he hadn't had those successes in the 1950s perhaps all this would have happened even earlier. When he went through those depressions, he kept saying to me, "I really don't understand these depressions. I don't know what they are and I hope someday people will know." And I think that he overcame them for a time. The theater gave that to him. But the theater then became everything—his family, his life. If something was written about him in the newspapers, it was as though his mother or father had said something to him, or his deepest love. And I think that finally he just wasn't getting the recognition; America worships success.

If you become a success in America and you have something to fall back on like a family, they can see you through it. But Bill had nothing to fall back on. We Americans don't pay attention, we don't care; people do their show, they exit, they go to the wings; we don't care what happens to them afterwards, where they go, how they live. If he had lived in France he would have been an honored citizen. If he had been in England he would be Sir William Inge. There would be that sort of recognition. But it is very crude and rough here in terms of artists.

There could have been a whole new cycle that could have come up later on. Ibsen wrote his great plays in his second cycle when he was in his sixties. But there isn't that kind of patience or support here. And there was this other thing, this illness, these depressions that were just constantly there. They got worse and worse. I've always thought of spending some time recalling specifically that time with Bill to try and define those depressions. I have had them myself and it is like a nausea and a sense of utter worthlessness and terrible pain. Everything that happens becomes terribly painful. When he went through these things Bill would isolate himself. He never wanted anybody to be a part of it. And I would force him to take drives, get out of the house, have dinner. It was sad towards the end to see the television going twenty hours a day. He couldn't break away from that tube; it became like a drug.

I was supposed to see Bill that last weekend and I said that I would take him for a drive because he liked to just take drives in the car. But there was a woman that I was interested in that I had been trying to seduce. Finally at last that Saturday night she decided to go to bed with me. And I was just thrilled about it because it had gone on for months, my trying to persuade her to go to bed with me. I was in bed with her and we had both fallen asleep when the phone rang. It was Helene and she said, "Jack, oh, my God, this time he really did it. This time he really succeeded. I don't know what to do." I said, "Helene, listen, I will be right over there, you just call the ambulance. Did you call the ambulance?" She said, "No, I have not." I said, "Call the ambulance. Have them come up immediately." I said, "I will be right there. I will probably beat them to it." I jumped out of bed; this woman sort of half woke up, and I didn't even tell her what was going on. I just said, "A friend of mine is in trouble."—because I didn't want to accept the fact that this had happened—and I jumped into my car and raced up the hill.

Helene said, "You go into the garage. He is in the garage." I went into the garage and I saw him sitting in the car. And he was sitting upright, very straight. He was in the driver's seat, and I sort of sat in the passenger seat. I noticed Bill's fist clenched tight. I sort of touched it, and I tried to see how it was like a determination. I felt like that was the last thing, even though he was struggling against it—that fist closed like that—that he was going to go through with it no matter what. He no longer wanted to be a part of what was going on here. I became aware of the massive strength of his body, just his whole presence, just this massive, massive strength. I couldn't believe that he was dead; I still felt this energy inside him. I was in shock myself after that. I was simply trying to help Helene take care of everything. I went back I think once more to look at him in the car before the ambulance arrived. And that is the most vivid thing, that clenched fist.

There were people around Bill, friends that were hangers-on. He always had people like that, handsome young cowboys and people he had very little in common with, but I guess it was sort of relaxing for him to have people like that. I was a little concerned about how the suicide was going to be handled. That is when I called Dan Sullivan and felt that he should be the one to write about it and report on it, rather than it becoming a story Bill's friends were—not making up because it was their sense of reality—but a story of blaming Hollywood, the theater, a very superficial way of looking at his life and his work, which they didn't really understand. So I talked to Helene and said, "I think it is very important that we have Dan Sullivan." I felt that because it was Hollywood that the person who was writing about the theater and knew Bill's work should write about him. And I called Clive Barnes in New York to tell him that the *Times* should do a story about what had happened. I didn't want it to become gossipy. I called Dan early in the morning.

Bill's works are the expression of the middle-class American, and the American of the Midwest. And a thousand years from now when they want to know how that man spoke and how that man thought they are going to have to turn to Bill Inge.

Notes on Contributors

Thomas P. **Adler** is a professor emeritus of English at Purdue University, where he taught dramatic literature and film for almost 40 years. His numerous publications on American drama include *Robert Anderson* (1978), *American Drama, 1940–1960: A Critical History* (1994), and *Tennessee Williams—A Streetcar Named Desire/Cat on a Hot Tin Roof: A Reader's Guide to Essential Criticism* (2013).

Robert **Anderson** (1917–2009) was one of the leading playwrights on Broadway for more than four decades, best known for *Tea and Sympathy* (1953) and *I Never Sang for My Father* (1968). His other plays include *Come Marching Home* (1946), *All Summer Long* (1953), and *Free and Clear* (1983). He also wrote screenplays, including *Until They Sail* (1957), *The Nun's Story* (1959), and *I Never Sang for My Father* (1970), each nominated for an Academy Award. He is a member of the Theatre Hall of Fame.

Philip **Clarkson** holds degrees from Wesleyan University, Columbia University, and Stanford University. He studied acting and directing at Central School in London, from which Laurence Olivier and Judy Dench graduated. His last academic appointment was as Dean of Arts and Sciences at SUNY Plattsburgh. In retirement he lives in Carmel, California, where he has directed and acted in local productions.

Helene Inge **Connell** (1907–90) was William Inge's older sister. After growing up in Independence, Kansas, she received a bachelor's degree and a master's degree in teaching from Peabody College in Nashville, Tennessee, where she was a high school art teacher from 1937 to 1970; among her students was Red Grooms. She was married to William Connell from whom she was later divorced. In 1971, she moved to Los Angeles and lived with her brother.

John **Connolly** served for six years as William Inge's secretary, assisting by typing drafts of Inge's typescripts, taking care of bills, correspondence and travel plans. His later career was as an Emmy Award–winning lighting designer for daytime television.

Jane **Courant** has an M.A. in English from Georgetown University, an M.L.S. from the University of Maryland, and a Ph.D. in Dramatic Art from the University of California, Berkeley. She is a theater director and teacher, and has also worked as an actor, archivist, and public librarian. Her dissertation was titled "The Drama of William Inge: A Critical Reassessment" and her articles include "Social and Cultural Prophecy in the Works of William Inge" in *Studies in American Drama, 1945–Present* (vol. 6, no. 2, 1991).

Notes on Contributors

Kerk **Fisher** was chair of the Theatre Department at Jefferson Community College in Louisville, Kentucky, where he used theatrical processes as interdisciplinary pedagogical tools. His most recent work as a playwright, a comedy written with Juergen K. Tossmann, *Holy Tolle Swallow That Ego*, premiered at Louisville's Banbury Theatre in 2010. Fisher's scholarship includes work on the theme of "the promise of mobility" in the plays of Eugene O'Neill, Tennessee Williams, and William Inge.

Horton **Foote** (1916–2009) had his first full-length play, *Texas Town*, produced in 1941; the last of his plays produced in his lifetime was *Dividing the Estate* (2007). Foote's many plays include *A Trip to Bountiful* (1953), *The Roads to Home* (1982), *The Young Man from Atlanta* (1995), which won the Pulitzer Prize, and *The Last of the Thorntons* (2000). Foote won Academy Awards for his film adaptations of *To Kill a Mockingbird* (1962) and *Tender Mercies* (1983).

Jack **Garfein** has had notable careers in stage and film and as an acting teacher. Born in Czechoslovakia, he survived imprisonment in Auschwitz and emigrated to the U.S. after World War II. On Broadway he directed *End as a Man* (1953), *Girls of Summer* (1956), and *The Sin of Pat Muldoon* (1957). He founded several acting studios around the world, including the Actors Studio, Los Angeles branch, and Le Studio Jack Garfein in Paris. He directed the films *The Strange One* (1957) and *Something Wild* (1961).

William **Gibson** (1914–2008) is best known for two successful and critically acclaimed plays, *Two for the Seesaw* (1958) and *The Miracle Worker* (1959). His other plays include *A Cry for Players* (1969), *American Primitive* (1971), *Golda* (1977), *Monday After the Miracle* (1982), *Handy Dandy* (1986), and *Golda's Balcony* (2002). He wrote the books for the musicals *Golden Boy* (1964) and *Raggedy Ann and Andy* (1984–86). He also published poetry, a novel, and several nonfiction books.

Richard H. **Goldstone** (1921–98) was a professor of English at the College of the City of New York. He is the author of *Thornton Wilder: An Intimate Portrait* (1975), editor of *Contexts of the Drama* (1968) and *Masterworks of Modern Drama* (1969), and co-editor of *The Mentor Book of Short Plays* (1969).

Barry **Gross** was a professor of English and the director of Jewish Studies at Michigan State University. His essays on Fitzgerald, Cather, Ellison, Baldwin, Roth, Hemingway, and Malamud, among others, have appeared in such periodicals as *Bucknell Review*, *Studies in the Novel*, *Arizona Quarterly*, *Western American Literature*, and *Midamerica*.

Luther C. **Inge** (1921–93) was the son of William Inge's brother Luther C. Inge and M. Marguerite Inge. He was born in Independence, Kansas, and after serving in the U.S. Marine Corps, lived for the last 25 years of his life in Oklahoma City, where he worked for the U.S. government. He is the author of *Travels in Search of the Past: The Ancestry of William Motter Inge, Playwright* (1991).

Therese **Jones** is an associate professor in the Department of Medicine and director of the Arts and Humanities in Healthcare Program for the Center for Bioethics and Humanities at the University of Colorado Anschutz Medical Campus in Denver. She is the editor of the *Journal of Medical Humanities* and has published widely in literature, film, and medical education.

Notes on Contributors 283

Jo Ann Mahan **Kirchmaier** (1925-2004), William Inge's niece, daughter of his sister Lucy, was born and raised in Toledo, Ohio, and attended Stephens College and the University of Toledo. She married Peter Kirchmaier and together they raised four children in Perrysburg, Ohio. She was very active in the Junior League and Planned Parenthood and worked extensively with families in the inner city.

Susan **Koprince** was formerly a professor of English at the University of North Dakota, where she taught courses in modern American fiction and drama. She is the author of *Understanding Neil Simon* (2002) and numerous essays on such American playwrights as Glaspell, Williams, Miller, and Wilson. Her essay, "Childless Women in the Plays of William Inge," appeared in *Midwest Quarterly* (Spring 2000).

Jerome **Lawrence** (1915–2004), in a 52-year collaboration with Robert E. Lee, co-wrote many plays including *Inherit the Wind* (1953), *The Gang's All Here* (1959), *A Call on Kuprin* (1961), *The Incomparable Max* (1971), and *First Monday in October* (1975; rev., 1978). They also wrote the books for the musicals *Look Ma, I'm Dancin'* (1948) and *Mame* (1966). Lawrence is also the author of the play *Live Spelled Backwards* (1970), *Actor: The Life & Times of Paul Muni* (1974), and the novel *A Golden Circle* (1993).

Robert E. **Lee** (1918–94), with his collaborator of 52 years, Jerome Lawrence, wrote many plays including *Auntie Mame* (1956), *Only in America* (1959), *The Night Thoreau Spent in Jail* (1970), *Jabberwock* (1972), and *Whisper in the Wind* (1990; rev., 1994). With Lawrence, he also wrote the books for the musicals *Shangri-La* (1956) and *Dear World* (1969). Lee is also the author of *Television: The Revolution* (1944) and was for 20 years an adjunct professor of playwriting at UCLA.

Joshua **Logan** (1908–88) was a director, playwright, musical book writer, and producer for close to 50 years. He directed and produced *Picnic* (1953), and wrote, directed, and produced the Pulitzer Prize–winning *South Pacific* (1949). He directed many plays, including *On Borrowed Time* (1938), and many musicals including *Annie Get Your Gun* (1946). He directed a number of movies, including *Picnic* (1955), *Bus Stop* (1956) and *Paint Your Wagon* (1969). Over the course of his career he won seven Tony Awards.

Robert A. **Martin** (1930–2008) was a professor of English at Michigan State University. He is the editor of *The Theatre Essays of Arthur Miller* (1978, 1994; rev. ed., 1996), *Arthur Miller: New Perspectives* (1982), *The Writer's Craft: Hopwood Lectures, 1965–81* (1982), and *Critical Essays on Tennessee Williams* (1997); the co-editor of *Rewriting the Good Fight: Critical Essays on the Spanish Civil War* (1989); and the author of numerous essays on modern American playwrights and fiction writers.

Jo **Mielziner** (1901–76) was one of the twentieth century's most prominent Broadway stage designers. He designed the set of more than 270 plays and musicals. His career began in the 1920s and flowered in the 1930s, 1940s and 1950s when he designed sets for such leading American playwrights as Maxwell Anderson, Robert E. Sherwood, Arthur Miller, Tennessee Williams, Robert Anderson, and Inge (*Picnic* [1953]). He received four Tony Awards for his designs, the first in 1949 and the last in 1970.

Jeanne Seymour **Mitcham** was a childhood friend and neighbor of the Inge family. After her marriage, she moved to San Antonio, Texas.

Notes on Contributors

N. Richard **Nash** (1913–2000), a prolific playwright and screenwriter, is best known as the author of the play *The Rainmaker* (1954), which he later adapted as a film (1956) and as a musical, *110 in the Shade* (1963). Among his other plays are *The Young and Fair* (1948), *Girls of Summer* (1956), and *Echoes* (1973); his other musicals are *Wildcat* (1960) and *The Happy Time* (1968). His screenplays include *Nora Prentiss* (1946), *The Vicious Years* (1950), *Top of the World* (1955), and *Porgy and Bess* (1959).

Robert **Patrick** was very active in the earliest days of the Off-Off-Broadway movement. His more than 60 published plays, which have been produced in theaters worldwide, include *The Haunted Host* (1964), *Fog* (1969), *Joyce Dynel* (1969), *Kennedy's Children* (1973), *My Cup Runneth Over* (1976), and *Untold Decades* (1988). More than 300 of his plays were produced in New York City in the 1960s; in 1972, the publishing company Samuel French called him "New York's Most-Produced Playwright."

David **Richman** is a professor of theatre and humanities at the University of New Hampshire, where in 2013 he received the Class of 1938 Professorship Award for excellence in teaching. He has directed 40 productions of classical and modern plays, among them *Picnic*, *All My Sons*, *Hamlet*, *Three Sisters*, *Old Times*, and *Phaedra*. He is the author of *Laughter, Pain, and Wonder: Shakespeare's Comedies and the Audience in the Theater* (1990) and *Passionate Action: Yeats's Mastery of Drama* (2000).

R. Baird **Shuman** (1929–2013) was an emeritus professor of English at the University of Illinois, Urbana-Champaign. He is the author of *William Inge* (1965; rev. ed., 1969), the first full-length critical biography of Inge, and of *Robert E. Sherwood* (1964). He also taught at the University of Pennsylvania and Duke University, among others, and as a visiting professor at King Faisal University in Saudi Arabia, Yarmouk University in Jordan, and the Bread Loaf School of English of Middlebury College in Vermont.

William **Stuckey** (1929–2007) was a professor of English at Purdue University, where he helped organize the creative writing program, served on the editorial board of *Modern Fiction Studies*, and was an advisor to the national literary magazine *Sycamore Review*. He is the author of *Caroline Gordon* (1972) and *The Pulitzer Prize Novels: A Critical Backward Look* (1981), as well as of numerous short stories, poems, and essays.

Ralph F. **Voss** is an emeritus professor of English at the University of Alabama. A native of Fort Hays, Kansas, he is a graduate of Fort Hays State University (B.A., M.A.) and the University of Texas (Ph.D.). He taught at Texas A&M University-Commerce, Atlanta (Georgia) Metro College, and the University of Utah. He is the author of *A Life of William Inge: The Strains of Triumph* (1989) and editor of *Magical Muse: Millennial Essays on Tennessee Williams* (2002).

Linda **Wagner-Martin** is the Frank Borden Hanes Professor Emerita of English and Comparative Literature at the University of North Carolina. She is the author of more than 40 books on American writers, including Faulkner, Stein, William Carlos Williams, Sexton, Frost, Plath, and Dos Passos. Her most recent books are *A History of American Literature from 1950 to the Present* (2013) and *Emily Dickinson: A Literary Life* (2013).

Albert **Wertheim** (1940–2003) was a professor of English and associate dean for research and graduate development at Indiana University, where he taught classic and contemporary British and American drama and won several teaching awards. He is the author of *The Dramatic Art of Athol Fugard: From South Africa to the World* (2000) and *Staging the War: American Drama and World War II* (2004) and co-editor of *Essays on Contemporary American Drama* (1981).

Robert **Whitehead** (1916–2002) was one of the leading producers on Broadway for nearly six decades. He produced, among many others, the premiere New York presentations of *The Member of the Wedding* (1950), *Orpheus Descending* (1957), *A Man for All Seasons* (1961), *A Texas Trilogy* (1976), *A Few Good Men* (1989), and *Master Class* (1995). He was the recipient of many awards including four Tonys. In 1960, he and Elia Kazan were appointed the heads of the first Lincoln Center theater company.

Audrey **Wood** (1905–85), Inge's theatrical agent, also represented playwrights Tennessee Williams, Robert Anderson, and Arthur Kopit, among others. Her autobiography *Represented by Audrey Wood* (1981) details her long career.

Jack B. **Wright** was artistic director of theatre at the University of Kansas from 1976 to 1994. He taught acting and directing at the University of Texas at Austin and the University of Oklahoma before coming to the University of Kansas. He has directed more than 150 plays and musicals. Wright is a member of the National Theatre Conference and a Fellow of the American Theatre. He tours the country with his one-person show about William Allen White, *The Sage of Emporia*.

Index

All titles not followed by an author name in parentheses are Inge's.

Academy Award 2, 11, 97, 162, 177, 230, 236, 246, 253
Actors and Directors Lab 273, 274
Actors Studio 274
Adler, Thomas 76
Albee, Edward 115, 116, 117
alcoholism: Inge's alcoholism 2, 97, 173, 179, 219, 222, 241, 245, 257, 258, 261, 270; in works (of Inge and of others) 16, 17, 19, 22, 27, 34, 35, 37, 39, 45, 51, 101, 102, 103, 109, 111, 121, 131, 132, 139, 141, 146, 157, 168, 170, 171, 179, 181, 198*n*14
Algonquin Hotel 269
All Fall Down (Inge adaptation of Herlihy novel) 11, 97–98, 163, 166–169, 171, 198*n*14, 267
All My Sons 138, 147, 155
American Dream 117, 144, 147
American Theatre Wing 223, 230
Anderson, Maxwell 14, 153, 154
Anderson, Robert 14, 18, 27, 223, 226, 229–230; *Tea and Sympathy* 14, 17, 27, 229
The Andersonville Trial (Levitt) 22
Antigone (Sophocles) 114
Ardrey, Robert 14
Arizona State University 270
Aronson, Boris 256
Atkinson, Brooks 3, 4, 13, 22, 50
Auden, W. H. 248
Austen Riggs Center 174, 245, 247, 248, 252, 259
The Autumn Garden (Hellman) 17, 154
Awake and Sing! (Odets) 155, 173

Barnes, Clive 279
Barry, Philip 153–154
Baxley, Barbara 96, 175, 251, 276
Bayer, Ronald 197*n*6
Beckham, Sue Bridwell 77–78
Behrman, S. N. 153–154
Bell, Book, and Candle (Van Druten) 28

Bentley, Eric 51, 98
Berkey, Ralph 22
Berkshire Theatre Festival 246, 247
Bieber, Irving 187, 190, 197*n*3
Blackmer, Sidney 223
Booth, Shirley 176, 205, 221, 223, 229, 248
"The Boy in the Basement" 46, 183–184*n*2, 198*n*9
Bradham, JoAllen 117
Brenman-Gibson, Dr. Margaret (Mrs. Wm. Gibson) 174, 245, 247
Brown Derby 270, 273
Brustein, Robert 6, 32, 96–118, 147, 157, 175–176, 182, 183*n*1, 251
Burgess, Charles 190
Bus Riley's Back in Town 12, 28, 97, 98, 163, 169–171
Bus Stop (film) 11, 22, 163, 173
Bus Stop (play) 1, 3, 4, 11, 12, 20, 21, 22, 26, 27, 28, 39, 41, 45, 46, 49, 50, 51, 56, 74, 97, 100, 109, 110, 111, 121, 122, 123, 125, 127, 133, 134, 135, 139, 144, 146, 147, 152, 157, 159, 174, 179, 227, 228, 240, 245, 252, 255, 256, 263

The Caine Mutiny Court Martial (Wouk) 22
The Call 198*n*9, 274
Camino Real (Williams) 17, 152
The Canterbury Tales (Chaucer) 144
Casebolt, Kathrene 91
Cassidy, Claudia 268, 269
Cat on a Hot Tin Roof (Williams) 16, 17, 58, 138, 147, 152, 155, 227
Chapman, John 50
Charlton, Richard 228
Chekhov, Anton/Chekhovian 127, 154; *The Cherry Orchard* 127, 131, 133, 134
The Cherry Orchard (Chekhov) 127, 131, 133, 134
Chicago Tribune 268–269
The Children's Hour (Hellman) 14, 154
Clarkson, Philip 74, 266–272

287

288   Index

Clurman, Harold 4, 5, 56, 63, 64, 65, 135, 156, 157, 193, 228, 255, 256, 267, 269, 273
Coe, Fred 223
Cold War 22, 40
Come Back, Little Sheba (film) 11, 163
Come Back, Little Sheba (play) 1, 3, 5, 11, 12, 13, 15, 17, 18, 19, 26, 27, 30–52, 74, 97, 100, 101–104, 109, 111, 115, 116, 121, 122, 123, 124, 128, 129, 130, 131–132, 139, 140, 142, 143, 144, 146, 147, 152, 155, 157, 159, 173, 174, 198n9, 205, 219–220, 221, 223, 224, 227–228, 229, 230, 231, 240, 241, 245, 257, 263, 275
Communism 14, 15, 22, 34
Como, Perry 246
Connell, Helene Inge 3, 198n10, 201–206, 208, 210, 211, 212, 250, 254, 260, 261, 262, 278, 279
Connolly, John 96, 198n13, 212, 248–254, 260
Cort Theatre 237
The Country Girl (Odets) 16, 17
Courant, Jane 99, 103, 115, 116, 117
Crane, Stephen 116
Crouse, Russel 137
The Crucible (Miller) 14, 15, 17, 22, 155
Custer, General George Armstrong 208

The Dakota (building) 174, 235, 238, 241, 273
Dansky, Steven 118
The Dark at the Top of the Stairs (film) 11, 163, 251
The Dark at the Top of the Stairs (play) 1, 2, 3, 11, 15, 19, 20, 26, 27, 28, 39, 41, 49, 74, 97, 100, 109, 111, 120, 122, 123, 124, 125, 128, 130, 131, 132–133, 139, 147, 149, 150, 152, 154, 155, 157, 158, 159, 167, 173, 174, 177, 183, 185, 186, 187, 188, 190, 191, 192, 197n7, 197n9, 198n13, 198n14, 205, 227, 228, 230, 240, 143, 246, 263
Death of a Salesman (Miller) 127, 129, 138, 147, 155
deKooning, Willem 270
Denker, Henry 22
"Departure" 198n9
depression 2, 3, 205, 265, 277
Desire Under the Elms (O'Neill) 129, 218
DeStefano, Lorenzo 183, 228
Diehl, Digby 2, 193
A Doll's House (Ibsen) 129, 131
Don't Go Gentle 276
Downer, Alan 32, 52n2
Dramatists Guild 230
Dumas, Alexandre 26
Dusenbury, Winifred 44

Esquire 1
Euripides 26

Fairbanks, Douglas 202, 203
Farther Off from Heaven 11, 174, 188, 189, 190, 191, 221, 223, 227

Fascism 14, 153, 154
Field, Betty 176
The Flowering Peach (Odets) 16, 22
Foote, Horton 223–225
Foucault, Michel 185
Frankenheimer, John 169
Freud/Freudian 30, 32, 122, 141, 142, 169, 177, 179, 180, 187, 189, 193, 195
Friedan, Betty 44, 103
"The Friends of Sir Galahad" 197n5, 198n9
Front Porch 56, 57, 63, 69, 73–93, 104, 174, 231
The Fugitive Kind (Williams) 28

Gage, Walter (Inge pseudonym) 12, 169
Gardner, R. H. 33, 52n1
Gassner, John 3, 142
Gazzo, Michael V. 16, 17
Gibson, William 6, 9, 96, 174, 175, 245–247; *The Miracle Worker* 16, 246
Gill, Brendan 152
The Glass Menagerie (Williams) 11, 28, 93, 114, 117, 138, 139, 142, 145, 147, 152, 154, 221
Glory in the Flower 242
Goff, Lewin 263, 264
Golden Boy (Odets) 155, 156
Goldman, Milton 227
Good Luck, Miss Wyckoff (film) 12
Good Luck, Miss Wyckoff (novel) 12
Gottfried, Martin 33, 52n7
Goyen, William 242
Granville-Barker, Harley 71
Great Depression 25, 34, 40, 137, 155, 166
Guardino, Harry 222

Hamlet (Shakespeare) 159, 192, 218
Haney, Carol 176
Harper's (magazine) 6, 96, 98, 115, 118, 157, 174, 175, 251
Hatch, Robert 4
A Hatful of Rain (Gazzo) 16, 17
Hayes, Richard 51
Hayworth, Rita 37, 44, 52n5
Heckart, Eileen 57, 61, 242
Hellman, Lillian 18, 154; *The Autumn Garden* 17, 154; *The Children's Hour* 14, 154; *Toys in the Attic* 17, 154; *Watch on the Rhine* 13, 154
Herlihy, James Leo 97, 163, 166–167, 168, 198n14, 242
Hingle, Pat 198n13
Holden, William 1
Hollywood 22, 29, 31, 32, 36, 37, 38, 39, 47, 50, 80, 84, 90, 91, 177, 225, 228, 244, 250, 251, 254, 258, 278, 279
homosexuality 2, 5, 6, 17, 25–29, 46, 91, 97, 98, 116, 117, 118, 179, 184, 186, 187, 189, 190, 192, 193, 195, 196n3, 197n4, 197n5, 197n6, 198n10, 198n12, 250–251, 276
Hopper, Edward 259
Howard, Sidney 46, 153
Hyman, Mac 22

Ibsen, Henrik 127, 131, 270, 277; *A Doll's House* 129, 131; *An Enemy of the People* 22, 155
"I'm a Star" 198
Independence Community College 3, 8, 9, 10, 52n4, 56, 57, 76, 150n1, 211, 259
Inge, Luther Clay 10, 139, 144, 148, 149, 150, 201, 202, 206, 213, 276
Inge, Luther Clayton 10, 150n1, 195, 198n11, 201, 202, 207, 210
Inge, Maude Gibson 10, 139, 180, 186–187, 188, 201, 210, 214, 215, 216, 249, 261, 276, 277
Inherit the Wind (Lawrence and Lee) 14, 227

Jackson, Charles 242; *The Lost Weekend* 258
JB (MacLeish) 16
Johnson, Jeff 30, 32, 49, 118
Jones, Margo 11, 188, 220, 223, 227
Jones, Therese 99, 103, 116, 117
Juhnke, Janet 99, 103, 116, 183n1

Kanin, Garson 226
Kansas Quarterly 99, 116
Kauffmann, Stanley 98, 116, 117
Kazan, Elia 58, 96, 164, 166, 175, 197n7, 230, 243, 252
Kernan, Alvin B. 98
Kerr, Walter 1, 115
"The Killing" 198n14
Kilroy, Thomas 127, 133
King Lear (Shakespeare) 71, 269
Kingsley, Sidney 14, 22, 153
Kinsey, Alfred 32
Knight, Shirley 197n4
Koestler, Arthur 14
Koprince, Susan 117
Korean War 22, 145

Lancaster, Burt 1
Langner, Lawrence 61, 75, 229
Lansbury, Angela 167
The Last Pad 12, 197n5, 198n9
Laurents, Arthur 26
Lawrence, Jerome 3, 6, 8, 227, 228; *Inherit the Wind* (with Lee) 14, 227
Lee, Robert E. 6, 8, 227, 228; *Inherit the Wind* (with Lawrence) 14, 227
Levitt, Saul 22
Lewis, Sinclair 153
Life (magazine) 39, 80
A Life of William Inge: The Strains of Triumph (Voss) 3, 74, 138, 227
Life with Father (Lindsay and Crouse) 137, 138
Lincoln Center 256
Lindsay, Howard 137
Logan, Joshua 6, 8, 55, 56–57, 58, 61–62, 63, 68, 73, 74–75, 76, 77, 79, 90, 91, 93, 108, 230, 231–234, 235, 236, 238, 242
Long Day's Journey Into Night (O'Neill) 114, 138, 147
A Loss of Roses 2, 3, 11, 28, 49, 97, 98, 115, 121, 122, 123, 152, 158, 163, 166, 167, 176, 177, 188, 197n5, 198n9, 240
The Lost Weekend (Jackson) 258
The Love Death 150, 198n14
Lysistrata (Aristophanes) 114

MacLeish, Archibald 22; *JB* 16; *The Trojan Horse* 14
Madison Avenue 36, 138
The Male Animal (Thurber and Nugent) 14
The Man in Boots 57, 77, 80, 82, 83, 84–85, 90, 92–93
Mann, Daniel 128, 221, 223, 259
Many a Glorious Morning 196n2
Marlowe, Christopher 26
Marshall, Armina 232, 242
McCarthyism 14, 22, 145
McCullers, Carson 27; *The Member of the Wedding* 28
McLuhan, Marshall 30
Meeker, Ralph 61, 63, 238, 242
The Member of the Wedding (McCullers) 28
"Memories of Green Summer" 188–189, 197n8
Merrick, David 61, 234
A Midsummer Night's Dream (Shakespeare) 21
Midwest/Midwestern 2, 18, 29, 79, 96, 99, 128, 135, 147, 148, 167, 175, 241, 246, 266, 279
Mielziner, Jo 79, 235–236
Miller, Arthur 22, 96, 127, 155, 156, 157, 162; *All My Sons* 138, 147, 155; *The Crucible* 14, 15, 17, 22; *Death of a Salesman* 127, 129, 138, 147, 155; *A View from the Bridge* 22, 155
Millstein, Gilbert 1
The Miracle Worker (Gibson) 16, 246
Mister Roberts (Logan) 231
Molière 270
Monroe, Marilyn 1, 21–22, 163, 173, 252
Moore, Marianne 248
Mourning Becomes Electra (O'Neill) 93
Music Box Theatre 11, 159, 227, 237
My Son Is a Splendid Driver 12, 117, 180, 185, 186, 193–196, 196n1, 197n5, 197n7, 197n9, 210

Nash, N. Richard 237–239
Nathan, George Jean 11, 52n6, 56
The Nation (magazine) 34
Natural Affection 2, 3, 5, 6, 12, 42, 46, 51, 97, 98, 115, 121, 122–123, 124, 125, 158–159, 173, 177–183, 188, 197n5, 198n9, 222, 227, 228, 240, 243, 244, 256, 266, 267
New York Daily News 50
New York Drama Critics' Circle Award 11, 233
The New Yorker 70, 71, 152
New York Times 13, 50, 116, 224, 242, 246, 274, 279
Newman, Paul 62, 234, 242
The Night of the Iguana (Williams) 28
Nightingale, Benedict 49
No Time for Sergeants (Hyman) 22
Nugent, Elliott 14

290   Index

Oakley, J. Ronald 34
Odets, Clifford 155, 156; *Awake and Sing!* 155, 173; *The Country Girl* 16, 17; *The Flowering Peach* 16, 22; *Golden Boy* 155, 156; *Paradise Lost* 155, 173; *Rocket to the Moon* 155, 156; *Waiting for Lefty* 155, 173
Oedipal (complex, bond, attraction, etc.) 112, 113, 148, 167, 177–180, 182, 185, 188–195, 197n8
Oedipus Rex (Sophocles) 114, 147
Off-Broadway (and off-off Broadway) 4, 5, 152, 153, 197n5, 225
O'Neill, Eugene 67, 153, 270; *Desire Under the Elms* 129, 218; *Long Day's Journey Into Night* 114, 138, 147; *Mourning Becomes Electra* 93
Orpheus Descending (Williams) 152, 155, 157
Our Town (Wilder) 27, 154
Out on the Outskirts of Town 12, 198n14
Overnight 4

Paradise Lost (Odets) 155, 173
Peabody College 10, 138, 211
People in the Wind 174
Picasso 91
Picnic (film) 11, 163, 236
Picnic (play) 1, 3, 4, 5, 11, 12, 20–21, 26, 27, 28, 33, 36, 38, 39, 41, 45, 46, 47, 48, 49, 50, 52n5, 55–71, 73–94, 96, 97, 100, 104–109, 116, 121, 122, 123, 124, 125, 128, 129, 130, 139, 142–145, 147, 148, 149, 152, 155, 156, 157, 159, 173, 174, 177, 179, 205, 206, 224, 227, 228, 230, 231–236, 237, 238, 239, 240, 241, 245, 256, 263, 267, 275
Pollock, Jackson 270
Porter, Katherine Anne 248
Pound, Ezra 30
Proust, Marcel 185, 242
psychoanalysis/psychotherapy 5, 173, 177, 179, 187, 188, 193, 196, 197n8
Pulitzer Prize 57, 96, 173, 227, 230, 233, 234, 236, 242

The Rainmaker (Nash) 237
Reader's Digest 39
Rice, Elmer 153, 154
Richardson, Tony 222, 228, 257
Riggs Center *see* Austen Riggs Center
Riley, James Whitcomb 152
Ripon College 268
Robertson, James Oliver 76
Rocket to the Moon (Odets) 155, 156
Rockwell, Norman 128
Rodgers and Hammerstein 99
Rorem, Ned 116
The Rose Tattoo (Williams) 17, 152, 155
Roussel, Raymond 185
Rule, Janice 237, 238, 242

St. Louis Star-Times 11, 31, 97, 138, 220, 221, 245
Saint-Subber, Arnold 242
Salmi, Albert 255–256

Sarotte, Georges-Michel 117–118, 179, 183–184n2, 196–197n3
Scanlan, Tom 78
Schary, Dore 16
Schlee, George 232
Sedgwick, Eve 198n12
Seldes, Gilbert 40, 42
Shakespeare 21, 26, 57, 146, 204, 218, 260, 270; *Hamlet* 159, 192, 218; *King Lear* 71, 269; *A Midsummer Night's Dream* 21; *The Taming of the Shrew* 109
Shaw, George Bernard 270
Sheaffer, Louis 4
Sheed, Wilfred 98
Shepard, Sam 117
Sheridan, General Philip 208
Sherwood, Robert E. 154
Shuman, R. Baird 45, 74, 130, 139, 166, 188
Simon, John 152, 157
Simon, Neil 152
Sing Me No Lullaby (Ardrey) 14
Sitwell, Dame Edith 248
The Skin of Our Teeth (Wilder) 154
Sombrero Playhouse 228, 266
Splendor in the Grass 2, 11, 51, 97, 115, 116, 117, 162, 163, 164–166, 169, 170, 171, 177, 198n13, 230, 242, 252, 258
Stanley, Kim 21, 22, 222, 223, 224, 242, 256, 257
Stephens College 10, 138, 211
A Streetcar Named Desire (Williams) 17, 28, 105, 152, 155, 157
The Stripper (film adaptation of *A Loss of Roses*) 11, 163
Stritch, Elaine 242
Styan, J. L. 133, 134
suicide: Inge's suicide 3, 93, 97, 173, 185, 196, 198n14, 213, 245–247, 261–262, 271–272, 278–279; in works (of Inge and of others) 49, 113, 120, 121, 138, 148, 157, 158, 165, 168, 170, 183, 192, 196, 197n5, 198n14
Sullivan, Dan 227, 278, 279
Summer and Smoke (Williams) 17, 152, 155, 157
Summer Brave 12, 21, 38, 52n7, 57, 69, 71, 73–94, 104, 108, 153, 230, 234, 247
Sunrise at Campobello (Schary) 16
Swanson, Gloria 202, 203
Sweet Bird of Youth (Williams) 21, 152, 155, 157

The Taming of the Shrew (Shakespeare) 109
Tarkington, Booth 152
Tea and Sympathy (R. Anderson) 14, 17, 27, 229
Theatre Arts (magazine) 45, 68
Theatre Guild 61, 75, 221, 222, 223, 224, 229, 232, 241
Theatre of the Absurd 2
They Knew What They Wanted (Howard) 46, 153
Thurber, James 14

Time Limit! (Denker and Berkey) 22
"The Tiny Closet" 46
Tony Awards 229, 230
Toys in the Attic (Hellman) 17, 154
The Trojan Horse (MacLeish) 14
Two Boobs 276
Tynan, Kenneth 98

Van Druten, John 26; *Bell, Book, and Candle* 28
"Venus in Therapy" 197n5, 198n9
Vidal, Gore 242
A View from the Bridge (Miller) 22, 155
Voss, Ralph 3, 56, 74, 90, 138, 190, 196n1, 227, 230

Wager, Michael 256
Waiting for Lefty (Odets) 155, 173
Waldo, Janet 228
Washington University, St. Louis 11, 138, 218, 219, 241
Watch on the Rhine (Hellman) 13, 154
Watts, Richard, Jr. 115
Weales, Gerald 52n1, 52n3, 98, 115, 144
Weissberger, L. Arnold 227
Welles, Orson 169
Wescott, Glenway 248
Where's Daddy? 2, 4, 12, 46, 97, 115, 183, 227, 228, 256, 263
Whitehead, Robert 228, 255–258

Wilde, Oscar 26
Wilder, Thornton 26, 241; *Our Town* 27, 154; *The Skin of Our Teeth* 154
Wilkinson, Rupert 38
William Inge Theatre Festival 3, 8, 98, 150n1, 226
Williams, Tennessee 1, 4, 11, 13, 17, 18, 21, 22, 26, 27, 96, 97, 98, 114–115, 116, 117, 127, 139, 152, 154, 155, 156, 160, 162, 169, 175, 190, 221, 227, 239, 242, 244, 250, 274; *Camino Real* 17, 152; *Cat on a Hot Tin Roof* 16, 17, 58, 138, 147, 155, 227; *The Fugitive Kind* 28; *The Glass Menagerie* 11, 28, 93, 114, 117, 138, 139, 142, 145, 147, 152, 154, 221; *The Night of the Iguana* 28; *Orpheus Descending* 152, 155, 157; *The Rose Tattoo* 17, 152, 155; *A Streetcar Named Desire* 17, 28, 105, 152, 155, 157; *Summer and Smoke* 17, 152, 155, 157; *Sweet Bird of Youth* 21, 152, 155, 157; *You Touched Me!* 152
Willson, Meredith 99
Winters, Shelley 256, 267
Wood, Audrey 8–9, 57, 93, 221–222, 225, 230, 251
World War II 1, 13, 14, 22, 25, 44, 48, 96, 137, 138, 240
Wouk, Herman 22
Wright, Teresa 230

You Touched Me! (Williams and Windham) 152

www.ingramcontent.com/pod-product-compliance
Lightning Source LLC
Chambersburg PA
CBHW020859020526
44116CB00029B/517